Beyond the Grand Tour

Travel in early modern Europe is frequently represented as synonymous with the institution of the Grand Tour, a journey undertaken by elite young males from northern Europe to the centres of the arts and antiquity in Italy. Taking a somewhat different perspective, this volume builds upon recent research that pushes beyond this narrow orthodoxy and which decentres Italy as the ultimate destination of European travellers. Instead, it explores a much broader pattern of travel, undertaken by people of varied backgrounds and with divergent motives for travelling. By tapping into current reactions against the reification of the Grand Tour as a unique and distinctive practice, this volume represents an important contribution to the ongoing process of resituating the Grand Tour as part of a wider context of travel and topographical writing. Focusing upon practices of travel in northern and western Europe rather than in Italy, particularly in Britain, the Low Countries and Germany, the essays in this collection highlight how itineraries continually evolved in response to changing political, economic and intellectual contexts. In so doing, the reasons for travel in northern Europe are subjected to a similar level of detailed analysis as has previously only been directed on Italy. By doing this, the volume demonstrates the variety of travel experiences, including the many shorter journeys made for pleasure, health, education and business undertaken by travellers of varying age and background across the period. In this way the volume brings to the fore the experiences of varied categories of traveller – from children to businessmen – which have traditionally been largely invisible in the historiography of travel.

Rosemary Sweet is Professor of Urban History at the Centre for Urban History, University of Leicester.

Gerrit Verhoeven lectures in Early Modern History at the universities of Antwerp, Ghent and Leiden.

Sarah Goldsmith is a Leverhulme Early Career Fellow at the University of Leicester.

Beyond the Grand Tour

Northern Metropolises and
Early Modern Travel Behaviour

Edited by
Rosemary Sweet, Gerrit Verhoeven
and Sarah Goldsmith

LONDON AND NEW YORK

First published 2017
by Routledge
2 Park Square, Milton Park, Abingdon, Oxon OX14 4RN

and by Routledge
711 Third Avenue, New York, NY 10017

Routledge is an imprint of the Taylor & Francis Group, an informa business

© 2017 selection and editorial matter, Rosemary Sweet, Gerrit
Verhoeven and Sarah Goldsmith; individual chapters, the
contributors

The right of Rosemary Sweet, Gerrit Verhoeven and Sarah
Goldsmith to be identified as the authors of the editorial material,
and of the authors for their individual chapters, has been asserted in
accordance with sections 77 and 78 of the Copyright, Designs and
Patents Act 1988.

All rights reserved. No part of this book may be reprinted or
reproduced or utilised in any form or by any electronic, mechanical,
or other means, now known or hereafter invented, including
photocopying and recording, or in any information storage or
retrieval system, without permission in writing from the publishers.

Trademark notice: Product or corporate names may be trademarks
or registered trademarks, and are used only for identification and
explanation without intent to infringe.

British Library Cataloguing-in-Publication Data
A catalogue record for this book is available from the British Library

Library of Congress Cataloguing-in-Publication Data
A catalog record for this book has been requested

ISBN: 978-1-4724-8580-9 (hbk)
ISBN: 978-1-315-56927-7 (ebk)

Typeset in Sabon
by Cenveo Publisher Services

Contents

List of figures and tables   vii
List of contributors   viii

1 Introduction   1
ROSEMARY SWEET, GERRIT VERHOEVEN
AND SARAH GOLDSMITH

PART I
Travel and elite formation   25

2 The Duc de Rohan's Voiage of 1600: Gallocentric
   travel to England in the formation of a French noble   27
EMMA PAUNCEFORT

3 Foubert's academy: British and Irish elite formation in
   seventeenth- and eighteenth-century Paris and London   46
RICHARD ANSELL

4 The social challenge: Northern and central European
   societies on the eighteenth-century aristocratic Grand Tour   65
SARAH GOLDSMITH

5 Abroad, or still 'at home'? Young noblemen
   from the Czech lands and the empire in the
   seventeenth and eighteenth centuries   83
EVA CHODĚJOVSKÁ AND ZDENĚK HOJDA

vi *Contents*

6   Between specialisation and encyclopaedic knowledge:
    Educational travelling and court culture in early
    eighteenth-century Germany   108
    MATHIS LEIBETSEDER

PART II
Travel for leisure and business   125

7   The Petit Tour to Spa, 1763–87   127
    RICHARD BATES

8   Amsterdam as global market and meeting place
    of nations: Perspectives of seventeenth- and
    eighteenth-century French travellers in Holland   147
    MADELEINE VAN STRIEN-CHARDONNEAU

9   The European 'Grand Tour' of Italian entrepreneurs   161
    CORINE MAITTE

PART III
New patterns of travel   183

10 Young cosmopolitans: Flemish and Dutch youths
    and their travel behaviour (from the late sixteenth
    to the eighteenth century)   185
    GERRIT VERHOEVEN

11 Revolutionary ruins: The reimagination of French
    touristic sites during the Peace of Amiens   203
    ELODIE DUCHÉ

    Index   222

Figures and tables

Figures

5.1	Selected urban destinations in the Holy Roman Empire of Grand Tours undertaken 1650–1700	88
5.2	Selected urban destinations in the Netherlands, England, Switzerland and the Duchy of Burgundy of Grand Tours undertaken 1650–1700	88
5.3	Average duration of sojourns at selected European *Residenzstädte* and at Leuven University, 1650–1700	89
5.4	Selected urban destinations in the Holy Roman Empire of Grand Tours undertaken 1700–50	92
5.5	Selected urban destinations in the Netherlands and the duchy of Lorraine, including Strasbourg and London, on Grand Tours undertaken 1700–50	93
5.6	Average duration of sojourns at selected European *Residenzstädte* and university (academy) towns, 1700–50	94
9.1	Map of Italian entrepreneurs' travels in Europe, 1766–1830	171
10.1	Netherlandish travellers and their age (1585–1750)	187
10.2	Netherlandish travellers and gender (1650–1750)	190

Tables

9.1	Numbers of cities visited by Italian entrepreneurs	168
9.2	Cities visited and described by Italian entrepreneurs	170

Contributors

Richard Ansell is a British Academy postdoctoral fellow at the Centre for Urban History, University of Leicester, working on education, travel and family strategy in Britain and Ireland, *c.*1650–1750.

Richard Bates is a PhD candidate in the School of History, University of Leicester, working on diplomacy and espionage in Spa during the eighteenth century. In an earlier life he was a chartered accountant.

Eva Chodějovská is a research assistant and map collection keeper at the Institute of History, Czech Academy of Sciences. She is a member of the International Commission for the History of Towns and the Historic Towns Atlas Trust. She is an expert on early modern cartography and has held fellowships in Rome, Vienna and Munster.

Elodie Duché is a lecturer at York St John University. She was the Alan Pearsall Research Fellow at the Institute of Historical Research, University of London, in 2015, and completed her PhD 'A passage to imprisonment: naval prisoners of war and transnational experiences in Napoleonic France' at the University of Warwick in 2014.

Sarah Goldsmith is a Leverhulme Early Career Fellow at the University of Leicester. She completed her AHRC-funded PhD, 'Danger, risk-taking and masculinity on the British Grand Tour to the European continent, 1730–1780' at the University of York in 2015.

Zdeněk Hojda studied at Charles University in Prague and was Archive Manager at the National Gallery in Prague. He has taught at Charles University and at the Univesrity of Liberec in the Department of History. His research interests focus on early modern cultural history, the history of collecting, visual culture, and the history of education and of travel.

Mathis Leibetseder works at the Prussian Privy State Archives in Berlin. He is a leading authority on the *Kavalierstour* in early modern Europe and has published widely on that subject, including the monograph

Die Kavalierstour. Adlige Erziehungsreisen im 17. und 18. Jahrhundert, Köln 2004 (Beihefte zum Archiv für Kulturgeschichte, 56).

Corine Maitte is professor of Modern History at the University of Marne la Vallée. She specialises in the economic and social history of early modern Italy, labour history and the history of migration. She recently published *L'entrepreneur et l'historien: deux regards sur l'industrialisation dans le textile (XVIIIe–XIXe siècle)*, Villeneuve d'Ascq, Presses du Septentrion, 2013.

Emma Pauncefort completed her PhD candidate in the School of European Languages, Culture and Society at University College London. Her thesis is entitled 'French travel writings on England 1698–1734: the audacious debate on Englishness'.

Madeleine van Strien-Chardonneau is a lecturer at the Centre for Arts and Society, France and the Low Countries at Leiden University. She is currently working on a project on tradition and renewal in French literature from the Romantic period. Her work has particularly focused upon the process of image creation through travel literature.

Rosemary Sweet is professor of Urban History at the Centre for Urban History, University of Leicester. She has published widely on eighteenth-century urban and cultural history, and her most recent book, *Cities and the Grand Tour: the British in Italy, c.1690–1820* was published by Cambridge University Press in 2012.

Gerrit Verhoeven lectures in Early Modern History at the universities of Antwerp, Ghent and Leiden. He specialises in social and cultural history of the Low Countries. His most recent book *Europe within Reach: Netherlandish Travellers on the Grand Tour and Beyond (1585–1750)* was published by Brill in 2015.

1 Introduction

*Rosemary Sweet, Gerrit Verhoeven
and Sarah Goldsmith*

In 1997 the Tate Gallery in London organised an exhibition on travel in the eighteenth century called 'Grand Tour: The Lure of Italy'.[1] Offering a compelling vision of who travelled, their destinations, their preoccupations, their entertainment, their collecting practices and the memorabilia of their travels, the exhibition, with its accompanying catalogue, provides a useful starting point for this volume, embodying as it does the dominant paradigm in Anglophone scholarship on early modern European travel: a British-led consumption of Italy's art, antiquities and history.[2]

Echoing numerous other scholarly works, the exhibition defined the Grand Tour as a northern European aristocratic practice. An extended voyage to Rome that represented the culmination of a youth's education and his passage to adult manhood, the Grand Tour involved sending young noblemen southwards to acquire a taste in the fine arts, to study the remains of Roman antiquity, to improve their command of French or Italian, to hone their diplomatic skills and to master the noble arts of dancing, fencing, horsemanship and conversation. As Bruce Redford argued in his important study *Venice and the Grand Tour*:

> A Grand Tour is not a Grand Tour unless it includes the following; first a young British male patrician (that is, a member of the aristocracy or the gentry); second, a tutor who accompanies his charge throughout the journey; third, a fixed itinerary that makes Rome its principal destination; fourth, a lengthy period of absence, averaging two or three years.[3]

The Grand Tour was supposedly established by the English and disseminated to other European countries and whereas scholars typically contend that English *milordi* outnumbered travellers from other nations for most of the eighteenth century, the attraction of Italy was clearly not limited to the English (or British) alone. Indeed, the concept of a 'Grand Tour' is recognisable across early modern European cultures and much of the scholarly literature has placed considerable emphasis upon what Cesare de Seta, in his introductory essay to *Lure of Italy*'s catalogue, referred to as its 'essentially cosmopolitan' character and universal qualities.[4]

2   *Sweet, Verhoeven and Goldsmith*

The dominance of Italy upon early modern patterns of travel – itself a perpetuation of the centrality of pilgrimages to Rome in medieval modes of travel – is impossible to ignore, whether in contemporary observations or modern scholarship. But in recognising the importance of Italy, and Rome in particular, as the ultimate destination of early modern travel, other itineraries and travelling agenda have tended to be overlooked. As Kay Dian Kriz observed in her review of *Lure of Italy*, the scholarship 'seems loath to situate the Tour within a larger network of international travel and exchange'.[5] Instead, an emphasis upon Italy's 'uniquely significant' status as a focus of travel and its 'unique riches'[6] has led to a prioritisation of the aesthetic agenda of the Grand Tour in Italy. Within the scholarship devoted to the Italian Grand Tour it is possible to identify two distinct and dominant scholarly discourses. First, the research agenda set by art historians has explored Italy's importance as the training ground for artists and architects, and stressed the relationship between taste, collecting and patronage, both in tracing the art trade's networks and in identifying the importance of the aesthetic and classical ideals in elite culture, and the enduring association between the visual arts,[7] classics and politics.[8] Second, building upon the works of Charles Batten and Percy Adams, who contended that travel literature formed its own eighteenth-century genre of writing, literature scholars have investigated travel literature's form, style, conventions and influence. Italy, and its role in the evolution of the novel, the Sublime, Gothic and Romantic literature, has provoked extensive commentary.[9] As Simon Ditchfield has recently observed, the field is dominated either by an 'old-fashioned' history of collecting and connoisseurship, or by a focus on 'travel *writing* (that is, narratives, their style and their conventions)', and questions of subjectivity and narrative. The actual experience of travel and the other dimensions of the history of travel have frequently been excluded.[10]

Important though the Italian Grand Tour undoubtedly was, this volume seeks to decentre its place in early modern European travel cultures, directing the focus instead upon other areas of northern, western and central Europe. Considering these regions as travel destinations in their own right, and in terms of the distinctive travel cultures of their inhabitants, it also builds upon recent scholarship that highlights the importance of travel for categories of traveller beyond the stereotypical aristocratic male. Collectively the chapters provide testimony of the growing diversity of different cultures of travel that co-existed alongside the extended itinerary of the traditional Grand Tour. The volume's objective is to provide a consistent focus upon the praxis and experience of travel as opposed to the research agenda set by art history or literature studies, through presenting a series of in-depth case studies that allows us to identify the diversity of early modern travel by focusing on neglected travellers, itineraries and destinations from France, the southern Netherlands, the Dutch Republic, the German territorial states, Bohemia, Italy and Britain. This builds upon and responds to

Introduction 3

research and anthologies that have been moving away from the canonical texts of travel literature or well-known editions of published correspondence, by delving into personal diaries, family papers, lists of travel expenses, scrapbooks, diplomatic reports, passport registers and other under-utilised archival sources, as well as printed ephemera on the early modern travel industry.[11] As will be discussed later, new themes and cultures of travel have been broached by reading these sources against the grain – for example, by looking for women, children, or domestic servants, who were travelling with, but were almost invisible in the journals written by the *patres familias.*

Although the existence of destinations beyond Italy has been routinely recognised by the principal studies of the Grand Tour, such recognition rarely goes beyond brief references or narrative-led discussion.[12] This is the more striking when we consider that, in terms of crude numbers, in so far as evidence survives, destinations such as Paris or Spa, the small but fashionably cosmopolitan resort in the Ardennes, attracted visitor numbers comparable or even superior to those to be found in any of the major Italian cities. Daniel Roche, for example, estimates that between 1772 and 1787 approximately 3,800 foreigners visited Paris annually, of which 25 per cent (950) were British, whereas Bates's analysis of visitor lists shows that during its peak years (1763–87) Spa could attract almost 350 British visitors in the summer months alone.[13] The same observation can be made for studies of German and Dutch travellers. From the 1980s onwards a flood of coffee-table books, anthologies and articles were published on the Netherlandish *Groot Tour*, yet Rudolf Dekker's 1994 detailed inventory of early modern travel manuscripts clearly demonstrates that Italy was being dwarfed by other destinations as early as the late seventeenth century. London and Paris were on the rise, while Dutch travellers also increasingly travelled eastwards to the Rhine, the spa of Aix-la-Chapelle, Berlin and Dresden.[14] For a long time, the German research programme was cut from the same cloth, as attention was primarily focused on Italy and the *Kavaliersreisen.* Joachim Rees, Winfried Siebers and Hilmar Tilgner's 2002 inventory of German travel journals from 1750–1800, however, broke new ground, demonstrating that France, not Italy, was the main destination for German nobles and commoners, followed closely by the Austrian Netherlands, the Dutch Republic and, from 1765 onwards, Great Britain.[15] Figures and findings such as these are suggestive of the distortion that the 'lure' of Italy has exercised over our understanding of the experience of travel.

Recent decades have seen a slowly developing, disparate but welcome body of scholarship that is less rigidly focused upon the Italian peninsula and which seeks to provide more detailed analysis of specific regions and countries. For example, following Michèle Cohen's pioneering work, Anglophone historiography has centred upon France's role within the education and refinement of young gentlemen, upon travel's role within

4   Sweet, Verhoeven and Goldsmith

contemporary debates concerning anti-French and Francophile tendencies, and upon the development of revolutionary travel.[16] Scholars such as Liesbeth Corens, Hugh Dunthorne and Kees van Strien have focused on the relationship between English Catholic institutions in the Low Countries and English travellers or on the close cultural ties between Britain, the Austrian Netherlands and the Dutch Republic.[17] Britain as a travel destination for French, German and other continental travellers, as represented in the accounts of foreign visitors to Britain of both sexes, from Sophie von la Roche and Johanna Schopenhauer to Count Lorenzo Magalotti and Louis Simond, has also received considerable attention.[18] These accounts have been mined by urban historians as well as scholars interested in the delineation of English manners and mores, but have been discussed less frequently from the perspective of patterns of travel behaviour and of the experience of travel.[19] Lucien Bély's analysis of French passport registers from 1712 offers a highly suggestive indication of this trend whereby, even in the early eighteenth century, Italy had been eclipsed by England – and above all by London – as the most popular travel destination for aristocrats.[20] As scholarly discussions of eighteenth-century Anglophilia and its admiration for political liberty and commercial and manufacturing progress demonstrates, a fascination with British culture and modernity was, in many cases, clearly a powerful motivation for travel, just as Italophilia and admiration for antiquity drew Englishmen southwards to Rome.[21] Admiration for novelty and the pursuit of knowledge and modernity could slip easily into industrial espionage, as meticulous notes were taken on industrial plants, mines, steam engines, agricultural systems, landscape parks and other things *was zu Hause Vortheil bringen könne* (meaning 'other things that could be of benefit back at home').[22]

The attention given to the different areas and topographies of northern Europe is, at present, uneven. Certain areas such as the German principalities and the Austro-Hungarian Empire have attracted only limited scholarly attention. David Worthington and Stephen Conway's recent studies of British and Irish ties with central Europe in the seventeenth and eighteenth centuries are a rare exception. However, whereas Worthington highlights detailed evidence for British travel to Austria-Hungary and Poland-Lithuania as early as 1560, and Conway's 'Grand Tour' chapter decentred Italy through drawing on a kaleidoscope of northern destinations, their discussions of travel are part of a wider exploration of the connections via trade, diplomacy, military service and intellectual exchange, and their role in shaping British and European identity.[23] In later eighteenth-century scholarship other areas, such as the Alps, spa towns and coastal destinations, have received more consideration. Yet again, this has tended to come from scholars less interested in travel per se than the discourse surrounding cultural and aesthetic attitudes towards mountains,[24] or historians of modern tourism seeking to trace back the lineages of the relationship between leisure, health and travel.[25] Equally, travel to and travel writing on areas designated as the 'periphery' of Europe, such as Russia, Scandinavia and the Levant have been the subject of discussions of the existence, inclusion and exclusion of a 'European identity', and the boundaries of civilisation, which have explored the overlap between European travel and the wider culture of exploration.[26]

As Bolton and McLoughlin recently observed, early modern European travel 'emerges as a vast panorama of opportunities and experiences far wider than any individual could take in'.[27] This observation remains as true for scholars as it did for travellers. Travel acts as an intersection for many disparate scholarly interests, making gaining a cohesive sense of the history and culture of European travel challenging. This volume fills certain lacunae through detailing historiographies, travel cultures and destinations of individual regions. As importantly, in focusing upon northern and central European destinations, these chapters also provide the opportunity to collectively reflect on the overall rationale behind travel to and the attractions of the 'north' of Europe. Montesquieu's theory of climate has often been used to explain the attraction of the north in terms of its characteristic industry and activity. However, this analysis has typically been binary in nature, comparing west to east, north to south, centres to peripheries, or Europe to colonial spaces, and has more often focused on what the north *was not*.[28] Focusing on travel as a central means of testing and consolidating a sense of self, Chloe Chard, for example, argues that European travel was essentially about understanding the north through comparison with the south, rather than in its own right: 'the traveller's own country – or the entire north of Europe – is assigned contrasting attributes, such as tameness, insipidness or mediocrity' in comparison to Italy as a place of escape, pleasure and exhilaration.[29]

Whereas in certain chapters the binary is reversed, this volume predominantly works against Chard's emphasis on the necessity of the south or other comparative elements through examining travel in the north, exploring how the north was understood by northern Europeans themselves and identifying a discourse that was capable of operating without a comparative element.[30] In identifying the central attractions of the north, this volume collectively finds that whereas art and antiquity were not unimportant – travellers, for example, were almost always fascinated by the burgeoning collections of the Louvre in Paris, the Palais Royal and Versailles, and the baroque paintings in churches and monasteries of the southern Low Countries – the evidence of 'modernity' was of equal or greater interest. This evidence was identified in programmes of urban renewal, in the architectural set-pieces of the modern city, in the business of commerce and manufactures, in centres of political and diplomatic power, in the pursuit of knowledge and its institutions (particularly legal and scientific), in the cosmopolitan social life and in the opportunities for leisure and recreation that were developing in the rapidly diversifying service sectors of cities such

6   *Sweet, Verhoeven and Goldsmith*

as London, Paris and Amsterdam. Whereas the chapters on educational travel by Pauncefort, Goldsmith, Leibetseder and Chodějovská and Hojda frequently note a response to the shifting loci of socio-political power and to the most current intellectual, educational options, Maitte, van Strien-Chardonneau and Verhoeven each demonstrate in different ways the tourist response to commercial, industrial and political might and modernity, whether expressed through an admiration for a wide array of consumer goods and shops, or the spectacle of Amsterdam's *Beurs* and London's Royal Exchange, or the most up-to-date means of textile manufacturing. Equally, as Maitte's chapter demonstrates, the appeal of northern innovation was shared not just by those already north of the Alps, but by Italians as well. This volume demonstrates that the fascination with contemporary culture and modernity was not just limited to Anglophile travel to Britain, as discussed earlier, but was a common feature of travel to, or within, the north.

In essence, whereas the traveller's fascination with Italy was fixated upon the past, travel culture to northern Europe was an overwhelming, enthusiastic engagement with contemporary power, society and culture in its multiple forms. In focusing on northern and central European metropolises, this volume therefore reveals a substantially different narrative of early modern travel culture, which questions the preoccupation with an Italian classical and aesthetic agenda. Travel was not simply a matter of affirming identity through experience of the 'other'; it could also be a confident affirmation, celebration and examination of modern society. Travel was a vivid engagement with contemporary *and* historic Europe, and a processes that was, as Duché so effectively explores in the final chapter, sensitive to contemporary shifts in power and influence.

Another characteristic of English-language historiography is its markedly Anglo-centric focus and the slight attention paid to other European cultures and attitudes towards travel. Whereas specific discussions of and comparisons with non-British travel cultures are lacking, travel scholarship is also more broadly characterised by a tendency to discuss cultures of early modern travel under the catch-all phrase 'Grand Tour'. The myth of an exclusively British Grand Tour has been challenged as abundant evidence from France, Germany, the Low Countries, Scandinavia and Central Europe illustrates a wider European trend of extended travel undertaken for educational purposes by the youth of the European elite. However, in arguing for the Grand Tour's 'cosmopolitan' nature and for the Grand Tour as a British 'export', numerous British and European scholars have, as Pauncefort and Leibetseder note, sought to impose a homophonic terminology, translating the Grand Tour to *'le Grand Tour'*, *'Groote Tour'*, *'Große Reise'* and so on. This is problematic not just on a national level. As scholars have begun to identify travellers from different social classes, genders and life stages, it has similarly been argued that the distinctions between different types of travellers should be collapsed, and eighteenth-century

Introduction 7

travel culture discussed under a generic title of 'Grand Tour', irrespective of social strata or travel practice.[31] Thus the term 'Grand Tour' and its derivatives have frequently been extended to a much broader range of eighteenth-century travellers.[32]

Yet, as Katherine Turner has demonstrated through her exploration of British published travel writing as a platform for the rising middling sorts, this practice may obscure some important social, gender and national differences.[33] The idea that every nation, region or social group in early modern Europe had its own travel culture, including meaningful variations in destinations, travel motives and the social profile of travellers, is, on one level, self-evident, but the implications of this for understanding histories of travel and contrasting histories of cultural formation have not been fully explored. This volume challenges the homogenising of early modern European travel, as its contributors undertake a more nuanced discussion of the terms, categories and cultures of travel undertaken and used by early modern travellers. In doing so, it allows for some meaningful conclusions to be drawn.

For example, in Part I, Pauncefort, Leibetseder and Chodějovská and Hojda suggest various alternative formulations to the Grand Tour in their studies of French, German and Bohemian education travel. Whereas Chodějovská and Hojda observe that *Länderreise* was the most common contemporary term applied to educational travel among the Bohemian nobility, Leibetseder affirms the recent resurgence in the use of *Kavalierstour*, a term coined in the late nineteenth century to refer to specifically German practices of educational travel, in order to explicitly accentuate the social heterogeneity of early modern travel culture.[34] Their discussion not only reveals the complexity of navigating the multiple terms used by contemporaries and scholars, but also highlights underlying methodological considerations. As Pauncefort's broader problematisation of scholars' selection of terms observes, the propensity 'to superimpose an homogenised interpretation of European noble travel practices from the sixteenth century onwards onto conventional understanding of the English custom' poses a central methodological issue. In the case of labelling French educational travel, Pauncefort argues that the use of 'le Grand Tour' makes little sense, given that it was not employed in early modern French travel writing or even included in lexicons until the late eighteenth century. Whereas the scholarly adoption of 'le Grand Tour' indicates a corresponding contemporary adoption of English pedagogy, Pauncefort argues that the contemporary French use of the educational 'voyage' contained very different, and uniquely French, connotations that emphasised the audacious, the bold and the experience of distant, far-off locations.

The British, French, German, Bohemian and Dutch variants of elite educational travel display distinctive similarities in terms of the social status and demographic of their participants, and a northern travel itinerary that focused upon formal educational opportunities via universities and

8   *Sweet, Verhoeven and Goldsmith*

academies, and a social, political and diplomatic engagement with certain rulers and ambassadors. Yet this apparent uniformity hides some significant differences.[35] Even though the label of the *Groote Tour* was frequently used, Dutch Reformed travellers were, for instance, less in thrall to Italy in the early seventeenth century than their counterparts in England or France. The *Groote Tour* was often limited to France, with a long visit to Geneva – the bulwark of Calvinism – as a solemn terminus.[36] Among others, Mathis Leibetseder's work has shown that the German *Kavaliersreise* had a strong northern focus from its inception, which only became stronger during the eighteenth century as the centre of gravity in Europe's economic and political power shifted steadily northwards away from the Mediterranean. These gradual shifts in focus can be partially explained by the influence of a country's political, diplomatic and confessional relationships which ensured certain courts and societies were more welcoming, appropriate and accessible than others, indicating that the country of origin of an educational traveller had far-reaching influence upon where he focused his attention. Equally, the evidence from Chodějovská and Hojda and from Leibetseder would suggest that travellers from the Holy Roman Empire and further east were shaped by a subtly different intellectual and religious culture, as religious and educational priorities took precedence over the refinement of taste or the pursuit of leisure. This could, of course, simply reflect a discursive strategy rather than reality: where parents or patrons were paying, there was always an incentive to tailor a travel narrative to suit the audience. However, this also held true for British, Dutch and French travellers, so the question remains, why the educational dimension of travel was apparently valued longer by German or Bohemian parents? Nonetheless, such narratives were not unmediated records of travel and negotiating the relationship between the represented experience of travel that survives in the archive through diaries and letters and what may actually have taken place presents a constant methodological challenge to any historian of travel.[37]

The enduringly narrow educational focus on the German and Bohemian travellers examined in this volume contrasts considerably with the increasingly widespread acceptance of travel for pleasure and recreation among the British, French and Dutch, whether on the Grand Tour, shorter continental tours, or even domestic travel. Such divergences raise the question of whether German elites adhered to the humanist paradigm of functional travelling rather longer than was the case further west. Whereas the different imperatives that lay behind ostensibly similar patterns of travel among the different elites of northern Europe is one of the key themes of the first part of this volume, the second and third parts explore travel patterns, cultures and motives that were fundamentally different from the elite culture of educational travel.

It is widely accepted among scholars that travel in the eighteenth century saw an increasingly diverse demographic and social profile. Even among

Introduction 9

those undertaking the traditional Grand Tour, the composition of the travelling body had been transformed by the end of the eighteenth century. In a ground-breaking article in 1985, the historical geographer John Towner analysed over 220 English travel narratives and demonstrated that, even in the supposed heyday of the classical Grand Tourist in the early eighteenth century, such young men were simply a subset of a larger group of travellers. By the second half of the eighteenth century they were increasingly outnumbered by well-heeled professionals, businessmen, scientists, artists, architects and other commoners.[38] Subsequent scholarship has built on these findings, particularly with regard to British travellers in Italy, but primarily focuses on the nature, purpose and influence of their travel writing.[39] The culture and growing significance of travel undertaken by women, family and middle-class groups still awaits full exploration.[40]

In terms of the current rather limited body of literature in English that deals with, first, travel to the prosperous northern European cities, such as London, Amsterdam and Paris, second, with non-anglophile European travel cultures and, third, with non-elite male travellers, Gerrit Verhoeven's examination of Dutch and Flemish travel culture provides an honourable exception and one which anticipates a number of themes in this volume. His analysis of manuscript and published travel literature identifies a substantially different pattern of travel from the lengthy Grand Tour and one which had very different aims consistent with a shorter duration of travel.[41] Narratives of *playsierreijsjes* (pleasure trips) and *somertogjes* (summer trips) proliferate from the late seventeenth century onwards; these were undertaken by a much more varied demographic than that traditionally associated with the Grand Tour and for reasons of leisure and pleasure as much as education or the refinement of taste.[42] Being shorter, they were also more affordable and did not require lengthy absences: they could therefore be undertaken by burghers as well as gentry; by women, children and the elderly as well as young men. Whereas many of these trips did not extend beyond national boundaries, others incorporated the major cities of the Austrian Netherlands, northern France, Germany and Britain.

Verhoeven's emphasis upon the shorter pleasure trips, particularly those which remained within national boundaries, and the much more inclusive social profile of those travelling can be paralleled with the growth of domestic travel in Britain during the eighteenth century. Strikingly, to date, there has been no comparative study of the development of domestic tourism across Europe during this period. Verhoeven aside, the English-language literature on the rise of domestic travel in early modern Europe is almost exclusively limited to the British experience.[43] Since the publication of Esther Moir's initial study of domestic travel in 1964, we have learned a great deal about the relationship between travel and national identity, the discovery of the British landscape, particularly its more picturesque elements, the role of travel as a vehicle for the construction of personal subjectivities, the emergence of the early tourist industry around the spas

10 *Sweet, Verhoeven and Goldsmith*

and resorts of eighteenth-century Britain and the opening of travel to wider social and gender groups.[44] As in the Dutch Republic, where nearly 80 per cent of the travel journals written between 1750 and 1800 had a domestic focus,[45] one of the striking aspects of domestic travel in Britain is the fact that it appears never to have been the preserve of men, and to have involved family groups and diverse backgrounds from an early period. Celia Fiennes, who travelled round England on horseback in the late seventeenth century, was exceptional, but as the spread of the turnpike network led to swifter, safer and cheaper travel, travel became increasingly accessible to a much wider social constituency. Looking beyond British and Dutch comparisons, van Strien-Chardonneau's discussion of French travel to the Netherlands and Dutch Republic goes some way towards rectifying the absence of detailed studies from other countries. However, the extent to which such developments were more pronounced among the British and the Dutch remains unclear. For example, despite the presence of Sophie von la Roche and Johanna Schopenhauer in London, the evidence of female travel companions on extended European tours, let alone independent travellers, among French, German and even Dutch travellers is scarce and circumstantial before the French Revolution.[46] Clearly, the prosperity enjoyed by the English middle class and Dutch *burghers*, as well as the greater degree of freedom that English and Dutch women were supposed to enjoy, may well have been a factor in generating more opportunities for women travellers both at home and further afield.[47]

Britain's status as an island has helped ensure that domestic travel is almost invariably considered in terms entirely distinct from European travel and in discrete publications. Richard Ansell's recent work, however, has led the way in attempting to break down what is, in many respects, an artificial binary. In his analysis of travel undertaken by Irish Protestant families in the late seventeenth and early eighteenth centuries, in his contribution to this volume and in his wider work, he demonstrates how domestic tours could become imbued with educational aims. They were very often perceived as preparation for a longer continental tour, or were the cheaper alternative, fulfilling some of the same educational purposes, for the younger son for whom European travel would have been an unjustifiable expense.[48] Equally, whereas leisure, recreation and health came to represent increasingly important motives for travel during the eighteenth century, it is important to remember that domestic travel was also frequently fuelled by sentiments of patriotism: Celia Fiennes, for example, was firmly of the view that it behove her as an Englishwoman to know something more about her country, its history and its manufactures,[49] and, as Verhoeven shows in this volume, travel was similarly seen as a means of inculcating sentiments of loyalty and patriotism by parents who toured the '*lieux de mémoire*' of the Dutch Republic's history with their children. Building on these insights, the relationship between domestic and foreign travel deserves closer attention across the period: how were patterns of travel behaviour

Introduction 11

learned in Britain, for example, extended to Europe? How were expectations of European travel shaped by experiences at home? To what extent was the increasing presence of British women undertaking a European tour in the second half of the eighteenth century a consequence of their early uptake of travel in Britain?

Finally, the issue of crossing borders aside, it could be argued that the rise of domestic travel and the developing British, French and Dutch 'Petit Tours' to the metropolises of the north were both tied to the same economic, structural and social factors. As Verhoeven, van Strien-Chardonneau and Bates each observe, at a basic structural level of transport infrastructure, the area of northern France, metropolitan England, the Austrian Netherlands and the Dutch Republic was particularly well integrated, cutting cost and adding considerably to ease and convenience.[50] More frequent and shorter journeys, which did not necessitate the lengthy journey to Italy or a drawn-out programme of study, appealed to the growing body of travellers who belonged to the increasingly prosperous urban elite across Europe. The close connection between travel, leisure and health lent itself to shorter recreational journeys and was also reflected in the increasing popularity of seaside resorts and spas across Europe.[51] In this sense travel can be considered alongside other 'luxury' goods, once the preserve of the aristocratic elite, but increasingly adapted and modified to suits the needs and demands of a far less homogeneous consumer market.[52] Considerations of time and money were clearly an important factor in the rising popularity of shorter journeys; so too was the increasing preference for travel as a family group, itself a reflection of broader shifts in social and familial relations.

Collectively, the chapters in this volume address three main themes. First, close attention has been paid to the evolving topography of travel behaviour and the different itineraries that were followed over the period. Second, due attention is paid to the social profile of travellers, as each chapter brings details on status, wealth, gender, age and other elements to the fore. Finally, the motivation for travel is considered: how important were education, art, religion, sociability and leisure? How did the balance between different priorities vary according to country of origin and to period? In putting together this volume our aim has been not only to chart evolving itineraries and patterns of travel but also to consider plausible explanations. In the course of the eighteenth century, Italy clearly lost some ground, whereas London, Paris and Amsterdam were on the rise. Yet, it remains unclear which factors tipped the balance. Within the traditional orthodoxy of research on the Grand Tour, *agents of change* have often been overlooked or downplayed. In examining how the consumer revolution, transport innovations, political upheaval, social ambition, urbanisation and the first stages of industrialisation, changing family relations, new moral values or enlightened educational ideals, to name just some of the factors, that (re)shaped early modern travel behaviour, *Beyond the Grand Tour* sets a new course by examining the crossovers between early modern travel

12   *Sweet, Verhoeven and Goldsmith*

behaviour and society in more detail. However, although economic and infrastructural factors were evidently important, the relative decline of Italy's significance as a destination cannot be explained simply in these terms. Over the course of the eighteenth century, Italy was increasingly associated with the past: a vision of former glory and faded magnificence, still to be admired, but not to be emulated. Commercial expansion, industrial growth and intellectual Enlightenment was taking place further across the Alps in the cities of northern France, the Low Countries and in Britain. The key to the European balance of power lay not in Italy but in the courts of Austria-Hungary, Prussia, France and Britain. Travel, even when ostensibly pursued for reasons of leisure or health, was also about the acquisition of useful knowledge and the observation of what was new or remarkable: and as northern Europe increasingly asserted both political and economic dominance, the attraction and the novelty of the cities of the northern tour was similarly enhanced. The appeal of Italy had always been constructed around its antiquities; modernity followed a different itinerary.

Part I: Travel and elite formation

The first part of the volume focuses upon travel as experienced by members of the European elite, but, rather than following them to Italy, these chapters highlight the very powerful motives for travel in northern and central Europe alongside analysis of how and why itineraries through these regions evolved during the seventeenth and eighteenth centuries.

Whereas urban historians have drawn attention to London's extraordinary growth in the eighteenth century as a modern commercial metropolis and the curiosity and admiration that this aroused in visitors, the significance of London as a destination for travellers has received less consideration from scholars of travel and travel writing. Emma Pauncefort and Richard Ansell's chapters outline the centrality of London, Edinburgh and Leith as destinations for European and British elite travellers. Focusing upon 1598 as a key turning point in the culture, construction and identity of the French *noblesse d'épée* and the subsequent importance of educational travel, Emma Pauncefort's chapter analyses the early-seventeenth century birth of a Gallocentric culture of instructive travel. Designed to bolster an underlying narrative of French eminence and consolidate a superior French sense of self, the importance of the 'tour en Angleterre' and Scotland within this culture has thus far been overlooked. Pauncefort pinpoints a growing desire to read about and experience England and its past, to the point that, by the 1650s, England was 'practically French'. Using the 1599–1600 travel and travel writings of Henri, Duc de Rohan, one of the first *nobles d'épée* to travel in the newly brokered peace, Pauncefort explores Rohan's rhetorical use of 'a glorious England as the stepping-stone to the brilliance of France' and distant Scotland as a grateful beneficiary of France's preeminence and alliance. Rohan's reflections on London, Edinburgh and

Introduction 13

Leith reveal a complex, nuanced narrative that was far more sophisticated than a straightforward 'othering'.

Moving forward to the late seventeenth and early eighteenth century, Richard Ansell's chapter adopts an innovative approach to the subject of travel by placing it in the context of familial strategy. Using the example of the Foubert family and their Parisian and London academies to approach British educational travel from several neglected angles, Ansell offers a new interpretation of contemporary cultures and strategies of education and travel. He highlights the role of the Huguenots, Solomon Foubert in particular, as crucial mediators in the Anglo-French cultural exchange, and the interplay of confessional, political and educational factors in shaping the ongoing contemporary debate surrounding the desirability and suitability of a foreign education. In exploring Foubert's role in wider family strategies of education and educational travel, Ansell brings London sharply into focus as a place where valuable worldly experience and education could be acquired at establishments like Foubert's eponymous academy before young men proceeded across the Channel. Arguing that London was 'the most underestimated northern metropolis in accounts of early modern English and Irish education travel', Ansell further demonstrates that London not only offered a means of preparing Grand Tourists for their foreign travels but also that for younger sons, and the provincial, Irish and Scottish gentry who could not afford to send their sons abroad, London was an affordable metropolitan alternative to foreign travel.

Whereas Italy was the undoubted centre of the arts and the study of classical virtù, it should not overshadow the fact that valuable skills were to be acquired elsewhere in Europe. As Sarah Goldsmith's chapter reveals, northern and central Europe was not just a territory to be travelled *through*, but was regarded by parents and tutors as an important training ground, particularly in terms of preparation for society and public life. The British Grand Tour's social agenda has seldom been scrutinised in detail, yet courtly and metropolitan sites such as the German courts and Vienna were highly valued for the opportunities they offered to develop masculine skills of judgement, polite conduct and sociability. Such attainments were as valued as the education in taste, antiquity and the arts gained in Italy. As Goldsmith demonstrates, these social encounters proved indispensable in the Grand Tour's aims in forming elite masculine identities, and in reinforcing the British elite's personal relationships with their European counterparts.

Drawing upon an analysis of 37 tours, Eva Chodĕjovská and Zdenĕk Hojda's chapter provides a unique insight into the travel behaviour of young Bohemian noblemen. Examining the continual evolution of the Habsburg Empire's education travel culture between *c.*1570–1750, Chodĕjovská and Hojda chart an increasingly decisive shift away from Italy and France towards more northern destinations, including the Holy Roman Empire's own metropolises. This shift was accompanied by changes in the

14   *Sweet, Verhoeven and Goldsmith*

consumption of university education, shifting from inter-university peregrinations to a prolonged study at one university institution, often in Leyden or Lorraine, and the rise of increasingly lengthy sojourns in the courts of *Residenzstätde*.

Chodějovská and Hojda hesitate to argue for a specifically Czech model of a Grand Tour, instead identifying their findings as part of a distinctive 'aristocratic' pattern of education. Yet whereas some of the changes identified are linked to Europe's evolving intellectual and educational culture, their analysis reveals the extent to which the pattern of young Bohemians' itinerary shifted to reflect new confessional, political and diplomatic configurations within the Empire. These aristocratic tours were not simply about the education offered by military academies and universities but about acquiring experience and contacts that would sustain a future career of political service to the Austro-Hungarian state. The dispersed character of the Habsburg territories from the southern Netherlands to eastern Europe meant that the young Bohemian noblemen were able to follow an itinerary based around the network of satellite courts of the empire, which was also, in many instances, a network of kinship and patronage. Elite education travel was therefore a direct manifestation of the Habsburg Empire's relationship with northern Europe at a national and familial level.

In his case study of Heinrich VI Reuß and Rochus Friedrich zu Lynar's 1731–2 *Kavalierstour*, Mathis Leibetseder illuminates the German culture of elite educational travel. Arguing that, from the early seventeenth century, there was a burgeoning focus upon the attractions of northern Europe, Leibetseder considers the shifting political, economic, confessional and intellectual factors behind this shift. In contrast to Chodějovská and Hojda, Leibetseder argues that the *Kavalierstour* was distinctive, shaped by domestic culture and concerns. He explores the combined impact of the German Enlightenment and Pietism upon the *Kavalierstour*'s intellectual aims, resulting in the conflicting demands of professionalisation versus an encyclopaedic breadth of knowledge, alongside the narrowing focus on social success in diplomatic circles. Leibetseder also draws attention towards the increased importance of the domestic *Kavalierstour* travel within the Holy Roman Empire. Whereas it was in part an opportunity to display and consolidate familial and personal affiliation, Leibetseder argues that this domestic travel was also an opportunity to recognise and celebrate the Holy Roman Empire's own history and prestige.

Part II: Travel for leisure and business

The second part of the volume moves away from patterns of travel dominated by elite males to consider the rapid expansion of other travel cultures. Richard Bates and Madeleine van Strien-Chardonneau's chapters discuss the rise in journeys for pleasure, which were undertaken by a much wider range of travellers, and draw attention to the increasingly sophisticated

Introduction 15

infrastructure that evolved to support the popularity of such leisured travel. Corine Maitte's chapter focuses upon the close relationship between travel and the acquisition of scientific and commercial information.

Richard Bates's chapter on Spa demonstrates the rising importance of alternative 'tours' of Europe which revolved around social, cultural and political centres of northwest Europe and which existed independently of the Italian itinerary. The intermingled rise of health and pleasure travel in the eighteenth century, and Spa's role within this, has frequently been alluded to by historians but remains a neglected area of travel history. Bates's tightly focused case study of the 'golden age' of Spa (1763–87) utilises under-considered resources, such as the visitor lists cross-referenced with the patient notes of one of Spa's resident doctors, to provide a detailed social profile of British travel to Spa. His analysis reveals the rich diversity of British travellers, featuring family groups, women, children, the elderly and unwell, and uses individual case studies to delineate patterns and cultures of travel that were fundamentally different to, and removed from, the practices and demography of the educational Grand Tour.

Bates contends that travel to Spa merged two different travel cultures: Spa evidently featured as an 'end' destination, visited principally for its attractions of medicinal wellbeing, scenic settings, cosmopolitan pleasures and exclusive society. However, the journey to Spa was an attraction in its own right. Facilitated by the French, Dutch and Netherlandish emergent travel industry, this journey was part of what Bates refers to as the 'Petit Tour', a short, six-week pleasure trip of the Low Countries' metropolises and cultural attractions. Briefer, safe and unburdened by the expectations of educational improvement, these Petit Tours were undertaken by family groups, older men with business and parliamentary responsibilities and even single women, rather than the gilded youth who dominate in the first section of this volume.

Central to Spa's appeal was its small size – a social world in miniature that was both exclusive and cosmopolitan. Amsterdam, as Madeleine van Strien-Chardonneau demonstrates, was similarly the focus for many Petit Tours made by French travellers. Focusing primarily on French published travel writing in the seventeenth and eighteenth centuries, van Strien-Chardonneau identifies a corresponding French culture of 'pleasure travel' to the Low Countries and the Dutch Republic, in which these destinations emerged as a distinctive travel route in their own right. Facilitated by a nascent tourist industry, and a developing travel culture of pleasure and leisure that was driven by a wider demographic of French travellers, this travel culture was distinct from the more narrow concerns and broader geographical remit of French elite educational travel. Van Strien-Chardonneau's specific focus upon Amsterdam further reveals how the French were fascinated by the city's contemporary nature and modernity. From the seventeenth century, French travellers were drawn by the fame of

16   *Sweet, Verhoeven and Goldsmith*

the Dutch Republic's political system and values, alongside its economic miracle and commercial wealth, as manifested in the city's public buildings, charitable institutions, merchant residences and leisure infrastructure. Amsterdam, argues van Strien-Chardonneau, offered French travellers the opportunity to view modernity as exemplified in its commercial and financial activities, its global networks, its highly developed welfare provision and its enlightened toleration. Equally, in contrasting the superiority of Amsterdam's world empire to Venice's more limited southern and Italian trade, French travellers saw Amsterdam as representing the relocation of power to the north of Europe. Through this, van Strien-Chardonneau presents the location of power and influence as an important factor in the pattern and focus of early modern travel.

Whereas van Strien-Chardonneau and Bates identify how centres of commercial and industrial power acted as a spectacle for pleasure travellers, Corine Maitte's chapter demonstrates the extent to which different travel agendas resulted in substantially different readings of northern Europe. Scholars have recognised the 'economic community', such as merchants and ship owners, as a body of travellers distinct from educational, pleasure or intellectual travellers, but Maitte provides a much-needed insight into their 'entrepreneurial' travels.

Reversing the traditional direction of travel by following Italian 'entrepreneurs' who went north of the Alps to France, Germany, the Low Countries and Britain in pursuit of commercial and technical knowledge, Maitte uses case studies of five manufacturers from Piedmont, Lombardy and Tuscany and their tours of northern industrial Europe between 1766 and 1830. Combining state-sponsored industrial espionage with efforts to expand family businesses through networking and exposure to northern European industrial practices, these 'entrepreneurial' itineraries, travel accounts and perspectives of northern Europe were primarily, if not exclusively, shaped by specialised manufacturing concerns. Her chapter opens up a culture of mercantile travel, focused upon the industrial cities of northwest Europe, in which the emphasis was upon evaluating cities in terms of their manufactures, competitive advantages and economic strengths, rather than sightseeing, observing the inhabitants or celebrating their cultural and political heritage.

Part III: New patterns of travel

This final part opens up new practices of travel and new itineraries. Gerrit Verhoeven's chapter undertakes a valuable exploration of the under-conceptualised field of children's travel. Challenging the presumption that travel was the exclusive preserve of adults, Verhoeven gathers compelling evidence of the increasing number of children and adolescents travelling with Dutch and Flemish families on shorter *speelreijsjes* (leisure trips) and *divertissante somertogjes* (pleasurable summer trips) around the Low

Introduction 17

Countries throughout the seventeenth and eighteenth centuries. Alongside providing insights into the age, gender and social status of early modern child travellers, Verhoeven correlates the eighteenth-century increase in family trips with the increased ease and safety associated with a developing travel industry, which made travelling with children safer and more feasible, and to changes in pedagogic theory and the conceptualisation of childhood. Nor should parental concern to inculcate sentiments of patriotism and national feeling through knowledge of their native country and the national *lieux de mémoire* be discounted.

Finally, Elodie Duché's chapter takes us beyond the French Revolution to consider a new phenomenon of revolutionary tourism, and to the shift in travel culture between the eighteenth and nineteenth centuries. As Duché notes, the impact of the Revolution and the subsequent Revolutionary and Napoleonic wars upon travel practices has frequently been alluded to, but her analysis of British and American travel to France during the 1802 Peace of Amiens presents a more precise exploration of the structural changes. Ranging from the efforts of merchants and tradesmen to re-establish and expand upon pre-war business networks to the American and British consumption of France's revolutionary ruins, Duché contends that the legacy of the Revolution was central to the construction of a new pattern of travel behaviour. Whether the sites of former monarchical glory, the mutilated fabric of domestic life, or the physical wreckage of the former confessional state, contemplation of the Revolution's ruins and the destructive forces that brought them about resulted in new sites of interest and patterns of behaviour. Traditional tropes, routes and modes of travel were subtly transformed to allow new emotional reflections on social unrest, war and the passage of time.

The French Revolution and the ensuing period of war are often identified with the end of the traditional Grand Tour, not least because of the physical barriers that were placed in the way of European travel. But as Duché's chapter demonstrates, just as important was the transformation that was engendered in contemporaries' own perception of the past and their relationship to it. The events of 1789, as travellers were well aware, had led to irrevocable change. The ruins of Rome were now overshadowed by the ruins of France, which were more accessible, more open to interpretation and of more compelling importance than the remains of classical antiquity.

Notes

1 The catalogue accompanying this exhibition, I. Bignamini and A. Wilton, eds, *Grand Tour: The Lure of Italy in the Eighteenth Century* (London, 1996), has become an indispensable part of the literature associated with the Grand Tour.
2 For recent academic literature, see J. Black, *Italy and the Grand Tour* (New Haven, 2003); C. Hornsby, *The Impact of Italy: The Grand Tour and Beyond*

18 *Sweet, Verhoeven and Goldsmith*

(London, 2000); R. Sweet, *Cities and the Grand Tour: The British in Italy, c. 1690–1820* (Cambridge, 2012). For a rather traditional synopsis, see E. Zuelow, *A History of Modern Tourism* (London, 2016), pp. 14–29.

3   B. Redford, *Venice and the Grand Tour* (New Haven, 1996), p. 15.

4   C. de Seta, 'Grand Tour: the lure of Italy in the eighteenth century', in Bignamini and Wilton, *Grand Tour,* p. 14. Every European country has its own tradition in research on early modern travel behaviour. For recent examples on Germany, see R. Babel and W. Paravicini, eds, *Grand Tour. Adeliges Reisen und Europäische Kultur vom 14.bis zum 18. Jahrhundert* (Ostfildern, 2005); M. Leibetseder, *Die Kavalierstour. Adlige Erziehungsreisen im 17.und 18 Jahrhundert* (Cologne, 2004); A. Stannek, *Telemachs Brüder. Die höfische Bildungsreise des 17. Jahrhunderts* (Frankfurt am Main, 2001). On France, see M.V. Castiglioni and G. Dotoli, *Le voyage français en Italie* (Fasano, 2006). On the Low Countries, see A. Frank-Van Westrienen, *De groote tour. Tekeningen van de educatiereis der Nederlanders in de zeventiende eeuw* (Amsterdam, 1983); G. Verhoeven, *Europe within Reach: Netherlandish Elites on Grand Tour and Beyond* (Leiden, 2015). The Italian scholarship tends to emphasise the tour's essential cosmopolitanism. See, for example, A. Brilli, *Il Viaggio in Italia. Storia di un granda tradizione culturale* (Bologna, 2006); C. de Seta, *L'Italia del Grand Tour da Montaigne a Goethe* (Naples, 2001). See also the texts cited in the chapter by Chodějovská and Hojda below.

5   K. Dian Kriz, 'Introduction: the Grand Tour', *Eighteenth Century Studies*, 31:1 (1997), p. 87.

6   F. Haskell, 'Preface', in Bignamini and Wilton, *Grand Tour*, p. 7.

7   The visual arts were, for instance, ubiquitous in Bignamini and Wilton, *Grand Tour*. Recent scholarship in which the visual arts forms a primary focus includes I. Bignamini and C. Hornsby, *Digging and Dealing in Eighteenth-Century Rome*, 2 vols (New Haven and London, 2011); E.P. Bowron and J.J. Rishel, eds, *Art in Rome in the Eighteenth Century* (London, 2000); E. Chaney, *The Evolution of the Grand Tour: Anglo-Italian Cultural Relations since the Renaissance* (London, 1998); E. Chaney and T. Wilks, *The Jacobean Grand Tour: Early Stuart Travellers in Europe* (London, 2014); P. Coen, 'Andrea Casali and James Byres: the mutual perception of the Roman and British art markets in the eighteenth century', *Journal for Eighteenth-Century Studies*, 34:4 (2011), pp. 291–313; C. Johns, *Papal Art and Cultural Politics: Rome in the Age of Clement XI* (Cambridge, 1993); D.R. Marshall, S. Russell and K. Wolfe, eds, *Roma Britannica: Art Patronage and Cultural Exchange in Eighteenth-Century Rome* (London, 2011); C. Paul, *The Borghese Collections and the Display of Art in the Age of the Grand Tour* (Burlington, 2008); Paul, ed., *The First Modern Museums of Art: The Birth of an Institution in 18th- and Early 19th-Century Europe* (Los Angeles, 2012); F. Salmon, *Building on Ruins: The Rediscovery of Rome and English Architecture* (Aldershot, 2000). Much of the research and literature on the Grand Tour arises directly or indirectly from exhibitions devoted to the artists, patrons and collectors connected with the Grand Tour. See, for example, E. Bowron and P.B. Kerber, *Pompeo Batoni: Prince of Painters in Eighteenth-Century Rome* (New Haven, 2007); A. Moore, *Norfolk and the Grand Tour* (Fakenham, 1985); C. Powell, *Italy in the Age of Turner: 'The Garden of the World'* (London, 1998); M.D. Sánchez-Jáuregui and S. Wilcox, eds, *The English Prize: The Capture of the Westmorland. An Episode in the Grand Tour* (New Haven, 2012); A. Sumner and G. Smith, eds, *Thomas Jones (1742–1803): An Artist Rediscovered* (New Haven, 2003); I. Warrell, *Turner and Venice* (London, 2003). For a similar trend in Dutch scholarship, see P. Schatborn, *Drawn to Warmth: Seventeenth-Century Dutch Artists in Italy* (Amsterdam, 2001).

Introduction 19

8 J.Wilton-Ely, '"Classic ground": Britain, Italy and the Grand Tour', *Eighteenth-Century Life*, 28:1 (2004), pp. 136–65. See, for example, V. Coltman, *Fabricating the Antique: Neoclassicism in Britain, 1760–1800* (Chicago, 2006); Coltman, *Classical Sculpture and The Culture of Collecting in Britain since 1760* (Oxford, 2009); R. Guilding, *Owning the Past: Why the English Collected Antique Sculpture, 1640–1840* (New Haven, 2015); I. Jenkins and K. Sloan, *Vases and Volcanoes: Sir William Hamilton and his Collection* (London, 1996); J.M. Kelly, *The Society of Dilettanti* (New Haven, 2009); J. Scott, *The Pleasures of Antiquity* (New Haven, 2003). For discussion of the importance of classical culture and education in elite identity, see D. Arnold, 'The illusion of grandeur? Antiquity, grand tourism and the country house', in D. Arnold, T. Clayton *et al.*, eds, *The Georgian Country House: Architecture, Landscape and Society* (Stroud, 1998), pp. 100–16; P. Ayres, *Classical Culture and the Idea of Rome in Eighteenth-Century England* (Cambridge, 1997); J. Morrison, *Winckelmann and the Notion of Aesthetic Education* (Oxford, 1996), pp. 1–19; W. Stenhouse, 'Visitors, display, and reception in the antiquity collections of late-Renaissance Rome', *Renaissance Quarterly*, 85 (2005), pp. 397–434.

9 C. Batten, *Pleasurable Instruction: Form and Convention in Eighteenth-Century Travel Literature* (Berkeley, 1978); P.G. Adams, *Travellers and Travel Liars, 1660–1800* (New York, 1980); Adams, *Travel Literature and the Evolution of the Novel* (Lexington, 1983). Seminal books and articles include E. Bohls, *Women Travel Writers and the Language of Aesthetics 1700–1830* (Cambridge, 1995); J. Buzard, *The Beaten Track: European Tourism, Literature, and the Ways to Culture, 1800–1918* (Oxford, 1993); C. Chard, *Pleasure and Guilt on the Grand Tour: Travel Writing and Imaginative Geography, 1600–1830* (Manchester, 1999); Chard, 'From the sublime to the ridiculous: the anxieties of sightseeing', in H.E.A. Berghoff, ed., *The Making of Modern Tourism: The Cultural History of the British Experience, 1600–2000* (Basingstoke, 2002), pp. 47-68; B. Korte, *English Travel Writing from Pilgrimages to Postcolonial Explorations*, transl. C. Matthias (Basingstoke, 2000); N. Leask, *Curiosity and the Aesthetics of Travel Writing, 1770–1840* (Oxford, 2002); D. Porter, ed., *Desire and Transgression in European Travel Writing* (Princeton, 1991); M.L. Pratt, *Imperial Eyes: Travel Writing and Transculturation* (London, 2008).

10 S. Ditchfield, 'Review of *The Jacobean Grand Tour: Early Stuart Travellers in Europe* (review no. 1777)', http://www.history.ac.uk/reviews/review/1777, DOI: 10.14296/RiH/2014/1777 [accessed 15 February 2016].

11 Exemplified by the recent rise in published and digitised manuscript collections that offer 'a view from the inside': J.T. Boulton and T.O. McLoughlin, 'Introduction', in Boulton and McLoughlin, eds, *News From Abroad: Letters Written by British Travellers on the Grand Tour, 1728–71* (Liverpool, 2012) p. 1. See also Adam Matthew's 'The Grand Tour' digital resource (http://www.grandtour.amdigital.co.uk [accessed 15 February 2016]); R. Pococke and J. Milles, *Letters From Abroad: The Grand Tour Correspondence of Richard Pococke and Jeremiah Milles*, Vols 1–3, ed. R. Finnegan (Piltown, 2011–13); M. Todd, *Matthew Todd's Journal: A Gentleman's Gentleman in Europe, 1814–1820*, ed. G. Trease (London, 1986).

12 See, for example, J. Black, *The British Abroad: The Grand Tour in the Eighteenth Century* (Stroud, 1985, 2003); C. Hibbert, *The Grand Tour* (London, 1969); J. Stoye, *English Travellers Abroad, 1604–1667: Their Influence in English Society and Politics* (London, 1989). Even publications delineating individual travellers' routes acknowledge but give no serious consideration to non-Italian destinations in their overall conclusions. For example, Sánchez-Jáuregui and Wilcox, 'The Westmorland: crates, contents, and owners', in Sánchez-Jáuregui and Wilcox, *English Prize*, pp. 17–25.

20   *Sweet, Verhoeven and Goldsmith*

13 D. Roche, *La Ville Promise* (Paris, 2000), pp. 236, 238; R. Bates, 'Spa and the "petit tour": British visitors to Spa, 1763–1787', University of Leicester MRes dissertation (2014). See Bates's chapter in this volume for further discussion.

14 R. Dekker, 'Van Grand Tour tot treur- en sukkelreis. Nederlandse reisverslagen van de 16e tot begin 19e eeuw', *Opossum*, 4 (1994), pp. 8–24; Dekker, R. Lindeman and Y. Scherf, *Reisverslagen van Noord-Nederlanders van de zestiende tot begin negentiende eeuw. Een chronologische lijst* (Rotterdam, 1994).

15 J. Rees, W. Siebers and H. Tilgner, 'Wahrnehmen in fremden Orten, was zu Hause Vortheil bringen und nachgeahmet werden könne. Europareisen und Kulturtransfer adeliger Eliten im Alten Reich, 1750–1800', *Das Achtzehnte Jahrhundert*, 26 (2002), pp. 35–62; Rees and Siebers, *Erfahrungsraum Europa. Reisen politischer Funktionsträger des Alten Reichs (1750–1800)* (Berlin 2005).

16 M. Cohen, *Fashioning Masculinity: National Identity and Language in the Eighteenth Century* (London,1996); Cohen, 'Manliness, effeminacy and the French: gender and the construction of national character in eighteenth-century England', in T. Hitchcock and M. Cohen, eds, *English Masculinities, 1660–1800* (London, 1999), pp. 44–62; R. Eagles, *Francophilia in English Society, 1748–1815* (Basingstoke, 1999); R. Tombs and I. Tombs, *That Sweet Enemy* (London, 2006).

17 L. Corens, 'Catholic nuns and English identities: English Protestant travellers on the English convents in the Low Countries, 1660–1730', *Recusant History*, 30:3 (2011), pp. 441–59; H. Dunthorn, 'British travellers in eighteenth-century Holland: tourism and the appreciation of Dutch culture', *British Journal for Eighteenth-Century Studies*, 5 (1982), pp. 77–84; C.D. Van Strien, *British Travellers in Holland during the Stuart Period: Edward Browne and John Locke as Tourists in the United Provinces* (New York, 1993); Van Strien, *Touring the Low Countries: Accounts of British Travellers, 1600–1720* (Amsterdam, 1998).

18 S. von La Roche, *Sophie in London, 1786: Being the Diary of Sophie von La Roche in London*, transl. C. Williams (London, 1933); R. Michaelis-Jena and W. Merson, transl. and eds, *A Lady Travels: Journeys in England and Scotland from the Diaries of Johanna Schopenhauer* (London, 1988); W.E. Knowles Middleton, *Lorenzo Magalotti at the Court of Charles II: His 'Relazione d'Inghilterra' of 1668* (Waterloo, ON, 1980); L. Simond, *Journal of a Tour and Residence in Great Britain During 1810 and 1811* (London, 1815).

19 C. Hancock, 'Your city does not speak my language: cross channel views of Paris and London in the early nineteenth century', *Planning Perspectives*, 12:1 (1997), pp. 1–18; J. Flavell, *When London Was Capital of America* (New Haven, 2012); P. Jones, 'Industrial enlightenment in practice: visitors to the Soho Manufactory, 1765–1720', *Midland History*, 33.1 (2008), pp. 68–96; E. McKellar, 'Tales of two cities: architecture, print and early guidebooks to Paris and London', *Humanities*, 2:3 (2013), pp. 328–50; McKellar, 'Guides, guidebooks and visitors to London, *c*.1650–1730: metropolitan literature in its continental context', in D. Arnold and J.-L. Cohen, eds, *Paris et Londres s'observant 1670–1970* (Paris, 2015); G. Ryden, 'Viewing and walking: Swedish visitors to eighteenth-century London', *Journal of Urban History*, 39:2 (2013), pp. 255–74.

20 L. Bély, *Espions et ambassadeurs au temps de Louis XIV* (Paris, 1990), p. 629.

21 I. Buruma, *Voltaire's Coconuts: Or, Anglomania in Europe* (London, 1999); L. Collison-Morley, 'The Georgian Englishman in contemporary Italian eyes', *The Modern Language Review*, 12:3 (1917), pp. 310–18; J. I. Cope, 'Goldoni's England and England's Goldoni', *The Modern Language Review*, 110 (1995),

Introduction 21

pp. 101–31; J. Grieder, *Anglomania in France, 1740–1789: Fact, Fiction, and Political Discourse* (Geneva, 1985); G. Stedman, *Cultural Exchange in Seventeenth-Century France and England* (Farnham, 2013).

22 Leibetseder, *Die Kavalierstour*, p. 153; Rees, 'Wahrnehmen in fremden Orten, was zu Hause Vortheil bringen und nachgeahmet warden könne. Europareisen und Kulturtransfer adeliger Eliten im Alten Reich, 1750–1800', in Babel and Paravinci, *Grand Tour*, pp. 513–39; Stannek, *Telemachs Brüder*, p. 83.

23 S. Conway, *Britain, Ireland and Continental Europe in the Eighteenth Century* (Oxford, 2011), chapter 7; D. Worthington, *British and Irish Experiences and Impressions of Central Europe, c.1560–1688* (Aldershot, 2012), pp. 27–32.

24 P. Hansen, *Summits of Modern Man: Mountaineering after the Enlightenment* (Cambridge, MA, 2013). For more pedestrian narratives, see P. Bernard, *Rush to the Alps: The Evolution of Vacationing in Switzerland* (Boulder, 1987); G. De Beer, *Early Travellers in the Alps* (London, 1966); R. Macfarlane, *Mountains of the Mind: A History of a Fascination* (London, 2003); J. Ring, *How the English Made the Alps* (London, 2000).

25 P. Borsay and J. Walton, eds, *Resorts and Ports: European Seaside Towns since 1700* (Clevedon, 2012); A. Corbin, *The Lure of the Sea: The Discovery of the Seaside in the Western World, 1750–1840*, transl. J. Phelps (Cambridge, 1994); R. Wrigley and G. Revill, eds, *Pathologies of Travel* (Amsterdam, 2000); J. Towner, *An Historical Geography of Recreation and Tourism in the Western World, 1540–1940* (Chichester, 1996), chapter 4; J.K. Walton, 'British tourists and the beaches of Europe, from the eighteenth century to the 1960s', in M. Farr and X. Guégan, eds, *The British Abroad Since the Eighteenth Century. Volume 1: Travellers and Tourists* (Basingstoke, 2013), pp. 19–37.

26 E. Adamovsky, *Euro-Orientalism: Liberal Ideology and the Image of Russia in France (c. 1740–1880)* (Oxford, 2006); G. Daly, *The British Soldier in the Peninsular War: Encounters with Spain and Portugal, 1808–1814* (Basingstoke, 2013); B. Dolan, *Exploring European Frontiers: British Travellers in the Age of Enlightenment* (Basingstoke, 2000); T. Lurcock, '*Not so Barren or Uncultivated*': *British Travellers in Finland, 1760–1830* (London, 2010); L. Wolff, *Inventing Eastern Europe* (Stanford, 1994).

27 Boulton and McLoughlin, 'Introduction', in Boulton and McLoughlin, *News From Abroad*, p. 1.

28 See, for example, Conway, *Continental Europe*, pp. 10–16; N. Davies, *Europe East and West* (London, 2006); Katarina Gephardt, *The Idea of Europe in British Travel Narratives, 1789–1914* (Farnham, 2014); R. Miles, *Gothic Writing, 1750–1820: A Genealogy* (London, 1993), pp. 87–9; F.A. Nussbaum, *Torrid Zones: Maternity, Sexuality, and Empire in Eighteenth-Century English Narratives* (Baltimore, 1995); A. Pagden, ed., *The Idea of Europe: From Antiquity to the European Union* (Cambridge, 2002).

29 Chard, *Pleasure and Guilt*, p. 43

30 See, for example, Maitte and Van Strien-Chardonneau's chapters.

31 Black, *British Abroad*, pp. v–vi; Chard, *Pleasure and Guilt*, pp. 11–13; Towner, 'The Grand Tour: a key phase in the history of tourism', *Annals of Tourism Research*, 12 (1985), p. 301.

32 See, for example, Black, *British Abroad*; Boulton and McLoughlin, 'The tourists and their letters', in Boulton and McLoughlin, *News From Abroad*, pp. 9–10; B. Dolan, *Ladies of the Grand Tour* (London, 2001).

33 K. Turner, *British Travel Writers in Europe, 1750–1800: Authorship, Gender and National Identity* (Aldershot, 2001), pp. 17, 46.

34 Accordingly, journeys undertaken by members of self-ruling dynasties (*Regenten- und Prinzenreise*) and by gentlemen-scholars and university men

22   Sweet, Verhoeven and Goldsmith

(*Gelehrten- und Gebildetenreise*) have come to the fore. See, for example, E. Bender, *Die Prinzenreise. Bildungsaufenthalt und Kavalierstour im höfischen Kontext gegen Ende des 17.Jahrhunderts* (Berlin, 2011); Rees, Siebers and Tilgner, 'Reisen im Erfahrungsraum Europa. Forschungsperspektiven zur Reisetätigkeit politisch-sozialer Eliten des Alten Reichs (1750–1800)', *Das achtzehnte Jahrhundert*, 26 (2002), pp. 35–62, especially p. 43. Although the term *Prinzenreisen* was not used, the concept is central to studies by C. Kollbach, *Aufwachsen bei Hof. Aufklärung und fürstliche Erziehung in Hessen und Baden* (Frankfurt/Main and New York, 2009), pp. 332–64, and Stannek, *Telemachs Brüder*. See also 'Funktionswandel und Erweiterung der kommunikativen Dimension', in Rees, Siebers and Tilgner, eds, *Europareisen politisch-sozialer Eliten im 18. Jahrhundert. Theoretische Neuorientierung – kommunikative Praxis – Kultur- und Wissenstransfer* (Berlin, 2002), pp. 41–66, especially p. 65; Siebers, 'Bildung auf Reisen. Bemerkungen zur Peregrinatio academica, Gelehrten- und Gebildetenreise', in M. Maurer, ed., *Neue Impulse der Reiseforschung* (Berlin, 1999), pp. 177–88; H. Tilgner, *Die Adelsreise im Kontext aufgeklärter Reformpolitik (1765–1800). Funktionswandel und Erweiterung der kommunikativen Dimension* (Berlin, 2002).

35 Key works from the extensive recent literature on the German Grand Tour include Babel and Paravicini, *Grand Tour*; Leibetseder, *Die Kavalierstour*; Stannek, *Telemachs Brüder*; Leibetseder, 'Vestis virum facit: fashion, identity, and ethnography on the seventeenth-century Grand Tour', *Journal of Early Modern History*, 7 (2003), pp. 332–42.

36 Verhoeven, *Europe within Reach*, pp. 31–81.

37 On this methodological challenge, see J. Adler, 'Travel as performed art', *American Journal of Sociology*, 94:1 (1989), pp. 1366–91; K. Haltunnen, 'Cultural history and the challenge of narrativity', in V.E. Bonnell and L. Hunt, eds, *Beyond the Cultural Turn: New Directions in the Study of Society and Culture* (Berkeley, CA, 1999), pp. 165–81; J. Martschukat and S. Patzold, 'Geschichtswissenschaft und "performative turn". Eine Einführung in Fragestellungen, Konzepte und Literatur', in Martschukat and Patzold, *Geschichtswissenschaft und 'performative turn': Ritual, Inszenierung und Performanz vom Mittelalter bis zur Neuzeit* (Keulen, 2003), pp. 1–31.

38 Towner, 'The Grand Tour', pp. 297–333; Wilton-Ely, 'Classic ground', p. 137.

39 See, for example, M. Agorni, *Translating Italy for the Eighteenth Century: British Women Novelists, Translators and Travel Writers 1739–1797* (Manchester, 2002); Bohls, *Women Travel Writers*; Dolan, *Ladies of the Grand Tour*; Turner, *British Travel Writers*, chapter 4; M. D'Ezio, 'Literary and cultural intersections between British and Italian women writers and *salonnières* during the eighteenth century', in H. Brown and G. Dow, eds, *Readers, Writers, Salonnières: Female Networks in Europe, 1700–1900* (New York, 2011), pp. 11–29; K. Lawrence, *Penelope Voyages: Women and Travel in the British Literary Tradition* (Ithaca, 1994). On middle-class travellers and the rise of the tourist see John Brewer, *The Pleasures of the Imagination: English Culture in the Eighteenth Century* (London, 1997), p. 171; E. Bohls and I. Duncan, *Travel Writing 1700–1830: An Anthology* (Oxford, 2005), pp. xv, 3, 96–7; J. Buzard, 'The Grand Tour and after (1660–1840)', in P. Hulme and T. Youngs, *The Cambridge Companion to Travel Writing* (Cambridge, 2008), pp. 42, 47–50; Turner, *British Travel Writers*.

40 The discussion of women travellers in Sweet, *Cities and the Grand Tour*, is an exception to this trend.

41 See, for example, Verhoeven, 'Foreshadowing tourism? Looking for modern and obsolete features – or some missing link – in early modern travel behaviour (1675–1750)', *Annals of Tourism Research*, 42:1 (2013), pp. 262–83 and *Europe*

Introduction 23

within Reach. On German cultures of travel see Leibetseder, 'Across Europe: educational travelling of German noblemen in a comparative perspective', *Journal of Early Modern History*, 14 (2010), pp. 417–49.

42 Verhoeven, 'Foreshadowing tourism', pp. 262–83; Verhoeven, 'In search for the new Rome: Europe's cultural hub(s) and early modern travellers (16th–19th century)', in A. Miles and I. Van Damme, eds, *Unscrewing the Creative City: The Historical Fabrication of Cities as Agents of Economic Innovation and Creativity* (Antwerp, 2016).

43 It is worth noting that there are some suggestive trends concerning German domestic tourism. Rees, Siebers and Tilgner found that domestic tourism within the pales of the *Alte Reich* was definitely on the rise in the late eighteenth century (see 'Reisen in Erfahrungsraum Europa', p. 57). For discussion of nineteenth-century French and German domestic travel, see P. Prein, *Bürgerliches Reisen im 19. Jahrhundert: Freizeit, Kommunikation und sozialen Grenzen* (Münster, 2005); P. Young, 'La vieille France as object of bourgeois desire: the touring Club de France and the French regions, 1890–1918', in R. Koshar, ed., *Histories of Leisure* (Oxford and New York, 2002), pp. 169–89.

44 The growing field on British domestic travel includes M. Andrews, *The Search for the Picturesque: Landscape, Aesthetics and Tourism, 1760–1800* (Stanford, 1989); S. Barton and A. Brodie, eds, *Travel and Tourism in Britain, 1700–1914* (London, 2014); Brewer provides an overview in *Pleasures of the Imagination*; B. Colbert, ed., *Travel Writing and Tourism in Britain and Ireland* (Basingstoke, 2012); K. Grenier, *Creating Caledonia: Tourism and Identity in Scotland, 1770–1914* (Aldershot, 2005); P. Hembry, *The English Spa 1560–1815: A Social History* (London, 1990); Z. Kinsley, *Women Writing the Home Tour 1682–1812* (Aldershot, 2008); E. Moir, *The Discovery of Britain: The English Tourists 1540–1840* (London, 1964); I. Ousby, *The Englishman's England: Taste, Travel and the Rise of Tourism* (Cambridge, 1990); A. Tinniswood, *The Polite Tourist: Country House Visiting in the Age of Jane Austen* (London, 1998).

45 G. Verhoeven, *Anders reizen? Evoluties in vroegmoderne reiservaringen van Hollandse en Brabantse elites (1600–1750)* (Hilversum, 2009), p. 360

46 Bély, *Espions et ambassadeurs*, p. 629; Leibetseder, *Die Kavalierstour*, pp. 28–52; Stannek, *Telemachs Brüder*, pp. 8–15; Verhoeven, *Europe within Reach*, pp. 123–8.

47 For literature on the freedom of Dutch women, see M. van der Heijden, E. van Nederveen Meerkerk and A. Schmidt, 'Terugkeer van het patriarchaat? Vrije vrouwen in de Republiek', *Tijdschrift voor Sociale en Economische Geschiedenis*, 6: 3 (2009), pp. 26–52.

48 See Richard Ansell's chapter in this volume.

49 C. Fiennes, *The Illustrated Journeys of Celia Fiennes 1685–c. 1712*, ed. C. Morris (London, 1982), p. 32.

50 On the improvements in travel infrastructure, see B. Blondé, 'At the cradle of the transport revolution? Paved roads, traffic flows and economic development in eighteenth-century Brabant', *Journal of Transport History*, 31:1 (2010), pp. 89–111; G. Livet, *Histoire des routes & des transports en Europe. Des chemins de Saint-Jacques à l'âge d'or des diligences* (Strasbourg, 2003); E. Pawson, *Transport and Economy: The Turnpike Roads of Eighteenth-Century Britain* (London, 1977); Verhoeven, '"Een divertissant somertogje": transport innovations and the rise of short-term pleasure trips in the Low Countries (1600–1750)', *Journal of Transport History*, 30:1 (2009), pp. 78–97.

51 P. Borsay and J. Hein Furnée, eds, *Leisure Cultures in Urban Europe, 1700–1870: A Transnational Perspective* (Manchester, 2016); J. Lowerson, 'Leisure, consumption, and the European city', *Urban History*, 30 (2003), pp. 92–7.

24   *Sweet, Verhoeven and Goldsmith*

52 On the increasing democratisation of luxury goods and the consumer (r)evolution, see M. Berg, *Luxury and Pleasure in Georgian Britain* (Oxford, 2005); J. de Vries, *The Industrious Revolution. Consumer Behaviour and the Household Economy: 1650 to the Present* (Cambridge, 2008); Roche, *Histoire des choses banales. Naissance de la consommation, XVIIe–XVIIIe siècles* (Paris, 1998).

Part I
Travel and elite formation

2 The Duc de Rohan's *Voiage* of 1600
Gallocentric travel to England in the formation of a French noble

Emma Pauncefort

In 1598, French canons fell momentarily silent. The Edict of Nantes, in the limited liberties it gave to French Huguenots, brought the bitter civil wars of religion to a fragile close. Meanwhile, the Treaty of Vervins ended hostilities between France and Spain. The end of conflict proved, however, to be a double-edged sword for the upper ranks of the French nobility – the *noblesse d'épée*. Although constant warfare had placed a considerable burden on the highest echelons of the nobility, it was from military service to the king that the pride and status of this elite had conventionally been derived. Soldiering had, moreover, gained all the greater importance once ministerial and household positions in the king's service began to be opened up to the lower elite orders – the bureaucratic *noblesse de robe* – in the later sixteenth century. With peace therefore came the removal of an edifying occupation and a failsafe means by which loyalty to the king could be demonstrated and – of central import for the upper French elite – differentiation from inferior nobles asserted. In turn, the economic and social crisis which scholarship has long identified as having faced the upper nobility in this period was rendered all the more acute.[1]

This chapter is concerned with one response to this existential plight as the seventeenth century dawned: the accelerated methodisation, practice and record of a new confirmatory form of noble travel to England. In this, it identifies the formulation of a specifically French social practice that sought to equip young nobles with the necessary geographical expertise to take up a position in the king's service, as well as to encourage them to positively self-differentiate against even their most eminent elite European counterparts.

By the end of the sixteenth century, travel practices were already undergoing significant transformation. One consequence of the French philosopher Petrus Ramus's advocacy of the systematisation of knowledge had been the chastisement of the medieval figure of the wandering knight.[2] While nevertheless offering eulogies to the roaming heroes of antiquity, the Bible and myth, humanist writers had instead begun to advocate a more regulated and ordered elite social practice.[3] Explorers in the king's service such as Jacques Cartier, André Thevet and Nicolas de Nicolay had

28   *Emma Pauncefort*

furnished the prefaces of their travel writings on the New World with – to draw on Rubiés' terminology – 'meta-cultural discourses' on travel.[4] Their eulogies to travel had sought to goad those aspiring to the highest positions of state of the continued relevance of travel if undertaken according to the guidelines advised.[5] Cartier, Thevet and Nicolay's call to travel targeted ambitious social equals rather than social superiors – all three commentators came from families who had enjoyed a recent rise in status due to non-military service to the monarch. Yet, their vigorous exhortations to travel, teamed with the narratives of valour and adventure contained in the main body of their texts, provided the justification for those nobles of the sword who later found themselves increasingly at leisure to undertake their own course of fruitful discovery, albeit through more localised intra-European travel. Indeed, the evidence put forward here suggests that the upper elite harnessed appropriate elements of a fast-developing social practice for its new educative and occupational needs.

Initially, elite travel southwards to visit the ancient ruins of Rome and the surrounding cities predominated, leading contemporary commentators such as Michel de Montaigne to equate the notion of foreign travel with visits to Italy.[6] Nevertheless, an alternative itinerary of travel northwards, with the incorporation of a sojourn in England, was increasingly undertaken as a means of complementing travel to other points of the compass. Diplomatic embassies to England continued to account for a significant proportion of noble visitors.[7] Nevertheless, a culture of extra-diplomatic travel across the Channel, stimulated in part out of an intellectual interest in England's past, was on the ascendancy. In his survey of sixteenth-century French writing on England, Charles Giry-Deloison contends that the closing decades of the sixteenth century witnessed a 'lack of real interest in English history and in England among the French population'.[8] The literary record, however, suggests quite the opposite. The publication in 1579 and again – which Giry-Deloison fails to note – in 1587 of a road-book entitled *La Guide des chemins d'Angleterre*, a volume headed by a didactic survey of English history, testifies not only to an elite market for literature relating to France's channel neighbour, but also to a growing desire to see as well as read about England.[9] Viewing England through the lens of the past would, in fact, become championed as a prop in the narration of contemporary French greatness.

Importantly, this alternative course of travel also spawned its own species of travelogue. This was a form that expediently redacted the experience of travel to England for the fruitful consumption of other members of the French elite. The section of these accounts dealing with visits across the Channel facilitated armchair travel to a distanced northern neighbour and acted as a further impetus to visit England. Both functions were, moreover, underpinned by one core objective: to cast the practice of travel to England, in person or vicariously, as a privileged means of formulating

The Duc de Rohan's Voiage *of 1600*   29

a sense of a superior French self – that is, to advocate what is here termed as 'Gallocentric' travel to England in the formation of a French upper noble. So great was the magnetism England came to exert on members of a French nobility desperately looking to assert themselves in a competitive social sphere that, in 1650, the eccentric noble writer François du Soucy would describe England as 'practically French', so overrun was the country with travellers.[10] Du Soucy's comment is no doubt a gross exaggeration. Nevertheless, his remark bears witness to the mushrooming and consolidation of a new direction of travel in the seventeenth century. In addition, it highlights the French hubris that coloured discussions of travel and the emerging concentric view of Europe that travel helped to construct.

This chapter explores the birth of this little-studied culture of travel and its documentation, as recorded in the travelogue of a *noble d'épée*. Through analysis of the duc de Rohan's 'Description de mon voiage', which was written up in 1600 after he returned from his travels, it offers a revised interpretation of the development of French travel. It identifies in travel to England and its capital, London, a hitherto unacknowledged component of the education of the French elite that came into being as the seventeenth century dawned.[11] Whereas scholarship has recognised the complementary role of travel in the development of new modes of education, such as that offered by noble academies, discussed by Richard Ansell in this volume, little attention has been paid to the formative experience of travel to the northern English metropolis, and the particularity of this direction of travel as the French elite renegotiated a sense of social identity in a period of fast-changing geopolitics, both within France and in Europe.[12] The propensity in historiography has been, at worst, to relegate French travel to England and the records such travel produced solely to the study of English social history and, at best, to homogenise French travel writings on England spanning over a century and penned by a variety of travellers – from exiles to savants, from diplomats to nobles at leisure. As a result, both the individual circumstances of travellers and the cultural and social contexts in which they were travelling and writing have been ignored.[13] Perhaps the most distorting framework imposed by scholarship has been, however, to consider all instances of noble French travel a species of the English 'Grand Tour', as indeed Rohan's *Voiage* has been repeatedly categorised.[14] Scrutiny of the presumptions brought to bear on French noble travel by this label is required if the current scholarly narrative is to be revised. Hence, this chapter seeks not only to examine the intricacies of a hitherto neglected record of travel; through its analysis of a rare early record of elite travel, this chapter also considers a revised theoretical framework for the study of French noble travel, at least that to England, in the seventeenth century. It is to this revised conceptualisation, in light of the distortions here identified in the general application of the term the 'Grand Tour', which this chapter first turns.

30 *Emma Pauncefort*

The distortions of the 'Grand Tour'

First coined by Richard Lassels in 1670 to refer to the travels to France and Italy undertaken by young English nobles as the final stage of their education, the term the 'Grand Tour' is now commonly employed by scholars to denote instructive travel undertaken by the young European nobility in general.[15] Although the label goes some way in accounting for the rise of intra-European noble travel, methodological issues arise in its application in studies of the increasingly itinerant French nobility. The effect is to superimpose a homogenised interpretation of European noble travel practices from the sixteenth century onwards onto conventional understanding of the English custom, thus distorting analysis of both English forms of travel and of parallel European trends. Jean Boutier's analysis is typical of the tendency to conceptualise the Grand Tour as a cross-European rather than exclusively English and complex practice.[16] He narrates the development of noble travel as a practice that grew independently of increasing territorial cohesion and the growing sense of national loyalties that was germinating in early modern Europe. The Grand Tour was, Boutier contends, 'une expérience partagée', which concerned 'l'ensemble des aristocraties européennes'.[17] In his view, if restrictions are to be placed on the term, these are to be conceived of in typological rather than geographical terms: his use is thus limited to 'le voyage d'éducation, pratiqué le plus souvent, mais pas exclusivement, par les fils de la noblesse' as opposed to the other types of tour – that of the older wealthy individual or that of the intellectual – as categorised by Robert Shackleton.[18] Moreover, if the practical details of elite travel differed, the ideology that underpinned it – that is, to educate an elite not yet initiated into adult society – remained, in Boutier's opinion, consistent.[19] The suggestion that the model of noble educative travel originated in England has, in turn, received endorsement by Gilles Bertrand in his study of European elite travel to Italy. Gilles Bertrand explains that the Grand Tour was a pedagogical tool conceived by the English in the sixteenth century and later developed in the seventeenth century which, the implication is, was then adopted by continental elites.[20] As for the terminology of the Grand Tour, elsewhere he advocates the utility of the notion as 'un concept à valeur opératoire' and 'un mot valise qui englobe l'histoire des transferts culturels'.[21] Strikingly, alongside such open endorsements of the term, both Boutier and Bertrand acknowledge the need for scholars to nuance current conceptualisations. Boutier, in particular, concedes that further research is required to consider divergences as well as convergences from the core model of elite travel and, additionally, notes that travel could, in fact, sharpen national affiliations and reinforce difference.[22] However, although both scholars seem to admit the methodological fault-line that a rigid Anglocentric framework creates, the notion of the Grand Tour continues to control their interpretations of elite travel, as well as those of others.[23]

The Duc de Rohan's Voiage *of 1600*   31

Through study of the French example, the aim here is to dispense with currently obfuscating terminology in an attempt to sketch one branch of the particularised cultures of elite travel to which Boutier and Bertrand nod. The alternative conceptualisation of Gallocentric travel put forward here more closely reflects the specific cultural requirements travel fulfilled for an early modern French elite in a state of flux. For there was no part of a French noble's itinerary that could be categorised as simply another species of the Grand Tour. The term was not employed in early modern French travel writing; nor does it appear to have been assimilated into French culture, given its absence as a compound lexical unit even in the later eighteenth-century editions of the *Dictionnaire de l'académie française*.[24] In a telling indication of the extent to which the term lacked resonance for a contemporary French audience, the 1671 French translation of Lassels' travelogue rendered the now much-cited phrase 'the Grand Tour *of* France' as 'le tour de France'.[25] Meanwhile, the term to which most travellers had recourse was not 'tour' at all, but a word with quite different resonances: 'voyage'.

This leads to a second point that highlights the importance of studying past travel practices through appropriate contemporary terminology, rather than through notions borrowed from disjunct cultural contexts. Contrary to current scholarly conceptualisations of the Grand Tour as a practice which sought to transcend the geographical separation of Europe's elite, the French 'voyage', as witnessed in the complementary formulation of travel northwards with travel southwards, served quite a different purpose; one which capitalised upon space and distance in the formation of an unique identity. As recorded by contemporary French dictionaries, unlike the term 'tour', which designated localised and restricted displacement, as indeed the construal of Lassels' comment in relation to France demonstrates, the term 'voyage' carried connotations of adventure and was coloured by an emphasis on the experience of distant, far-off locations.[26] In his French translation of the Flemish scholar Justus Lispius's renowned Latin treatise advising a noble how to conduct his visit to Italy, for example, Le Brun chose the term 'voyage' to translate the Latin *peregrinatio* and its connotations of exotic travel.[27] The 'voyage' was, therefore, both in terms of the original experience and the account subsequently authored for fellow elite consumption, perceived to designate encounters and the record of encounters with distanced others. Study of elite travel within Europe demands, therefore, the same appreciation of hierarchies and narratives of power that have been identified in early modern narratives on New World peoples in the extreme east and west in the wake of Saïd's *Orientalism*.[28] The 'voyager "entre soi"' and journey of self-exploration was not, as Boutier explains, a paradox of elite travel. Rather, it was intrinsic to it.[29] The designation the Grand Tour thus masks the fierce division within a seemingly cosmopolitan European nobility conventionally studied within the framework of the republic of letters. Whereas the term seems appropriate, given accepted understanding

32   Emma Pauncefort

of inter-elite literary contact, contemporary formulations of French travel highlight that visiting other lands and peoples was a social practice, at least among the elite, that sought to accentuate difference rather than knit closer cultural ties.

The birth of the particularised Gallocentric form of instructive French noble travel at the start of the seventeenth century was a culture of travel which, as Boutier has rightly emphasised, did indeed share many elements with the educative peregrinations of Europe's elite. Similar to that mode of travel increasingly executed by English, Dutch, Italian and German nobles, French elite travel developed out of scholarly modes of displacement. As the practice became a central component of a noble's education, it maintained strong links with antiquarianism. However, unlike the antiquarian reliance on the written text and the meticulous recording of inscriptions, Gallocentric travel sought to endow young noble travellers with privileged knowledge that could not be acquired from books. The education it gave ensured fledgling courtiers experienced and witnessed for themselves the cultures and courts of their European counterparts, as much to lay the foundations of a noble network as to be in a position to report back to counterparts with eyewitness accounts on matters of import for the nature and functioning of that elite. Well-directed French travellers were to become better versed in the nature of their European counterparts and, ultimately, to return from their travels better equipped to serve the French monarch and with a confirmed and superior sense of self.

Gallocentric travel achieved a particularly potent formulation in the experience of a 'tour en Angleterre' and its subsequent redaction in the travel account. The 'educational and social value' of new courses of noble travel was not, as Justin Stagl espouses, 'almost negligible'.[30] In the example of French elite travel to England can be witnessed a vigorous process of self-exploration through contact with an intra-European other. Behind the veil of acclaimed humanist universalism and elite sociability lay a fractured European society. This was a society whose dispersed elites sought out a localised sense of identity, one which was loosely tied to a territorial entity before being later recast as national. In the case of the French elite, this impulse was developed through travel to a little-navigated European nation separated by a seaway, which, in posing a considerable obstacle to travel, contributed at once to the imagining of travel to a distant land and French visions of superiority over distant flourishing nations. Travel did not, as Mark Motley contends, place 'distance between young nobles and their family and friends [and] national customs'.[31] While lip-service was paid by contemporary thinkers to the role of travel in shedding prejudice, an underlying narrative of French eminence was being woven through first-hand experience of travel to England and the account that was later composed.

Two further points of contention in use of the English Grand Tour as a benchmark bring discussion back to this chapter's case study of the *Voiage*

The Duc de Rohan's Voiage of 1600   33

of the duc de Rohan: the first issue concerns who undertook such travel; the second, how such travel came to be developed. A royal servant who returned to education, albeit while still only 18 years old, the duc de Rohan affords an example of an individual who defies the categorisation suggested by Shackleton: as an adult noble with financial means, Rohan, nevertheless, remained part of the younger elite who self-invested in travel as an instructive tool.[32] This identifies fluidity between different cultures of travel which is distorted by the application of typologies.[33] Moreover, examination of Rohan's *Voiage* highlights that travelogues are of historical value, not only by virtue of the record of individual itineraries they document, but also on account of the evidence they provide of the reformulated practices noble travellers-turned-writers encouraged among their social equals. Currently, understanding of the development of French noble travel is caught between two interpretations. On the one hand, there is Bertrand's suggestion that the English model came to be rolled out across Europe. On the other, cross-European studies of the art of travel or *ars apodemica* such as that by Stagl reinforce Boutier's transnational approach in marking the methodisation of travel cultures as a European phenomenon.[34] The issues posed by such interpretations are further compounded by the suggestion that travel practices were developed by treatises alone. Meanwhile, the travel account is assumed to be simply a record of the implementation of travel rather than a potential contributor to the evolution of the practice.[35] Yet, like earlier accounts of voyages to exotic lands, descriptions of travel to England owe their existence to a desire to inform an eager audience, to whet the appetites of compatriots and to exert an instructive force even if, as Rohan's *Voiage* exemplifies, this audience was limited to the inner elite. They also attest to an early impulse to regulate the practice of travel that came from within the highest ranks. Indeed, Rohan's *Voiage* boasts particular importance in that it plugs a 40-year void that currently exists in the scholarly account of the French *art de voyager*.[36] Multiple devices were employed to achieve such ends. However, the careful configuration of the relationship between geography and history examined by this chapter stands, it is argued, at the core of Rohan's endeavour to place travel to England at the service of a French elite concerned to maintain its status and identity. Far from being, as Jonathan Dewald contends, 'proudly cosmopolitan as he moved about Europe', Rohan evidently traversed neighbouring states with a rigid hierarchy of nations in mind.[37] It is this hierarchy, bolstered through careful marrying of the past with the present landscape, he set down and promulgated in his *Voiage*.

The Duc de Rohan's confirmatory travel to England: a blueprint of noble travel and travel writing

Henri, duc de Rohan, was born into one of the most illustrious Breton families of the period. In 1595, aged 16 years old and having been educated

34   *Emma Pauncefort*

by his widowed mother, a revered intellect of her time and Huguenot heiress, Catherine de Parthenay, Rohan left his native region of Brittany to be presented at court. As befitted his status as a member of the *noblesse d'épée*, and given the bitter conflicts that still loomed large for France, he was allocated a post in the French army. When peace ensued three years later, however, he became redundant in the service of the king. Bereft of his soldiering function and aware that, despite having seen active military service, at 18 years old he remained 'for the moment, more suited to learning than serving one's homeland', he was impelled, as he observed in the opening of his travelogue, to embark upon a period of travel. In the manuscript account of his travel across southern and northern European states, which he laid out in the style of printed travel works through adding summary margin notes, and which was later published, Rohan gives paltry detail on the trials, tribulations, pleasures and daily intricacies of his journey. Only by turning to records kept by a member of his entourage, the well-reputed physician Theodore de Mayerne, is it possible, for example, to discern the make-up of the travelling party.[38] Nevertheless, his account is of greater import than current critique allows.[39] Setting out from Paris on 8 May 1599, Rohan was one of the first, if not the first, to embark upon a period of instructive travel under the newly brokered peace. In so doing, he rejected the Protestant movement at the end of the sixteenth century which had dismissed the benefits of travel and had advocated attendance at noble academies in its place.[40] Moreover, the account of travel he gave in the *Voiage* stands as the earliest extant record of noble travel to England for pleasure and instruction rather than diplomacy, as well as one of the few extant records of a seventeenth-century noble sojourn in England.[41]

This is not to suggest this direction of travel had not been undertaken by Rohan's noble travelling forebears, nor that Rohan's chosen course was an anomaly in seventeenth-century elite French travel culture. The Huguenot writer and one-time refugee in England Philippe Duplessis-Mornay sent his son on a tour of Europe, including to England. So convinced was Duplessis-Mornay of the benefits to be reaped from such travel that he even bequeathed funds so that his grandsons might undertake a similar itinerary.[42] As for later travel, the records of lower-ranking members of their entourage document that the duc de Chevreuse and the duc de Chavigny crossed the Channel for pleasure and instruction in 1663 and 1676 respectively.[43] By the late seventeenth century, according to an anonymous young courtier writing in 1671, travel to England as part of a Europe-wide itinerary had become established as a rite of passage for the nobility. Explaining why he had travelled round Italy, Germany, Holland and England between 1669 and 1671, the noble remarked that, in addition to peace in Europe and the completion of his formal education, he had understood that the knowledge obtained from such an experience was 'very useful for a man of [his] lineage'.[44]

The Duc de Rohan's Voiage *of 1600*   35

Nevertheless, the record of noble travel to England is, to borrow William Sherman's phrase, 'haunted by missing persons and texts'.[45] A reasonably prolific record of French antiquarian travel to England exists, especially from the latter half of the seventeenth century.[46] The nature of French noble travel, however, as a practice of exploration by adherents of a hermetic French elite, and with records normally only produced for personal use or elite counterparts, meant that accounts rarely made it to print.[47] As a case in point, Rohan expressed the hope that his account might act as an aide-mémoire solely for the benefit of himself and his noble acquaintances. It was of particular importance to Rohan that the readership of the *Voiage* should be restricted: in the address to his mother at the close of his account, he reiterated his desire that only his closest friends and others whom his mother might deem worthy of learning from him might peruse his travelogue.[48] The redaction of his travelogue thus had a greater purpose than simply serving as a personal record. He had no intention, however, of adding to the growing number of published travel texts.

Rohan's *Voiage* offers a rare window onto a widely attested culture of elite travel and thus helps to elucidate the nature of this practice. Contrary to the narrative that describes noble travel – including that undertaken by Rohan – as the final stage of education, the example of Rohan confirms that travel was also utilised as a vehicle of further education by existing members of the French court.[49] That Rohan was not an aberration from the norm is, moreover, highlighted in the example of the duc de Chavigny, who was 26 years old when he embarked upon his travels.[50] Finally, Rohan's *Voiage* gives a sense of the central importance of travel to England in the continuing education of a French noble. To the end of his travelogue Rohan appended a series of comparisons between European nations. He opened by contrasting the climates of Germany and Italy and went on to compare the characteristics of each nation's ruler.[51] He also drew comparisons between Scotland and Bohemia and Venice and Holland respectively.[52] In the case of England, however, rather than selecting another European nation, he pitted it against France and proceeded to present a highly favourable sketch of French customs in contradistinction to the lowly English character.[53] Rohan thus left little doubt as to which nation was of the greatest import for elevating the greatness of France and to what end his account of the northern kingdoms was ultimately to serve. The rarity of the travel account to England is not, therefore, to detract from the centrality of confirmatory travel northwards in seventeenth-century French culture.

A geo-historical account of England and Scotland to narrate French eminence

If there was one form of travel Rohan was adamant that his *Voiage* would not endorse, that was antiquarian travel and its exhaustive chronicling of curiosities. Throughout the *Voiage* Rohan took great pains to present his

36   *Emma Pauncefort*

account as a selective record. He would, he remarked in his comments on Strasbourg, only describe an object 'worth being commented upon' and worth being remembered.[54] He was not, he also affirmed elsewhere, interested in giving lengthy histories of towns.[55] Nevertheless, artfully chosen moments from the past were to be endowed with a formative role in the redaction of his experience of northern cities. Responding to a contemporary trend that conceived of geography as a discipline to be subordinated to history, Rohan layered his description of selected English and Scottish cities with highly charged historical references.[56] This stratagem was central to his bid to envision a France as glorious in its past as in its present and future exploits, as well as to advocate the sight of foreign cities as a means of mapping such eminence. In Wilson Harris's theorisation, Rohan's *Voiage* thus engages in a form of 'fossilisation' according to which palimpsestic modes of writing testify to the continued importance of the past for the present.[57] Though a Protestant travelling with memories of the staunch religious loyalties that had underpinned internal French conflict, a socio-geographical identification as a noble Frenchman seems to have superseded any religious and regional loyalties. Unlike the religious universalism Tony Claydon identifies in English travel writing on Europe later in the century, Rohan's *Voiage* exhibits a wish to formulate a cross-denominational elite French self as it weaves a narrative of a superlative Christian nation of France in geo-historical terms around which his social equals might rally.[58] To this end, the account of travel to England and Scotland afforded a ripe opportunity to employ pointed geographical references and bring historical events to bear on topographical descriptions of cities. Like Bernard before him, Rohan was to use events in English history to French advantage.

England and Scotland presented Rohan with distant lands to which he could travel. If narrated with his eyewitness authority as inferior to France, they could also bolster a vision of French eminence.[59] In a rare commentary on his personal experience of travel, Rohan separated his opening survey of English and Scottish history and his description of London with a striking report on the perilous channel crossing from Holland to England. He relayed an account of nearly thwarted travel, detailing how the travelling party were kept at sea for four days and nights before finally reaching port by nothing other than 'the Grace of God'. Conspicuous by their inclusion, such remarks allowed Rohan to recast his travels to the capital city of London as a voyage of courageous exploration and discovery akin to that undertaken by adventurers to the east and the New World. Moreover, their incorporation into an otherwise seemingly detached account was also to exert a determined rhetorical effect: to foreshadow his subsequent presentation of England as a nation in a state of decline, and Scotland, a distant nation which owed its fortuitous position to the steadfastness and might of its ally, France. Together, these descriptions served to underpin a climactic affirmation of a France on the verge of a golden age, a statement itself

The Duc de Rohan's Voiage *of 1600*   37

subjugated to the greater cause of providing the firm foundations of a commendable elite identity.

With reference to the English historian William Camden, Rohan headed the end section of his travel account with a survey of English history and geography and reinforced his characterisation of a mighty England. A nation bestowed with honour by virtue of being descended from the Gauls – an early glimmer of French partiality, England was contrasted with the 'more sterile' regions that constituted Scotland.[60] Rohan emphasised England's natural good fortune by designating it a country 'most fertile, most populous, and most rich'.[61] He went on to reiterate such praise in the opening of his account of London. London was, he proclaimed with a generous application of adjectives reinforced with quantifiers, 'comparable with the greatest, richest and most populous' of all Christian nations. The port city boasted without doubt an 'extremely beautiful' situation, being located in an 'extremely good place' on the banks of the River Thames, itself described as 'extremely big and beautiful'.[62] Rohan was equally reverent of the historical military strength of London, as well as of other English cities. No town, Rohan underlined, had ever fallen victim to an invading force. London was an impenetrable capital whose Roman walls had, he declared, saved it from being 'ransacked, burnt and razed to the ground' or from suffering any number of misfortunes commonly endured by cities under siege.[63] The final component of the apparent paean to London came in his account of architecture. London was a city, he related, 'adorned with many beautiful buildings'. Having marked out the Royal Exchange as particularly noteworthy, Rohan also commended Saint Paul's, Cheap Street and London Bridge. Together, these observations constructed an image of London as wondrous by virtue of its natural and physical landscape.

In terms of its governance and people, however, Rohan had a very different story to tell. His depiction of an awesome city served to accentuate the other half of the starkly dichotomised vision of England he sought to peddle. This alternative view presented England as a nation whose people inhabited a splendid environment but fell far short of their illustrious ancestry. To bring such a vision into focus, Rohan tempered his superficially favourable sketch of London by refusing to overlay the cityscape with complementary historical colouring. Although he admired the historically proven strength of English city defences, particularly in the capital, Rohan denied London any continued significance. To curb his discussion of the city's history after his comments on its walls, he declared that since little of note had recently taken place in London, he was compelled to move on to speak of the city's architecture.[64] His brief and pointed description of the area linked to the monarch – Westminster – similarly presented the city as a locale that had stagnated since its glory days. Whereas his praise of the physical environment, both natural and manmade, had been unbridled, his account of Westminster was abrupt, with remarks on the English court and its head, the queen who had been fawned upon by his travelling Huguenot

38 Emma Pauncefort

predecessors, notably absent.[65] Declaring that the only object worthy of remark was the church by virtue of the royal tombs it contained, he drew his report on London to a close while again acknowledging the superb location of the city. Such reiteration further underlined the disjuncture between the nation's geographical prosperity and its insignificant political status: now only the sepulchres of past monarchs were worthy of observation.[66] Meanwhile, the decision to eschew description of the English court was soon highlighted for its rhetorical effect. In the digression that followed his review of London, Rohan declared that he had undertaken his travels for the purpose of observing both courts resident on 'this island'.[67] Yet, whereas English governance and custom featured prominently in his later discussion of different political systems, in his travel account proper, Rohan denied England any political prominence through omission of a description.[68] This image of decline, in great part constructed through presenting England as a country of historically insurmountable military, was to lay the foundation for exalting former and continuing French greatness in his subsequent account of Scotland.

In a further elucidation of his reasons for travel, Rohan explained that to facilitate comparisons between nations, it was of paramount importance not only to observe the external form of governments, but also to penetrate their inner nature.[69] Whereas his remarks on England had not engaged in such scrutiny in a bid to underline the disparity between the geographical and political landscape, his account of Scotland triumphed the complementarity between natural and civil prosperity. Though dedicating less space to this final stage of his travels, the concentration of praise of Scotland is marked. He revised his earlier designation of Scotland as sterile by designating it 'more fertile than other nations'. This acted as a fitting preface to his presentation of Scotland as a kingdom whose elite were worthy of admiration and whose monarch was the paragon of a good and virtuous leader and was thus, in contrast to the English queen, worth observing in the flesh.[70] Nevertheless, notwithstanding his apology of Scottish greatness, Rohan was careful to frame his discussion so as to suggest that the northern state was neither a true equal to other European nations nor solely responsible for its current prosperity. In the opening of his commentary, he stopped short of placing Scotland in the same rank as – what he termed – 'his nation', noting that such a comparison would only have been possible if motivated by natural affection. In addition, in contrast to the muted interest he had shown in the suburbs of London, following his concise survey of Edinburgh, he chose to conclude his account of Scotland by marking out the importance of the neighbouring town of Leith where, with French support, the Scots had withstood the besieging English. This was not to expand upon Scottish strengths. Rather, it was to superimpose temporal references onto a Scottish cityscape in a bid to narrate French greatness. The reading of the historical past in cities was an impulse Rohan had demonstrated in his earlier description of

The Duc de Rohan's Voiage of 1600   39

Milan and Pavia. A visit to Milan's fortress had triggered a note of regret that the city had been lost and had been succeeded by an expression of hope that one day French forces would retake the city.[71] Similarly, a brief sojourn in Pavia had resurrected the sorrow Rohan had felt on seeing in a cabinet of curiosities in Munich the very sword and tabard that had been lost by the French king in the Battle of Pavia in 1526.[72] Yet, here the opportunity was afforded not to mourn but to celebrate past French exploits and, concurrently, to affirm the continued greatness of France in contrast to a languishing English nation. Thus, in his account of Leith Rohan commented upon 'the memorable siege that the French maintained', an event he characterised as 'most honourable' for France and highly advantageous for the Scots. It was in Leith that the French 'not only stopped the fury of the English ... but also saved the entire kingdom'.[73] With this, Rohan revealed the driving objective of his lengthy panegyric on Scotland: to anticipate a celebration of the Auld Alliance in which he could erect France as the pre-eminent ally of a great nation. If the sight of Pavia had reminded him of French failings, reaching Leith had allowed him to present a historicised description of a Scottish town in which France's strength on foreign soil and over a formidable English enemy could be declared supreme.

Once confirmed in the narrative of his travel to English and Scottish urban centres, the image of a victorious and superlative French nation was maintained for the remainder of the *Voiage*. In his account of the return journey to Brittany, Rohan declared his delight at being back on French soil, only to proceed to describe Calais and Amiens by virtue of the French victories that had occurred there.[74] Meanwhile, he coloured his closing comparative analysis of nations with a further pointed historical reference which used England's present to rectify a shameful episode in France's past. Such was the bellicosity and cruelty of the English, he declared, it exonerated the French of most wrongdoing in one of their darkest moments – the St Bartholomew's Day M[assacre].[75] Consequently, England, he contended, was coming to the end of its golden era. It was not, as Trevor Roper suggests, Scotland that would take its place, but rather its old and venerable ally, France.[76] 'If it pleases God,' he declared triumphantly, 'we are ready to enter into the ownership of a better fate, which will begin when the fortune of England comes to an end'.[77]

Conclusion

The immediate impact of Rohan's *Voiage* is difficult to assess. Nevertheless, it is striking that in 1604, just a few years after Rohan's return to France, Thomas Pelletier's treatise on noble education, *La nourriture de la noblesse*, valorised and exhorted, not just travel in and of itself, but the germ of noble travel northwards that Rohan had recently undertaken.[78] In the revised programme of humanist education he set out for the nobility, Pelletier

40   *Emma Pauncefort*

endorsed the development of noble academies, such as that newly established by Antoine Pluvinel in Paris, which favoured practical education. However, contrary to those who saw in the academies a means of curbing foreign travel, Pelletier identified travel as a way of reinforcing a formal noble education.[79] Equipped with a rudimentary understanding of geography as a discipline which bolstered one's knowledge of history, Pelletier hoped the young noble would embark upon a fruitful course of travel during which he would seek to penetrate 'the soul' rather than just 'the body' of those things he saw.[80] In a further attempt to rail against the prevailing attitude of his contemporaries, he also expressed his scepticism at the benefits of travel to Italy. Belying his own Gallocentric bent, he condemned the failure of such practices to produce the 'French gentleman' as opposed to an Italianised noble corrupted by foreign manners.[81] This led him to declare that 'if it were not the custom of the French to race straight to Italy', he would rather 'advise [a French noble] to see the nations of the North'.[82] This preference for travel northwards rather than southwards was one he developed in his outline of a noble itinerary. He was damning of Rome, which, in a remark that mirrored the link Bernard and, in his turn, Rohan had forged between history and travel to Europe's cities, he saw as a poor image of its former greatness. Instead, he lavished praise on the flourishing nation of England, now under the rule of James I whom he characterised 'as wise, virtuous, learned and full-spirited' as any other king of Europe. Yet, like Rohan, Pelletier's praise came at a price. James I was a useful figure, for adulation of a widely revered monarch could provide a marked point of comparison with a superlative French king. The sight of the great English monarch would, Pelletier explained, be cast into shadow by the dazzling vision of the French king whom the young noble would behold on his return to the French court.[83] Incorporating travel into noble instruction, Pelletier identified travel to England as not just a further stage on a noble's European itinerary, but – to draw on Bourdieu – confirmed that it was an 'interested' social practice whose 'symbolic profit' derived from the unshakeable sense of French superiority it afforded.[84] It is not clear whether Pelletier was aware of Rohan's *Voiage*. However, as an individual 'highly implicated in his period' and who employed his writings to ruminate on currents and shifts in French society, it is possible to conjecture that his ruminations on travel in *La nourriture* were a response to the changing practices Pelletier had discerned among his social superiors.[85]

Whether or not Pelletier was indeed endorsing a practice of which he was aware, the implications of his discussion of travel for study of Rohan's *Voiage* remain the same; considerable weight is given to the thesis, here put forward, that noble actors themselves effected the reformulation of social practices. Indeed, if, taking the survival and attested circulation of Rohan's manuscript among the elite as supporting evidence, Dewald's contention that Rohan is 'an important example for understanding what mattered to seventeenth-century aristocrats' is accepted, then it is even

The Duc de Rohan's Voiage of 1600   41

possible to suggest that Rohan set the tone for the later discussion and practice of travel.[86] Either way, in the example of Rohan can be witnessed a noble who reshaped travel so as to establish a practice that could contribute to the quest to build a sense of French cohesion after years of tumult, to build a community, not within Europe, but within a much smaller elite French grouping. In so doing, Rohan extended the 'meta-cultural discourses' that had previously adorned the prefaces of travel writings to the travel account proper.[87] This was a bid to make present practices capitalise upon past events to lay the foundations, at least in rhetoric, for the great continental power of France of the future. It was a bid that, in the wake of the later publication of Rohan's *Voiage* in 1646 evidently appealed, not just to the upper elite, but to members of the lesser nobility as well. Writing in 1666, the scholar and son of a noble of the robe, Samuel Chappuzeau, testified to the continuing impulse to present a glorious England as the stepping-stone to the brilliance of France following a period of travel.[88] It would be a bid that would come under fire in pre-Enlightenment thought by a new species of traveller who reacted against the culture of travel writing of England that had been brought into being by Rohan and which had become a common prop to an elite sense of French identity.[89] For the moment however, Gallocentric travel to England and the narratives woven by its exponents would remain central to the formation of a French noble.

Notes

1 See D. Bitton, *The French Nobility in Crisis, 1560–1640* (Stanford, CA, 1969).
2 See J. Stagl, *A History of Curiosity: The Theory of Travel, 1550–1800* (London, 2004), pp. 68–9.
3 See N. Doiron, 'Voyage et humanisme', *Liberté*, 35:4–5 (1993), pp. 37–48; Doiron, 'L'être et l'espace', *Dix-Septième Siècle*, 3:252 (2011), pp. 489–500.
4 J.P. Rubiés, 'Instructions for travellers: teaching the eye to see', *History and Anthropology*, 9:2–3 (1996), p. 141.
5 See the dedicatory epistle 'au roy tres chrestien' in J. Cartier's *Brief récit* (Paris, 1545), the preface of A. Thevet's *Cosmographie de Levant* (Lyon, 1554), and the dedication to Charles IX and the 'preface a la louange des peregrinations et observations estranges' in N. de Nicolay's *Les quatre premiers livres des navigations et peregrinations orientales* (Lyon, 1568).
6 See M. Montaigne, 'De l'institution des enfants', in *Essais*, P. Villey and V.L. Saulnier, eds, (Paris, 1965), p. 153.
7 For a survey of diplomatic travellers see C. Giry-Deloison, 'France and Elizabethan England', *Transactions of the Royal Historical Society*, 14 (2004), pp. 223–43.
8 Ibid., p. 238.
9 J. Bernard, *Discours des plus memorables faits des roys & grands seigneurs d'Angleterre* (Paris, 1587); Giry-Deloison draws on Bernard's text as evidence of a declining interest, erroneously stating that it was never republished (see 'France and Elizabethan England', pp. 238–9).
10 F. du Soucy, *L'Art de voyager utilement où l'on apprend à se rendre capable de bien servir son Prince, sa patrie & soy-mesme* (Paris, 1650), p. 2.

42   Emma Pauncefort

11 For Rohan's manuscript, see Bibliothèque Nationale de France, Ms 17173, 1599–1600 Voyage d'un gentilhomme français en Italie, Allemagne, Pays-Bas, Angleterre et Écosse; signé 'H.D.R.'. The text was later published as the *Voyage du Duc de Rohan en Italie, Allemaigne, Pays-Bas Uni, Angleterre, & Escosse* (Amsterdam, 1646). All citations are taken from the later and more widely available printed version.

12 J. Boutier argues a bilateral relationship existed between the establishment of noble academies and the itineraries and pace of travel (see 'Le Grand Tour des gentilshommes et les académies d'éducation pour la noblesse: France et Italie, XVIe–XVIIIe siècle', in R. Babel and W. Paravicini, eds, *Grand Tour. Adeliges Reisen und Europaïsche Kulter vom 14. Bis zum 18 Jahrhundert* (Ostfildern, 2005), pp. 237–53).

13 Examples of such studies include G. Ascoli, *La Grande-Bretagne devant l'opinion française au XVII siècle* (Paris, 1930), and P. Langford, *Englishness Identified: Manners and Character 1650–1850* (Oxford, 2000).

14 E. Bates, *Touring in 1600: A Study in the Development of Travels as a Means of Education* (Boston and New York, 1911), p. 31; H. Trevor-Roper, *Europe's Physician: The Life of Sir Theodore de Mayerne, 1573–1655* (New Haven, 2006), p. 44; J. Dewald, *Status, Power, and Identity in Early Modern France: The Rohan Family, 1550–1715* (University Park, PA, 2015), p. 52.

15 R. Lassels *The Voyage of Italy* (Paris, 1670), preface.

16 For example, J. Black, 'Grand Tour', in A. Kors, ed., *Encyclopedia of the Enlightenment*, Vol. 2 (Oxford, 2003), pp. 151–3.

17 J. Boutier, 'Le Grand Tour: une pratique d'éducation des noblesses européennes (XVIe–XVIIIe siècles)', *Bulletin de l'Association des Historiens modernistes des Universités*, 27 (2004), p. 8.

18 R. Shackleton, 'The Grand Tour in the eighteenth century', *Studies in Eighteenth-Century Culture*, 1 (1971), pp. 127–42.

19 Boutier, 'Le Grand Tour', p. 12.

20 G. Bertrand, *Le grand tour revisité: pour une archéologie du tourisme: le voyage des français en Italie, milieu XVIIe siècle–debut XIXe siècle* (Rome, 2008), p. 2.

21 G. Bertrand, 'Le Grand Tour: une expression problématique pour désigner les pratiques du voyage des élites en Europe à l'époque moderne?' (2009) (http://www.crlv.org/conference/le-grand-tour-une-expression-problém atique-pour-désigner-les-pratiques-du-voyage-des) [accessed 18 November 2015].

22 Boutier, 'Le Grand Tour: une pratique d'éducation', pp. 9-10, 20-1.

23 See note 14 above.

24 In references to a 'Grand Tour' in the entries for 'tour' in the *Dictionnaire*'s first, fourth and fifth editions (1694, 1762 and 1798 respectively) 'grand' is employed as a qualifying adjective rather than a constituent of a compound term or well-defined cultural concept. Entries for 'voyage' also do not reference the term 'Grand Tour'.

25 R. Lassels, *Voyage d'Italie ..., traduit de l'anglais*, 2 vols (Paris, 1671), preface.

26 J. Nicot, *Le Thresor de la langue françoyse* (Paris, 1606), lists examples of travel to Jerusalem and Germany for war. Later seventeenth-century dictionaries emphasised the extensive undertaking of a voyage. See for example, 'voyage' in the *Dictionnaire de l'académie française* (Paris, 1694).

27 A. Le Brun, *Le Choix des épistres de Lipse traduites de Latin en François par Anthoine Brun, de Dole en la Franche Comté* (Lyon, 1650), pp. 17–33. Throughout his translation, first published in 1619, Le Brun translates the noun and verb – 'peregrinatio' and 'peregrinari' – with the terms 'voyage' and 'voyager' respectively.

The Duc de Rohan's Voiage *of 1600*   43

28 See, for example, M. Duchet, *Anthropologie et histoire au siècle des lumières* (Paris, 1995), and N. Bisaha, *Creating East and West: Renaissance Humanists and the Ottoman Turks* (Philadelphia, 2004).
29 Boutier, 'Le grand tour: une pratique d'éducation', p. 20.
30 Stagl, *A History of Curiosity*, pp. 83–4.
31 Motley, *Becoming a French Aristocrat*, p. 191.
32 See note 18 above.
33 See E. Pauncefort, 'Review of *La République en voyage, 1770–1830*, ed. by G. Bertrand and P. Serna', *French History*, 29:1 (2015), p. 122.
34 See Stagl, *A History of Curiosity*.
35 See J. Stagl, *Apodemiken: Eine räsonnierte Bibliographie der reisetheoretischen Literatur des 16., 17. und 18. Jahrhunderts* (Paderborn, 1983). There are a number of striking omissions of French texts in Stagl's bibliography.
36 Normand Doiron's key study passes over all material between Lipsius's 1578 letter and Le Brun's 1619 French translation (*L'art de voyager: Le déplacement à l'époque classique* (Paris, 1995)).
37 Dewald, *The Rohan Family*, p. 38.
38 Trevor-Roper, *Europe's Physician*, pp. 45, 52. Mayerne's notes reveal that Rohan was accompanied by his younger brother Benjamin, the later duc de Soubise, Armand Nompar de Caumont, heir to the highest-ranking Protestant family in Guyenne, and several other unnamed Huguenot young nobles.
39 Ibid. Trevor-Roper dismisses Rohan's account as having 'the dry character of Baedeker'.
40 For a fierce criticism of unregulated travel, see F. de La Noue, *Discours politiques et militaires* (Basle, 1875), pp. 8, 143–51, 244–5, 272–3, 557–8.
41 For a bibliography of foreign travel writing on England, see E.G. Cox, *A Reference Guide to the Literature of Travel: Including Voyages, Geographical Descriptions, Adventures, Shipwrecks and Expeditions* (Seattle, 1949), Vol. 3, pp. 84–90.
42 For a record of Duplessis-Mornay's refuge in England, see the account given by his wife (C. Duplessis-Mornay, *Les Mémoires de Madame de Mornay*, ed. N. Kuperty-Tsur (Paris, 2010), pp. 91, 97, 147–50). See also R. Patry, *Philippe du Plessis-Mornay. Un huguenot, homme d'état, 1549–1623* (Paris, 1933), pp. 10–19.
43 See, for example, B. de Monconys' posthumous *Iournal des voyages de Monsieur de Monconys, conseiller du Roy en ses Conseils d'Estat & Privé & lieutenant Criminel au Siege Presidial de Lyon*, 2 vols (Lyon, 1665–6), and François Brunet's manuscript travelogue (British Library Add Ms 35177, 1767, 'Voyage d'Angleterre').
44 BnF, Ms 13375 f. 1, 1671, [anon], 'Voyages d'Italie, Allemagne, Pays-Bas et Angleterre, par un jeune seigneur de la cour de Louis XIV' (1669–71).
45 W. Sherman, 'Stirrings and searchings (1500–1720)', in P. Hulme and T. Youngs, eds, *The Cambridge Companion to Travel Writing* (Cambridge, 2013), p. 17.
46 For example, S. Sorbière, *Relation d'un voyage en Angleterre* (Paris, 1664); C. Patin, *Relations historiques* (Lyon, 1674); C. Jordan, *Voyages historiques* (Paris, 1692).
47 Rohan's trip is testimony to this. No other member of his travelling party produced a travel record (see note 38 above). A further contextual point is that authors endured an uneasy status before the eighteenth century, with writing for an occupation denigrated by the upper classes.
48 Rohan, *Voyage*, pp. 2, 255. The subsequent ownership of the manuscript copy – the manuscript bears the ex-libris of Balthasar-Henry de Fourcy – suggests that, in fact, the lesser elite took an equal interest in Rohan's travelogue.

44   Emma Pauncefort

(De Fourcy was a statesman of lower noble stock who rose to multiple positions of eminence.)

49 Motley, *Becoming a French Aristocrat*, pp. 187–92.
50 Internal evidence in Brunet's *Voyage* suggests the Duke de Chavigny to whom he refers was Jacques-Léon, who was born in 1640.
51 Rohan, *Voyage*, pp. 226–32.
52 Ibid., pp. 239–53.
53 Ibid., pp. 232–9.
54 Ibid., pp. 9–10, 33.
55 See his description of Rome (ibid., pp. 58–9).
56 In his 1599 treatise on history, La Popelinière had advised that the narration of past events ought to create a sense of grandeur and that such relations were to colour discussion of geography: L.V. de La Popelinière, *L'idée de l'histoire accomplice* (Paris, 1599), quoted in Doiron, *L'art de voyager*, p. 37.
57 W. Harris, 'Creoleness: the crossroads of a civilization?', in A.J.M. Bundy, ed., *Selected Essays*, cited in B. Ashcroft, G. Griffiths and H. Tiffin, eds, *Key Concepts in Post-Colonial Studies* (London, 1998), p. 174.
58 See T. Claydon, *Europe and the Making of England, 1660–1760* (Cambridge, 2007), pp. 7, 61, 66.
59 Rohan, *Voyage*, p. 180.
60 Ibid., p. 184.
61 Ibid., p. 190.
62 Ibid., pp. 194–5.
63 Ibid., pp. 195–6.
64 Ibid., p. 196.
65 In contrast, Charlotte Duplessis-Mornay recorded how her husband, Philippe, ripped up and hid a poem he had written for the English monarch in case he was intercepted during his 1572 mission to the English court, which he undertook to entreaty Elizabeth I to champion the Protestant cause (Duplessis-Mornay, *Mémoires*, p. 91).
66 Rohan, *Voyage*, p. 198.
67 Ibid., p. 199.
68 See note 53 above.
69 Rohan, *Voyage*, p. 200.
70 Ibid., pp. 206–8, 217, 218.
71 Ibid., p. 42.
72 Ibid., pp. 22–3, 43.
73 Ibid., pp. 214–15.
74 Ibid., pp. 221–2, 224.
75 Ibid., pp. 234–5.
76 Trevor-Roper, *Europe's Physician*, pp. 47–8.
77 Rohan, *Voyage*, pp. 238–9.
78 T. Pelletier, *La nourriture de la noblesse* (Paris, 1604).
79 See note 40 above.
80 Pelletier, *La nourriture de la noblesse*, pp. 90r–90v, 98v–99v.
81 Ibid., pp. 966f–96v.
82 Ibid., p. 100r.
83 Ibid., pp. 101f, 106f.
84 D. Swartz, *Culture and Power: The Sociology of Pierre Bourdieu* (Chicago, 1997), p. 42.
85 I. Flandrois, *L'institution du prince au début du XVIIe Siècle* (Paris, 1992), p. 46.
86 Dewald, *The Rohan Family*, p. 37; see note 48 above.

The Duc de Rohan's Voiage of 1600   45

87 See note 4 above.
88 See the dedicatory epistle addressed to Charles II and Louis XIV, who are designated 'the sovereign powers of Christianity', in S. Chappuzeau, *L'Europe vivante ou relation nouvelle historique et politique de tous ses États* (Geneva, 1666). Chappuzeau wrote *L'Europe vivante* following multiple trips to England. For a study of Chappuzeau's travels, see N. Jennings and M. Jones, *A Biography of Samuel Chappuzeau, a Seventeenth-Century French Huguenot Playwright, Scholar, Traveller, and Preacher: An Encyclopedic Life* (Lewiston, NY, 2012).
89 For a preliminary study of the challenge mounted against noble and antiquarian cultures of travel and the narratives of these modes of travel, see E. Pauncefort, 'Capitalising on the English urban model: the writings of Miège (1685/1725) and Muralt (1725) and the pitting of economic capital against the "cultural capital" of Paris', *L'Esprit Créateur*, 55:3 (2015), pp. 29–44.

3 Foubert's academy

British and Irish elite formation in seventeenth- and eighteenth-century Paris and London

Richard Ansell

An exploration of early modern travel culture offers the chance to consider diverse outlooks and practices related to European voyages, rather than simply to examine journeys in isolation. The opportunity is welcome because historians tend to remove travellers from the contexts in which they understood and undertook foreign experience. Studies of travel from seventeenth- and eighteenth-century England or Britain usually begin as young men arrive in continental Europe and typically end as they re-cross the Channel.[1] Journeys appear divorced from family circumstances and strategies, which dictated whether young men left home at all and shaped the forms of travel pursued by those who ventured abroad. Why did some undertake continental travel while others did not? How did travellers prepare for foreign encounters? What alternatives were there for those who remained in Britain and Ireland? Such questions rarely appear in studies of travel, but they should feature prominently in explorations of travel culture.[2]

One way in which to look beyond the Grand Tour is to examine the context of domestic preparations and alternatives within which foreign voyages took place. From this perspective, London is arguably the most underestimated northern metropolis in accounts of early modern British and Irish travel culture. According to one Anglo-Irish landowner, Robert Molesworth, the English capital was an 'Epitome of the World'. Weighing the benefits and risks of educational travel, Molesworth felt that London afforded some of the advantages of foreign experience to those who had not been 'very conversant with the World'.[3] Charles Petty, teenage son of the political economist William, similarly argued that he might inform himself 'of every Crick and Corner of the Habitable World' without leaving Piccadilly.[4] The educational opportunities of the English capital were prominent in contemporary thinking about the value, purpose and form of foreign travel.

The Fouberts, a family of Huguenot immigrants, offer an opportunity to explore the centrality of London to a travel culture that thrived in the higher reaches of British and Irish society. Solomon Foubert taught noble and gentlemanly 'accomplishments', with an emphasis on horse-riding, at

Parisian academies from at least the late 1650s. Little evidence remains of his background, save for his Protestantism and his likely origins in Normandy, but Foubert moved his establishment to London in 1679, fleeing religious persecution. When Solomon died in 1696, his son, Henri, assumed control until his own death in 1743. Instruction in riding, increasingly without pretention to a fuller 'academy' formation, continued under descendants until 1778.[5] The Fouberts remained prominent in family strategies and wider debates over several generations, offering access to contemporary thinking, at the levels of government, civil society and family, about the purposes and desirability of educational travel.

This chapter begins with an account of the Foubert family's educational endeavours in late seventeenth- and early eighteenth-century Paris and London, setting them in the context of a broader academy movement and its bodily theories of nobility. Existing institutional histories would be difficult to surpass, given a lack of official records, but manuscript correspondence allows an unprecedented emphasis on parents and students. Searches for 'Foubert' and its variant spellings in British, Irish and American archives have indicated useful sources, as have mentions in the *Oxford Dictionary of National Biography*, the *History of Parliament*, *Early English Books Online*, *Eighteenth Century Collections Online* and the Burney Collection of contemporary newspapers. Manuscript references to fellow students have, in turn, suggested further archival exploration, compiling evidence for parental thinking and student experience. The second half of the chapter draws on these sources to assess the ways in which families used the academy, establishing its position in early modern British and Irish travel culture. The Fouberts offer a chance to explore the function of mediators in Anglo-French 'cultural exchange', currently a developing field of enquiry, and help to gauge the position of that exchange in British and Irish elite formation.[6]

'Master of an Academy at Paris'

When Solomon Foubert arrived in London in early 1679, he had already 'been Master of an Academy at Paris during the space of about twenty years'.[7] In the heyday of such institutions, between 1600 and 1680, there were seven or eight in the French capital and between 18 and 20 in the provinces. Academies prioritised horsemanship, dancing, fencing and military mathematics (often known as 'fortification'), but they complemented this core with languages, history, civil law or particular specialities. The emphasis lay on developing the body as a social symbol: dancing masters, for instance, taught pupils how to walk and greet company. The perfection of nobility through behavioural training flowed from the Italian Renaissance, but France supplanted Italy as a centre of 'academy improvements' over the late sixteenth and seventeenth centuries. Frenchmen founded institutions to teach accomplishments at home, leading a continental trend that sought to

48   *Richard Ansell*

save young noblemen from the supposed moral and physical dangers of Italian travel.[8]

Academies are an under-represented aspect of early modern travel culture. The tendency to see the Grand Tour as an 'invisible academy' or an 'informal' addition to domestic education overshadows the integral and early part that situated learning played in elite, adolescent, male voyages. Here was another way in which early modern travel was an urban experience, involving lengthy settlement in academy towns, and a more northern undertaking than scholarship on the 'lure of Italy' would allow.[9] Some families from France sought an alternative to Italian journeys, while others attended in preparation for southerly travel, but the use of French academies was a shared aspect of travel culture among British, Irish Protestant, Dutch and German families.[10] These institutions prepared young men to make a good impression in continental high society, but travellers like the teenage earl of Orrery, who would have been 'asshamed to return' to Ireland in 1689 'without knowing my exercises', also recognised that these accomplishments carried their own prestige.[11]

Since academies aimed to alter bearing and even body shape, developing both stature and constitution, experts recommended attendance in the mid- to late teens.[12] One tutor advocated a nine- or ten-month stay and an English traveller reported that French wisdom 'counted twelve months enough to perfect al yt is learnt in accademye'.[13] Besides Paris, the towns of the Loire Valley, including Orléans, Blois, Saumur and Angers, proved popular for their plentiful masters and pure spoken French.[14] Throughout the seventeenth century, French, German and Dutch students outnumbered travellers from Britain and Ireland, who would dominate, especially by the Loire, later in the eighteenth century.[15] Foubert's Royal Academy, on the Rue Sainte-Marguerite in the Faubourg Saint-Germain, particularly attracted fellow Huguenots like the marquis d'Ausson, who listed teachers and students in 1668, but the institution stood at the centre of an academy movement that represented a shared aspect of travel culture among a spread of European elites.[16]

Foubert later recalled that, in Paris, he had been 'intrusted with the Education of severall of the Nobility and Gentry of England as well as of other Nations'.[17] He took English lodgers during the 1650s, when Cromwell's ambassador to France suggested 'preferment as a rider of his Highness' horses', but evidence is clearest for the 1670s, when Foubert welcomed sons of the duke of Hamilton, the marquis of Halifax and the earls of Clarendon and Bath.[18] The Hamiltons and the Rawdon family, from Lisburn in Ireland, suggest that parents and tutors chose Foubert for his good horses, his range of masters and his 'sober' students, but also because staff and pupils worshipped 'in the protestant way' amid the 'temptations' of Paris.[19] John Rawdon, for whom Foubert was a budgeted alternative to Cambridge, joins Caleb Banks, the son of a prominent London merchant, and John Norborne, a Wiltshire gentleman, as evidence for attendance below the nobility.[20] These young men brought tutors, who presumably numbered among the learned Englishmen whom Solomon Foubert thanked in his 1666 translation of Gervase Markham's *The Perfect Horseman*, and servants, among whom one tutor counted 'near 30 footmen'.[21] Foubert was already a cultural mediator at the heart of an English-speaking community in Paris.

The combination of Protestantism and educational expertise attracted domestic and foreign students, but it also placed Foubert under threat. Parisian Huguenots had co-existed in a Catholic city for much of the seventeenth century but, as royal policy grew more hostile in the two decades after 1661, Foubert faced 'great & frequent allarms of being suppressed (by reason of his professing the [r]eformed Religion)'.[22] Royal edicts forbade Protestant masters from teaching exercises and, when an *ordonnance* of 16 January 1679 recognised that Foubert had maintained his academy regardless, city authorities backed up the king's orders in a year of intensifying moves against reformed religion.[23] Foubert was not 'allowed one hour's time for putting off his numerous equipage of horse', an expulsion that Huguenots cited as another set-back for their community.[24] Some Englishmen, however, saw an opportunity. John Brisbane, a diplomatic secretary in Paris, immediately suggested to government officials that Foubert 'ought to be encouraged to set up an academy in London, as these establishments have been of great service in France'.[25]

The move to London

John Brisbane was only the latest Englishman to suggest the establishment of an 'academy' at home. Historians apply the term to diverse institutions, but confusion is nothing new: what is an academy, asked one Oxford don in 1700, if the great schools of London and the ancient universities do not count?[26] This chapter focuses on the bodily and mental formation of the nobility and gentry, continuing along Italian Renaissance lines. The reigns of Elizabeth and James I saw several court-centred projects, from Sir Humphrey Gilbert's 1570s design for an expanded school of wards to a 'college' in the household of Prince Henry. Under Charles I and the Commonwealth, a series of projectors like Sir Francis Kynaston and Sir Balthazar Gerbier failed to gain official support but enjoyed brief, modest success in smaller London premises. These establishments, whether planned or executed, claimed to address the inability of the grammar schools, universities and Inns of Court to provide practical education for a social and governmental elite, hoping to end dangerous and expensive foreign travel by providing instruction at home. Proposals usually failed because of inadequate official backing, the opposition of the universities and the growing cachet of educational travel.[27]

Existing accounts of English 'academies' end before the restoration of monarchy in 1660, but two decades of renewed Stuart rule produced a

50   *Richard Ansell*

distinctive context for Foubert's arrival in London. Gentlemen from Britain and Ireland had, during the civil wars and the interregnum, broadened experience of continental travel beyond the nobility, while Charles II had spent the 1650s abroad and now sat at the centre of a 'network of cultural mediators' who encouraged Restoration 'Gallomania'.[28] Projectors seeking royal and elite patronage could no longer pretend that the avoidance of foreign educational travel was possible or desirable, arguing only that it was 'Troublesom, Dangerous and Costly' for young men to be sent 'too early into France'. Grounding in 'Languages, Exercises, and competent Judgment' would allow them 'to use their Travels with Advantage'.[29] Investigations into the 'origins' of the Grand Tour reach beyond this chapter, but the years after the Restoration may have confirmed foreign educational travel as a cultural fixture to be improved rather than denied.[30]

Foubert also entered an immediate confessional context. The fear that journeys to Catholic Europe risked the mass conversion of the English elite, though perhaps informing the earliest academy proposals, had declined since the 1570s. Opponents of travel instead stigmatised the conduct and demeanour of returned young men.[31] Over the 1670s, however, royal policies revived English wariness of 'popery and arbitrary government', which now focused on the prospect of a French counter-reformation led by Louis XIV. Fears culminated in the autumn of 1678, when revelations surfaced of a supposed 'Popish Plot' to assassinate Charles II. Hundreds of tracts attacked Jesuits, the presumed instruments of counter-reformation, and Catholics were executed for membership of the Society of Jesus.[32] Against this backdrop, Brisbane hoped that Foubert would settle in England not only because academies had 'been of great service in France', but also because, with the closure of Protestant institutions, which Foubert himself blamed on 'the reiterated Instances of the French Clergy', English educational travellers were now 'exposed to the wiles of the Jesuits'.[33]

Brisbane's suggestions obviously received official encouragement. Foubert arrived in London and laid his proposal for a 'Royall Academy for Military Exercises' before the Privy Council in May 1679, a month before his possessions, including 'large folios relating to the academy and horse-manship', reached the Thames.[34] He proved sensitive to English debates, proposing to educate the nobility and gentry in 'Martial and vertuous Exercises befitting their Quality' and according to 'the manner of the best disciplined Academies beyond the seas'. Foubert would teach all exercises 'commonly' found abroad, from riding, bearing arms, vaulting, fencing and dancing to history, mathematics, fortification, navigation and geography. Masters, servants and a chaplain would speak French, so that students might 'Learn and improve' the language through lessons and 'familliar common discourse'. Preparation 'of the mind and of the Body at home' would render young men 'fitter to improve' abroad, but the academy would also serve domestic purposes. Foubert would offer some 'stricktness and Discipline' between university and travel, 'the most dangerous step of youth', and keep

Foubert's academy 51

'vast sums of Money' in England. He might, rather than preventing travel, attract 'other Protestants from abroad as Germans, Dutch, and even the french themselves of the same communion', who might 'bring their money with them, and becom English men both in affection and Liking'.[35]

Most compellingly, Foubert recognised the confessional climate. The 'dangerous necessity' of adolescent travel to France, where Jesuits had 'ingrossed' education, risked exposure to 'pernicious Impressions and Contagious Principles', since the teachings of 'Popish Seminaries, Schools, and Academies' were 'contrary and unessencial to all true English-men'. Foubert would, though, ensure that his family, servants and masters were 'Known sincere, and true' Protestants. Desires for a London academy were motivated by more than anti-Catholicism, looking to encourage domestic spending and attract foreign students, but fear of 'popery', and particularly of Jesuit educators, shaped early English attitudes towards Foubert. At a sensitive time, he would avoid 'making shipwreck of the Protestant Religion'.[36]

Foubert's calculated proposals, so attuned to national debates for a recent arrival, suggest involvement by English friends and former students.[37] He certainly forged relationships with fellows of the Royal Society like Sir Robert Southwell, the Privy Council secretary present for his proposals, and John Evelyn. The society suggested that Foubert take over the vacant Chelsea College, a fixture of previous plans for a London academy, and Evelyn helped to assess other houses in the capital.[38] The Royal Society continued the Hartlib Circle's support for educational projectors, but their advocacy of Foubert also sits amid diverse engagement with travel.[39] Fellows encouraged long-distance voyages, recruiting sailors, merchants and diplomats into their observational approach to natural history, and planned shorter educational journeys, including periods at French and Dutch academies, in their own families.[40] The Royal Society backed Foubert in the hope that an academy 'built by subscription of worthy gentlemen and noblemen for the education of youth' would 'lessen the vast expense the nation is yearly at by sending children into France to be taught military exercises', but their economic justification of a London academy by no means rejected educational travel.[41]

These proposals met with qualified royal support. Charles appointed Foubert Supernumerary Equerry, a position for which he received four and a half years of backdated salary in December 1684, but the king also offered informal 'bounty', including at least £540 between 1681 and 1683.[42] The family had the means to occupy two houses on Sherwood Street in Soho before June 1679 and took students immediately, using adjoining fields for riding before railing in a permanent space in 1684.[43] Foubert employed the London press to advertise his arrival, display his Parisian credentials and declare his 'readiness to receive such Noble Persons as shall be pleased to come into his Academy', though his exploitation of print fell short of Gerbier's prolific self-promotion two decades earlier.[44]

52   *Richard Ansell*

The earl of Ossory hoped that his son might study with Foubert as early as April 1679 and prospective parents noted that, by July 1680, the academy taught 'divers persons of quality'.[45] Foubert's reputation spread through correspondence and conversation in court circles, but his use of print suggests a determination to attract the gentry represented in his early student body.

Neither royal promises nor the Royal Society's assistance yielded the public establishment that Foubert craved. The reign of the Catholic James II is an archival blind-spot, perhaps because Foubert lost official backing, but the family subsequently pursued alternative sources of income. In 1695, Solomon joined attempts to fund an academy through a public lottery, a method in which many projectors saw a panacea during the early financial revolution, but the failed scheme featured impractically broad tuition for women and men. It notably recognised, however, that French and Italian noblemen were not 'Born Soldiers, and Virtuosi' but 'Made so'.[46] William III paid Henri Foubert, with whom he had fought at the Boyne, an annual subsidy of £500 to leave the army and run the academy upon his father's death in 1696, but the situation was still insecure.[47] Henri participated in ill-fated plans to found an Oxford riding school in 1702 and had turned to former pupils by 1710, seeking help with the construction of new premises on Swallow Street. The latter project was successful, but the buildings were eventually demolished to make way for Regent Street in the early nineteenth century.[48]

Over the eighteenth century, attempts to make ends meet encouraged a shift from broad academy improvements to practical military training. The army offered a logical clientele for Henri Foubert as the horsemanship of the *haute école* declined among an aristocracy more interested in racing and hunting.[49] Cavalry officers attended for brief periods to hone their technique, as Henri's appearances in family accounts narrow to riding tuition and the supply of equipment, though the attendance and patronage of Prince William Augustus, the duke of Cumberland, suggests renewed royal support during the 1730s and 1740s.[50] The story of the Fouberts is a common one in the history of attempts to found a French-style academy in England, despite its longevity: from ambitious beginnings and the promise of royal establishment, the academy ended up a more focused institution that sought to finance itself. The family also stand among other Huguenot educators who set up schools or academies, particularly in and around London, during the 1680s and 1690s.[51] The Fouberts, however, occupied an unusually prominent and revelatory position in British and Irish travel culture, especially in the early London decades explored in the rest of this chapter.

Life at Foubert's academy

Student numbers shaped daily life at the London academy, but figures are rarely clear. Letters by parents and pupils refer only to 'divers persons of

Foubert's academy   53

quality', while promotional materials seem reluctant to set numerical limits. French institutions offer a guide, since the Fouberts determined to copy their approach, and examples from the early seventeenth to the mid-eighteenth centuries suggest between 20 and 40 pupils at any one time.[52] Solomon Foubert's student body likely expanded and contracted across a similar range, requiring larger accommodation than the houses acquired in 1679, but it narrowed under the direction of Henri. His 15 or 16 pupils in 1737, seven in 1738 and 'very few scholars' in 1739 offer evidence of decline.[53] The London institution nevertheless saw high turnover, as students usually paid quarterly bills for a few months of boarding and tuition.

Riding dominated the academy, where pupils built up 'a martial look, posture, and countenance' through 'emulation', and the Fouberts occasionally held 'carousels' in which current and former students publicly demonstrated their skills.[54] Horsemanship took pride of place in the morning, as in France, leaving afternoons for other exercises, learning and London engagements.[55] The academy also offered fencing, dancing, handling of arms and mathematics in 1680, though Foubert presumably tailored the curriculum to supply and demand.[56] One 1686 publication asserts that he boasted 'the best Masters for all sorts of Exercises', but there is no London equivalent of d'Ausson's 1668 list.[57] Foubert surely brought Huguenot masters with him, given his promise of reformed, French-speaking tutors, and the Parisian closure certainly left Protestant teachers out of work, but evidence is limited to a handful of French names in student correspondence and printed advertisements over decades.[58]

Beyond teaching, student experience involved engagement with the metropolitan and courtly opportunities of London. If Renaissance-style academies ideally turned young men into courtiers, establishments like the *Accademia Reale* in Turin cemented this connection by building at the centre of power.[59] Foubert initially hoped for something similar in the 'City of Westminster near and about the Court', but his premises near the Haymarket still allowed him to supervise the social lives of young noblemen like the teenage Baron Kingsale, for whom 'ye nearness of Whitehall seems to sweeten ye apprehensions of ye discipline of an Academy'.[60] Foubert departed from Parisian practice by preventing students from bringing tutors, attaining a level of control that George Hastings, the son of the earl of Huntingdon, tried to avoid by living out of the academy.[61] The institution supervised first adolescent experiences of London, allowing young gentlemen like Maurice Johnson of Spalding in Lincolnshire to visit antiquarians and the Royal Society alongside riding and French lessons.[62] Foubert offered a structured option to families who had previously used the Inns of Court as informal finishing schools.[63]

The supposed 'discipline' of the academy attracted parents and guardians, but it was not always firm.[64] The poor reputation of French institutions, notorious for gambling and prostitution, travelled to England with

54 Richard Ansell

Foubert.[65] A character in Thomas Otway's 1684 play, *The Atheist*, arrives in London and demands to know 'what Sins are stirring in this Noble Metropolis', hearing of Foubert among the talking points of a new 'Race of Vermin they call Wits'.[66] Otway's depiction has some basis in student behaviour, though evidence is scarce in family letters. One pupil, Edward Nicholas, reported to Robert Harley, who had recently departed in 1682, that the academy seemed 'like a Sodome, that you have left for fear of a punisment on your selfe'. Unspecified misbehaviour had killed one student, Samuel Fenwick, whose peers were far from 'a thorough reformation'. Foubert had blamed his 'most miserable Accademists' for 'many & great disorders of Late', warning that friends and even the king 'had taken ye freedom to tell him of ye loosenes his Academy was in'.[67] William, the teen-age Lord North and Grey, ironically undertook Italian travel in 1696 to avoid debts and corrupting company gathered over a year with Foubert in London.[68] Some parents realised this reputation, withdrawing their sons, but in these 'disorders' lay the roots of networks that would serve students in later life.[69]

Foubert's academy in travel culture

The ways in which parents and guardians used Foubert's academy indicate its position in travel culture, but family strategies were the products of trade-offs between means and ambitions. The cost of attending the Parisian institution was daunting, whether the £150 that the earl of Arran spent in his first three months or John Rawdon's projected £170 a year, despite the presumption that no 'person, of what qualité soever should live high, so long as he is in an Academy'.[70] Expenses fell with the move to England, offering a new possibility to families unable to afford foreign travel, but they remained prohibitive. Riding tuition cost between three and five guin-eas a month in the 1720s and 1730s, with a guinea worth a pound and a shilling, but families also paid an entrance fee of four to six guineas and, if boarding, provided 'Furniture of a Chamber, riding-Equipage &c.'[71] George Hastings suggests various additional costs, accounting for 28 pounds and 13 shillings spent at Foubert's in the last quarter of 1695 besides living expenses, servants' wages and, controversially, alternative accommodation.[72] Wealthy noblemen like Hastings's father answered such sums easily, but other families found Foubert at the limits of their spending power. Even Sir Donat O'Brien, reputedly the richest commoner in Ireland, reminded his son, Lucius, that his expenses were 'very heavy upon me', but promised to keep him with Foubert for a year, sticking 'at nothing I can by any means compass for your education & advantage'.[73] Differing finances, as well as divergent religious and cultural outlooks, led families to incorpo-rate the academy into various educational strategies.

During his earliest London years, Foubert allowed some to avoid French travel in the context of the Popish Plot. Charles II plucked the young Baron

Kingsale from his Irish Catholic family and marked him for an English Protestant upbringing in the late 1670s and early 1680s, but financial short-comings and religious dangers precluded foreign travel. The king instead demanded that Kingsale end a troubled period at Oxford and board with Foubert, a recent arrival from France offering his best hope of Protestant Anglicisation.[74] Robert Harley, the son of a godly Hertfordshire gentry family who criticised the vice and luxury of London, is similarly unlikely to have contemplated foreign travel, particularly amid confessional tensions.[75] The future earl of Oxford moved in mid-1680 from a dissenting academy to Foubert, whom his father chose after visits and consultations.[76] Robert left for Inner Temple in late 1682, perhaps driven away by the Huguenot academy's lax morality, but Foubert nevertheless offered a managed engagement with metropolitan and cosmopolitan opportunities to a family who might otherwise have rejected such accomplishments.[77] The academy catered for 'hotter' Protestants and conversion risks alike, offering some of the cultural advantages of French travel without its religious dangers.

Other families, particularly among the nobility, incorporated Foubert into educational repertoires alongside continental travel. George Savile, first marquis of Halifax, sent his eldest son, Henry, to Foubert's Parisian institution in 1675; William, the middle brother, spent 1679–81 in Geneva before matriculating at Oxford; and George, the youngest, also went to Geneva but afterwards began at Foubert's London premises in his mid-teens.[78] Decades later, the academy worked similarly for the Spencers. Charles, the future third duke of Marlborough, and his brother, John, both left Eton in 1722 for Foubert, but John remained when Charles left for Geneva the following year. The brothers then travelled together through France and Italy between 1725 and 1728, including nine months at the duke of Lorraine's military academy at Lunéville.[79] Foubert functioned as a stop-gap for the wealthiest families, complementing periods of 'settlement' at foreign institutions.

The academy also entered the calculations of the gentry, whether in preparation or substitution for continental travel. The Nicholas family, Dorset and Surrey landowners with a strong London presence, sent Edward to Foubert between Oxford and a continental voyage in the early 1680s, but his younger brother, John, rode at institutions in Saumur and Angers.[80] The Yarburghs of Yorkshire similarly sent their eldest son, James, to Foubert in 1681, but their third son, Blague, probably attended the academy at Orléans around 1701. Perhaps Lady Yarburgh remembered Foubert when she reminded James that she had surrendered ten pounds of her yearly allowance to fund his studies at 'a Southen Scoule'.[81] Other aspiring provincial families, of insufficient means to compass foreign travel for any of their sons, considered Foubert as a new option, though evidence of calculations at this level is scarce. Early pupils surely foreshadowed Maurice Johnson, who recognised in 1730 that 'it will cost my ffather a great deal of money my being here' and so minded his 'riding & ffrench as

56   *Richard Ansell*

much as I possibly can'.[82] For such families, Foubert offered new access to accomplishments previously restricted to those who could afford foreign travel. Whether students attended in preparation for continental voyages or as an alternative, Foubert's academy formed part of a broader travel culture that English families embraced differently according to household economies and educational ambitions.

Families from Ireland and Scotland lacked nearby options for academy learning. A plan to repurpose the Irish school of wards into a broader Protestant institution, imparting 'all Good Literature, and Noble Qualities' to the nobility and gentry in Dublin, never progressed beyond its proposal to Charles II in the early 1660s. The scheme would have kept young men from 'the danger of Travayle, and Corruption of their Religion & Manners in Forraigne parts by their Education Abroad', but privileged sons ventured from Ireland to continental academies throughout the seventeenth century.[83] Wealthy Scottish students might approximate such learning through private tuition at university, as did the earl of Arran in the 1670s, or at one of the handful of dancing schools that rose and fell in Edinburgh during the late seventeenth and early eighteenth centuries, but institutional options for riding and fencing only appeared in Glasgow and the capital from the 1760s.[84] Families from Ireland and Scotland continued to send sons abroad, especially while local alternatives remained limited, but Foubert added a new and more convenient possibility.

London was already an educational centre for Protestants and Catholics from Ireland, who particularly frequented the Inns of Court, and the English capital often acted as a 'staging post' for further travel.[85] For the wealthiest, invariably Protestant under the Cromwellian settlement, Foubert added a new metropolitan option between university and a continental voyage, where 'there was formerly the Inns of Court alone'. In 1683, Sir Robert Southwell informed correspondents in Limerick of a new and 'very famous Academy in London Governed by a french Gentleman Monsr. Faubert, where riding, ffrench, Mathematicks, & all exercises are tought which are usually learnt in Travell'. Southwell's kinsman, Sir Thomas, might 'passe 6 Monthes' with Foubert, 'as many Englishmen doe, ye better to prepare them for the improovemt. of Travell', though continental experience ultimately lay beyond the family's means.[86] Even without further travel, however, Foubert offered a managed introduction to London. William, Lord O'Brien and later earl of Inchiquin, boarded at the academy in 1681 and looked fondly on his metropolitan adolescence once Irish adulthood had taken him 'out of ye World'.[87] Inchiquin's 20-year-old kinsman, Lucius O'Brien, similarly learnt with Foubert in 1695, but left to acquire an 'ornamentall' knowledge of the law at Middle Temple. The O'Briens sought social accomplishments at Foubert's academy and the Inns of Court, but both institutions also provided bases for London exploration. Sir Donat, who had visited the English capital in his youth, found Lucius's letters 'short & Barren', but warned that the 'Courts at Westminster, ye

Foubert's academy 57

Parliament house, ye Kings monumts neare it, ye tower, & other places' were 'things another would take some notice of'.[88] Foubert facilitated shorter-distance educational mobility that, alongside continental travel, increasingly offered common touchstones to British and Irish elites.

The Scottish Graham family enjoyed a long-standing relationship with the Fouberts that demonstrates how far the Huguenot family were embedded in British and Irish travel culture. James, marquis of Montrose, boarded in 1699 at the Parisian academy of Longpré, which had taken over Solomon Foubert's premises on the Rue Sainte-Marguerite, but he engaged Henri to supply a groom and convey his horses back to Edinburgh after further continental travel, along with a 'Large hunting saddle such as ye king'. Montrose's son would spend the summer of 1722 at Foubert's academy, visiting court and taking riding lessons that left him 'sensillie taller' for his onward travel to Geneva.[89] For two generations of Grahams, the Foubert family acted as educators, mediators and facilitators, arranging the practicalities of travel, conveying courtly fashions and teaching an appropriately noble bearing.

Solomon Foubert repeatedly promised to attract 'Forreign Gentry hither as formerly into France', but British and Irish students mention no foreign contemporaries.[90] One example is Philipp Christoph Graf von Königsmarck, a Swedish count who arrived in 1682 before an intended period at Oxford. Philipp Christoph boarded with his travelling tutor, suggesting that Foubert sometimes relaxed personal control, and he enjoyed the plays and sociability of London alongside his studies. Evidence appears in the trial of his elder brother, Karl Johann, who stood accused of ordering the murder of a love rival, Thomas Thynne, while visiting the English court. Karl Johann swore to the jury, amid fears of the Popish Plot, that he had brought Philipp Christoph 'into England to be brought up into the Protestant Religion to shew my Inclination to the Religion, and the English Nation'.[91] If he accurately represented his brother's purposes, at least one foreigner met Foubert's lofty promises.

Little trace otherwise remains of foreign students at the London academy, although they may await discovery in northern European archives. The closure of popular Huguenot institutions in France certainly opened a gap in the market, as Protestant students avoided the territories of Louis XIV after the 1685 Revocation of the Edict of Nantes and the outbreak of war in 1687, but continental options like Geneva and Turin proved more attractive than Foubert in London.[92] One travelling tutor praised the educational entrepreneurs of Geneva, who had 'taken care to draw other Strangers thither, by establishing Masters of all Exercises that young Gentlemen are us'd to perform'. Genevan institutions attracted 'many of the Protestant Countries, as, Germany, Swedeland, Denmark, &c. who for Religion's Sake chuse rather to go to Geneva (where they may speak French) than to France'.[93] Neither, perhaps, could the Fouberts compete with the *Accademia Reale* of Turin, founded in 1680 at a 'truly bilingual'

58   *Richard Ansell*

court that united French-speaking Savoy and Italian-speaking Piedmont.[94] Students may have avoided France on political and confessional grounds but, in their continued pursuit of Francophone culture, they sought more immersive options than London. One 1710 guide for German and French visitors to the English capital presented a trip to see Henri Foubert and his students as a minor attraction rather than an educational option.[95] Into the eighteenth century, the moment was lost as French academies recovered pre-eminence.[96]

Conclusions

An examination of Foubert's academy and its position in British and Irish travel culture adds to the idea that Huguenots were 'England's cultural intermediaries *par excellence*'.[97] The family demonstrates the centrality of 'mediators' in Anglo-French 'cultural exchange', as recently outlined by Gesa Stedman, but they also begin the process of going further, suggesting how aspects of French culture interacted with British and Irish society. Patrons of the academy incorporated its teachings into the menu of attributes expected of the English Protestant gentleman, an ideal pursued by families throughout Britain and Ireland. Foubert's riding tuition, which afforded 'a more manly and disingag'd Air', features alongside 'University Learning' and foreign travel in the careful educational plan proposed by 'an honest English Gentleman' in Charles Davenant's *New Dialogues* of 1710.[98] Much as Michèle Cohen shows for educational voyages to France, families pursued French-style academy accomplishments in London as part of the broader 'construction' of the English gentleman.[99] If Stedman finds contemporaries who feared the 'disruption of indigenous culture and social order' that might accompany cultural exchange, many elite families in fact drew on the same process to bolster their prestige.[100] Neil Kenny establishes the cohesive force of 'travel-talk' among the French and German nobilities, but the Fouberts encourage historians to consider the binding power that shared patterns of gesture and comportment also offered elites in Britain, Ireland and beyond.[101]

The academy has provided an opportunity to contextualise educational voyages from Britain and Ireland, placing continental journeys within a broader travel culture. The transplanted institution particularly demonstrates the untenable nature of divisions that historians continue to maintain between domestic and foreign travel, as continental voyages overlapped with journeys to London in diverse educational strategies. For some families, Foubert approximated the cultural advantages of French travel without its confessional risks; for others, the relocated academy allowed young men to prepare for onward journeys in a safer and cheaper environment; still more parents and guardians saw a new chance to pursue accomplishments previously beyond their geographical and financial reach. But for all families, Foubert rivalled the Inns of Court as a managed introduction to

London's burgeoning social and cultural scene and an opportunity to develop influential metropolitan connections. Though young Robert Harley may have left the academy scandalised at its immorality, the earl of Oxford would receive fond reminiscences from Yorkshire and Irish contemporaries seeking patronage in the decades to come.[102] Historians of Britain and Ireland identify an increasingly homogeneous elite in the late seventeenth and eighteenth centuries, but are yet to examine many of the mechanisms by which this coalescence took place.[103] The Foubert family, their patrons and their students suggest that a comprehensive account of educational mobility, both at home and abroad, may shed light on profound social and cultural change. Mediators like Solomon and Henri Foubert will undoubtedly be central.

Notes

1 J. Stoye, *English Travellers Abroad, 1604–1667: Their Influence in English Society and Politics* (London, 1989); J. Black, *The British Abroad: The Grand Tour in the Eighteenth Century* (Stroud, 2003).

2 R. Ansell, 'Educational travel in Protestant families from post-Restoration Ireland', *Historical Journal*, 58:4 (2015), pp. 931–58.

3 R. Molesworth, *An Account of Denmark, as it was in the Year 1692* (London, 1694), sig. C4v.

4 H.W.E. Petty-FitzMaurice, marquis of Lansdowne, ed., *The Petty-Southwell Correspondence, 1676–1687* (New York, 1967), p. 303.

5 W.H. Manchée, 'The Fouberts and their Royal Academy', *Proceedings of the Huguenot Society of London*, 16 (1937), pp. 77–97; J.D. Aylward, *The English Master of Arms from the Twelfth to the Twentieth Century* (London, 1956), pp. 92–107; G. Worsley, *The British Stable* (London, 2004), p. 70.

6 G. Stedman, *Cultural Exchange in Seventeenth-Century France and England* (Farnham, 2013).

7 British Library (hereafter BL), Harley Ms 7614 f. 101, Commons Petition of Solomon Foubert [*c.* 1685].

8 E. Schalk, *From Valor to Pedigree: Ideas of Nobility in France in the Sixteenth and Seventeenth Centuries* (Princeton, 1986), pp. 177–201; M. Motley, *Becoming a French Aristocrat: The Education of the Court Nobility, 1580–1715* (Princeton, 1990), pp. 123–67; C. Doucet, 'Les académies équestres et l'éducation de la noblesse (XVIe–XVIIIe siècle)', *Revue historique*, 628 (2003/4), pp. 817–36.

9 R. Sweet, *Cities and the Grand Tour: The British in Italy, c.1690–1820* (Cambridge, 2012); I. Bignamini and A. Wilton, eds, *Grand Tour: The Lure of Italy in the Eighteenth Century* (London, 1996).

10 J. Dewald, *Aristocratic Experience and the Origins of Modern Culture: France, 1570–1715* (Oxford, 1993), p. 85; G. Verhoeven, 'Calvinist pilgrimages and popish encounters: religious identity and sacred space on the Dutch Grand Tour (1598–1685)', *Journal of Social History*, 43:3 (2010), p. 619; M. Leibetseder, 'Across Europe: educational travelling of German noblemen in a comparative perspective', *Journal of Early Modern History*, 14 (2010), pp. 437–9.

11 National Library of Ireland (hereafter NLI), Ms 36 f. 724, 5 Feb. 1688/9, Lionel Boyle, 3rd Earl of Orrery, Geneva, to Margaret Boyle, Dowager Countess of Orrery.

12 Bodleian Library (hereafter Bodl.), Carte Ms 128 f. 387v, 17 Aug. 1680, Henry Bennet, 1st Earl of Arlington, London, to James Butler, 1st Duke of Ormond;

60   *Richard Ansell*

NLI Ms 2493 f. 57, [Peter] Drelincourt, 'About education of men of family' [1670s].

13 J. Gailhard, *The Compleat Gentleman*, 2 vols (London, 1678), II, pp. 45, 137; BL Add Ms 70013 f. 116, 12 Jul. 1682, [Lady Abigail Harley], [Brampton], to Sir Edward Harley.

14 Gailhard, *Compleat Gentleman*, II, p. 33.

15 Doucet, 'Académies équestres', p. 831; D. Julia, *Atlas de la Révolution Française: 2. L'enseignement* (Paris, 1987), p. 53; S. Conway, 'Christians, Catholics, Protestants: the religious links of Britain and Ireland with continental Europe, c.1689–1800', *English Historical Review*, 124:509 (2009), p. 363.

16 I. Dumont de Bostaquet, *Memoirs of Isaac Dumont de Bostaquet, a Gentleman of Normandy Before and After the Revocation of the Edict of Nantes*, D.W. Ressinger, ed. and transl. (London, 2005), pp. 62–4, 304–5.

17 BL Harley Ms 7614 f. 101, Foubert's Petition.

18 M.A.E. Green, ed., *Calendar of State Papers, Domestic Series, [Commonwealth], 1649–60*, 13 vols (London, 1875–86), X, p. 359; G. Savile, *The Life and Letters of Sir George Savile, Bart., First Marquis of Halifax*, H.C. Foxcroft, ed., 2 vols (London, 1898), I, p. 116; H. Savile, *Savile Correspondence*, W.D. Cooper, ed. (London, 1858), p. 42.

19 National Records of Scotland (hereafter NRS), GD406/1/5979, 13 Jul. 1676, James Forbes, Blois, to William, 3rd Duke of Hamilton; GD406/1/5997, 3 Mar. 1677, Forbes, Paris, to Hamilton; Huntington Library (hereafter HL), HA 15264, 6 Jul. 1674, Humphrey Maunsell, Paris, to Lady Dorothy Rawdon.

20 HL HA 14526, 17 Apr. 1674, Edward, Earl of Conway, Ragley, to Sir George Rawdon; J. Lough, ed., *Locke's Travels in France, 1675–1679* (Cambridge, 1953), p. 195n; Anon, *The Visor Pluckt Off from Richard Thompson of Bristol, Clerk* [London, 1681].

21 NRS GD406/1/5995, 10 Feb. 1677, Forbes, Paris, to Hamilton; G. Markham, *Le nouveau et sçavant mareschal*, transl. [S.] Foubert (Paris, 1666), sig. O1v.

22 D. Garrioch, *The Huguenots of Paris and the Coming of Religious Freedom, 1685–1789* (Cambridge, 2014), pp. 24–5; M. Prestwich, 'The Huguenots under Richelieu and Mazarin, 1629–61: a golden age?', in I. Scouloudi, ed., *Huguenots in Britain and their French Background, 1550–1800* (Basingstoke, 1987), pp. 188–90; BL Harley Ms 7614 f. 101, Foubert's Petition

23 O. Douen, *La Révocation de l'Edit de Nantes à Paris d'après des documents inédits*, 3 vols (Paris, 1894), I, pp. 241–2, 331; R. Mettam, 'Louis XIV and the persecution of the Huguenots: the role of the ministers and royal officials', in Scouloudi, *Huguenots in Britain*, pp. 208–9.

24 Aylward, *English Master of Arms*, p. 95; BL Add Ms 46956A f. 11v, 15/25 Jan. 1679, Alexandre de Rasigade, Paris, to Sir Robert Southwell; P. Bayle, *Inventaire critique de la correspondance de Pierre Bayle*, E. Labrousse, ed. (Paris, 1961), letter 165; Anon, 'Extraits de la Gazette de Haarlem sur les persécutions dirigées contre les protestants français de 1679 à 1685', *Bulletin de la Société de l'Histoire du Protestantisme Français*, 28 (1879), p. 403.

25 Aylward, *English Master of Arms*, p. 95.

26 T.W. Jackson, ed., 'Dr Wallis' letter against Mr Maidwell', in C.R.L. Fletcher, ed., *Collectanea, First Series* (Oxford, 1885), p. 324.

27 P.-A. Lee, 'Some English academies: an experiment in the education of Renaissance gentlemen', *History of Education Quarterly*, 10:3 (1970), pp. 273–86; T. Raylor, 'Milton, the Hartlib Circle and the education of the aristocracy', in N. McDowell and N. Smith, eds, *The Oxford Handbook of Milton* (Oxford, 2011), pp. 382–406; R. Cust, 'Charles I's noble academy', *The Seventeenth Century*, 29:4 (2014), pp. 337–56.

Foubert's academy 61

28 M.G. Brennan, ed., *The Origins of the Grand Tour: The Travels of Robert Montagu, Lord Mandeville (1649–1654), William Hammond (1655–1658), Banaster Maynard (1660–1663)* (London, 2004), pp. 30–6; K. Lambley, *The Teaching and Cultivation of the French Language in England during Tudor and Stuart Times* (London, 1920), pp. 361–80; Stedman, *Cultural Exchange*, p. 63; M.R.F. Williams, *The King's Irishmen: The Irish in the Exiled Court of Charles II, 1649–1660* (Woodbridge, 2014).

29 E. Panton, *A Publick and Pious Design for the Preserving the Generous Youth, and Consequently the Nation from Ruine* (London, 1676), p. 1.

30 E. Chaney, *The Evolution of the Grand Tour: Anglo-Italian Cultural Relations since the Renaissance* (London, 1998); Brennan, *Origins of the Grand Tour*; E. Chaney and T. Wilks, *The Jacobean Grand Tour: Early Stuart Travellers in Europe* (London, 2014).

31 S. Warneke, *Images of the Educational Traveller in Early Modern England* (Leiden, 1995).

32 J. Scott, 'England's troubles: exhuming the Popish Plot', in T. Harris, P. Seaward and M. Goldie, eds, *The Politics of Religion in Restoration England* (Oxford, 1990), pp. 107–31; T. Claydon, *Europe and the Making of England, 1660–1760* (Cambridge, 2007), pp. 223–41.

33 Aylward, *English Master of Arms*, p. 95; BL Harley Ms 7614 f. 101, Foubert's Petition.

34 W.A. Shaw, ed., *Calendar of Treasury Books, Volume 6: 1679–1680* (London, 1913), pp. 126–40.

35 The National Archives (hereafter TNA), SP29/411 ff. 417–20, 14 May 1679, 'The Humble Proposalles of Solomon de Fobert Esqr'.

36 TNA SP29/411 ff. 417–20, 'Humble Proposalles'.

37 Aylward, *English Master of Arms*, p. 97.

38 Royal Society, London, CMO/1/263, 14 Jan. 1680, Minutes of Meeting; J. Evelyn, *The Diary of John Evelyn*, A. Dobson, ed., 3 vols (London, 1906), III, p. 72.

39 Raylor, 'Milton, the Hartlib Circle and the education of the aristocracy'.

40 D. Carey, 'Compiling nature's history: travellers and travel narratives in the early Royal Society', *Annals of Science*, 54 (1997), pp. 269–92; Ansell, 'Educational travel'.

41 Evelyn, *Diary*, III, p. 87.

42 J.Y. Akerman, ed., *Moneys Received and Paid for Secret Services of Charles II and James II from 30th March, 1679, to 25th December, 1688* (London, 1851), pp. 41, 57, 68, 116.

43 Manchée, 'Fouberts', pp. 80, 82; Worsley, *British Stable*, p. 70.

44 *London Gazette*, 23–27 Oct. 1679, issue 1454; 28 Nov.–1 Dec. 1681, issue 1673; J. Peacey, 'Print, publicity and popularity: the projecting of Sir Balthazar Gerbier, 1642–1662', *Journal of British Studies*, 51:2 (2012), pp. 284–307.

45 Aylward, *English Master of Arms*, p. 98; BL Add Ms 70013 f. 40, 6 Jul. 1680, Sir Edward Harley, [London], to Lady Harley.

46 A.L. Murphy, 'Lotteries in the 1690s: investment or gamble?', *Financial History Review*, 12:2 (2005), pp. 227–46; Anon, *The Royal Academies. By the King's Authority* [London, 1695]; Anon, *From the Undertakers of the Royal Academy* [London, 1695].

47 Aylward, *English Master of Arms*, p. 105; *General Evening Post*, 12–15 Feb. 1743, issue 1468.

48 Manchée, 'Fouberts', pp. 85–6.

49 G. Worsley, 'A courtly art: the history of haute école in England', *Court Historian*, 6:1 (2001), pp. 29–47.

62   Richard Ansell

50 B. Greenwood, *The Case of Mr Bartholomew Greenwood* (London, 1740), p. 18; *Read's Weekly Journal or British Gazetteer*, 11 Dec. 1731, issue 351; *General Evening Post*, 2–4 Sep. 1735, issue 301; *Grub Street Journal*, 19 Aug. 1736, issue 347; *Daily Advertiser*, 4 Jan. 1744, issue 4045.

51 [H. Misson], *Mémoires et observations faites par un voyageur en Angleterre* (The Hague, 1698), p. 99; T.V. Murdoch, *The Quiet Conquest: The Huguenots, 1685 to 1985* (London, 1985), pp. 89, 94.

52 Motley, *Becoming a French Aristocrat*, p. 156; Commandant de La Roche, 'Les académies militaires sous l'ancien régime d'après des documents inédits', *Revue des études historiques* (1929), p. 417.

53 J.J. Cartwright, ed., *The Wentworth Papers, 1705–1739* (London, 1883), pp. 536, 540–1.

54 NRS GD406/1/5981, 5/15 Aug. 1676, Forbes, Paris, to Hamilton; Gailhard, *Compleat Gentleman*, II, p. 51; *London Gazette*, 28 Nov.–1 Dec. 1681, issue 1673; Evelyn, *Diary*, III, p. 134.

55 Motley, *Becoming a French Aristocrat*, p. 142.

56 BL Add Ms 70013 f. 40, 6 Jul. 1680, Sir Edward Harley to Lady Harley.

57 R. Blome, *The Gentlemans Recreation*, 2 vols (London, 1686), II, p. 5.

58 Bayle, *Correspondance*, letter 165; NLI Ms 45293/6, 22 Mar. 1694/5, Sir Donat O'Brien, Dromoland, to Lucius O'Brien; *Daily Post*, 8 Feb. 1739, issue 6058.

59 M.D. Pollak, *Turin, 1564–1680: Urban Design, Military Culture, and the Creation of the Absolutist Capital* (London, 1991), p. 234.

60 TNA SP29/411, ff. 417–20, 'Humble Proposalles'; Christ Church, Oxford Ms 426, 14 Aug. 1681, John Benson, Oxford, to Sir Robert Southwell.

61 BL Add Ms 46956C f. 98, 11 May 1680, John Perceval, London, to Sir Robert Southwell; HL HA 3334, 11 Feb. 1695/6, Jean Gailhard, London, to Theophilus Hastings, 7th Earl of Huntingdon.

62 Spalding Gentlemen's Society, letter 105, 21 Mar. 1734/5, Maurice Johnson, London, to Richard Faulkner.

63 W.R. Prest, *The Inns of Court under Elizabeth I and the Early Stuarts, 1590–1640* (London, 1972), pp. 21–45; D. Lemmings, *Gentlemen and Barristers: The Inns of Court and the English Bar, 1680–1730* (Oxford, 1990), pp. 8–30.

64 Bodl. Carte Ms 128 f. 387v, 17 Aug. 1680, Arlington to Ormond; HL HA 14526, 17 Apr. 1674, Conway to Rawdon; Historical Manuscripts Commission (hereafter HMC), *Report on the Manuscripts of the Earl of Egmont*, 2 vols (London, 1905–9), II, p. 142.

65 Motley, *Becoming a French Aristocrat*, pp. 162–3; J. Black, *France and the Grand Tour* (Basingstoke, 2003), pp. 135–6.

66 T. Otway, *The Atheist* (London, 1684), p. 6.

67 BL Add Ms 70013 f. 137, 9 Jan. 1682/3, Edward Nicholas, London, to Robert Harley.

68 R. North, *The Lives of the Right Hon. Francis North, Baron Guilford; the Hon. Sir Dudley North; and the Hon. and Rev. Dr John North … Together with the Autobiography of the Author*, A. Jessopp, ed., 3 vols (London, 1890), III, pp. 235–6, 296.

69 L. Ellinghausen, 'University of vice: drink, gentility and masculinity in Oxford, Cambridge and London', in A. Bailey and R. Hentschell, eds, *Masculinity and the Metropolis of Vice, 1550–1650* (Basingstoke, 2010), pp. 45–66.

70 NRS GD406/1/5981, 5/15 Aug. 1676, Forbes to Hamilton; GD406/1/5986, 2 Dec. 1676, Forbes to Hamilton; HL HA 14526, 17 Apr. 1674, Conway to Rawdon.

71 NRS GD220/6/1217/10, 23 Aug. 1722, Financial accounts of Dukes of Montrose; GD406/1/5981, 5/15 Aug. 1676, Forbes to Hamilton; BL Add Mss

Foubert's academy 63

61445 ff. 90, 119, Apr. 1722–Aug. 1727, Educational and travelling expenses of Charles and John Spencer; 70013 f. 77, 10 Jun. 1681, Sir Edward Harley, Brampton, to Robert Harley; Christ Church, Oxford Ms 426, 25 Sep. 1681, Benson to Southwell; *Wentworth Papers*, p. 536.

72 HL mss HAF, Box 26, Folder 25, 8 Jan. 1693–24 Dec. 1695, Expenses of Lord Hastings.

73 NLI Ms 45293/6, 22 Mar. 1694/5, Sir Donat O'Brien to Lucius O'Brien.

74 National Art Library, London, Forster Ms 47.A.40 f. 83, 19 Feb. 1680, Ormond, Dublin, to Southwell; TNA SP44/62 f. 255, 11 Aug. 1681, Sir Leoline Jenkins, Whitehall, to John Fell; Christ Church, Oxford Ms 426, 25 Sep. 1681, Benson to Southwell.

75 I. Warren, 'The English landed elite and the social environment of London, *c*.1580–1700: the cradle of an aristocratic culture?', *English Historical Review*, 126:518 (2011), p. 68.

76 BL Add Ms 70013 f. 40, 6 Jul. 1680, Sir Edward Harley to Lady Harley.

77 W.A. Speck, 'Harley, Robert, first earl of Oxford and Mortimer (1661–1724)', in H.C.G. Matthew and B. Harrison, eds, *Oxford Dictionary of National Biography* (Oxford, 2004).

78 *Savile Correspondence*, p. 228.

79 BL Add Ms 61445, ff. 84–184, Apr. 1722–Aug. 1727, Spencer bills and expenses.

80 BL Egerton Ms 2540 f. 43, 3 Jan. 1682/3, John Nicholas, Saumur, to Sir John Nicholas; J.P. Ferris, 'Nicholas, Edward II (1662–1726)', in B.D. Henning, ed., *The History of Parliament: The House of Commons, 1660–1690* (London, 1983). Published correspondence names 'Edmund' Nicholas, affecting other works on Foubert, but the manuscript reads 'Edwd': HMC, *The Manuscripts of His Grace the Duke of Portland, Preserved at Welbeck Abbey*, 10 vols (London, 1891–1931), III, p. 374; BL Add Ms 70013 f. 137, 9 Jan. 1682/3, Nicholas to Harley.

81 Borthwick Institute for Archives, York, YM/CP/M/6, [after 1 Dec. 1700, Lady Henrietta Maria Yarburgh to James Yarburgh]; YM/CP/1/26, 2 Dec. [1701?], Blague Yarburgh, Orléans, to Lady Yarburgh; YM/CP/1/30, 13 Aug. 1698, Richard Yarburgh, London, to Lady Yarburgh.

82 Spalding Gentlemen's Society, letter 7, 5 Mar. 1734/5, Maurice Johnson, London, to Maurice Johnson; letter 105, 21 Mar. 1734/5, Johnson to Faulkner.

83 NLI Ms 2493 f. 383, 'Project for the Erecting of an Academy for the Education of Youth in Ireland' [*c*.1660]; J. Ohlmeyer, *Making Ireland English: The Irish Aristocracy in the Seventeenth Century* (New Haven, 2012), pp. 442–4; Ansell, 'Educational travel', pp. 955–7.

84 R.K. Marshall, 'Hamilton, James, fourth duke of Hamilton and first duke of Brandon (1658–1712)', in *Oxford Dictionary of National Biography*; W. Forbes Gray, 'An eighteenth-century riding school', *Book of the Old Edinburgh Club*, 20 (1935), pp. 111–59; R.A. Houston, *Social Change in the Age of Enlightenment: Edinburgh, 1660–1760* (Oxford, 1994), pp. 221–2; R.L. Emerson, *Academic Patronage in the Scottish Enlightenment: Glasgow, Edinburgh and St Andrews Universities* (Edinburgh, 2008), p. 185.

85 T. Barnard, *A New Anatomy of Ireland: The Irish Protestants, 1649–1770* (London, 2003), pp. 113–28; J. Bergin, 'Irish Catholics and their networks in eighteenth-century London', *Eighteenth-Century Life*, 39:1 (2015), pp. 66–102.

86 NLI Ms 664, 5 Oct. 1683, Sir Robert Southwell, Kingsweston, to Sir William King; Christ Church, Oxford Ms 427, 23 Dec. 1682, Southwell to [Solomon Foubert]; 22 Jan. 1682/3, Southwell to Henry Aldrich; HMC, *Egmont*, II, p. 142.

64   Richard Ansell

87   BL Add Ms 70028 ff. 103–6, 27 Jul. 1711, William O'Brien, 3rd Earl of Inchiquin, Dublin, to Robert Harley, 1st Earl of Oxford; Inchiquin to [Martha] Lundie.

88   NLI Ms 45293/6, 22 Mar. 1694/5, Sir Donat O'Brien to Lucius O'Brien; E. M. Johnston-Liik, *History of the Irish Parliament, 1692–1800: Commons, Constituencies and Statutes*, 6 vols (Belfast, 2002), V, p. 371; Ohlmeyer, *Making Ireland English*, pp. 439–40.

89   NRS GD220/5/839/6, 12 May 1722, James Graham, 4th Marquis of Montrose, London, to Mungo Graham; GD220/5/839/23, 26 Jun. 1722, Montrose to Graham; GD220/5/840/7, 26 Jul. 1722, Montrose to Graham; GD220/5/1867/2-3, 7 Nov. 1700, Henri Foubert, London, to Montrose; GD220/6/99, Account book for Montrose's travels, 1698–1700; GD220/6/1217/10, 16 Jul.–26 Sep. 1722, Vouchers of Andrew Gardner's accounts; *Mercure Galant*, Mars 1679, p. 296.

90   BL Harley Ms 7614 f. 101, Foubert's Petition.

91   Anon, *The Tryal and Condemnation of George Borosky, alias Borotzi, Christopher Vratz, and John Stern* (London, 1682), pp. 17, 20–7, 42, 46–7; W.H. Wilkins, *The Love of an Uncrowned Queen* (New York, 1901), pp. 104–11; R.B. Manning, *Swordsmen: The Martial Ethos in the Three Kingdoms* (Oxford, 2003), pp. 163–5.

92   K. Maag, 'The Huguenot academies: preparing for an uncertain future', in R.A. Mentzer and A. Spicer, eds, *Society and Culture in the Huguenot World, 1559–1685* (Cambridge, 2002), pp. 139–56; H. de Ridder-Symoens, 'Mobility', in de Ridder-Symoens, ed., *A History of the University in Europe*, II: *Universities in Early Modern Europe* (Cambridge, 1996), p. 437.

93   F.M. Misson, *A New Voyage to Italy*, 4 vols (London, 1714), IV, pp. 421–2.

94   R. Oresko, 'The Duchy of Savoy and the Kingdom of Sardinia: the Sabaudian court, 1563–c.1750', in J. Adamson, ed., *The Princely Courts of Europe: Ritual, Politics and Culture under the Ancien Régime, 1500–1750* (London, 2000), pp. 231–53; P. Bianchi, 'In cerca del moderno: studenti e viaggiatori inglesi a Torino nel Settecento', *Rivista storica italiana*, 115:3 (2003), pp. 1021–51.

95   F. Colsoni, *Le guide de Londres pour les estrangers* (London, 1710), p. 30.

96   Black, *France and the Grand Tour*, pp. 39–41.

97   G.C. Gibbs, 'Huguenot contributions to England's intellectual life, and England's intellectual commerce with Europe, c.1680–1720', in Scouloudi, ed., *Huguenots in Britain*, p. 35.

98   [C. Davenant], *New Dialogues upon the Present Posture of Affairs* (London, 1710), pp. 5, 15–16.

99   M. Cohen, 'The Grand Tour: constructing the English gentleman in eighteenth-century France', *History of Education*, 21:3 (1992), pp. 241–57.

100   Stedman, *Cultural Exchange*, p. 125.

101   N. Kenny, *The Uses of Curiosity in Early Modern France and Germany* (Oxford, 2004), pp. 245–6.

102   BL Add Mss 70028 f. 103, 27 Jul. 1711, Inchiquin to Oxford; 70029 f. 231, 16 Jul. 1712, James Yarburgh, Heslington, to Oxford.

103   L. Colley, *Britons: Forging the Nation, 1707–1837* (London, 1992), pp. 147–93; J.M. Rosenheim, *The Emergence of a Ruling Order: English Landed Society, 1650–1750* (London, 1997).

4 The social challenge

Northern and central European societies on the eighteenth-century aristocratic Grand Tour[1]

Sarah Goldsmith

In 1755, the tutor William Whitehead defended the German itinerary of his two charges, George Bussy Villiers, later 4th earl of Jersey, and George Simon Harcourt, Viscount Nuneham and later 2nd earl Harcourt, protesting to Villiers' father that:

> Your Lordship seems very apprehensive that we prefer things to men, which is by no means our case; we hardly ever see things but merely out of Complaisance to the several Courts as we pass ... Our whole time is spent in Company.[2]

Given the tendency of Grand Tour scholarship to focus upon 'things' rather than 'men', Whitehead's vehement denial of this preference is perhaps surprising. The current scholarship on the eighteenth-century elite masculine British Grand Tour presents a conundrum. Scholars are unanimous in identifying the Tour as a form of educational travel that was an important rite of passage into adulthood. Ideally, it developed the adult masculine identities of participants, endowing them with the skills and virtues most highly prized by the elite.[3] Correspondingly, survey studies list the Tour's ambitious array of destinations and activities, in which social formation and activity, alongside non-Italian destinations, are often fleetingly mentioned. In practice, as discussed in the Introduction, a far more limited investigation has taken place. The traditional focus on Italy and its itinerary of arts, antiquities and architecture has been partially rectified by some consideration of France's role in the formation of a polite masculine identity, but overall a significant proportion of the Tour's route and activities remains neglected.[4] This has resulted in the perception that the Tour represented a limited, ineffective element in the formation of elite masculinity, and one that focused primarily upon its polite and virtuoso elements. As recent revisions of eighteenth-century masculinity have increasingly moved beyond the hegemonic theory of politeness to acknowledge more complex interactions between multiple, co-existent masculine identities, a reappraisal of the Grand Tour's overall aims, itineraries and its role in masculine formation becomes necessary.[5]

66 *Sarah Goldsmith*

This chapter contributes to this reappraisal through three interlinked means. First, it uses the manuscript correspondence and journals of seven groups of British Grand Tourists, tutors and their families, *c.*1740–80, to identify how the Grand Tour was conceptualised in dialogues internal to elite society, as opposed to published discourses.[6] Second, it focuses on the Grand Tour's northern and central European branch. Villiers, Nuneham and Whitehead's letters and diaries reveal that their Grand Tour took place between June 1754 and September 1756. It lasted 27 months, 19 of which were spent outside Italy. The amount of time dedicated to the northern and central European part of the Grand Tour indicates this was more than just a route into Italy. It contained destinations that were important in their own right. Without giving them due attention, it becomes difficult for scholars to comprehend the full extent of the Grand Tour's aims and importance.

As other chapters in this volume, particularly those by Richard Bates, Madeline van Strien-Chardonneau, Corine Maitte and Gerrit Verhoeven, demonstrate, these destinations held numerous attractions. However, this chapter's third focus is on the Grand Tour's prioritisation of the social itinerary in northern and central Europe. As Rosemary Sweet notes, the Tour was 'a prolonged journey based around the principal cities of Europe' and was therefore essentially structured around opportunities for social interaction.[7] Scholars routinely give brief attention to the Tour's social activity but remain uneasy in pinpointing its actual importance. Socialising was far from a 'holiday' activity.[8] It formed a fundamental part of the Grand Tour's structure and rationale. Extending the most common scholarly assertion that the Tour's social dimension was educational in nature, this chapter argues that travel through northern and central Europe exposed Tourists to a varied array of social cultures. Rather than teaching participants to adhere to a single form of polite sociability, the Grand Tour purposely formed participants in multiple cultures of masculinity and sociability, and in skills of adaptability and social judgement. By placing these findings within the wider context of recent scholarly work concerning the complexities of the eighteenth-century social and political world, this chapter also argues that the Tour had serious socio-political aims and should be viewed as a key tool within elite strategies of pan-European networking. Identifying the Grand Tour's social, political and educational aims surrounding sociability not only allows us to rethink the nature and purpose of the Grand Tour. It further explores the powerful influence of social concerns upon the formation of elite masculine identity and wider dynamics of elite socio-political culture.

Courts and metropolises: the social attractions of northern and central Europe

Instructed by his uncle, Philip Yorke, 2nd earl of Hardwicke, 'to mention in yr letters what attentions are shewn you at the different places you visit',

The social challenge 67

Philip Yorke, later 3rd earl of Hardwicke's letters and journals throughout his 1777–9 Grand Tour acted as an account book of social interaction. They also give insight into the staggering effort devoted to socialising.[9] He listed stays in over 30 key social centres in the Low Countries, Germany, Austria and Switzerland, and recorded hundreds of names and social activities, ranging from formal court presentations and balls to salon parties, private dinners and riding expeditions.[10] His socialising peaked in Vienna in October 1777–May 1778 where he made 50 social calls on his first day alone.[11] Even when only recording unusual events, he noted over 290 engagements and 60 political, diplomatic and fashionable hosts.[12] One of the most notable features of Yorke's social life is its swift decline upon entering Italy. Having had too much to record in Vienna, Yorke found that there was so little to say in Venice that he stopped keeping a daily diary of social events.[13] Equally, it was only upon entering Italy that Yorke began to prioritise aesthetics over men.

Yorke's experience was not uncommon. In 1753, Lord Frederick North, later 2nd earl of Guilford, was part way through a Grand Tour with his stepbrother, William Legge, the 2nd earl of Dartmouth. Writing from Rome, he reflected that:

The principal pleasure a Traveller has in Italy, consists, in the first place, in viewing the Antiquities of the country, & in the second, in seeing the great perfection to which the Italians have push'd the arts of Painting, Sculpture, & Architecture; In point of Society I think the tour of Italy inferior to that of Germany.[14]

While 'civil, obliging & polite enough', North unfavourably compared Italians against the Germans' 'easy manner of inviting Foreigners to their houses & tables'.[15] Even when amenable, Italian society was held to a northern and central European standard. Yorke wrote that 'After Milan we must I believe bid adieu to agreeable societies & no longer expect to receive so many civilities as we have been accustomed to meet with at Vienna and in the rest of Germany: this is one of the few towns in Italy that are on that footing.'[16]

As Yorke's experience in Milan suggests, a straightforward divide between a welcoming north and inhospitable south is over-simplistic. Tourists sometimes castigated German society as dull, rigid or old-fashioned.[17] In contrast, Florence was often described as a welcoming city when ruled by Anglophiles, like the Grand Duke Cosimo III, and with the energetic, hospitable ambassador, Sir Horace Mann.[18] Political circumstance substantially affected a city's social tone; particularly as the *corps diplomatique* was essential to the Grand Tourist's social experience.[19] For example, the Vatican's support of the Stuart cause meant that Rome had no British ambassador and Venice's ban on fraternisation between its elite and foreign ambassadors curtailed diplomats' social abilities.[20] Despite these nuances,

68   *Sarah Goldsmith*

Yorke and North broadly characterised Italy as the ideal site to develop their status as gentlemen-classicists, but championed northern and central European society as welcoming and fashionable.

An analysis of Grand Tours between 1750 and 1780 indicates that Paris, The Hague, Brussels, Hesse-Cassel, Hanover, Mannheim, Wolfenbüttel, Brunswick, Berlin, Potsdam, Brandenburg, Dresden, Prague and Vienna were rarely missed. Leiden, Leipzig, Geneva, Lausanne and various French towns also attracted lengthy stays due to their universities and academies, while towns devoted to trade and commerce, like Rotterdam, Amsterdam and Utrecht, were often quickly visited with no socialising.[21] As this list suggests, travelling through northern and central Europe exposed Tourists to a spectrum of social centres, ranging from large metropolises to smaller urban sites, country courts and university towns. Size substantially affected social experiences. As Yorke observed, 'In such great Courts as Vienna one knows less of the Princes than in the small courts of Germany which indeed are the only places where a stranger becomes acquainted with them.'[22] Visits to country courts, like Hesse-Cassel, Mannheim, Brunswick and Ansbach, were characterised by close contact with rulers. Intimate pastimes, like chess and dances in the private interiors of orangeries and salons, formed the main entertainment.[23] For example, at Hesse-Cassel, William VIII invited Villiers and Nuneham to his private country residence and personally guided them around his cabinet of curiosities.[24]

The Hague, Brussels, Berlin and Dresden were small urban centres with prominent courts. Describing Dresden as 'a sort of little London', North and Dartmouth's letters noted that direct access to rulers was limited but royal families remained relatively accessible.[25] This was often accompanied by more public entertainments, like balls, ridottos and theatres, and a wider society of diplomats and nobility. In larger cosmopolitan centres, like Paris and Vienna, social intimacy with the courts disappeared entirely. However, the best company was now the elite *beau monde*, rather than royalty.[26] Dartmouth reflected from Paris in 1754 that they had got 'among the best company', but that was not Versailles. The Parisian nobility 'amuse themselves better, as they have greater variety both of company & publick diversions'.[27] Similarly, Whitehead wrote from Vienna that the diplomat, the elder Robert Keith, had not yet presented Villiers and Nuneham at court but they had 'been introduced to most of the people of fashion'.[28]

Northern and central Europe provided a rich, varied social experience and Tourists aimed to be well received in each society. However, certain destinations were favoured as families directed their sons towards social and political cultures related to their own.[29] Republican and burgher university towns, like Leiden, Leipzig, Geneva and Lausanne, were valued for their educational institutions, but families were wary of Tourists imbibing inappropriate ideals and social norms. In 1752, Charles Lennox, 3rd duke of Richmond, was removed from a Genevan academy after several years residence. Fearing he had been 'Geneva'd' by a 'low' Geneva woman

The social challenge 69

and observing that the 'Style in his Letters' had changed for the worse, his guardians felt he had 'learnt too much there, already', indicating concern that he was becoming influenced by republican principles.[30] A more suitable location for 'a Man of Quality' was sought, and the merits of Hanover, other German courts and Paris, more aristocratic societies that shared many cultural values and norms with British elite society, discussed.[31]

Worthy of stays lasting several months to a year, the 'metropolis' of Paris, Vienna and Turin were particularly fashionable. They combined the multiple attractions of a royal or imperial court with sophisticated cosmopolitanism, elite society *and* educational opportunities. As scholars have noted, throughout the eighteenth century Paris was held in high regard as a fashionable Tour destination.[32] Yet, until at least the 1750s, Turin vied with Paris as an influential centre of courtly politeness. While technically an Italian city, it was often viewed as northern in nature. Its kings held international political reputations, and fostered a welcoming court and one of Europe's premier noble educational institutes, the *Accademia Reale*.[33]

From the 1750s onwards, Paris and Turin were increasingly eclipsed by Vienna in the estimation of Tourists, tutors and parents.[34] In 1754, Dartmouth was disillusioned by Paris's sociability. Having expected 'chearfullness & vivacity', he instead found 'it is not at present the fashion to speak much'.[35] In contrast, Vienna was a lively place for learning and 'pleasure'. North enthused, 'We receive great civilities & politeness from all hands.'[36] Vienna's reputation strengthened throughout the 1760s and 1770s, until Dartmouth's son, George Legge, Viscount Lewisham and later 3rd earl of Dartmouth, eagerly anticipated his arrival in 1776: 'We have every reason to think that our stay in that metropolis will be very agreeable – English are in general very well received, the society is considerable, and Sir R: M: Keith our Embassador [sic.] a most excellent man.'[37] His expectations were exceeded. Four months later he wrote 'It is really amazing how well we are received here – the houses of all the first nobility are open to us.'[38] Leaving seven months earlier, Yorke lamented 'I assure you that excepting my own home in the midst of my friends & family, I cannot conceive a more agreeable situation.'[39]

In considering what made destinations like Vienna so attractive, a couple of reasons can be suggested. As Jennifer Mori has argued, ambassadors were a central factor. Launching young gentlemen into the court and noble circles of European societies was part of their mandate. Acting as mediators and instructors, they were an identifiable part of the Grand Tour's educational process. Some ambassadors resented this role, but between 1748–57 and 1772–88, the father and son Robert Keith and Robert Murray Keith provided Vienna and the Grand Tour with two diplomats who worked extremely hard on their social mandate. Murray Keith even called his embassy a 'school' and claimed that by 1785 he had presented at least 400 'pupils'.[40] Regularly cited as outstanding hosts and attentive mentors, the Keiths played an important part in Vienna's rising status.[41]

70   *Sarah Goldsmith*

High value was also placed on the Viennese nobility's extraordinarily open sociability, which, by combining open houses with a sense of exclusivity, was at the heart of the Austrian Enlightenment.[42] In 1778, Yorke exclaimed: 'I do not believe there is a town in Europe where the Society is so universally agreeable or where one has so many opportunities of passing ones time in the best company.'[43] Yorke's hosts included Vienna's premier aristocracy, such as Prince Wenzel von Kaunitz, Maria Theresa's chief minister whose social gatherings were attended by the Emperor, Count Rudolf Colloredo and Prince Nikolaus Esterházy I, who opened their houses every evening. Some of the 'best houses' hosted weekly assemblies, including Count Carl and Madame Charlotte Hatzfeldt-Gleichen, Count Ernst and Madame Maria Josepha von Harrach and the French Ambassador. Yorke regularly dined with the Dutch ambassador and his wife, Count and Madame von Degenfeld, and attended salons run by Maria Wilhelmine von Thun and by Countess Philippina Pergen, wife of the influential Habsburg statesman, Count Joseph Pergen.[44] Vienna's society was viewed as a sophisticated, cosmopolitan and elegant aristocratic society and therefore the ideal place to develop equivalent traits.

Finally, it is clear that the fluctuating popularity of cities was partially linked to a country's political status. For example, following the final resolution of the Habsburg–Bourbon contest for control of the Mediterranean in 1720, Italy became a second-rank political theatre.[45] Wining and dining Italy's elite became less important. Equally, as Savoy rose to prominence under Victor Amadeus II in the first half of the eighteenth century and as Prussia grew in power and fame under Frederick the Great in the mid-eighteenth century, Turin, Berlin and Potsdam became more popular destinations.[46] Accompanying developments in cultural and aesthetic ascendancy also formed an added attraction.[47] This indicates that the Grand Tour's social itinerary was politically responsive in seeking out and cultivating relationships with emerging arenas of political power.[48]

Vienna's rising popularity from the 1750s is therefore intriguing, given that the 1756 'Diplomatic Revolution' allied the Habsburgs with the Bourbons and broke the older alliance with Britain. Austria held a special status in Court Whig political theory as the chief ally in securing European acceptance of the 1688 Revolution. Mori suggests that as the Court Whigs hankered to return to the 'Old System' in which Vienna had been a jewel in the crown of diplomatic service, the court remained an attractive place for sons of the establishment whom it was impossible for ambassadors to turn away.[49] If Tourists were directed to visit certain courts in order to cement political and diplomatic relations, they could also be used to maintain or recover them. Read in this light, Vienna's rising popularity was perhaps part of a wider effort to return to the 'Old System'. Lewisham, for example, was well aware that Prince Kaunitz's chief interest had been 'bringing about the alliance was France'. His report of Kaunitz's subsequent declaration that Lewisham and his fellow Tourists were Vienna's 'chere colonie' and

The social challenge 71

'la nation favorite' could be read as a politically hopeful statement regarding the positive diplomatic impact of young Tourists.[50] Furthermore, as the following section will explore, elite families were also interested in maintaining their own continental networks that maintained older connections while also following rising power and influence.

'Our whole time is spent in Company': the social rationale of the Grand Tour

It could be argued that the Grand Tour's social dimension assumed a greater importance in northern and central Europe because of the dearth of arts, antiquities and architecture. However, the pressure, time and effort involved suggests an impetus beyond filling a vacuum. For example, during Lewisham's 1775–6 winter residence in Paris, his father, Dartmouth, was concerned 'that you are not yet a part of some good French Circles, I want you to lose no time in getting into that Society'.[51] Lewisham had been hampered by his fellow countrymen's poor behaviour, which had resulted in the French refusing to allow the British ambassador to make introductions.[52] He redoubled his efforts and soon his correspondence was filled with the names of the French elite.[53]

In seeking to understand this preoccupation with social success, scholars have typically and fleetingly viewed it as educational in nature.[54] In discussing the rationale behind the Grand Tour's social itinerary, it is clear that Grand Tourists learnt through a process of observation and immersed participation that taught vital skills in social versatility. This was reflected in the personalised nature of their observations about the individuals they encountered. These could be examples to be wary of, like the 'capricious' Wilhelmina Karolina, Landgravine of Hesse-Cassel, and the boorish, uneducated Bavarian Prince Radziwiłł.[55] Alternatively, there were admired models like Emperor Joseph II of Austria, who talked so 'inimitably well' that he became Yorke's model for polite conversation.[56] However, the Grand Tour's social agenda also was part of a wider social-political strategy that linked the British elite to their continental counterparts.

Contemporaries perceived the Grand Tour as a series of social challenges. As Lewisham developed his social confidence in Paris, Dartmouth set him more complex tasks, such as rectifying an embarrassing mistake that had excluded his tutor from elite circles.[57] On his 'Dutch Tour' and 'Round of the German Courts', Lewisham encountered new tests.[58] At Mannheim, an absent contact and the Elector Palatine's unexpected removal to a summer residence meant he failed to be presented, but Colonel Fawcett, a minister at Hanover, subsequently instructed him on 'how to act in similar circumstances' and avoid future 'awkwardness'.[59] As Mori observes, as living exemplars of the Grand Tour's cosmopolitan ideal, diplomats played an important role as mediators and instructors.[60]

72   Sarah Goldsmith

The Grand Tour is often associated with polite, cosmopolitan sociability; however, variation formed a key feature of its social curriculum. Hardwicke instructed Yorke:

> You will (I believe) find a great sameness in the Lesser German Courts till you come to Berlin & Vienna ... You will not fail to observe the Variations in the ways & fashions wch prevail at the different Courts; you will find those in Germany a good deal on the same Grounds, but with different shades. I take Italy & France to be very different.[61]

The Grand Tour did not simply involve observing differing social cultures. Its immersive approach forced participants to develop skills in social adaptability. For example, in the early 1750s, Henry Herbert, 10th earl of Pembroke, Dartmouth and North encountered social situations that forced them to embrace different etiquettes. In 1751, Dartmouth and North were startled by the Leipzig practice of kissing all the ladies at table. Dartmouth 'was obliged to follow his [the host's] example; not without some reluctance ... it was sad clammy work'.[62] In 1752, Pembroke was deeply offended by his reception at Potsdam as Frederick the Great 'passed very briskly by, & took no notice of us'.[63] This transgressed Pembroke's social codes and honour ideals so much that he resolved to leave. When an apologetic aide explained that the King had ignored him because he disliked receiving people in a military setting, he let the insult pass. The aide was important in helping Pembroke navigate a social etiquette characterised by military brusqueness but, desirous of a military career and of making a good impression on a figure he deeply admired, Pembroke nevertheless suspended personal codes of etiquette.[64]

Even within one location, Tourists continually moved between different social spheres, including local elite society, the *corps diplomatique* and other British travellers. Within these overlapping groups, they encountered different generations and sexes. For example, the playful correspondence and diaries of the Common Room club – a homosocial friendship group of English, Scottish and German Tourists and tutors in Geneva in the early 1740s – reveals a wide variety of social behaviours that was dependent on their various social spheres. Alongside hiring a communal space, they drank, dined, toasted and used other club structures like voting, fining and keeping a logbook.[65] This homosocial society was characterised by high-spirited, impolite behaviour.[66] They farted, belched, played practical jokes, shared sexual advice and gossiped. One fellow Tourist was so lovelorn that an exasperated Robert Price exclaimed they needed 'to cut his Cock off & give it to the Cat'.[67]

Yet the Common Room also successfully conformed to other social standards. They participated in Geneva's more intellectual circles, attending the university and engaging their professors in social calls and experiments.[68] One tutor, John Williamson (a frequent farting offender), was an

The social challenge 73

excellent mathematician and a member of Geneva's 'Beaux Esprits', a classic example of Enlightenment sociability.[69] The Common Room moved in Geneva's straight-laced polite society. Richard Aldworth and William Windham both contracted engagements, and departed Bloods (their term for club members) punctuated letters with greetings to a wide range of Genevan families. They put on highly popular plays, attended by the Magistrates, almost all 'persons of distinction' and foreigners at the Academy, including the Princes of Anhalt.[70] While unconventional, this demonstrated a very successful engagement with Geneva's international society.

As these examples demonstrate, the Grand Tour exposed the elite young male to a variety of social standards as they constantly shifted between country, urban, polite, impolite, cosmopolitan, martial, aristocratic, republican, male, mixed, young and old social groups. Each group made different demands on their social abilities. Tourists were expected to succeed in all; therefore, rather than teaching participants to adhere to one culture of sociability, the Grand Tour's social curriculum primarily taught social adaptability and judgement – skills that would enable them to respond appropriately to numerous social settings. To a certain extent, this could be seen as the embodiment of polite sociability as Tourists adapted their behaviour to please others. Terms like 'polite' and 'civil' certainly appeared frequently as approbation, but other traits were also admired. For example, Yorke's admiration for General Martin Ernst von Schlieffen and Prince Ferdinand of Brunswick's martial reputations more than equalled his admiration for their politeness.[71] Just as important, as the Common Room demonstrates, this adaptability often resulted in behaviours that either meant politeness had a broader meaning than scholars acknowledge or that social versatility was an elite trait that went beyond politeness.

In the past scholars have dismissed these discrepancies as illicit or the sowing of wild oats abroad, but the shifting, conflicting standards and complexities of the Grand Tour's social world sketched here directly mirrored the elite adult social world, and were often legitimated by older authority figures, such as tutors, parents and diplomats.[72] As scholars have identified polite sociability as the pinnacle of social behaviour, homosocial, impolite, rowdy and libertine social cultures have often been downplayed as subversive. Recent scholarship, however, has repeatedly highlighted their legitimacy in eighteenth-century British culture. For example, despite their 'impoliteness', homosocial societies were vital to the affirmation of masculinity, social bonding and the transaction of business, politics and information exchange, and were validated by wider society.[73] The eighteenth-century elite world encompassed a plurality of 'sociabilities'. Some of these contained conflicting codes of conduct, yet providing the individual did not transgress codes of acceptance, through undertaking the wrong social behaviour in the wrong social sphere, these discrepancies did not invalidate opposing expressions of sociability.[74] It was expected that men would move

74 *Sarah Goldsmith*

between social groups; the resultant changes in behaviour were proof of their prowess in these skills.[75] As long as an individual retained the social skill and discernment to keep these different spheres of social behaviour separate, he could fully partake in all without invalidating his standing in any. This behaviour was not just tolerated. The critical social lessons encompassed in the Grand Tour through moving constantly between different modes and codes of sociability reveal that the masculine skills of social adaptability and judgement were highly valued.

The formative dimension of the Grand Tour's social itinerary was fundamentally important. However, to simply view the Grand Tour as (to use Jason Kelly's term) a laboratory for social learning is problematic.[76] It reduces the scope of its role within wider elite networking and underplays the extent to which the Tour was a highly public, protracted international debut. Failure to adequately judge one's social behaviour could result in severe castigation. For example, the Common Room's letters routinely attacked 'that Wonderful Knight', Sir Bourchier Wrey, who consistently broke multiple codes of etiquette in order to inflate his importance.[77] For example, on being asked to dine with two Common Room members, the 'German Counts', William, count of Schaumburg-Lippe, and his brother George, 'he took upon Him to be master'.[78] Wrey's transgressions turned him into an international figure of ridicule as he was mocked by British, German and Dutch society. Judgements were not just made by one's peers. While Grand Tourists watched, judged and admired their European counterparts, elite society observed them in return. For example, throughout Lewisham's Tour, Dartmouth received a number of reports from ambassadors on his son's social progress, while reports of his and North's own Tour circulated among political and diplomatic circles.[79] Their Tour was an undeniable social success, as they caught the attention of the duke of Newcastle in Hanover. Newcastle discussed them extensively, describing them as:

> Two different Beauties here of the soft, & of the rough kind ... My Ld D is y prettiest, most agreeable, best behav'd, Comical little Creature ... Ld North the oddest, most entertaining, best hearted man.[80]

Newcastle and his correspondents frequently discussed Grand Tourists and not everyone was so enthusiastically received. The earl of Albermarle, ambassador in Paris, lukewarmly described a Mr Buckingham as 'a very odd one', while glowingly referring to Dartmouth and North as 'of a different kind'.[81] The connections and reputations established on the Grand Tour could have long-lasting ramifications. Upon their return to England, North and Dartmouth's political careers were furthered by Newcastle.[82] Equally, Kelly's study of the Society of the Dilettanti demonstrates the long-lasting nature of the Tour's networks.[83] While an illustrious example, the longevity of this connection was not unusual.[84]

The social challenge 75

The Grand Tour was deeply embedded in contemporary aristocratic culture and made an important contribution to its societal networks and strategies of power. These connections were not just made with fellow British. The elite regarded the Grand Tour as an essential opportunity for 'direct and personal contact' with their continental counterparts.[85] Essentially, the Tour was a crucial means of displaying and maintaining influential networks between British and continental elites.[86]

For aristocratic Grand Tourists, the Tour's social dimension was often encompassed within existing familial networks. Thus, it was an opportunity to reaffirm and expand networks on a transgenerational basis. For example, Dartmouth and Pembroke travelled in the 1750s; their sons, Lewisham and George Herbert, later 11th earl of Pembroke, travelled around 20 years later in the 1770s.[87] In each case, the son's social itinerary was directly shaped by his father's Grand Tour social network. Herbert had his face twisted 'bout for ¼ of an hour' by the famous Parisian hostess, Amélie de Boufflers, Duchess de Lauzun, before she recognised him as 'the petit George'.[88] At Paris, Hanover and Brunswick, Lewisham regularly described meeting 'your old acquaintances', ranging from old servants to the duchess of Brunswick.[89] At Vienna, he exclaimed: 'I meet a great deal of your old friends here,' before listing 'Sottby, an officer in Charles' regiment, M: de Hason the Saxon minister Mad:e de Borkhausen, the Collorédo &c &c'.[90] The success of Dartmouth's Tour directly influenced Lewisham's reception. Keith wrote, '[I've] introduced them to the Ministers & People of Fashion in Town, who were prepared to receive them with Distinction both for your Ldships sake & their own.'[91] In 1754, Villiers even boasted that his family connections were so strong that he had no need of an ambassador's hospitality, 'For I am entirely of Papa's Opinion that one should have recommendations enough to stand upon one's own Legs at every Court.'[92]

While old connections were reaffirmed, new relationships were also established. In 1754 Richmond was extremely touched by his friendship with the duc de Belle Isle, the powerful French General and statesman, and his son, de Gisors. Upon hearing that de Gisors was visiting England during his educational *voyage*, Richmond asked Newcastle that his stay be made as agreeable as possible, concluding that 'I am miserable not to be now in England to go about with him myself.'[93] De Gisors and Richmond had a great deal in common and evidently expected their friendship to endure beyond Richmond's Tour. Both had fathers with considerable military reputations and both desired to follow in their footsteps. Conducted during the lead-up to the Seven Years War, their friendship is a striking example of the strong commonality between British and continental aristocrats. As Stephen Conway observes, national and European identities were not mutually exclusive but existed alongside one another. Far from perceiving continental Europe as an alien 'other', Tourists often embraced their place within a pan-European 'high elite culture'.[94] Such friendships could

76   Sarah Goldsmith

transcend but not overcome national tensions. Belle Isle's hospitality came after a year in British captivity during the War of Austrian Succession (1740–8) and de Gisors was to be killed in 1758 at the Battle of Krefeld, between French and Prussian-Hanoverian forces.

The pressure surrounding socialising was only partially due to its educational virtues. The Grand Tour was a debut in which an elite young man simultaneously sought to prove his social standing and affirm his family's socio-political connections. It was an opportunity to meet the continental leaders that they would eventually make treaties, fight and trade with. As Elaine Chalus has noted, the 'operation of a highly personal, influence-based form of politics that took place outside of parliament in social situations' is stubbornly unquantifiable, but understanding such operations is crucial to understanding the maintenance and exercise of elite power and influence.[95] While this chapter begins to demonstrate the Grand Tour's potential political influence upon European power plays through contributing towards an exclusive trans-European network of socio-political elite, European scholarship is identifying similar aims and activities in the continental equivalents of the Grand Tour. For example, Paola Bianchi's investigation into Turin's *Accademia Reale*'s alumni has traced a high percentage of Habsburg and German nobility, which reflected an entwined, international aristocratic network across Europe that created diplomatic, military and family ties between, for example, Turin and Vienna.[96] Equally Mathis Leibetseder's and Eva Chodějovská and Zdeněk Hojda's analysis of Bohemian and German nobility also links their shifting itinerary to family kinship, social networks, cliental bonds at kindred courts and shifts in political alliances in a manner similar to my own findings.

Conclusion

Whereas this chapter has focused primarily upon aristocratic Grand Tourists, material from gentry Tourists, such as Edward Gibbon or John Holroyd, later 1st earl of Sheffield, suggests that, while far more challenging and fraught, the Grand Tour's social dimensions remained extremely important for gentry participants in offering the opportunity for social advancement.[97] Equally, Richard Bates's chapter on Spa demonstrates that the opportunity to socialise with the international elite remained a major attraction for older male and female elite travellers. In contrast, I would speculate that the developing travel cultures of the middling and mercantile sort reflected a growing divergence between the professional, social and touristic itineraries of travel. The Italian 'entrepreneur-travellers' described by Corine Maitte parallel the socio-political efforts of British elite Grand Tourists, in responding to emerging centres of (industrial and economic) power and in seeking to develop contacts relevant to their trade, yet their travel was distinctly business-like in nature. In contrast, the

The social challenge 77

developing Dutch and French 'pleasure' trips explored by Verhoeven and van Strien-Chardonneau and the travel to the revolutionary ruins described by Elodie Duché focused upon an itinerary of viewing and gazing that increasingly distinguished a middling culture of travel from its aristocratic counterpart.

The itinerary of northern and central Europe was fundamental to the success and purpose of the elite Grand Tour in enabling the social and masculine formation of its participants. The Tour was more than just a low-stakes trial period for becoming a man or an institution limited to aesthetic and polite agendas; it taught important masculine social skills of versatility and judgement, and was a chance to create bonds on an international level that would ideally benefit the Tourist for the rest of his life. The men considered here sought to form lasting ties of friendship that transcended national tensions, and to attend to the collective socio-political power of the European elite which relied on, among other factors, transgenerational displays and affirmations of transcontinental networks.

The Tour's social rationale also points to the crucial role of sociability and society in the forming and affirming of masculine identity. Social and masculine formations are distinct categories but as identities require validation, social interactions play an important role in establishing ideal standards and expressions of masculinity. Families and wider society were extremely powerful agents in this, but, as John Tosh observes, homosociability, all-male groups and peer approval played an equally important role.[98] Addressing the complex social and homosocial dynamics and pressures of the Grand Tour brings further insight into the eighteenth-century elite masculine world and masculine formation.

Notes

1   I would like to thank my fellow editors and contributors, alongside Amy Milka, Catriona Kennedy, Claire Canavan, Mark Jenner, Michèle Cohen, Natasha Glaisyer, Robin Macdonald and Valerie Capdeville, for their generous, thoughtful and formative feedback on this chapter in its various stages of evolution. The material pertaining to the Dartmouth family is used by permission of the Dartmouth Heirlooms Trust and Staffordshire Record Office.
2   London Metropolitan Archives (hereafter LMA) Acc. 510/242, 7 June 1755, William Whitehead, Hanover, to William Villiers, 3rd earl of Jersey.
3   For example, B. Redford, *Venice and the Grand Tour* (New Haven and London, 1996), pp. 7–9, 14–5; J.M. Kelly, *The Society of Dilettanti: Archaeology and Identity in the British Enlightenment* (New Haven and London, 2009), pp. 12–14; H. French and M. Rothery, *Man's Estate: Landed Gentry Masculinities 1660–1900* (Oxford, 2012), pp. 137–43; M. Cohen, *Fashioning Masculinity: National Identity and Language in the Eighteenth Century* (London, 2002), pp. 54–63.
4   For the importance of Paris and France as a centre of polite cosmopolitanism, see Cohen, *Masculinity*, pp. 55–6; Cohen, 'The Grand Tour: constructing the English gentleman in eighteenth-century France', *History of Education*, 21:3 (1992), pp. 241–57; Cohen, '"Manners" make the man: politeness, chivalry and

78   *Sarah Goldsmith*

the construction of masculinity, 1750–1830', *Journal of British Studies*, 44:2 (2005), pp. 312–29.

5 See, for example, K. Harvey and A. Shepard, 'What have historians done with masculinity? Reflections on five centuries of British history, circa 1500–1950', *Journal of British Studies*, 44:2 (2005), pp. 274–80; French and Rothery, *Man's Estate*, pp. 3–15; J. Tosh, 'Hegemonic masculinity and the history of gender', in S. Dudink, K. Hagemann and J. Tosh, eds, *Masculinity in Politics and War: Gendering Modern History* (Manchester, 2004), p. 52.

6 This builds upon the methodology furthered by French and Rothery, *Man's Estate*, and French and Rothery, '"Upon your entry to the world": masculine values and the threshold of adulthood among landed elites in England 1680–1800', *Social History*, 33:4 (2008), pp. 403–22.

7 R. Sweet, *Cities and the Grand Tour: The British in Italy, c.1690–1820* (Cambridge, 2012), p. 2.

8 J. Black, *The British Abroad: The Grand Tour in the Eighteenth Century* (Stroud, 1992), p. 331.

9 British Library (hereafter BL) Add. Ms. 35378 f. 59, 29 Jun. 1777, Philip Yorke, later 3rd earl of Hardwicke, London, to Philip Yorke, 2nd earl of Hardwicke.

10 See BL Add. Ms. 36258-60, 1777–9, Grand Tour journals of Yorke.

11 BL Add. Ms. 36258, 31 Oct. 1777, Yorke's journal.

12 BL Add. Ms. 36258-59, 30 Oct. 1777–11 May 1778, Yorke's journal.

13 BL Add MS 36259, 2–5 Jun. 1779, Yorke's journal.

14 BL Add. Ms. 32731, fols 198–9, 8 Feb. 1753, Lord Frederick North, Rome, to Thomas Pelham-Holles, the duke of Newcastle.

15 BL Add. Ms. 32731, fol. 198–9, 8 Feb. 1753, North, Rome, to Newcastle.

16 BL Add MS 36259, 24 Aug. 1779, Yorke's journal.

17 Black, *British Abroad*, pp. 55–60. For example, Centre for Buckinghamshire Studies Ms. D-LE-E2-7, [undated, *c.*1754–5], George Simon Harcourt, Viscount Nuneham and later 2nd earl Harcourt, [Germany?], to his sister, Lady Elizabeth Harcourt.

18 Sweet, *Cities and the Grand Tour*, pp. 68, 79, 177–8.

19 J. Mori, 'Hosting the Grand Tour: civility, enlightenment and culture, *c.*1740–1790', in M. Hilton and J. Shefrin, eds, *Educating the Child in Enlightenment Britain: Beliefs, Cultures, Practices* (Farnham, 2009), pp. 117, 119; Sweet, *Cities and the Grand Tour*, pp. 138–40, 207.

20 Sweet, *Cities and the Grand Tour*, pp. 138–40, 207.

21 H. de Ridder-Symoens, 'Mobility', in Ridder-Symoens, ed., *A History of the University in Europe. Volume 2: Universities in Early Modern Europe (1500–1800)* (Cambridge, 2003), pp. 432–3. See also M. Rosa di Simone, 'Admission', in *Universities in Europe*, pp. 318–24.

22 BL Add. Ms. 35378 f. 202, 2 Jun. 1778, Yorke, Venice, to Hardwicke.

23 BL Add. Ms. 35378 f. 74, 5 Aug. 1777, Yorke, Carlsmuche, to Hardwicke; BL Add. Ms. 32733 f. 230, 9 Nov. 1753, Charles Lennox, 3rd duke of Richmond and Lennox, Leyden, to Newcastle.

24 LMA Acc. 510/239, 5 Oct. 1754, Villiers, Cassel, to Lady Jersey.

25 BL Add. Ms. 62114 K ff 69, 9 Mar. 1752, William Legge, 2nd earl of Dartmouth, Leipzig, to Rev. Edward Stillingfleet; BL Add. Ms. 32728 fols 163–4, 12 Jul. 1752, North, Dresden, to Newcastle.

26 H. Greig, *The Beau Monde: Fashionable Society in Georgian London* (Oxford, 2013), p. 3. See her appendix, 'Uses and meaning of Beau Monde: a supplementary essay', pp. 243–58, for further details.

27 BL Add. Ms. 32734 fols 144–5, 16 Feb. 1754, Dartmouth, Paris, to Newcastle.

28 LMA Acc. 510/245, 16 Sep. 1755, Whitehead, Vienna, to Lord Jersey.

The social challenge 79

29 See, for example, BL Add. Ms. 33087 fols 6–7, 16 Feb. 1747, J. Pelham, London to Thomas Pelham, 1st earl of Chichester.
30 BL Add. Ms. 32727 fols 220–3, 9 Jun. 1752, Henry Fox, London, to Newcastle; BL Add. Ms. 32727 fols 428–9, 12 June 1752, Fox, London, to Newcastle; BL Add. Ms. 32727 fols 88–9, 24 June 1752, Newcastle, Hanover, to Fox.
31 BL Add. Ms. 32727 fols 220–3, 9 Jun. 1752, Fox, London, to Newcastle; BL Add. Ms. 32727 fols 428–9, 12 June 1752, Fox, London, to Newcastle; BL Add. Ms. 32727 fols 88–9, 24 Jun. 1752, Newcastle to Fox.
32 Black, *British Abroad*, pp. 6–9; For contemporary opinions, see Staffordshire Record Office (hereafter SRO) D(W)1778/V/886, 4 Jan. 1776, David Stevenson, Paris, to Dartmouth.
33 C. Storrs, *War, Diplomacy and the Rise of Savoy, 1690–1720* (Cambridge, 1999), p. 236; P. Bianchi, 'Una palestra di arti cavalleresche e di politica. Presenze austro-tedesche all'Accademia Reale di Torino nel Settecento, in M. Bellabarba and J.P. Niederkorn, eds, *Le corti come luogo di comunicazione: gli Asburgo e l'Italia (secoli XVI–XIX)* (Berlin, 2010), pp. 1021–51; J. Spence, *Joseph Spence: Letters from the Grand Tour*, ed. S. Klima (Montreal, 1975), pp. 223–35.
34 S. Conway, *England, Ireland and Continental Europe in the Eighteenth Century* (Oxford, 2011), p. 211; LMA Acc. 510/245, 16 Sep. 1755, Whitehead, Vienna, to Lord Jersey; BL Add. Ms. 32731, fols 127–8, [?] Jan. 1753, Henry Herbert, 10th earl of Pembroke, Vienna, to Newcastle; BL Add. Ms. 35378 f. 59, 29 Jun. 1777, Hardwicke, London, to Yorke; Wiltshire and Swindon History Centre (hereafter WSHC), Ms. 2057/F4/27, 1 March 1776, Elizabeth Herbert, Countess of Pembroke, Whitehall, to Reverend William Coxe; WSHC Ms. 2057/F4/27, 28 Mar. 1777, Lady Pembroke, Wilton House, to Coxe.
35 BL Add. Ms. 32734 fols 144–5, 16 Feb. 1754, Dartmouth, Paris, to Newcastle.
36 BL Add. Ms. 32729 fols 128–9, 30 Aug. 1752, North, Vienna, to Newcastle.
37 For praise of the Keiths, see SRO D(W)1778/V/874, 4 Sep. 1776, George Legge, Viscount Lewisham, later 3rd earl of Dartmouth, Dresden, to Lady Dartmouth.
38 SRO D(W)1778/V/874, 12 Dec. 1776, Lewisham, Vienna, to Lady Dartmouth.
39 BL Add. Ms. 35378 f. 190, 18 May 1778, Yorke, Trieste, to Hardwicke.
40 Mori, 'Hosting', pp. 117, 119, 125, 127; Mori, *The Culture of Diplomacy: Britain in Europe, c.1750–1830* (Manchester, 2011), pp. 153, 155.
41 See, for example, BL Add. Ms. 32730 fols 163–4, 25 Oct. 1752, North, Milan, to Newcastle; BL Add MS 36258, 14 Dec. 1778, Yorke's journal; WSHC Ms. 2057/F4/27, 1 March 1776, Lady Pembroke, Whitehall, to Coxe; WSHC Ms. 2057/F4/27, 28 March 1777, Pembroke, Wilton House, to Coxe.
42 Mori, 'Hosting', p. 126.
43 BL Add. Ms. 35378 f. 202, 2 Jun. 1778, Yorke, Venice, to Hardwicke.
44 All of the above was taken from analysis of BL Add. Ms. 36258-9, 30 Oct. 1777–11 May 1778, Yorke's journal.
45 Mori, *Diplomacy*, p. 158.
46 See, for example, Storrs, *Rise of Savoy*, pp. 1–5; P. Dwyer, ed., *The Rise of Prussia 1700–1830* (Harlow and New York, 2000). See Black, *British Abroad*, pp. 54–5 for similar observations about Hanover.
47 Black, *British Abroad*, pp. 59–60.
48 See Eva Chodějovská and Zdeněk Hojda's and Mathis Leibetseder's chapters for similar points regarding the Bohemian Grand Tour and the German *Kavalierstour*.
49 Mori, 'Hosting', p. 126.
50 SRO D(W)1778/V/874, 18 Feb. 1777, Lewisham, Vienna, to Lady Dartmouth; SRO D(W)1778/V/874, 12 Dec. 1776, Lewisham, Vienna, to Lady Dartmouth.

80 *Sarah Goldsmith*

51 SRO D(W)1778/V/852, 18 Dec. 1775, Dartmouth, London, to Lewisham.
52 SRO D(W)1778/V/874, 16 Aug. 1775, Lewisham, Upon the Loire, to Dartmouth; 28 Jan. 1776, Lewisham, Paris, to Dartmouth.
53 SRO D(W)1778/V/874, 22 Dec. 1775, Lewisham, Paris, to Dartmouth; 28 Jan. 1776, Lewisham, Paris, to Dartmouth.
54 See, for example, G.C. Brauer, *The Education of a Gentleman: Theories of Gentlemanly Education in England, 1660–1775* (New York, 1959), pp. 156–9; J. Towner, *An Historical Geography of Recreation and Tourism in the Western World 1540–1940* (Chichester and New York, 1996), p. 100; French and Rothery, *Man's Estate*, pp. 137–8; Redford, *Venice*, pp. 8, 11; Sweet, *Cities and the Grand Tour*, pp. 23, 278; Kelly, *Dilettanti*, pp. 17–18. For more extensive, thoughtful analysis of the Tour's social education, particularly the role of academies, see Cohen, *Fashioning Masculinity*, pp. 60–2; Bianchi, 'Una palestra', pp. 1021–51; R. Ansell, 'Irish Protestant travel to Europe, 1660–1727', University of Oxford D.Phil. thesis (2013), chapter 6, pp. 222–48.
55 BL Add. Ms. 35378 f. 84, 1 Sep. 1777, Yorke, Gottingen, to Hardwicke; BL Add. Ms. 35378 f. 3, 3 Jan. 1777, Yorke, The Hague, to Hardwicke.
56 BL Add. Ms. 35378 f. 109, 21 Nov. 1777, Yorke, Vienna, to Hardwicke.
57 SRO D(W)1778/V/852, 3 Jan. 1776, Dartmouth, London, to Lewisham.
58 SRO D(W)1778/V/874, 30 Jul. 1776, Lewisham, Hanover, to Lady Dartmouth.
59 SRO D(W)1778/V/886, 2 Aug. 1776, David Stevenson, Hanover, to Dartmouth.
60 Mori, 'Hosting', pp. 121–3.
61 BL Add. Ms. 35378 f. 59, 29 Jun. 1777, Hardwicke, London, to Yorke.
62 BL Add. Ms. 62114 K, 13 Aug. 1751, Dartmouth, Leipzig, to Stillingfleet.
63 BL Add. M. 32730 fols 116–17, 15 Oct. 1752, Pembroke, Leipzig, to Newcastle.
64 Ibid.
65 BL Add. Ms. 22998, 4–15 Jun. 1741, Richard Pococke's travel journals.
66 See the Common Room's correspondence with one another in NRO WKC 7/46/9-19; BL Add. Ms. 22998, Richard Pococke's travel journals; William Coxe, *Literary Life and Select Works of Benjamin Stillingfleet* ... (London, 1811); R.W. Ketton-Cremer, *Felbrigg: The Story of a House* (London, 1962), p. 145.
67 NRO WKC 7/46/11, 9 Nov. 1741, Robert Price, Paris, to the Bloods.
68 BL Add. Ms. 22998, 2–13 Jun. 1741, Richard Pococke's travel journals.
69 Ibid.
70 Coxe, *Literary Life*, pp. 75, 78–9.
71 BL Add. Ms. 35378 f. 84, 1 Sep. 1777, Yorke, Gottingen, to Hardwicke; BL Add. Ms. 36258, 11 Sep. 1777, Yorke's journal.
72 Black, *British Abroad*, pp. 217, 225; I. Littlewood, *Sultry Climates: Travel and Sex* (London, 2001), pp. 11–15, 21.
73 For scholarship on the complexities of the adult elite world, see J. Tosh, *Manliness and Masculinities in Nineteenth-Century Britain: Essays on Gender, Family, and Empire* (Harlow and New York, 2005), p. 70; Tosh, *A Man's Place: Masculinity and the Middle-Class Home in Victorian England* (New Haven and London, 1999), chapter 6, p. 128; P. Higgins, '"Let us play the men": masculinity and the citizen-soldier in late eighteenth-century Ireland', in C. Kennedy and M. McCormack, eds, *Soldiering in Britain and Ireland, 1750–1850: Men of Arms* (Houndmills, 2013), pp. 180, 182, 184; R. Carr, 'The gentleman and the soldier: patriotic masculinities in eighteenth-century Scotland', *Journal of Scottish Historical Studies*, 28:2 (2008), pp. 105–6, 110; K. Harvey, 'Ritual encounters: punch parties and masculinity in the eighteenth century', *Past and Present*, 214:1 (2012), pp. 200–1; H. Berry, 'Rethinking politeness in eighteenth-century England: Moll King's coffee house and the

The social challenge 81

significance of "flash talk"', *Transactions of the Royal Historical Society*, 11 (2001), pp. 65–81; V. Gatrell, *City of Laughter: Sex and Satire in Eighteenth-Century London* (London, 2006), p. 316; French and Rothery, *Man's Estate*, pp. 125–7.

74 For further discussions of elite society's mercurial codes of acceptance, see Greig, *Beau Monde*, pp. 193–4, 202, 209–15; J. Kelly, 'Riots, revelries, and rumour: libertinism and masculine association in enlightenment London', *Journal of British Studies*, 45:4 (2006), pp. 774–5, 788–90; Gatrell, *City of Laughter*, p. 178.

75 See, for example, Yorke's admiration for one French ambassador's social virtues. BL Add. Ms. 35378 f. 143, 11 Feb. 1778, Yorke, Vienna, to Hardwicke.

76 Kelly, *Dilettanti*, pp. 17–18.

77 NRO WKC 7/46/12, 24 Oct. 1741, Price, Lyon, to the Bloods; NRO WKC 7/46/11, 9 Nov. 1741, Price, Paris, to the Bloods; NRO WKC 7/46/13-4, 17 Mar. 1741, Benjamin Tate and William Dampier, Strasbourg, to the Bloods; NRO WKC 7/46/19, 19 Apr. 1741, Dampier, Rotterdam, to the Bloods; French and Rothery, *Man's Estate*, p. 110.

78 NRO WKC 7/46/19, 19 April 1741, Dampier, Rotterdam, to the Bloods.

79 For example, SRO D(W)1778/V/895, 28 Jun. 1776, Sir Joseph Yorke, The Hague, to Dartmouth; SRO D(W)1778/V/896, 30 Jul. 1775, Colonel Fawcett, Hanover, to Dartmouth.

80 BL Add. Ms. 32727 fols 214–5, May 1752, Newcastle, Hanover, to Lord Ashburnham.

81 For example, BL Add. Ms. 32723 f. 46, 28 Sep. 1750, S.A. Richmond, London, to Newcastle; BL Add. Ms. 32724: f. 18, 13 Jan. 1750, Lord Albemarle, Paris, to Newcastle; BL Add. Ms. 32729 fols 91–2, [undated] Newcastle, Hanover, to his brother; BL. Add. Ms. 32730 fols 256–7, 11 Oct. 1752, earl of Rochford, Turin, to Sir Hans Younge; BL Add. Ms. 32733 f. 381, 6 Dec. 1753, Newcastle, London, to Albermarle; BL Add. Ms. 32733 fols 429–30, 12 Dec. 1753, Albermarle, Paris, to Newcastle. See also Mori, 'Hosting', p. 120.

82 See P.D.G. Thomas, 'North, Frederick, second earl of Guilford [Lord North] (1732–1792)', *Oxford Dictionary of National Biography (ODNB)* (OUP: online edn, January 2015), doi:10.1093/ref:odnb/20304 [accessed 28 May 2015].

83 See Kelly, *Dilettanti*.

84 For example, the Common Room remained in close contact throughout their adult lives, as they brought 'the Common Room from Geneva to London'. In their early career, they sought to exert a collective influence over London's cultural taste, by sponsoring new artists, musicians and scientists. In later life, they gave each other preferment in promotions and careers and acted as will executors and trustees.

85 Conway, *Continental Europe*, pp. 210–13.

86 See R. Eagles, *Francophilia in English Society, 1748–1815* (Basingstoke, 2000). Similar points are made by French and Rothery, *Man's Estate*, p. 140; D. Bell, *The First Total War: Napoleon's Europe and the Birth of Warfare as we Know it* (Boston, 2007), p. 36.

87 SRO D(W)1778/V/874, 3 Oct. 1777, Lewisham, Geneva, to Lady Dartmouth. Lewisham reported that he met up with Francis North, North's second son, in Lausanne.

88 WSHC Ms. 2057/F5/7, 1 May 1780, Herbert's journal.

89 SRO D(W)1778/V/874, 10 Dec. 1775, Lewisham, Paris, to Dartmouth; 11 Aug. 1776, Lewisham, Berlin, to Dartmouth.

90 SRO D(W)1778/V/874, 11 Aug. 1776, Lewisham, Berlin, to Dartmouth; SRO D(W)1778/V/874, 10 Dec. 1775, Lewisham, Paris, to Dartmouth.

82 *Sarah Goldsmith*

91 SRO D(W)1778/V/858, 21 Sep. 1776, Keith, Vienna, to Dartmouth.
92 LMA Acc. 510/239, 5 Oct. 1754, Jersey, Cassel, to Lady Jersey.
93 BL Add, Ms. 2734 f. 81, 25 Jan. 1754, Richmond, Leyden, to Newcastle.
94 Conway, *Continental Europe*, pp. 192–3, 213; Bell, *The First Total War,* pp. 28, 36. See also G. Newman, *The Rise of English Nationalism: A Cultural History, 1740–1830* (New York, 1987). R. Babel and W. Paravicini, eds, *Grand Tour. Adeliges Reisen und Europaïsche Kultur vom 14. bis zum 18. Jahrhundert* (Ostfildern, 2005) makes similar observations in its discussions of the German *Kavaliersreisen* to Italy.
95 E. Chalus, 'Elite women, social politics, and the political world of late eighteenth-century England', *Historical Journal*, 43:3 (2000), p. 672.
96 P. Bianchi, 'La caccia nell'educazione del gentiluomo. Il caso sabaudo (sec. XVI–XVIII)', in P. Bianchi and P. Passerin d'Entrèves, eds, *La caccia nello Stato sabaudo I. Caccia e cultura (sec. XVI–XVIII)* (Turin, 2010), pp. 19–37; Bianchi, 'Una palestra', pp. 135, 144–8, 150.
97 See, for example, BL Add. Ms. 34887 f. 138, 9 Jan. 1764, John Holroyd, later 1st earl of Sheffield, Lausanne, to Mrs Atkinson; BL Add. Ms. 34887 f. 140, 2 Feb. 1764, Holroyd, Lausanne, to Mrs Baker; BL Add. Ms. 34887 f. 178, 3 Oct. 1765, Holroyd, Vienna, to Mrs Baker; BL Add. Ms. 34883 f. 85, 19 Mar. 1765, Edward Gibbon, Rome, to Edward Gibbon; BL Add. Ms. 34883 f. 87, 22 Apr. 1765, Gibbon, Venice, to Dorothea Gibbon née Patton.
98 Tosh, *Manliness*, pp. 70–1.

5   Abroad, or still 'at home'? Young noblemen from the Czech lands and the empire in the seventeenth and eighteenth centuries

Eva Chodějovská and Zdeněk Hojda

Between 1570 and 1750 numbers of young noblemen from the Holy Roman Empire travelled hundreds of miles through the cities of western and southern Europe, taking two to four years, and exceptionally more. The course of their itineraries, however, did not remain the same but underwent distinct evolutions.[1] Throughout the seventeenth century their journeys took them through France and Italy among the most densely urbanised parts of the European continent. However, after 1700 the itineraries of the noblemen from the Habsburg Monarchy show a decisive shift towards more northern destinations (the Netherlands, England, the duchy of Lorraine, but also towns in the Empire). Taking inspiration from the subtitle of the present book – 'northern metropolises and early modern travel behaviour' – this chapter examines the reasons for this reorientation in travel culture towards the north and analyses how these changes were linked with the new perception of the sense and purpose of the Grand Tours.

Since a high percentage of these aristocrats were from the Czech lands, the analysis is based on a sample of 37 Tours by Bohemian noblemen[2] undertaken between 1650 and 1750 – that is, between the end of the Thirty Years' War and the restriction of the Grand Tours after Maria Theresa's ascent to the Austrian throne. There were several conditions used as the criteria for inclusion: the Tour lasted at least 18 months; the young nobleman visited several countries[3] and originated from the Czech lands or, respectively, owned some landed property there and, of course – the surviving written sources allow for substantial documenting of his travels. The good condition of the surviving sources[4] – travel diaries, correspondence, travel bills (accounts of expenses), instructions issued for the hofmeisters, passports and, exceptionally, also memoirs – offer rich potential for Czech historical research. In addition, no such research based on a similarly extensive sample has yet been carried out.[5]

There naturally arises the question whether there was a specifically Czech model of a Grand Tour. Probably not – as far as an itinerary or a Tour's duration are concerned. The Tours of the young Bohemian or Moravian men did not differ significantly from those of their Austrian and German contemporaries. However, some characteristic features can be

84   *Eva Chodějovská and Zdeněk Hojda*

traced in their motivation – especially in the case of the members of the families which, after 1620, gambled on the way towards the fastest possible integration into the cosmopolitan milieu developing around the Viennese court. These saw their chance for social mobility among the elite in pursuing an upswing in the court milieu[6] – which distinguished them from, for example, British aristocrats.[7]

The present chapter unfolds in three parts. The first part describes the phenomenon of the Grand Tour as it has hitherto been understood by Czech, Austrian or German historiography – as a journey undertaken by central European aristocrats for the sake of knowledge in order to complete their education.[8] The Grand Tour is examined chronologically as it developed from the sixteenth century, along with the aims and programme which it had in the period of its greatest influence – that is, in the seventeenth century. In the second part, the itineraries and the programme of a typical Grand Tour taken in the second half of the seventeenth century will be analysed on the basis of our sample. The shift towards a more northern focus in the itineraries of the central European Grand Tour after 1700 will be analysed in the third and closing section.

A Grand Tour of central European aristocrats: characteristic features, aims and itineraries

The Grand Tours of the young Bohemian and German noblemen can also be defined as a certain kind of 'rite of passage'. An aristocrat would take the journey after completing his education at home, and in the company of his hofmeister. He was viewed as an adult only upon his return when he could marry, begin climbing up the career ladder of service to the state and take charge of controlling the family property. This model of Grand Tour became a customary part of aristocratic education not only in the lands of the Habsburg Monarchy[9] and in other territories of the Holy Roman Empire;[10] it was also adopted by young aristocrats from Poland,[11] Scandinavia[12] and the Netherlands.[13]

The principal objective of a Tour for education and knowledge undertaken by young noblemen, usually aged between 16 and 20, was to embrace the cultural habitus which would later facilitate their smooth integration into the society of the west and central European courts. The Grand Tour as the final stage of a distinctive 'aristocratic' pattern of education thus represented an exemplary case of cultural transfer in the sense of not only specific patterns of behaviour and manners,[14] but also particular cultural forms, ideas and objects.[15]

The nobility, who provided the backbone of the state establishment, faced new qualification claims presented by the early modern state. In line with the humanist requirements described by Erasmus of Rotterdam in his *Institutio principis Christiani* (1517), an aristocrat was expected to acquire the kind of intellectual and social accomplishments that only a humanistic university could offer in the sixteenth century. The conclusion of the process of a young nobleman's education and the crowning point of his curricula, was not only his university studies but also his 'round trip' of foreign courts. The Grand Tours were therefore based on two crucial elements: the highly traditional, 'knightly' travelling from court to court, when a young aristocrat would mature from the boyish page into an adult man, and the humanist-conceived *peregrinatio academica* from university to university.

University residency was not – as in the case of numerous students from the bourgeois ranks – focused on acquiring an academic degree. Its duration varied from a few months to two or three years and its aim was to acquire a certain amount of philosophical knowledge and, usually, also the rudiments of law. Students of noble origin, however, would soon try to set themselves apart from their lower-class fellows. They did not partake in collective education, but sought private lessons with the university tutors; they did not limit themselves to the nearby German universities frequented by their bourgeois contemporaries but could afford to travel to more remote Italian (mainly Padua and Siena) or French institutes. It was not exceptional, either, for non-Catholic aristocrats to attend strictly denominational universities of Calvinist orientation (such as Heidelberg, Basel, or Geneva) prior to 1620. All this, then, gradually helped to develop a specific 'aristocratic' model of university education.[16]

Around the mid-sixteenth century, the ideal that an aristocrat should receive the highest possible humanist schooling was influenced by a new concept, the *cortegiano* – a courtier modelled after the protagonist of the hugely successful book by Baldassare Castiglione (first published in 1528).[17] *Il Cortegiano* spread out from the milieu of the north Italian high-Renaissance courts when northern Italy was a cultural doyen to the whole of Europe, and the success of Castiglione's text can be credited with enabling Italy to retain its prestige and cultural influence, even when the economy and politics of most of its states were already in decline. Such an educated, socially seasoned courtier of wide purview and noble carriage, who was perfectly acquainted with the ceremonial conventions and qualified to flawlessly discuss in the court anterooms the complete range of all imaginable subjects in several appropriate languages and to the expected level, could rise to the higher stages of the state or, respectively, court services.[18] The Grand Tour was, in the terms of Pierre Bourdieu, a crucial source of social and cultural capital, justifying thereby the considerable expenses of the undertaking.[19]

If we look at the curricula of the aristocratic education during the period under discussion in detail, we can trace the gradual evolution of the so-called 'noble disciplines',[20] encompassing political science, law, history, geography and contemporary modern (in practice, mainly Romance) languages[21] and, finally, mathematics and especially geometry. The latter two were adapted to the purposes of the military sciences and were thus often simply described as fortification studies or fortification and structural engineering. This selection of subjects was designed to train an aristocrat for his future career in either the army or administration or, in the most general

86   Eva Chodějovská and Zdeněk Hojda

sense, for court service which could, for example, lead to diplomatic assignments.[22] With the continuing proliferation of travel throughout all strata of the nobility, however, the differential advantage of the journey was somehow reduced from the objective of gaining additional social and cultural credit, and the Grand Tour gradually turned into an elementary – necessary, but not sufficient – precondition for future progress in one's career.

Another crucial aspect in elevating young noblemen to the highest status had always been the requirement to learn traditional noblemen's exercises – that is, mastery of the arts of horse-riding, dancing and fencing. This triad was based upon well-founded principles. If training in the stables leads to the perfect control of a horse, one must also control one's own body. This was, furthermore, supported by dance lessons, serving to achieve absolute control of motion and gesture.[23] The language of movement and deportment in the court milieu held the same significance as verbal and intellectual skills. Fencing, then, represented a traditional martial art being, again, formalised and refined enough via an array of rules to make it yet another attribute of aristocratic upbringing. The young noblemen could further supplement their theoretical studies and physical training with other, more 'artistic' activities according to their taste – most often playing musical instruments or taking practical lessons in drawing or observing architecture.

As mentioned above, the second pillar of aristocratic education, complementing the academic studies and physical drill, was a sojourn at the courts of 'Residenzstädte', which allowed for the observation of court life or – in the case of smaller residences – direct participation.[24] This aspect became more significant to the upbringing of a young nobleman than his curriculum of study in the course of the seventeenth century. The success of such a strategy was naturally influenced by the class, property and political status of the young aristocrat's family and the influential friends of his relatives but, in general, it was an irreplaceable constituent of each and every Grand Tour. The individual sojourns differed according to the 'atmosphere' prevailing in this or that court milieu. At the helpful and accommodating courts, such as the Medici in Florence or the Savoy in Turin, the visiting young noblemen were not only able to master the art of conversation in the anterooms but also to attend court balls, dance and theatre performances and rides.[25] Some courts in the Empire and courts of the Habsburgs (Innsbruck) and their governors (Brussels) were friendly in a similar manner. Rather different conditions prevailed, for instance, in Rome where social life mostly revolved around the courts of individual cardinals and where the young noblemen could only gain access to significant ceremonies and church services, blessed by the presence of the head of the Catholic Church, through cardinals or imperial diplomats. Participation in the life of the grand royal courts in Paris[26] or Madrid[27] was of a similarly 'long-distance' character. Nevertheless, there were differences between the latter two. While in Paris it was relatively easy to 'visit' – to 'stay with' the court (however, because it resided in Versailles it was not always easy to coordinate attendance there with lessons at the Paris riding academies) – penetrating the narrow circle around the ruler often required persistent effort and the influential intercessions of imperial or Spanish diplomats for the noblemen from the Habsburg lands. But it held true in both cities that the main goal was to achieve one or more audiences with the ruler and his relatives; otherwise, the young noblemen mainly acquired knowledge by observation.

As mentioned above, a particular type of aristocratic journey for education began to develop in central Europe about the mid-sixteenth century.[28] Most features of this Grand Tour pattern remained intact until the early Enlightenment, although it underwent several development stages, especially with regard to the methods of achieving the educational goals during the seventeenth and early eighteenth centuries which we will now summarise briefly. The turning point for the nobility from the Czech lands was the year 1620, which closed the 'golden age' of the inter-university peregrinations when there were no significant political or confessional restrictions on travelling. The rise of Counter Reformation Catholicism effectively restricted freedom of movement to the non-Catholic parts of Europe, and endemic warfare was a further constraint. Nevertheless, patterns which would emerge fully in the later seventeenth century were already discernible. Having graduated from a Jesuit school or, having completed legal studies at Leuven University, an aristocrat would set off to do the rounds through the Apennine Peninsula and often to Spain and, in the periods when the Emperor was not at war with the French king, also naturally to France.[29] Non-Catholic countries (the Netherlands, England) were not totally proscribed zones, either, but in the seventeenth-century itineraries they featured as short-term visits at most.

From the 1660s then the interest in studying at Leuven faded; instead, the young men from the Czech lands began appearing at the newly established aristocratic academies. The absence of university studies may misleadingly encourage the assumption that the Grand Tours actually equated to some kind of leisure travelling. It was not so – it is just that their main focus shifted towards longer sojourns at the courts where the young noblemen could refine their conversation and other social skills. Simultaneously, they would hire private tutors in the given towns (or enter academies where available). Such a Tour was not a matter of alternating study and the highly valued *exercitia* with visits to cities and courts,[30] but rather it developed into 'ambulatory' studies which were closely tied to the continuous acquisition of social ease and dexterity.

The next stage in the evolution of Grand Tours can be identified around 1700, although the new elements only became fully apparent after the War of the Spanish Succession. The *exercitia* slowly gave way to 'sciences' and a firm place on the programme was occupied *exercitia* by a longer sojourn to a single place (usually Leiden or the Lunéville/Nancy academy in Lorraine), devoted to studying law with a renowned lecturer. Only then followed the Grand Tour as such, the duration of which was thus reduced. Developments in the Habsburg Empire towards the end of this period were influenced by the ruler's restrictions imposed on this kind of travel, partly for political reasons, but also in response to contemporary Enlightenment criticism of 'excessive expenses'. At the same time that these restrictions were being imposed domestic educational establishments were also being established such as the Theresianum in Vienna. This stage can be justly called that of early Enlightenment.[31]

Central European aristocratic destinations in the second half of the seventeenth century

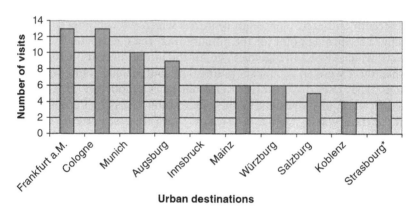

Figure 5.1 Selected urban destinations in the Holy Roman Empire of Grand Tours undertaken 1650–1700, not including Ratisbon and Nuremberg which served mainly as transit towns (based on 21 travels)

Note: A visit constituted a stay of at least two nights in any given place.

* From 1681 Strasbourg was occupied by France.

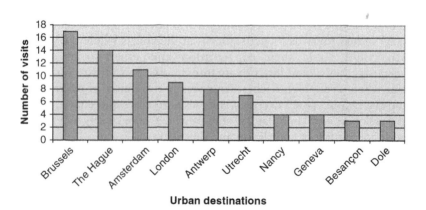

Figure 5.2 Selected urban destinations in the Netherlands, England, Switzerland and the Duchy of Burgundy of Grand Tours undertaken 1650–1700 (based on 21 travels)

Note: A visit constituted a stay of at least two nights in any given place.

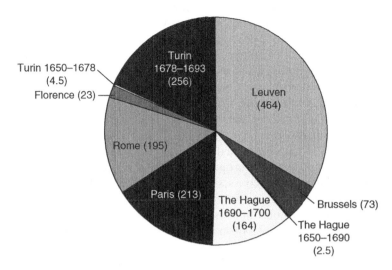

Figure 5.3 Average duration of sojourns at selected European *Residenzstädte* and at Leuven University, 1650–1700

Note: It was not possible to establish the exact duration of particular sojourns for the towns listed below from all itineraries, therefore the data presented is provisional only.

Leuven 464 days (based on 8 study sojourns)
Brussels 73 days (12 travels)
The Hague 1650–1690 2.5 days (10 travels)
The Hague 1690–1700 164 days (5 travels)
Paris 213 days (20 travels)
Rome 195 days (19 travels)
Florence 23 days (13 travels)
Turin 1650–78 4.5 days (7 travels)
Turin 1678–93* 256 days (9 travels)
* between the opening of *Accademia Reale* and the war with France

Reconstructing a typical Grand Tour taken in the latter half of the seventeenth century is quite a difficult task. Although the cavaliers usually moved along well-trodden tracks, the itinerary of each Tour was quite individual, determined by the father's instructions, the experience of the hofmeister and, naturally, also the financial resources of the gentlemen. Let us thus at least look at the places they visited most often during this time.

Universities did not generally adapt swiftly or very effectively to meet the requirements of the new noble clientele. Some gradually established adjoining aristocratic colleges for their accommodation (these were mainly the Jesuit universities, which were more responsive and flexible); at other places aristocratic needs were accommodated on a more informal and ad hoc basis, with private tutors offering that which a university could not provide. Several university towns, however, remained significant for aristocratic education, on the strength of their intellectual reputation and also because

90 *Eva Chodějovská and Zdeněk Hojda*

the institutions of the 'university nations',[32] for example, maintained their prestige.[33] This was the case for Siena in Tuscany and, to a certain extent, Padua, as well as Leuven in the Netherlands. Siena was frequented from the first half of the seventeenth century and its popularity was at a peak between the 1650s and 1680s, when sojourns to the city lasted from three to 12 months. Prolonged sojourns in Siena could, in addition, be combined with visits to the Medici in Florence. This, nevertheless, holds true for only some aristocrats documented by entries in the Sienese register *nationis germanicae*, whereas many others merely enrolled, stayed in the city for just a few days and then swiftly proceeded to Rome. As far as the southern Netherlands is concerned, central Europeans mainly favoured the university in Leuven due to its high-quality courses in law; the young noblemen would often stay there for more than a year.[34] Yet another temptation was the proximity of the governor's court in Brussels. It must be noted, though, that the Leuven institute was viewed as too conservative from the 1660s. The rapid decline in interest in Leuven and travels to the southern Netherlands in general is evident in the period of the War of Devolution of the 1670s and during the French occupation of Brussels between 1695 and 1697.

From the late sixteenth century, a new concept of the aristocratic academy appeared which would offer training in the 'noble disciplines' and exercises, so to speak, under the same roof.[35] In Italy, several minor local colleges (*collegi*) or private academies, which began gradually appearing in the travelling itineraries after the mid-seventeenth century, were followed by the Savoyard *Accademia Reale* in Turin, established in 1678. This was the only one to enjoy full success right from its foundation.[36] Young gentlemen, arriving mainly from central Europe, but also the Netherlands and north Italy, would usually spend six to 14 months there. The academy had to close due to the war with France in 1693 and then reopened for six years after the Peace of Rijswijk of 1697, but the onset of war forced it to close again soon after in 1703. It never managed to win back its previous renown in the eighteenth century.

The long sojourns in Paris (lasting a year or more) were linked with visits to riding academies (*académies d'équitation*)[37] and, naturally, with hiring more tutors. But education (horse-riding aside) was certainly not the main reason for visiting Paris. Besides the court of the 'Sun King', which set the tone for all other courts in Europe, the city had a generous selection of splendid theatre and ballet productions to offer. Between 1688 and 1697 and then during the War of the Spanish Succession, however, trips from countries in the Empire to France were extremely rare. Paris aside, some young noblemen frequented Angers and Orléans, chiefly in the 1680s and 1690s; in Spanish Burgundy the aristocratic academies in Dole (during the 1650s to 1665) and Besançon (between 1664 and 1674) were highly popular until they were occupied by the French. Academies were rather unstable institutions in which periods of prosperity were often quickly followed by decline or even extinction. Despite this, as Richard Ansell's chapter in this volume

Abroad, or still 'at home'? 91

also shows, they played a more important role in the programme of the Grand Tours than has traditionally been thought. However, the overriding problem continues to be the lack of any lists or registers of their clients.[38]

A young nobleman, moreover, acquired knowledge and experience by participating in or even merely observing life at court governed by ceremonial rules and through social interaction with local elites in the cities through which he passed. This type of learning was actually the most important purpose of staying in cities with a court, although it did not mean that a cavalier had to resign his studies and *exercitia*. Hiring teachers in law, maths, geometry, languages and other disciplines, as well as tutors in aristocratic skills was commonplace in all large *Residenzstädte*. In effect they offered almost the same educational opportunities in the noble disciplines as the towns where there were universities or academies. Florence was typical in this respect, as it represented a comparable 'study' to the university in Siena. Here the court of the future Cosimo III, successor to the Grand Duke Ferdinand, was especially attractive and the young Transalpine aristocrats not only directly partook in the court life but also attended the local private academy or, after 1689, the *Istituto dei nobili*.

Next to be examined is the nature of travel throughout the Holy Roman Empire, which served mainly as a transit region in the latter half of the seventeenth century. Journeying across the imperial areas was reduced to the fastest possible transfer from either Czech or Austrian lands to the west – the Netherlands or France – or, eventually, to shorter routes via southern German territories to Italy. Such journeys usually did not take more than four or five weeks. This, however, does not mean that the young noblemen did not seek audiences with the princes of the Empire, either secular or ecclesiastical. Nor did they omit to visit places of interest in the *Reichsstädte*, even when travelling at this fast pace.[39] The most frequented route meandered from Nuremberg, Würzburg, Frankfurt am Main, Mainz, Koblenz, Cologne and Düsseldorf to the Netherlands. Another choice was more south-bound, through Ratisbon, Munich, Augsburg, Ulm, Stuttgart and Rastatt, with the final destination being France. Swiss cities, too, served as places of transit. Only a few chose a somewhat slower pace when crossing Germany (such as Johann Maximilian Thun in 1695). The clear exception is Herman Jacob Czernin (1679),[40] who spent a month in Ratisbon (the permanent seat of the Imperial Diet) and then proceeded to those in Munich and Salzburg. The correspondence of Herman's father, Humprecht Johann Czernin, reveals that these 'layovers' were conceived as an opportunity for Herman Jacob to prepare for his social role in more prestigious destinations, especially in Italy or Spain.

Visits to the United Provinces and England were similarly of only very brief duration. Journeys to England exclusively meant visits to London.[41] In the case of the Netherlands, the young gentlemen would set off on short roundabout trips which usually did not exceed two weeks. The short duration of these trips should not lead to the conclusion that they were perceived as somehow marginal or even a dispensable part of the programme.[42] Only

92 *Eva Chodějovská and Zdeněk Hojda*

four of the 21 Tours between 1650 and 1700 which have been researched in this sample omitted north Netherlands from their plan. A typical example is Herman Jacob Czernin, who had to return from his Grand Tour hastily in 1682 due to his father's death; two years later, having become the head of the family, he set off again for several months, including the countries and cities in his programme which had previously been unvisited – Amsterdam, The Hague and London, and also Berlin and Dresden.[43]

The United Provinces began to play a different role in the travel programmes from the early 1690s at the latest.[44] Undoubtedly, the important fact here was the political alliance between the Netherlandish Estates and the Habsburgs against France.[45] Thus, sojourns to The Hague, the seat of the Dutch governor, government and an array of diplomats, often as long as several months, became commonplace during that period. There, the young noblemen could also undertake aristocratic training as they had in the previously well-tested cities of Paris and Brussels. In some years (mainly before the signing of the Peace of Rijswijk in 1697), The Hague was even a substitute when travel to Paris was impossible.

Where did the central European aristocrats travel to and where did they receive their education in the first half of the eighteenth century?

The War of the Spanish Succession did not bring an end to making Grand Tours but it did act as a brake. Opportunities to travel west revived after 1715, but it was to a different Europe: Vienna gained its share of territory on the Spanish Succession – the Southern Netherlands and the north Italian provinces – and, after 1723, the fates of the Habsburg and Lorraine

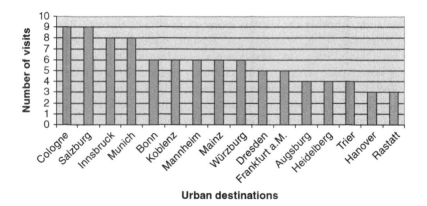

Figure 5.4 Selected urban destinations in the Holy Roman Empire of Grand Tours undertaken 1700–50, not including Ratisbon and Nuremberg, which served mainly as transit towns (based on 16 travels)

Note: A visit constituted a stay of at least two nights in any given place.

Abroad, or still 'at home'? 93

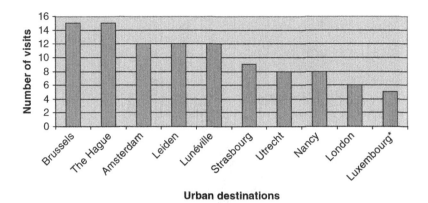

Figure 5.5 Selected urban destinations in the Netherlands and the duchy of Lorraine, including Strasbourg and London, on Grand Tours undertaken 1700–50 (based on 16 travels)

Note: A visit constituted a stay of at least two nights in any given place.

* From 1714 Luxembourg was administered as a part of the Austrian Netherlands.

dynasties became more intertwined due to the promised future marriage of Franz Stephan, son of the duke of Lorraine, with the oldest daughter of Emperor Charles VI, Maria Theresa. The new trends in travelling, which had begun to emerge in the late seventeenth century, could now assert themselves in full. The journeys became rationalised and were shorter – usually from two to two and a half years – and their core element was a period of at least six months at some of the most renowned schools of law or, more precisely, at the lectures provided by the most outstanding lawyers, such as Johann Jacob Vitriarius in Leiden or his pupil de Begnicour in Lunéville. Here, the cavaliers would listen to lectures mainly in public law – the latter being a novelty – and also Roman law, thus consistently training for their future political careers. And there was yet one more very distinct novelty: the cultural language of the eighteenth century was French, to which even the Viennese court 'yielded' after the death of Emperor Joseph I, albeit with some delay in comparison with other German territories. This necessarily influenced the overall cultural orientation of the young aristocrats as well as their correspondence and records. Perfect mastery of French was a precondition for any further professional progress; moreover, the lectures in law noted above were naturally given in French.

Although, as already discussed, the United Provinces had been regularly frequented in the previous century, the country acquired a reputation as a sought-after destination for study only in the early eighteenth century.[46] The most attractive town was Leiden and its law school: eight aristocrats from the sample used in this study were enrolled in the Leiden register

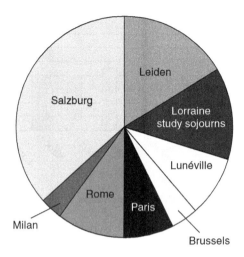

Figure 5.6 Average duration of sojourns at selected European *Residenzstädte* and university (academy) towns, 1700–50

Note: It was not possible to establish the exact duration of particular sojourns for the towns listed below from all itineraries, therefore the data presented is provisional only.

Leiden 203 days (based on 8 study sojourns)

Lorraine (study sojourns*) 163 days (8 sojourns)

Lunéville (all visits) 108 days (10 travels)

Brussels 50 days (12 travels)

Paris 93 days (12 travels**)

Rome 122 days (8 travels***)

Milan 41 days (8 travels****)

Salzburg 452 days (4 study sojourns)

* in Lunéville, Nancy and Pont-à-Mousson

** this does not include the extended sojourn of the Chotek brothers (16 months, 1728–30)

*** this does not include the two extended sojourns of the Nostitz brothers (54 months, 1721–6) and the Buquoy brothers (17 months, 1729–30)

**** this does not include the extended sojourn of the Buquoy brothers (*c*.20 days 1728–9 and 9 months 1730–1)

between 1721 and 1730.[47] What made the law schools there so attractive to students from the imperial countries? It was not just a matter of the modern reputation of the education and the truly individual and almost fatherly guardianship with which Vitriarius pampered his students;[48] a very important role was also played by the pro-imperial orientation of Vitriarius's legal writings. And if studying law was one of the main reasons for travelling to the Netherlands, it was far from being the only one. The political climate, its traditions of liberty and the relatively low-key observance of formal ceremonials, as well as the splendid supply of information – all enjoyed a renowned reputation, as is illustrated, for instance,

Abroad, or still 'at home'? 95

by the advice provided by Franz Joseph Czernin to his nephews: *Hollandt [...] ist das Landt, woh am allerfreyeßten geredet wirdt, [...] so kann* [ein junger cavalier] *viel omni scibili erfahren, nacher durch kleine hien und her Reyßen in Hollandt vieles sehen, undt ein Fructum ziehen; dann erstlichen weillen Hollandt eine freye Republic ist, so wirdt da von allen Regierungen von ganz Europa, von allen Intriquen, deren bey verschiedenen Höffen befündlichen Ministern frey und clar gesprochen.* The openness and informality of the Dutch thus sharply contrasted with the French secretiveness: *die Oerther als [...] Paris, [...] haben viel ein künstlichere, verschwiegenere Lebensarth, daß mann da lang seyn kann, ehe ein junger Mensch was erfahret, nacher aber doch nicht alles weyß, woh in der freyen Republique Hollandt einem gleich alles zu Ohren kommt, da Leuthe von keinem Caeremoniel seyn folgsamb, der Access leicht und mann baldt mit Ihnen in Confidentz kommet.*[49] This, however, did not exhaust the benefits of visiting the Dutch Republic: the cavaliers would also visit the headquarters of the East India Company or the porcelain manufactory in Delft,[50] interests which were in keeping with the contemporary spirit of mercantilism.

Some young men continued in their journeys from the Netherlands via Dunkirk and Calais to England. The numbers who did so – approximately one third[51] – were no higher than in the preceding 50 years; but some did stay longer than the usual two weeks and some did not even limit themselves to London and the adjoining royal palaces.[52] Upon graduating from the Dutch lesson of republicanism, their studies of political systems could thus continue by exploring the English parliamentary system, as again Franz Joseph Czernin recommended to his protégés: *dann von Callais in Gottesnahmen nach Engellandt, umb nachdehme mann in Hollandt das Gouvernium democraticum gesehen, mann Species aristocratici seu Monarchiae limitatae in bonum Subditorum sehen, undt ist in Engellandt [...] so viel zu erfahren, weillen eben alle Affairen durch das Parlament undt durch viel Köpf, also nicht so secret gehandelt werden.*[53]

French cultural dominance was also naturally reflected in the particular itineraries. Between 1688 and 1697 and then during the War of the Spanish Succession, no one from the Habsburg Empire would travel to France, and new problems also arose with the 1733 War of the Polish Succession. Between 1715 and 1733, however, Paris remained as one of the main destinations of each and every Grand Tour. Sojourns to Paris were not as long as in the previous century – most cavaliers got by with two to five months, for they did not attend the local *académies d'équitation* as their predecessors had done. Some of them, nonetheless, conceived their sojourn as a certain kind of political practice, as did the Chotek brothers, who spent 14 months in the French metropolis,[54] attended the Paris Court of Appeal and closely observed the negotiations at the international Congress of Soissons, while Johann Karl Chotek even passed an 'administrative practice' with the Paris imperial envoy, Stephan Wilhelm Kinsky.[55] In 1733 Adam Franz Sternberg apparently adopted a similar plan, as can be judged from his

96 *Eva Chodějovská and Zdeněk Hojda*

resolution in the introduction to his *Mémoires des mes voyages:[...] la plus grand etude doit être de bien s'instruir de la manier du gouvernement etant differant l'une de l'autre païs.*[56] His intention was unfortunately halted by the outbreak of the Polish War of Succession in October 1733 after merely two months spent in Paris.

But a young aristocrat from the Habsburg Monarchy, who desired to master good French and French manners, had two more options to choose from for their travels – the court of the Austrian governor at Brussels, which none of the gentlemen from our sample omitted, and the court of the duchy of Lorraine in Nancy and Lunéville. Lorraine exceptionally appeared on the itineraries as early as the 1670s, but more considerable numbers of young noblemen from the Monarchy travelled there in the period after 1723. The reason for this upsurge in interest was the dynastic connection between the dukes of Lorraine and the Habsburgs. Léopold V de Lorraine (1679–1729) was the nephew of Emperor Leopold I, and his son Franz Stephan, as the promised husband of Maria Theresa, received his upbringing in Vienna between 1724 and 1729. This made Lorraine an attractive goal for the young noblemen arriving from the imperial countries. The court and the aristocratic academy would commute between Nancy and the new residence in Lunéville,[57] and sojourns at the two towns between 1714 and 1733 are documented in 13 of the 16 Grand Tours in our sample. Some travellers spent only a month at the court of Lorraine, while six- or 12-month courses of study can be identified in at least six cases. The local legal authority was Monsieur de Begnicour, who could boast 16 years of practice as a *répétiteur* with the legendary Vitriarius.[58] Lorraine was simultaneously a good springboard for discovering the French border fortresses, of which the most admired was Luxembourg.

Finally, how did the itinerary around the cities of the Holy Roman Empire evolve? The rise of a number of ducal houses resulted in the development of new centres of power and culture. The previously exceptional interest in either the Brandenburg or Saxon metropolises gradually changed and Dresden, Berlin or Hanover turned into regular stops of the Grand Tours. And they were not the only ones. Both the secular and ecclesiastic electors in the Empire built monumental baroque castles and even new *Residenzstädte* – which similarly drew attention to new destinations, such as Mannheim, Bonn and Koblenz. This did not, however, mean that cities that had previously been frequented, such as Frankfurt am Main, where the Emperor's coronation took place, vanished from the noble itineraries.

The archiepiscopal city of Salzburg was a very specific case. It had been favoured even before the eighteenth century, especially by the aristocrats from the Czech lands, due to the welcoming court milieu, excellent riding school and also thanks to the numerous family bonds between the Bohemian nobles and the local bishops and canons. From the turn of the century, it, however, developed a new and distinctive profile as a popular place of study thanks to the local Benedictine university which succeeded in fostering high-quality law studies. Salzburg would thus satisfy the study

Abroad, or still 'at home'? 97

demand during the period when travelling further west was impossible due to war, although it remained popular until as late as 1730.[59]

The key factors affecting the evolution of the post-1700 Grand Tour itineraries were the specific political environment (notably war), family traditions, family kinship and social networks,[60] as well as the cliental bonds at kindred courts. The itineraries were also determined by structural factors, such as the network of postal routes (which facilitated ease of travel) and travel literature. Many of these factors could also impose limitations upon the route taken, whether on account of military conflict or the financial resources of particular families.

The process of de-confessionalisation and new political coalitions from the early eighteenth century allowed even aristocrats from the imperial countries to sojourn at non-Catholic countries and non-Catholic universities. Law studies were unambiguously viewed as a professional training for the career of a state official[61] and, as such, transcended all religious controversies. This can be clearly observed in the example of Leiden, where the decisive factors were the high quality of education, the opportunity to study modern disciplines of law and the political loyalty of teachers – that is, the pro-imperial orientation of Johann Jacob Vitriarius.[62] After all, his clientele from the Habsburg lands enjoyed unlimited access to the private Catholic services in Leiden.[63]

The question of the practical value of such 'reformed' Grand Tours[64] can be answered by pointing to the illustrious political careers of several of those who undertook a Tour,[65] and the even larger numbers of the 'nameless' whose careers did not even start. A more exhaustive response certainly would require extensive prosopographical research which has not been carried out yet. It is, however, without doubt that a Grand Tour of this type at least guaranteed a decent purview and a decent starting position. But in the early eighteenth century an alternative option to expensive travel abroad also emerged: these were the aristocratic academies newly opened by some Church institutions (the Benedictine Academy in Ettal, 1711), as well as, for example, the bi-confessional Royal Noble Academy in the Silesian Liegnitz (1707), which owed its existence to an initiative of the Silesian Estates. A similar initiative was adopted by the traditional Jesuit universities which began founding special aristocratic colleges, such as the Ferdinandeum in Olomouc, in the 1730s. Apart from Ettal, however, the impact of these ventures was unfortunately relatively insignificant.

The trend of establishing domestic institutions, which were intended to save the high costs which Grand Tours usually entailed, soon fused with the political interests of the state. The outbreak of the War of the Austrian Succession in 1740, following the accession of Maria Theresa to the throne, turned out to be a decisive impetus for the attempts of the Viennese court to restrict and exercise more control over travel abroad.[66] The year 1746 witnessed the establishment of the *Theresianische Akademie* in Vienna.[67] Yet although the Theresian travelling restrictions represented a significant turning point in the history of the Grand Tours, they were far from bringing them to an end. On the one hand, most young aristocrats went abroad

98 Eva Chodějovská and Zdeněk Hojda

equipped with an imperial passport even before 1743 (because it made their journeying much easier), and the travels undertaken by sons of high court officials had always been subject to some degree of state control.[68] From the 1740s however, imperial approval became a necessary precondition for crossing the border, while the Empress neither wanted to nor, in fact, was able to ban it completely. In the long term, her measures simply accelerated the transition to the next stage in the history of the Grand Tours – the separation of academic studies from the Tour itself and the convention of making the Tour at an older age than had been customary before.

It seems appropriate, in closing, to return to the title of this chapter: 'Abroad, or still "at home"'? It certainly is a metaphor, but it simultaneously expresses the obvious tension between the fascinating and expansive Baroque Grand Tour and its more or less rationalised eighteenth-century version. The issue of the strangeness or, on the contrary, the feeling of the intimately known, based on researching the surviving travel diaries, would make for a separate historical and psychological study. The fact is that a touring aristocrat arriving from the Czech lands in the eighteenth century would have spent more time in the Empire or, more precisely, in the territory of the German states. He was often tied to them by family relations or was even steered by the chance of inspecting his own family estates (as was the case with the Kaunitzs and Schwarzenbergs). He would also frequently encounter his relatives and acquaintances in the company of the state officials or at the military garrisons at the governor's court in Brussels, Milan or Naples (until 1735). And whereas the duration of the sojourns at these places gradually extended, the distances on the map of Europe on the contrary psychologically shortened due to the family ties and points of contact discussed above. Last, but not least, by the end of the reign of Charles VI there was, indeed, a decrease in travelling abroad and many youngsters would indeed literally stay 'at home'.

Summary list of Grand Tours on which this chapter is based, including dates and archival deposit

1650–1700

1. Maximilian Andreas and Ferdinand Josef of Dietrichstein, 1649–52. MZA Brno, RA Ditrichštejnů, inv. no. 1583, box 358
2. Adam Franz of Waldstein, 1649–53. MZA Brno, RA Ditrichštejnů (related families), inv. no. 3017, box 661; RA Berchtoldů, Buchlov, inv. no. 141, box 10
3. Maximilian of Trauttmansdorff, Österreichisches Staatsarchiv, Allgemeines Verwaltungsarchiv, FA Trauttmansdorff, inv. no. 50, box 147
4. Franz Ferdinand and Anton Pankraz of Gallas, 1657–9. SOA Litoměřice, dep. Děčín, Historická sbírka (rodinný archiv) Clam-Gallasů, inv. no. 155, box 61

Abroad, or still 'at home'? 99

5. Johann Christian and Johann Seyfried of Eggenberg, 1660–3. SOA Třeboň, dep. Český Krumlov, Sbírka rukopisů no. 39
6. Wenzel Adalbert, Johann Norbert and Ignaz Karl of Sternberg, 1662–4. KNM Praha, sign. VIII G 18
7. Ignaz Karl of Sternberg and Peter of Rziczan, 1664–5. NK ČR Praha, sign. VIII A 25
8. N. of Waldstein, 1664–5. SOA Praha, RA Valdštejnů, Mnichovo Hradiště, (manuscripts) inv. no. 273/1
9. Johann Ignaz Dominik Putz of Adlerthurn/Turraquila, 1667–70. SOA Praha, RA Putzů z Adlerthurnu, box 3
10. Dominik Andreas of Kaunitz, 1671–4. MZA Brno, RA Kounicú Slavkov, inv. no. 827, box 84
11. Ferdinand August of Lobkowicz, 1673–4 and 1675–6. Nelahozeves, Lobkowicz Collections – Archives, sign. A 36 and sign. D 177–182
12. Herman Jacob Czernin of Chudenitz, 1678–82 and 1684. NK ČR Praha, sign. XXIII F 30 and XXIII F 43; SOA Třeboň, dep. Jindřichův Hradec, RA Černínů z Chudenic, Jindřichův Hradec, box 258 and unnumbered file of correspondence 1665–1690
13. Leopold Ignaz of Dietrichstein, 1679–85. MZA Brno, RA Ditrichštejnů, inv. no. 1587, box 362
14. Walter Xaver of Dietrichstein, 1683–6. MZA Brno, RA Ditrichštejnů, inv. no. 1586, box 361
15. Johann Maximilian of Thun 1692–5. SOA Litoměřice, dep. Děčín, RA Thun-Hohensteinů, Klášterec nad Ohří, inv. no. 826, sign. W 14/2, box 89
16. Johann Karl and Otto Wenzel of Nostitz, 1695–1700. SOA Plzeň, dep. Klášter, RA Nostitzů, Planá, inv. no. 87, box 32; inv. no. 222, box 61–62; inv. no. 225, box 64
17. Johann Adam of Questenberg, 1696–9. MZA Brno, Ústřední správa a ústřední účtárna Kouniců, inv. no. 9720, box 2423
18. Philipp Hyazinth and Josef Anton of Lobkowicz, 1697–1701. Nelahozeves, Lobkowicz Collections – Archives, sign. A 36, A 38 and D 181
19. Adam Franz of Schwarzenberg 1697–1701. SOA Třeboň, dep. Český Krumlov, RA Schwarzenberků, Hluboká nad Vltavou, fasc. 416
20. Franz Karl and Wratislaw Maximilian Wratislaw of Mitrovic, 1697–1700. Dírná, RA Vratislavů z Mitrovic, Dírná, inv. no. 249, box 71

1700–50

1. Franz Josef Czernin of Chudenitz, 1715–17. SOA Třeboň, dep. Jindřichův Hradec, RA Černínů z Chudenic, Jindřichův Hradec, box 330
2. Amand Anton Peterswaldzky of Peterswald, 1715–19. MZA Brno, RA Berchtoldů, Buchlov, inv. no. 136, box 9

100 *Eva Chodějovská and Zdeněk Hojda*

3. Karl Maximilian and Johann Leopold of Dietrichstein, 1719–24. MZA Brno, RA Ditrichštejnů, inv. no. 1591, box 364
4. Philipp Josef of Gallas, 1721–5. SOA Litoměřice, dep. Děčín, Historická sbírka (rodinný archiv) Clam-Gallasů, inv. no. 1544–1545, box 437–438
5. Josef Wilhelm and Anton Christoph of Nostitz, 1721 and 1726–9. Archiwum Państwowe Wrocław, Akta majątku Nostitzów i Wolkensteinów w Luboradzu, sign. 158
6. Herman Jacob Czernin of Chudenitz, 1725–7. SOA Třeboň, dep. Jindřichův Hradec, RA Černínů z Chudenic, Jindřichův Hradec, box 342–347
7. Franz Josef Georg of Waldstein, 1726–7, SOA Třeboň, dep. Jindřichův Hradec, RA Černínů z Chudenic, Jindřichův Hradec, box 346
8. Franz Leopold and Karl Jakob de Longueval, count of Buquoy, 1726–31. SOA Třeboň, RA Buquoyů, inv. no. 589, box 95
9. Franz Anton Czernin of Chudenitz, 1726–31, SOA Třeboň, dep. Jindřichův Hradec, RA Černínů z Chudenic, Jindřichův Hradec, box 345–347, 352
10. Johann Karl and Rudolf Chotek of Chotkow and Wognin, 1727–30. SOA Praha, RA Chotků, Veltrusy, inv. no. 489, box 24; SOA Třeboň, dep. Jindřichův Hradec, RA Černínů z Chudenic, Jindřichův Hradec, box 350, 352, 353
11. Maximilian Wenzel and Karl Josef Laziansky of Bukowa, 1729–31. SOA Třeboň, dep. Jindřichův Hradec, Cizí rody, box 35; RA Černínů z Chudenic, Jindřichův Hradec, box 351–352
12. Johann Josef of Thun, 1730–1. SOA Litoměřice, dep. Děčín, RA Thun-Hohensteinů, Klášterec nad Ohří, inv. no. 880, sign. Y 4/11, box 138; inv. no. 866, sign. Y 2/2, box 123
13. Wenzel Anton of Kaunitz, 1731–4. MZA Brno, RA Kouniců Slavkov, inv. no. 2256–2257, box 261
14. Johann Karl of Waldstein, 1731–3. RA Valdštejnů, Mnichovo Hradiště, inv. no. 3255, box 24
15. Adam Franz of Sternberg, 1732–4/5 [?], *Mémoires des mes voyages*, 7 vols, SOA Praha, fond RA Šternberků, Český Šternberk, inv. no. 138, box 9
16. Prokop Adalbert Czernin of Chudenitz, 1744–6. SOA Třeboň, dep. Jindřichův Hradec, RA Černínů z Chudenic, Jindřichův Hradec, box 380–382

Abbreviations

FA – Familienarchiv
KNM – Library of National Museum
MZA – Moravian Land Archives
N. – unknown

Abroad, or still 'at home'? 101

NK ČR – National Library of Czech Republic
RA – Family Archives
sign. – signature
SOA – State Regional Archives

Notes

1 The term 'Grand Tour', describing educational journeys undertaken by young aristocrats between the sixteenth and eighteenth centuries (and defined below), is used in this chapter in accordance with the practice dominant in Anglophone and Francophone literature (but also often used in German and Italian scholarship). In German the more usual concept is *Kavalierstour*, while its more archaic German alternative is *Kavaliersreise*, from which the Czech *kavalírská cesta* is also derived. The most commonplace contemporary German term was, however, *Länderreis(e)*. The authors are aware that the British generally link the term 'Grand Tour' with the Enlightenment type of early tourist behaviour, which did not have study as its primary purpose. Nevertheless, even British historians use the concept Grand Tours for the journeys undertaken by the English nobility in the seventeenth century, which were of a similar character to the central European journeys. See E. Chaney, *The Evolution of the Grand Tour: Anglo-Italian Cultural Relations since the Renaissance* (London, 2000); M. Brennan, *The Origins of the Grand Tour. The Travels of Robert Montagu, Lord Mandeville (1649–1654), William Hammond (1655–1658), Banaster Maynard (1660–1663)* (London, 2004); E. Chaney and T. Wilks, *The Jacobean Grand Tour: Early Stuart Travellers in Europe* (London and New York, 2014).

2 These 37 journeys were undertaken by 51 individuals – quite often groups of two or three young noblemen travelled together. The sample used in the research includes 21 journeys (30 individuals) from between 1650 and 1700 and 16 journeys (21 individuals) from between 1700 and 1750. For a list of the noblemen, see summary list above.

3 Not, for example, only Italy, as happened in many cases.

4 These are documents from the family archives usually deposited in the network of the State Regional Archives (hereafter SOA); only some family archives were returned to the original owners or, respectively, their heirs in the framework of the post-1990 restitutions. The direct sources, however, report only a mere fragment of the completed Grand Tours. The fact that many more journeys were undertaken is, for example, documented by the records in the university registers (the records were not necessarily linked with genuine studies) or the scattered references to having encountered countrymen found in travel correspondence and diaries.

5 For example, I. Cerman, 'Bildungsziele – Reiseziele. Die Kavalierstour im 18. Jahrhundert', in M. Scheutz, W. Schmale and D. Štefanová, eds, *Orte des Wissens*, Jahrbuch der Österreichischen Gesellschaft zur Erforschung des achtzehnten Jahrhunderts, vol. 18/19 (Bochum, 2004), pp. 49–78. Cerman compared the development of the eighteenth-century Grand Tours based on the example of three generations of two noble families, the Choteks and the Dietrichsteins.

6 On the careers of the Bohemian nobility at the court in Vienna, see P. Maťa, 'Der Adel aus den böhmischen Ländern am Kaiserhof 1620–1740. Versuch, eine falsche Frage richtig zu lösen', in V. Bůžek and P. Král, eds, *Šlechta v habsburské monarchii a císařský dvůr 1526–1740*, Opera historica 10 (České Budějovice, 2003), pp. 213–33; P. Vokáčová, *Příběhy hrdé pokory* (Prague, 2014). Certainly not all aristocrats who returned from the Grand Tour strove purposefully for

102   Eva Chodějovská and Zdeněk Hojda

positions at court or a diplomatic career. Many were content to manage their estates; others saw their future in the army and some in a Church career. Not even the less ambitious, however, denied themselves the Grand Tour because, to them, it was the fulfilment of the social convention appropriate to their status.

7   See note 1 above. The traditional British approach to the phenomenon of the Grand Tour is represented by J. Black, *The British and the Grand Tour* (Beckenham, 1985); Black, *The British Abroad. The Grand Tour in the Eighteenth Century* (Stroud, 1992).

8   On the most important aspects of the central European approach to the Grand Tour phenomenon, see A. Stannek, *Telemachs Brüder. Die höfische Bildungsreise des 17. Jahrhunderts* (Frankfurt am Main and New York, 2001); M. Leibetseder, *Die Kavalierstour. Adlige Erziehungsreisen im 17. und 18. Jahrhundert* (Cologne, Weimar and Vienna, 2004); for other important papers, see R. Babel and W. Paravicini, eds, *Grand Tour. Adeliges Reisen und europäische Kultur vom 14. bis zum 18. Jahrhundert* (Ostfildern, 2005). The most recent Czech books are J. Kubeš, *Náročné dospívání urozených. Kavalírské cesty české a rakouské šlechty (1620–1750)* (Pelhřimov, 2013), and Z. Hojda and E. Chodějovská, eds, *Heřman Jakub Černín na cestě za Alpy a Pyreneje*, 2 vols (Prague, 2014). A comparison with non-aristocratic travellers was attempted by T. Grosser, 'Reisen und soziale Eliten. Kavalierstour – Patrizierreise – bürgerliche Bildungsreise', in M. Maurer, ed., *Neue Impulse der Reiseforschung* (Berlin, 1999), pp. 135–76.

9   The Grand Tour, however, became noticeably less widespread in the Hungarian part of the Habsburg Monarchy, which did not belong to the Holy Roman Empire and, moreover, was a Turkish battlefield for most of the seventeenth century.

10 From the literature on travel in the individual countries of the Empire, the following are particularly significant: K. Keller, 'Von der Nützlichkeit des Reisens. Bemerkungen zum Erscheinungsbild und Konsequenzen der Kavalierstour am Beispiel kursächsischer Befunde', in Babel and Paravicini, *Grand Tour*, pp. 429–54; S. Kolck, *Bayerische und pfalz-neuburgische Prinzen auf Reisen: Kavalierstouren weltlicher und geistlicher katholischer Prinzen vom Ende des 16. bis zur Mitte des 18. Jahrhunderts im Vergleich* (Münster, 2010).

11 See, for example, A. Markiewicz, *Podróże edukacyjne w czasach Jana III Sobieskiego. Peregrinationes Jablonovianae* (Warsaw, 2011).

12 L. Niléhn, *Peregrinatio academica. Det svenska samhället och de utrikes studieresorna under 1600-talet* (Lund, 1983); V. Helk, *Dansk-norske studierejser 1661–1813* (Odense, 1991).

13 A. Frank-van Westrienen, *De Groote Tour. Tekening van de educatiereis der Nederlanders in de zeventiende eeuw* (Amsterdam, 1983); G. Verhoeven, *Anders reizen: evoluties in vroegmoderne reiservaringen van Hollandse en Brabantse elites (1600–1750)* (Hilversum, 2009).

14 This particularly concerned mastering the principles of the court ceremonial. For research on this issue, see the several studies published in *Zeremoniell als höfische Ästhetik in Spätmittelalter und Früher Neuzeit*, ed., J. Jochen Berns and T. Rahn (Tübingen, 1995), particularly the bibliography; for more information, see the editions of the Viennese *Zeremonialprotokolle*: I. Pangerl, M. Scheutz and T. Winkelbauer, eds, *Der Wiener Hof im Spiegel der Zeremonialprotokolle (1652–1800). Eine Annäherung* (Innsbruck, Vienna and Bozen, 2007). Extensive literature is available on Spanish court ceremonial, while D. Carrió-Invernizzi, *El gobierno de las imágenes: ceremonial y mecenazgo en la Italia española de la segunda mitad del siglo XVII* (Madrid and Frankfurt am Main, 2008), is especially thought-provoking from among the most recently published works.

Abroad, or still 'at home'? 103

15 Z. Hojda, '*Le Grandezze d'Italia*. Die Kavalierstouren der böhmischen Adeligen, die Kunstbetrachtung und die Kunstsammlungen im 17. Jahrhundert', in H.-B. Harder and H. Rothe, eds, *Studien zum Humanismus in den böhmischen Ländern*, Teil III. *Die Bedeutung der humanistischen Topographien und Reisebeschreibungen in der Kultur der böhmischen Länder bis zur Zeit Balbíns* (Cologne, Weimar and Vienna, 1993), pp. 151–60. The direct influence of Grand Tours on aesthetic preferences and collecting activities of Polish visitors to Italy was analysed by M. Wrześniak, *Roma sancta, Fiorenza bella. Dzieła sztuki w diariuszach polskich podróżników do Włoch w XVI i XVII wieku* (Warsaw, 2010); in the Czech lands, the impact of Grand Tours on later building activities of the Sternberg family was closely analysed by J. Kropáček through the example of Wenceslas Adalbert of Sternberg, 'Architekt J.B. Mathey a zámek Trója v Praze', *Acta Universitatis Carolinae – Philosophica et Historica*, 1 (1987) (Příspěvky k dějinám umění IV).

16 See, for example, M. Holý, *Zrození renesančního kavalíra. Výchova a vzdělávání šlechty z českých zemí na prahu novověku (1500–1620)* (Prague, 2010).

17 K. Ley, 'Castiglione und die Höflichkeit. Zur Rezeption des Cortegiano im deutschen Sprachraum vom 16. bis zum 17. Jahrhundert', *Chloe* 9 (1990), pp. 3–108; P. Burke, *The Fortunes of the Courtier: The European Reception of Castiglione's Cortegiano* (Cambridge, 1995).

18 E. Bender, 'Das höfische Comportement', in *Die Prinzenreise. Bildungsaufenthalt und Kavalierstour im höfischen Kontext gegen Ende des 17. Jahrhunderts* (Berlin, 2011), pp. 240–310; there is also an inspiring essay by S.C. Pils, 'Identität und Kontinuität. Erziehung für den Hofdienst am Beispiel der Familie Harrach im 17. Jahrhundert', in W. Paravicini and J.Wettlaufer, eds, *Erziehung und Bildung bei Hofe*, Residenzenforschung 13 (Stuttgart, 2002), pp. 89–106. For the court society see: *Hofgesellschaft und Höflinge an europäischen Fürstenhöfen in der Frühen Neuzeit (15.–18. Jh.) / Société de cour et courtisans dans l'Europe de l'époque moderne (XVe–XVIIIe siècle)*, ed. K. Malettke (Münster, 2001). On courtesy, see M. Beetz, *Frühmoderne Höflichkeit, Komplimentierkunst und Höflichkeitsrituale im deutschen Sprachraum* (Stuttgart, 1990).

19 P. Bourdieu, *Le Sens pratique* (Paris, 1980); Bourdieu, *La noblesse d'Etat: grandes écoles et esprit de corps* (Paris, 1989); the concept of Bourdieu directly inspired Petr Maťa in his synthetic study of early modern nobility in the Czech lands: Maťa, *Svět české aristokracie* (Prague, 2004).

20 See, for example, G. Heiss, 'Standeserziehung und Schulunterricht. Zur Bildung des niederösterreichischen Adeligen in der frühen Neuzeit,' in H. Knittler, G. Stangler and R. Zedinger, eds, *Adel im Wandel. Politik – Kultur – Konfession 1500–1700* (Vienna, 1990), pp. 391–427; Heiss, 'Ihro keiserlichen Mayestät zu Diensten ... unserer ganzen fürstlichen Familie aber zur Glori. Erziehung und Unterricht des Fürsten von Liechtenstein im Zeitalter des Absolutismus', in E. Oberhammer, ed., *Der ganzen Welt ein Lob und Spiegel. Das Fürstenhaus Liechtenstein in der frühen Neuzeit* (Vienna and Munich, 1990), pp. 155–81.

21 On the significance of various languages, especially Italian, at the Viennese court, see W.-M. Wuzella, 'Untersuchungen zu Mehrsprachigkeit und Sprachgebrauch am Wiener Kaiserhof zwischen 1658 und 1780', in Bůžek and Král, *Šlechta v habsburské monarchii a císařský dvůr 1526–1740*, pp. 415–38.

22 For a thorough analysis of a single Grand Tour and of the later diplomatic activity of its protagonist, see F. Polleroß, *Die Kunst der Diplomatie. Auf den Spuren des kaiserlichen Botschafters Leopold Joseph Graf von Lamberg (1653–1706)* (Petersberg, 2010).

23 R. Braun and D. Gugerli, *Macht des Tanzes – Tanz der Mächtigen. Hoffeste und Herrschaftszeremoniell 1550–1914* (Munich, 1993). As far as Czech literature

104 Eva Chodějovská and Zdeněk Hojda

is concerned, see V. Bůžek and R. Smíšek, 'Tanec v každodenním životě šlechty počátkem novověku', in *Tance a slavnosti 16.–18. Století*, Exhibition catalogue (Prague, 2008), pp. 27–38.

24 A. Stannek, 'Exempla & Imitatio. Medien und Methoden höfischer Standeserziehung im 17. Jahrhundert', in Paravicini and Wettlaufer, *Erziehung und Bildung bei Hofe*, pp. 107–23.

25 For summary information on Cisalpine travellers to the Apennine Peninsula, see L. Schudt, *Italienreisen im 17. und 18. Jahrhundert* (Vienna and Munich, 1959); Lucia Tresoldi, *Viaggiatori tedeschi in Italia, 1452–1870: saggio bibliografico*, 2 vols (Rome, 1975–7). On the Bohemian journeys to Rome, E. Chodějovská, 'I giovani nobili provenienti dalle Terre ceche nel loro viaggio d'educazione a Roma: topografia della loro vita quotidiana nella Città eterna del XVII secolo', *Bollettino dell'Istituto Storico Ceco di Roma*, 8 (2012), pp. 87–114. See also G.P. Brizzi, 'La pratica del viaggio d'istruzione in Italia nel Sei-Settecento', *Annali dell'Istituto storico italo-germanico in Trento*, 2 (1976), pp. 203–91; C. de Seta, 'L'Italia nello specchio del Grand Tour,' in de Seta, ed., *Storia d'Italia – Annali 5: Il paesaggio* (Turin, 1982), pp. 127–264. The most recent summary is provided by K. Keller, 'Die italienische Reise. Pilgerfahrt, Kavalierstour, Bildungsreise', in W. Huschner, E. Bünz and C. Lübke, eds, *Italien – Mitteldeutschland – Polen. Geschichte und Kultur im europäischen Kontext vom 10. bis zum 18. Jahrhundert* (Leipzig, 2013), pp. 601–26.

26 On Tours to France see T. Grosser, *Reiseziel Frankreich. Deutsche Reiseliteratur vom Barock bis zur Französischen Revolution* (Opladen, 1989); on the Bohemian aristocrats in France, see Kubeš, *Náročné dospívání urozených*, pp. 48–68.

27 On Tours to Spain, see H. Kürbis, *Hispania decripta. Von der Reise zum Bericht. Deutschsprachige Reiseberichte des 16. und 17. Jahrhunderts über Spanien. Ein Beitrag zur Struktur und Funktion der Frühneuzeitlichen Reiseliteratur* (Frankfurt am Main, 2004); on Spanish journeys undertaken by Bohemian noblemen, see, for example, P. Marek, 'Los viajes al sur. Sdenco Adalberto Popel de Lobkowicz y sus primeros encuentros con el mundo hispano', in *Las relaciones checo-españolas*, Ibero-Americana Pragensia, supplementum, 20 (Prague, 2007), pp. 119–36; Z. Hojda, 'El viaje español de Jiří Adam de Martinitz', ibid., pp. 137–50.

28 On the Bohemian nobility, see Holý, *Zrození renesančního kavalíra*.

29 Caution, however, was always desirable, as Humprecht Johann Czernin instructed his son's hofmeister before they entered the French territory: SOA Třeboň, Department Jindřichův Hradec, RA [Family Archives] Černín, box 260, 27. 6. 1681.

30 See, for example, G. Klingenstein, *Der Aufstieg des Hauses Kaunitz. Studien zur Herkunft und Bildung des Staatskanzlers Wenzel Anton* (Göttingen, 1975).

31 This is how the Grand Tour is defined by Cerman, 'Bildungsziele – Reiseziele'.

32 The university nations were corporations associating students from a certain area which developed on a territorial rather than an ethnic basis. They played an important role at medieval universities (for example, Paris and Prague), but continued at universities in Italy (for example, Padua and Siena) into the seventeenth century. All aristocrats originating from the Holy Roman Empire – that is, including Czech ones – ranked among the members of the 'German nation'. Membership in a 'nation' was prestigious but also had practical value, when a 'nation' advocated for its members in disputes with university or municipal authorities.

33 See G. Heiss, 'Bildungs- und Reiseziele österreichischer Adeliger in der Frühen Neuzeit,' in Babel and Paravicini, *Grand Tour*, pp. 217–36; on Siena, see, for

Abroad, or still 'at home'? 105

example, F. Weigle, ed., *Die Matrikel der deutschen Nation in Siena (1573–1738)*, 2 vols (Tübingen, 1962).

34 Georg Adam of Martinitz spent 30 months there between 1620 and 1623, Maximilian of Trauttmansdorff 39 months between 1651 and 1655, Johann Norbert and Ignaz Karl Sternbergs spent 18 months between 1661 and 1663 and Walter Xaver of Dietrichstein 35 months between 1683 and 1686. The university in Leuven was sought after only until the 1660s; Dietrichstein's sojourn there in the 1680s was thus highly exceptional.

35 The most important monograph on noble academies (literally knightly academies) is N. Conrads, *Ritterakademien der frühen Neuzeit* (Göttingen, 1982). See also J. Boutier, 'Le Grand Tour des gentilshommes et les académies d'éducation pour la noblesse: France et Italie, XVIe–XVIIIe siècle', in Babel and Paravicini, *Grand Tour*, pp. 237–53.

36 On German cavaliers at the Turin *Accademia Reale*, see P. Bianchi, 'Una palestra di arti cavalleresche e di politica. Presenze austro-tedesche all'Accademia Reale di Torino nel Settecento', in M. Bellabarba and J.P. Niederkorn, eds, *Le corti come luogo di comunicazione. Gli Asburgo e l'Italia (secoli XVI–XIX)/Höfe als Orte der Kommunikation. Die Habsburger und Italien (16. bis 19. Jh.)* (Bologna and Berlin, 2010), pp. 135–53.

37 See, for example, M. Dumolin, 'Les Académies Parisiennes d'Équitation', *Bulletin de la Société Archéologique, Historique & Artistique le Vieux papier pour l'étude de la vie et des moeurs d'autrefois*, 16, fasc. 111 (May 1925), pp. 417–28, fasc. 112, 485–94, fasc. 113, 556–72; Corinne Doucet, *Les académies d'art équestre dans la France d'Ancien régime* (Paris, 2007).

38 The historian therefore has to rely on laborious reconstructions based on incidental reports recorded in individual ego-documents. For example, the list attached to the letter addressed by Herman Jaccob Czernin to his father and sent from Turin on 12 July 1681 contained 85 names of the *accademisti* enrolled at the time and their hofmeisters, of which seven were noblemen from the Czech lands. SOA Třeboň, Department Jindřichův Hradec, RA Černín, correspondence 1665–90.

39 An illustrious example of this is the notes in the travel itinerary designed by hofmeister Gottfried Zurmöllen for Philipp Sigismund von Dietrichstein. MZA [Moravian Land Archives] Brno, RA Dietrichstein, box 360, sign. 740.

40 The first names of the Czech aristocrats mentioned in this text are always given in German form as was the usual practice at the time. If they wrote letters in Italian, French or Czech, however, they adapted the spelling of their names to the respective language.

41 A total of nine out of 21 aristocrats from the authors' sample visited the English metropolis as part of their programme.

42 J. Kubeš, 'Friendship, admiration, or hatred? The image of the United Provinces in the travel diaries of the Czech nobility (1650–1750)', *Theatrum historiae*, 4 (2009), pp. 215–33. For the German nobility, see A. Chales de Beaulieu, *Deutsche Reisende in den Niederlanden. Das Bild eines Nachbarn zwischen 1648 und 1795* (Frankfurt am Main, 2000).

43 SOA Třeboň, Department Jindřichův Hradec, RA Černín, box 262. The itinerary of this journey can be reconstructed thanks to 24 letters written by Václav Hruška, a secretary to Herman Jacob Czernin. They were sent from Prague 17 Jun.–16 Nov. 1684.

44 See Kubeš, *Náročné dospívání urozených*, pp. 85–6.

45 See, for example, N. Conrads, 'Politische und staatsrechtliche Probleme der Kavalierstour', in A. Mączak and H.J. Teuteberg, eds, *Reiseberichte als Quellen*

106 Eva Chodějovská and Zdeněk Hojda

europäischer Kulturgeschichte, Wolfenbütteler Forschungen 21 (Wolfenbüttel, 1982), pp. 45–64.

46 See note 42 above and W. Siebers and H. Tilgner, eds, *Europareisen politisch-sozialer Eliten im 18. Jahrhundert* (Berlin, 2002).

47 See W. de Rieu, ed., *Album studiosorum Academiae Lugduno-Bataviae I, 1575–1875* (The Hague, 1875). Franz Joseph Czernin studied with J.J. Vitriarius in 1715 when the lawyer tutored in Utrecht.

48 For example, the correspondence of Franz Joseph Czernin includes a personal and very cordial letter from Vitriarius, which he sent to Czernin approximately one year after the aristocrat completed his studies in Leiden and when he was still travelling. SOA Třeboň, Department Jindřichův Hradec, RA Černín, box 330.

49 SOA Třeboň, Department Jindřichův Hradec, RA Černín, box 351, 22 Apr. 1730. ('Holland is the country, where one can discuss matters most freely [...] a young gentleman can discover much and benefit greatly from short journeys to and fro. First, Holland is a free republic, so they speak about all European governments, all sorts of machinations, all ministers at various courts frankly and free ... Places such as Paris have a much more affected and secret lifestyle, so a young man has to stay for a while before he picks up some rumours, but even then he never gets to the bottom of things. By contrast, in the Dutch Republic, he hears all sorts of things, as people are not restrained by ceremony and take someone into confidence lightly').

50 For example, Johann Karl von Waldstein. See J. Hrbek, *Barokní Valdštejnové v Čechách, 1640–1740* (Prague, 2013), pp. 512–18.

51 Six of the 16 itineraries dated 1700–50 also included a stage in England.

52 For example, Johann Karl von Waldstein in 1732 not only visited London but also Rochester, Dartford and Canterbury.

53 See note 50. ('Then from Calais, for heaven's sake, to England, after one has seen the democratic government of Holland, one sees the aristocratic type of a monarchy restrained for the good of its subjects, and there is much to discover in England, as all affairs of the state are treated by parliament and by many heads, and thus not in secret').

54 From Dec. 1728–Mar. [?] 1730.

55 I. Cerman, *Chotkové. Příběh úřednické šlechty* (Prague, 2008), pp. 71–97, and SOA Třeboň, Department Jindřichův Hradec, RA Černín, boxes 350 and 353.

56 Franz Adam Sternberg, 'Mémoires des mes voyages', vol. I, p. 2, SOA Prague, RA Sternberg, inventory. no. 138. ('The most important branch of study must be to instruct oneself in the different styles of government that exist in other countries'.)

57 See R. Zedinger, 'Chantons Leopold à jamais. Herzog Leopold von Lothringen und sein Hof (1698–1729)', in V. Bůžek, ed., *Život na dvorech barokní šlechty* (České Budějovice, 1996), pp. 129–49.

58 Probably Philipp Reinhard Vitriarius (1647–1720). The Laziansky brothers studied with Begnicour from Dec. 1729 to Jun. 1730 in Pont-à-Mousson, while other aristocrats were lectured by him in Lunéville.

59 See J. Kubeš, 'Rudolf Josef Colloredo z Wallsee a jeho studium v Salcburku v letech 1723–1725', in Kubeš, ed., *Šlechtic na cestách v 16.–18. století* (Pardubice, 2007), pp. 163–92.

60 For example, Franz Joseph Czernin, who took his Grand Tour between 1715 and 1717, financed the Grand Tour of his nephew, Herman Jacob Czernin (1725–7) only eight years later. He also covered all Grand Tour expenses for the sons of his cousin, the Laziansky brothers (1729–31), for whom he compiled a comprehensive volume of travelling advice (see note 49). His correspondence

Abroad, or still 'at home'? 107

also includes several series of letters from young gentlemen undertaking travels, whom he supported and for whom he was a respected authority.

61 *Je remarque principalement dans Monsieur le Comte Laschanski l'Ainé, une extraordinaire Passion pour les Etudes, et une inclination singuliere à les aprofondir d'une maniere qui me donne lieu d'esperer que ce jeune Seigneur sera un jour un tres digne Ministre d'Etat,* as de Begnicour wrote to Franz Joseph Czernin on 19 Dec. 1729 about the prospects for Czernin's relative. SOA Třeboň, Department Jindřichův Hradec, RA Černín, box 351. ('In the eldest son of Earl Laschanski, I descry an extraordinary passion for study and a specific inclination to broaden his horizons, which arouses the expectation that he will be a worthy secretary of state one day.')

62 The same also holds for de Begnicour, who was, however, most probably a Catholic. On 31 Jan. 1729, Begnicour sent Franz Joseph Czernin his treatise on the inadmissibility of a Protestant duke being elected by the Roman Emperor. SOA Třeboň, Department Jindřichův Hradec, RA Černín, box 350.

63 For a comparative perspective, see L. Corens, 'Catholic nuns and English identities. English Protestant travellers on the English convents in the Low Countries, 1660–1730', *Recusant History*, 30 (2011), pp. 441–59.

64 N. Conrads, 'Tradition und Modernität im adligen Bildungsprogramm der Frühen Neuzeit', in W. Schulze, ed., *Ständische Gesellschaft und Soziale Mobilität* (Munich, 1988), pp. 389–403.

65 For example, Rudolf Chotek became the Supreme Chancellor and Wenzel Anton Kaunitz the Prime Minister to Maria Theresa, in which capacity he determined the foreign policy of the monarchy.

66 The restrictive policy of Maria Theresa resulted in the imposition of limitations on 'useless' educational journeys abroad in a decree dated 23 Jan. 1743; see *Codex Austriacus*, vol. 5 (Vienna 1777), p. 96. A further ban *ohne landesfürstliche Erlaubnis ins Ausland zu reisen* was published and sent to regional governors on 17 Jun. 1752. See also Christoph Beidtel, *Geschichte der österreichischen Staatsverwaltung 1746–1814*, vol. 1 (Innsbruck, 1896), p. 51; the memo is held in the Austrian State Archives (Österreichisches Staatsarchiv, Wien, Allgemeines Verwaltungsarchiv, Bestand Inneres, Hofkanzlei, IV A 7, box 496). On the attempts to curtail travel, see also G. Klingenstein, 'Vorstufen der theresianischen Studienreformen in der Regierungszeit Karls VI', *Mitteilungen des Instituts für Österreichische Geschichte*, 76 (1968), pp. 327–77; J. Rees, '"Wahrnehmen in fremden Orten, was zu Hause Vortheil bringen und nachgeahmet werden könne": Europareisen und Kulturtransfer adeliger Eliten im Alten Reich 1750–1800', in Babel and Paravicini, *Grand Tour*, pp. 513–40.

67 See I. Cerman, 'Habsburgischer Adel und Theresianum in Wien 1746–1784. Wissensvermittlung, Sozialisation und Berufswege', in I.Cerman and L. Velek, eds, *Adelige Ausbildung. Die Herausforderung der Aufklärung und die Folgen* (Munich, 2006), pp. 143–68.

68 For example, Ferdinand August von Lobkowicz deliberately gave up visiting France in order not to compromise his father, Wenceslas Eusebius, who had lost his position at the court of Leopold I due to his pro-French policy. See T. Foltýn, 'Druhá kavalírská cesta a zejména římský pobyt Ferdinanda Augusta z Lobkovic (1675–1676)', in J. Kubeš, ed., *Šlechtic na cestách v 16.–18. století* (Pardubice, 2007), pp. 99–127.

6 Between specialisation and encyclopaedic knowledge

Educational travelling and court culture in early eighteenth-century Germany

Mathis Leibetseder

This chapter is about the changing perspectives of German travel culture in the age of Enlightenment.[1] I will highlight the transformation and adaptation that the classical, late-seventeenth-century *Kavalierstour* had to undergo to meet the intellectual settings of Enlightenment culture on the basis of *one* selected journey or rather travel account.[2] As to the actual purposes of going abroad, my analysis will reveal the seemingly opposing agendas of a growing need for professionalisation[3] or rather professional specialisation, on the one hand, and the demand for wide-ranging, encyclopaedic knowledge collecting, on the other.[4] Moreover, I will show how travellers who were heavily influenced by Pietism opened up new fields of investigation in long-familiar travel destinations.

Although the travel account I am discussing here is, in religious terms, not representative at all, in social terms it fits neatly into the traditional patterns of the *Kavalierstour* as a privilege of influential and well-to-do members of the *Land-* and *Reichsadel*, as well as of the urban *Patriziat*. The *Kavalierstour* evolved from the sixteenth century onwards as a form of journey for educational purposes undertaken by members of the social elite being connected in one way or another to courts and princes. As a social practice, the *Kavalierstour* as a distinctive practice was defined through numerous individual acts of travelling and travel writing rather than by learned or other discourses. Since there is no technical term which contemporaries used to refer to the *Kavalierstour*, it is essential to discuss what terminology they used to describe what they were doing and, as a corollary, how *we* should term their doings in an academic context. During the first decades of the seventeenth century, the term *grosse tour*[5] was occasionally used by German travellers to designate a circular trip through the provinces of France, whereas the excursion through Italy was rather known as *giro d'Italia*.[6] But, more frequently, educational travellers referred to what they were doing unspecifically as *Länderreise*[7] or *seine Reisen machen*.[8] Late nineteenth-century historiography, however, coined *Kavalierstour* as a technical term for educational travelling. Only when the history of travel culture and literature became a field of study organised along transnational lines did historians become convinced that it would be appropriate to

Educational travelling and court culture 109

replace *Kavalierstour* by the internationally more recognised catchword Grand Tour.[9] There is, however, an opposing trend, which takes the concept of *Kavalierstour* as a point of departure for accentuating more explicitly the social heterogeneity of early modern travel culture.[10] Since differentiations of class as much as nationality and gender lie at the heart of cultural history, it is essential to reflect upon and cultivate a more sophisticated and nuanced vocabulary than the umbrella-term 'Grand Tour',[11] or, in other words, to keep the *Kavalierstour* in mind while talking about educational travellers coming from German territorial states.

Enlightenment, Pietism and a *Kavalierstour*

The *Kavalierstour*, I am going to explore, was conducted in 1731/2. At about that time, the German Enlightenment started to spread outwards from the philosophical arena and to gain force as a social movement seeking fulfilment in practical reforming activities.[12] Typical topics on reforming agendas were the encouragement of industry and craftsmanship, developing the rural and manorial economy, encouraging the immigration of foreign specialists (*Peuplierung*), improving public hygiene, controlling poverty, reforming the penal system and establishing equality before the law.[13] The movement rested on an academically trained elite of civil servants and educated men (and women), as well as with princes (and princesses), being themselves educated in enlightened principles. This elite was a recent social formation which transcended or rather overarched traditional class barriers comprising academically trained men from all strata of middle- and upper-class society who strove to put their ideas into practice as members of public bureaucracy.[14]

Against this background, the whole value system of enlightened absolutist court society started to shift: the seminal figures of the *cortegiano* and *honnête homme* were replaced by the social ideal of the 'upright man at court', as Johann Michael von Loen put it in the title of a novel published in 1740.[15] A new kind of civility (*Bürgerlichkeit*) was hailed, bearing undertones of criticism directed against 'effeminate' French polite society and fostering instead sober 'manly' values such as diligence, order, austerity, fidelity, probity, modesty and sincerity.[16] No longer were techniques of dissimulation deemed adequate within the framework of an expanding civil service running through a process of professionalisation and specialisation.[17] From an early point, this movement was supported by German Pietism, a religious movement that challenged Lutheran orthodoxy with its quest for a more inward and upright, but less ritualistic fidelity and its zeal for improving social conditions culminating in the *Franckensche Stiftungen* at Halle.[18] Though moderate Pietism acquired a semi-official status in some territories of the Holy Roman Empire during the first half of the eighteenth century, it never completely lost the subversive potential of its precarious beginnings.

110   *Mathis Leibetseder*

It is within this particular context that in 1731/2 the *Kavalierstour* of two counts, Heinrich VI Reuß[19] and Rochus Friedrich zu Lynar,[20] took place. Rochus Friedrich, who was left fatherless at the age of eight, was raised by his mother at the family's estate at Lübbenau, situated in the lands of the margrave of Lower and Upper Lusatia which belonged to the territories of the dukes of Saxony-Merseburg. When Lynar reached the age of 16, it was deemed that the time was ripe to send him to a higher-ranking court for educational refinement. The court of choice was Köstritz, the so-called *paragium* of Heinrich XXIV Count Reuß j. L., which held a semi-independent self-ruling status without the right to vote at the imperial diets. In constitutional terms, the situation of the Reuß family was actually weaker than that of other families belonging to the *Reichsadel* and, in addition, their independence was constantly threatened by the neighbouring electors of Saxony. But, despite this precarious quality in the Reuß-Köstritz family, the Lynar family clearly ranked lower in terms of status, reputation and honour.[21] This and the fact that both families nurtured Pietistic principles of the moderate, reform-oriented kind were crucial in determining the decision to send Rochus Friedrich to Köstritz.[22]

Heinrich VI, son of Heinrich XXIV, was raised at Köstritz too. He was only one year senior to Lynar and hence his 'natural playmate' and future travel companion. Lynar stayed at Köstritz for about two years before moving to Jena, where he started university studies and from where he visited the neighbouring courts at Weimar, Eisenach and Gotha. At length, he resumed studies at Halle (Saale), which in the early eighteenth century was not only a 'highly modern' university, but also held a top-ranking position in training the socio-political elites of Brandenburg-Prussia.[23] After completing his formal education at Halle, Lynar started travelling in 1730/1, roaming Denmark and Sweden before visiting Berlin, a town, his family was traditionally attached to, on his return trip in April 1731. In the same year he set off on his *Kavalierstour*, together with Heinrich VI, and took himself to Copenhagen after the tour had come to an end. In Denmark, both counts were employed in the German Chancery. For Lynar, this was the starting point for a brilliant diplomatic career, whereas Heinrich VI's career culminated in the directorate of the Sorø knightly academy.[24]

Of course, the two counts did not set off untutored. They were escorted through western Europe by Anton von Geusau. Geusau received his first initiation into court life and ritual as a page to Henriette Christine Duchess of Brunswig-Wolfenbüttel, abbess of Gandersheim, and completed his education by visiting the *Pädagogium* at Glaucha and subsequently the University of Halle. After leaving university, he entered the service of Heinrich XXIV Count Reuß in 1716 and acted as tutor for two consecutive *Kavalierstouren* of Reuß family members.[25] He was a gentlemen-scholar with excellent connections to intellectual circles in Berlin. Many years later his biography would be written by Anton Friedrich Büsching.[26]

Educational travelling and court culture   111

The journey started on 27 July 1731, when the party left Eger (there is no hint as to what they had been doing there) and progressed in a stately fashion towards the German-Dutch border. Once they entered the Netherlands, they rested at Utrecht from 16–20 August, at Amsterdam for another five days, at Leiden from 24–29 August and spent almost three weeks at The Hague. Then, they set off at a leisurely pace to the Austrian Netherlands where they rested about a fortnight at Brussels. The French capital, where Reuß, Lynar and Geusau arrived on 20 October, was selected to serve as wintering grounds. It was the main destination of their voyage and they did not depart until 25 March 1732. Heading northwards, they spent six days in London, visited Oxford, but did not venture any further into Britain. On 20 May they arrived back at Paris once again. There, the company split – Lynar headed southwards in order to see Nancy, Lunéville and Strasbourg – only to reunite at Wetzlar in order to visit the petty-courts of the Wetterau to which Reuß held family ties. This was the terminus of their *Kavalierstour*.

On the whole, this was an itinerary that was typical of Protestant German elite travellers since the second half of the seventeenth century. Until around 1620 itineraries had been clearly stamped with the dominance of Italy as a travel destination, after this point the Thirty Years' War initiated a swing to northern countries such as the Netherlands and northern France.[27]

The Netherlands and England were perceived as advanced countries in economic terms, and their constitutional development was of interest too.[28] In contrast, the magnetism of France rested on its position as the dominant European power after the end of the Thirty Years' War as much as on the magnificence of its crown and court.[29] These countries were long since familiar to German travellers and they usually preferred them to Italy and other southern European countries.[30] The reason for this was not a general lack of interest but was rather dictated by confessional prejudice. In Paris during the winter of 1731 Reuß and Lynar had considered continuing southwards, but plans to travel to Italy were blocked by Reuß's parents at Köstritz, who considered Italy too much of a hotbed of sin for their offspring to venture upon.[31]

Knowledge collecting between generalisation and specialisation

Reuß, Lynar and Geusau kept a communal travel diary. Rotating weekly, each of them had to draw up reports, which were sent home to inform the Köstritz court about the journey's progression. The reports contained minute accounts of the day-to-day proceedings and conversations of the travelling party, amounting to a total of about 200 pages filled with the authors' narrow, miniscule script. Their narrations did not reveal individual predilections; all three of them tried to record what they heard and saw as precisely and impartially as they could.

112   *Mathis Leibetseder*

Despite a generally broad scope of locations to visit and persons to contact, the travellers' notes reflected a marked preference for certain themes and topics. Particular emphasis, for instance, was put on the religious or rather confessional condition of the towns through which the party passed. Whereas other travellers only stated briefly that they had been attending services of their own confessional denominations in order to present themselves as faithful Christians, the weekly reports of Reuß, Lynar and Geusau are distinguished by a vivid interest in confessional heterogeneity and differences. They would reproduce entire sermons including detailed philological exegesis in Hebrew and Ancient Greek.[32] The travel companions were not only keen church-goers but were also interested in municipal social institutions intended to relieve the shortcomings of early modern society. At Amsterdam, for example, they went to see several social institutions, among others an orphanage, allegedly the *burgerweeshuis* in the *Kalverstraat*. Given that such institutions were genuine indispensable viewing for all travellers to Amsterdam,[33] the travel companions tried to give a substantial account of the conditions they found there. Thus, they reported on the boys and girls raised there and on the layout of the building, as well as on disciplinary methods, its governors and pedagogical goals. They inspected its kitchen, refectory, dormitory and sickroom, but, at the end of the day, preferred the arrangements of August Hermann Francke's Halle Orphanage to what they saw in Amsterdam.[34] This hints at the role of Pietism as the referential framework of this particular trip. In this respect, the journey of Reuß and Lynar pioneered the realignment of the *Kavalierstour* during the second half of the eighteenth century, when travelling took place within the context of enlightened absolutist reforming policy.[35]

As a field of study, religion mattered not only in a country like the United Provinces that was marked out by confessional heterogeneity, but also in a largely homogeneously Catholic metropolis like Paris. Assuming parallels to the Pietist movement in Germany, Reuß, Lynar and Geusau eagerly gathered information on the Jansenist movement in Paris. Attending the table of the imperial envoy, they got to know a certain Abbé Ferrus, who instructed them on the life and death of the so-called Diacre de Parîs. François de Parîs was an ascetic man who, after an untimely early death, was venerated by many adherents of the Jansenist movement in Paris as a saint. His tomb at the cemetery of Saint-Médard quickly became a place of pilgrimage for the *convulsionnaires*.[36] It was Ferrus, too, who provided the travel companions with the *Nouvelles ecclésiastiques*, the most important polemical publication of the Jansenist movement.[37] He also informed them how the journal was distributed by an underground network of agents (the diarists inserted a diagram of this network in their account). Printing, distributing and reading the journal, which had been founded in 1728, was officially strictly forbidden. Yet neither Reuß nor Lynar were the least afraid about being provided with or reading such pieces of underground literature, nor did

Educational travelling and court culture   113

their tutor forbid them to do so. Ecumenical impulses and an alleged convergence between Jansenist and Protestant principles[38] operated more strongly than the threat of being prosecuted by French authorities. Accordingly, Reuß, Lynar and Geusau did not hesitate to read the *Nouvelles ecclésiastiques* to each other and to copy excerpts from selected articles to the diaries they sent back home. One can only speculate as to the extent to which the politically precarious status of the Köstritz court might have inspired a hightened sensibility for this kind of dangerous knowledge in the travelling party.[39]

Thus, confessional pluralism and heterodox movements were clearly top of the list of this travel party's agenda. But there was a second theme that was no less important, namely intercourse with diplomatic circles. For reasons of furthering their own careers, as well as of making contact with fellow travellers,[40] Lynar and Reuß regularly frequented the Paris household – and Protestant chapel – of the Danish minister. They visited the Swedish minister at Paris eight times and were honoured with two return visits. Occasionally, they attended services in his house too. Other diplomatic points of contact were the imperial and the Dutch envoy's housholds. The latter they appreciated above all for the illustrious *assemblées* that were given approximately every fortnight. As to imperial diplomats, two ministers were in residence at Paris during the two counts' stay in the capital. They visited them 16 times and were invited to attend the minister's table. Apart from that, they regularly met with the ambassador's doctor and one imperial secretary. Other diplomats residing in Paris were visited occasionally, but not very frequently. Of course, being introduced to inter-court relationships and international politics had belonged to the traditional features of princely tours since the seventeenth century.[41] But in this particular case, contacts with the diplomatic *milieu* abroad bore rather the trait of preparing the travellers for future diplomatic service. It was this trend towards professional specialisation that made Lynar pay a visit to Johann Daniel Schöpflin at the University of Strasbourg, who engaged himself in educating future diplomats.[42]

The accounts of Reuß, Lynar and Geusau offer deep insights into their encounters with diplomats in Paris as elsewhere. They recorded the ceremonial arrangements according to which they were received as minutely as they did the services and sermons that they attended. When visiting the French minister at The Hague, they were pleased to note that they were received in the minister's cabinet and were seated on the same *fauteuils* that he himself sat on.[43] They were welcomed even more warmly by the British ambassador, who made them sit on a *canapé* [sofa] while he himself humbly took a seat on an ordinary *tabouret* [stool].[44] Such encounters regularly resulted in an invitation to the 'table', an indispensable social institution of any eighteenth-century diplomatic household. At the table the minister hosted both persons with diplomatic backgrounds (not necessarily of his own staff) and selected members of the local society and travellers

114 *Mathis Leibetseder*

passing through. These tables were definitely institutions of polite society as well as places of informal conversation concerning current political events, including matters of foreign policy. In The Hague, for example, the imperial ministers held forth at his table on the differences between the Emperor and the United Provinces with regard to the *Compagnie d'Ostende* (the East India Company of the Austrian Netherlands) referring to Hugo Grotius's dictum *mare esse liberum* and the peace treaty of Westphalia.[45] Of course, such discussions of matters of state were of fundamental interest to Lynar and Reuß.[46]

Apart from professional training, there was a second aspect to contacting diplomatic circles which was closely linked to their practice of diary writing. All three authors carefully put down what they could recall of such table talks. Usually, they would reproduce discussions in indirect speech reflecting the speaker's opinion without commenting on it. Accordingly, the accounts convey the impression that the counts and their tutor were rather reticent and did not themselves engage in discussions, thereby demonstrating their impartiality. This absence of commentary would have enabled the Köstritz court to evaluate the political attitudes of the members of the socio-political elites the travellers were in touch with abroad. Thus, the minuteness of the weekly accounts responded to the Köstritz court's thirst for knowledge and compensated, at least in part, for the dearth of information that confronted a self-ruling petty-court which had neither the need nor the means to establish and entertain a full-scale diplomatic service.[47]

Social interaction at ambassadorial households was not, however, free of perils. A particularly disreputable social practice, from the point of view of the two cavaliers (as well as their parents), was gambling. Games of hazard had become a central practice of polite society since the time of Louis XIV. For the local elites, it was closely connected to the system of social rivalry prompted by French court culture. Being in itself highly competitive and requiring tactical skills, gambling became a way of excelling at court as well as in metropolitan society.[48] For non-locals like Reuß and Lynar, taking part in this competition did not make any sense at all. Social disfunctionality aside, Pietistic principles played their part in restraining the two counts from gambling. Yet social pressure to partake in gambling was as high as the young counts' appetite to concede to it under the pretext of assimilation to the social customs of the local elite. Being their tutor, it was Geusau's task to evade such morally despicable but nonetheless compelling activities. Attending the Dutch ambassador's *assemblée* at Paris, he luckily noted one evening, that because of the quantity of other guests there were few 'contestations of gambling'.[49] At times, concerts were preferred to the *assemblées* because they offered them the opportunity to come into contact with the *monde* and to partake in conversation without running the risk of being forced into gambling.[50] However, Pietistic travellers were not the only ones with a reluctance to play. Catholic travellers on their *Kavalierstour* similarly commented that they would rather spend money going to theatres

Educational travelling and court culture 115

than losing it through gambling. To gamble is to lose, while '*aller aux Spectacles c'est gagner*',[51] as one Bavarian tutor put it. Of course, such comments were designed to ease parental concern and should not necessarily be taken as representative of the traveller's real actions while abroad. At times, however, small sums for gambling are to be found in travel expense accounts and small losses are mentioned in letters and travel accounts.[52]

The *Kavalierstour* of Reuß and Lynar needs to be understood in terms of the objectives of both the travellers themselves and the court that despatched them. In addition to preparing Reuß and Lynar for a career in Danish diplomatic service and making them more perceptive of religious matters, their *Kavalierstour* adhered to the nascent encyclopaedic endeavour of Enlightenment culture. The travel party was expected to study a wide range of fields. In Leiden, for example, where they stayed from 25–28 August 1732, they arrived during the University vacation. Hardly any students were to be seen in the streets and those who were, were dressed 'in nightgowns'.[53] Visits to the academic collections and institutions, however, were at the top of the party's list. Though formal university training had already been completed before leaving Germany, making contact with leading intellectuals and seeing famous scientific collections still remained a key reason for travel. In the medical garden they observed, for instance, a technique to prevent ants from inflicting damage on oranges and marvelled at the exotic palms and trees. Afterwards they visited the adjoining *Wunderkammer*, duly enumerating 32 curiosities, including beasts and plants from overseas, deformed animals, ethnic artefacts, singular foetuses and other oddities like the leather boots of Charlemagne. They also went to see the cabinet of anatomical curiosities, where similar items and trophies from exotic regions were on display, as well as the theatre of anatomy 'famous for its gruesome display of death–skeletons some of which were stuffed men in quaint postures'.[54] The inspection of natural history collections was completed by a tour through the adjacent library, where the *Leidse Sphaera*, given by the Rotterdam burgomaster Sebastiaen Schepers to the University of Leyden in 1710, aroused their interest. But after having seen it, they preferred the model of the heliocentric system they had seen in August Hermann Francke's Halle Orphanage.

Probably even more important than sightseeing was the experience of listening to leading scholars lecturing, or conversing with them in person. The library, for instance, was shown to the party by the university rector Pieter Burman, with whom they had discussed literary criticism and studies in Germany the day before. They also attended Johann Jacob Vitriarius, son of the famous Leiden jurist Philipp Reinhard, who talked to them principally about matters of state. But the social apex of the stay in Leyden was the visit to the aged Herman Boerhaave, the celebrated professor of medicine, whose discourse ran on the interdependencies between a person's sickness, his soul and the 'machine of his body'.[55] Taking both contacts to intellectual circles in Paris and Leyden into consideration, the travel

116 *Mathis Leibetseder*

companions strode across the world of learning from 'precarious knowledge workers' like Abbé Ferrus to the 'mandarins of bourgeois knowledge' like Herman Boerhaave.[56]

Sightseeing Germany – new destinations on the *Kavalierstour*'s map

The journey of Reuß, Lynar and Geusau highlights a further chapter in the evolution of the *Kavalierstour*. Over the course of the eighteenth century, the Holy Roman Empire increasingly became a travel destination in its own right, not only for foreign but also for domestic travellers. A '"patriotization" of destinations'[57] occurred. It is difficult, however, to identify the actual moment when travellers started to *visit* Germany instead of merely passing through. Though travellers had never completely done without sightseeing in either German residential or imperial cities, for centuries the tendency had been to travel hastily through Germany. For the typical seventeenth-century aristocrat on a *Kavalierstour*, visiting the territories of the Holy Roman Empire was definitely not the actual intention of educational travelling.[58]

Among the spectacles in Germany fascinating travellers, those presented by the Rhine valley were top of the list. Travellers appreciated panoramic voyages down the Rhine, since they provided an excellent combination of aesthetic pleasure and speedy progress to the south. A quantitative analysis of Grand Tour itineraries has shown that travelling down the Rhine between Cologne and Frankfurt was also a preferred route south for English travellers.[59] Apart from that, the Schaffhausen cascade had been known as a major landmark since the late seventeenth century to domestic travellers too.[60] A century later, romantic tastes refuelled the appreciation for travelling along the Rhine and British travellers, in particular, came to see the Rhine valley as distinct travel destination rather than a mere transit zone.[61]

As the travel narrative of Reuß, Lynar and Geusau shows, German aristocrats followed this general trend too. Heading from Eger to Utrecht at the beginning of their tour, they took the chance and embarked at Mainz in order to sail down the Rhine to Cologne. They adhered to the same mixture of practical and aesthetic reasons for choosing this means of transportation as British travellers. While 'routes over land became from now on quite troublesome and mountainous', sailing down the Rhine was considered 'better value for money' and 'quick'.[62] Of course, ships were equipped to meet the aristocratic traveller's demands, being ready to accommodate the travel companions, their baggage and their carriage. The travellers' impression of the Rhine valley was expressed not through an elaborate description but rather a brief statement that one 'passed through the most beautiful quarters and spots of the Rhine'.[63] Historical monuments were duly enumerated and commented upon, as well as vineyards and natural spectacles,

Educational travelling and court culture 117

especially waterfalls, cataracts and whirlpools. Thus, they marvelled at the Binger Loch, 'where the waters blasting over the rocks, some of which tower above the strand, are causing strong noises and waves'.[64] The three diarists were especially fond of historical monuments in a picturesque setting that could best be admired from the privileged perspective of a river cruise, such as the Pfalzgrafenstein (the customs facilities at the castle of the Pfalzgraf) close to the smallish town of Kaub, on one of the Rhine islands. They admired the castle as 'an old-fashioned palace made from building blocks and supplied with many pitched roofs',[65] mistaking the whole structure as the ancestral seat of the counts palatine. Scenery and history seemed to blend into each other in a particularly alluring way. Lynar, whose turn it was to keep that week's diary, was so impressed by the view, that he sketched Pfalzgrafenstein as seen from the south. (The second monument he portrayed was the Mouse Tower that also stood on a small island.)

Despite the attractions of the Rhine, travelling through the Holy Roman Empire basically meant visiting its numerous *Residenzstädte*. Traditionally, courts exerted a strong pull especially on princes of self-governing petty-dynasties who sought to establish themselves within the networks of the 'society of princes'.[66] The choice of which courts to visit, depended on the travellers' individual affiliations, bonds and choices. For Reuß and Lynar, their passage through Germany was characterised by an emphasis upon the medieval heartland of the Holy Roman Empire rather than visiting the numerous secular and ecclesiastical self-governing rulers and bodies. Accordingly, while travelling down the Rhine, they noted with interest to whom the towns and villages they saw laying on the river banks actually belonged. Where Reuß and Lynar made longer stays, it was understood that their primary objective was to visit courts and governing bodies. Having arrived at Frankfurt am Main, their first object was to call on the *Römer* in a mixture of paying respect to the *Rat*, as ruling body of the imperial city, and sightseeing. This visit was clearly made as part of the travellers' introduction to matters of state, given that a *Ratsschreiber* (town secretary) showed them the Frankfurt copy of the Golden Bull of 1356 which contained the regulation for the coronation of the *rex romanorum*. Not only did they recognise it as 'fundamental law of the Reich',[67] but also they took great pains in describing the parchment it was written on and the manuscript hand, as well as the seal and its cords. Afterwards they visited rooms related to the election of the emperor – that is, the *Kaisersaal* – where the coronation banquets took place, and the *Konferenzstube*, where the electors voted for the emperor.[68] The antiquity of the Holy Roman Empire was matched by the old-fashioned *Kaisersaal*, whereas a series of portraits depicting the emperors gave visual expression to its dignity and continuity. Thus, by visiting the *Kaisersaal*, the travellers gained an impression both of *Kaiser* and *Reich* as a non-personal constitutional order and of empire as a dignity embodied by specific persons or rather dynasties. The visit was not only a constitutional lesson, but also a ritual envisioning the travelling

118   *Mathis Leibetseder*

counts' adherence to the Empire's established hierarchy. A close reading of the narrative, however, might suggest that the young travellers may have harboured reservations against the imperial dynasty whom they called Austrian emperors. This might reflect the growing gap between the Habsburgs, who were using their Austrian power base to extend their glory vis-à-vis the *Reich*, and the *Reich*, which laid claim to its alleged independence.[69]

In travelling through the power centres of the medieval Holy Roman Empire, Reuß, Lynar and Geusau also caught glimpses of conditions in the three most important ecclesiastical territories of Catholic Germany – in the electorates of Mainz, Cologne and Trier. At Mainz, they did not appear at court, presumably because the elector was not in residence. Instead, they visited the cathedral and the charterhouse, giving minutely detailed accounts of them, without denouncing them or depicting them as part of a particularly backward political system. However, they did not approve of the shops situated in alleys on either side of the cathedral: 'Thereby we remembered the words: "My house is a house of prayer etc"'.[70] Moreover, the treatment of Protestants was keenly observed. Apart from that, the diary shows no signs of reflecting the discourse of the Protestant Enlightenment with regard to Catholic territories and institutions. In fact, by marvelling at the splendours of the elector's recently built summer residence, La Favorite, near Mainz, the diarists were actually adhering to the value system of courtly society.

At first sight, the same applies to their account of their halt at Bonn, which was explicitly made only because the elector was in town. As soon as they heard that he was in residence, they decided to disembark and call on him. The visit was prepared as carefully as ever and followed the usual ceremonies. Reuß, Lynar and Geusau had to wait until the elector had finished attending mass before they could be introduced and they used this time to gather information on the vast electoral court. Then, the great moment arrived and the travellers were presented to the elector for a short conversation. Thereafter, August Clemens went to dine and the cavaliers were conveyed to a table in another chamber where they also ate and conversed with some of the elector's courtiers. After that, a lengthy visit of the palace followed, before, at about five o'clock, the travellers left the court and embarked again in order to continue their way down the Rhine.

At second sight, some features of their account raise suspicion vis-à-vis the travellers' alleged impartiality. This applies especially to the characterisation of the courtiers at the palace of La Favorite. The high-ranking court officials, who crowded the elector's antechamber, were described by the travellers as a row of sickly and semi-crippled individuals who somehow seemed misplaced within a courtly setting – the first was hobbled by gout, the second looked 'torrid'[71] and the third was marked by the consequences of alcohol consumption. The impression the elector himself left was not any better: August Clemens was a 'lord with a wispy body and face' who

Educational travelling and court culture 119

'according to the Bavarian princes' way left his mouth slightly open'.[72] Apart from that, his temperament was described as sanguine and choleric.

It is difficult to tell, whether there is any criticism hidden in the diarist's description of the electoral courtiers and the elector himself at all. Arguably, there was a tendency in their narrative to depict court society at Bonn as being odd. Unfortunately, the travellers did not visit any comparable court against which that description might contrast. However, there seems to be no criticism hidden in the description of either the French court at Versailles or the English court at London. Whereas it turned out to be quite difficult to be presented to the French King at all, religious alliances ensured a warm welcome at London, especially from Queen Caroline, to whom Reuß and Lynar had been recommended by the Pietist Count Albert Wolfgang von Schaumburg-Lippe.[73] Implied criticism or not, there clearly was no overall condemnation of the court of Cologne as such. This clearly emerges from the descriptions of court ceremonies and etiquette that are given as accurately and soberly as in many other instances in the diary. The table talks that were recorded at length suggest that all three travellers very much appreciated the members of polite society gathered there. Moreover, the elaborate account of the décor of the Bonn palace betrays how impressed they were by contemporary baroque architecture and princely splendour. Accordingly, one might conclude that the travel companions probably appreciated the court, in the first instance, for aesthetic reasons and as a place for polite conversation, whereas the elector and his leading court officials appeared rather moribund. Although there is no open criticism of August Clemens or his court to be found within the diary, Lynar's narration left little doubt that hardly any advancement of social issues or the public good could be expected from this elector.

Conclusion

Over the course of the eighteenth century, the social foundations on which the *Kavalierstour* rested, that is to say court culture itself, underwent a process of transformation. Increasingly, the court became an arena for a socially heterogeneous elite comprising academically trained men with both aristocratic and bourgeois backgrounds who subscribed to enlightened agendas for socio-economic reform and affiliated closely with transnational intellectual networks. Or, to put it differently, the Enlightenment as a social movement substantially altered the referential framework of the *Kavalierstour* and court society. As a consequence, travelling became more 'individualistic' in the sense that it was moulded along the lines of the individual traveller's or travelling party's specific needs rather than along those of social conventions serving the reproduction of social status in the first place. No longer was the value of travelling uncontested or self-evident; it unfolded only when individuals created meaning for themselves, usually by placing their travelling experiences in the service of the public good.

120   *Mathis Leibetseder*

As a consequence, the reasons for travelling multiplied as did the range of travel destinations and social classes travelling abroad.

The *Kavalierstour* that Reuß, Lynar and Geusau conducted in 1731–2 pioneered, in more than one respect, what became a general trend throughout the second half of the eighteenth century. By conversing with diplomatic circles, they sought informal training for future application in foreign service in which Lynar, at least, would later excel. Apart from this, they nourished a special interest in all issues confessional as well as philosophical, seeking, wherever they went, close contacts to reputable as well as controversial intellectuals. A trend towards professional specialisation was combined with large-scale knowledge collecting destined to the enhancement of the public good. Although the travel companions contacted underground writers in Paris, they did not contest the established constitutional order of the Holy Roman Empire, on which their social status as (imperial) counts depended. The role of courts as part of the established political system as much as court ritual and ceremony was not put into question either. Reading between the lines, one might, however, interpret some parts of their descriptions of German monarchs and court officials as criticism. Although they affirmed the constitutional order as the general framework for further social development, they portrayed rulers such as the Elector August Clemens of Cologne, as well as his leading court officials, as moribund persons who were not inclined to pursue a reforming agenda. The generally critical attitude displayed by Reuß, Lynar and Geusau could have resulted from their religious affiliation. Certainly, Pietism lay at the heart of this tour, with its minute recording of day-to-day events. Yet their reports should probably be seen in the light of the evolving encyclopaedic endeavour rather than Pietistic fondness for detailed introspection and self-exploration. Thus, enlightened principles started superimposing confessional creeds that helped to prepare a receptiveness for a new intellectual culture.

Notes

1   J. Rees, W. Siebers and H. Tilgner, eds, *Europareisen politisch-sozialer Eliten im 18. Jahrhundert: theoretische Neuorientierung kommunikative Praxis, Kultur- und Wissentransfer* (Berlin, 2002).

2   The most important document on the 1731/2 tour of Rochus Friedrich Count zu Lynar and Heinrich VI. Count Reuß is an autograph travel diary that is to be found in the Lynar family archive; BLHA [Brandenburgisches Landeshauptarchiv], Rep. 37, SchlossA [Schlossarchiv] Lübbenau, Nr 5065.

3   H. Sieg, *Staatsdienst, Staatsdenken und Dienstgesinnung in Brandenburg-Preußen im 18. Jahrhundert (1713–1806). Studien zum Verständnis des Absolutismus* (Berlin, 2003), pp. 365–8.

4   A. Meier, 'Von der enzyklopädischen Studienreise zur ästhetischen Bildungsreise. Italienreisen im 18. Jahrhundert', in P. Brenner, ed, *Der Reisebericht. Die Entwicklung einer Gattung in der deutschen Literatur* (Frankfurt am Main, 1989), pp. 284–305.

Educational travelling and court culture 121

5 '*Vermeine über 3 Monath mit meinem gnäd[igen] Herren die grosse Tour in Franckreich als Orleans Rochelle Tours Angiers Blois Saumurs Poictirer Lion Vnd Geneve &c. anzustellen*'; BHLA, Rep. 37 SchlossA Lübbenau, Nr 4537; Paul Bowers to Elisabeth Countess zu Lynar, [20/30 Jun.] 1633. The term crops up in letters of other travel companies too; see Thüringisches Staatsarchiv Greiz, Hausarchiv Schleiz D 15, fol. 485v, 621v, 634r and 639r.

6 A. Stannek, 'Perereginamur non ataranaese dutapes. Auslandserfahrungen im Kontext adliger Standeserziehung an der Wende vom 16. zum 17. Jahrhundert', in N. Hammerstein and G. Walther, eds, *Späthumanismus. Studien über das Ende einer historischen Epoche* (Göttingen, 2000), pp. 208–26, especially p. 208.

7 G. Klingenstein, *Der Aufstieg des Hauses Kaunitz. Studien zur Herkunft und Bildung des Staatskanzlers Wenzel Anton* (Göttingen, 1975), p. 220; N. Conrads, 'Politische und staatsrechtliche Probleme der Kavalierstour', in A. Maczak and H.-J. Teuteberg, eds, *Reiseberichte als Quellen europäischer Kulturgeschichte. Aufgaben und Möglichkeiten der historischen Reiseforschung* (Wolfenbüttel, 1982), p. 47; M. Weidner, *Landadel in Münster 1600–1760. Stadtverfassung, Standesbehauptung und Fürstenhof* (Münster, 2000), p. 57.

8 M. Leibetseder, *Die Kavalierstour. Adlige Erziehungsreisen im 17. und 18. Jahrhundert* (Cologne/Weimar/Vienna, 2004), p. 21.

9 At present, many researchers use the terms *Kavalierstour* and *Grand Tour* synonymously. A. Stannek, *Telemachs Brüder. Die höfische Bildungsreise des 17. Jahrhunderts* (Frankfurt am Main and New York, 2001); W. Paravicini, 'Vom Erkenntniswert der Adelsreise: Einleitung', in R. Babel and W. Paravicini, eds, *Grand Tour. Adliges Reisen und Europäische Kultur vom 14. bis zum 18. Jahrhundeert. Akten der internationalen Kolloquien in der Villa Vigoni 1999 und im Deutschen Historischen Institut Paris 2000* (Ostfildern, 2005), pp. 11–20, especially p. 12; R. Hachtmann, *Tourismusgeschichte* (Göttingen, 2007), p. 44.

10 Accordingly, journeys undertaken by members of self-ruling dynasties (*Regenten- und Prinzenreise*) as well as by gentlemen-scholars and university men (*Gelehrten- und Gebildetenreise*) come to the fore. J. Rees, W. Siebers and H. Tilgner, 'Reisen im Erfahrungsraum Europa. Forschungsperspektiven zur Reisetätigkeit politisch-sozialer Eliten des Alten Reichs (1750–1800)', *Das achtzehnte Jahrhundert*, 26 (2002), pp. 35–62, especially p. 43; E. Bender, *Die Prinzenreise. Bildungsaufenthalt und Kavalierstour im höfischen Kontext gegen Ende des 17. Jahrhunderts* (Berlin, 2011). Without employing the term, '*Prinzenreisen*' were in the focus of the studies by Stannek, *Telemachs Brüder* and C. Kollbach, *Aufwachsen bei Hof. Aufklärung und fürstliche Erziehung in Hessen und Baden* (Frankfurt/Main and New York, 2009), pp. 332–64. H. Tilgner, 'Die Adelsreise im Kontext aufgeklärter Reformpolitik (1765–1800). Funktionswandel und Erweiterung der kommunikativen Dimension', in Rees, Siebers and Tilgner, *Europareisen*, pp. 41–66, especially p. 65; W. Siebers, 'Bildung auf Reisen. Bemerkungen zur Peregrinatio academica, Gelehrten- und Gebildetenreise', in M. Maurer, ed., *Neue Impulse der Reiseforschung* (Berlin, 1999), pp. 177–88.

11 For the heuristic value as well as the limitations of the term 'Grand Tour', see R. Sweet, *Cities and the Grand Tour: The British in Italy, c.1690–1820* (Cambridge, 2012), p. 19.

12 W. Müller, *Die Aufklärung* (Munich, 2002), p. 11.

13 Ibid., pp. 57–61.

14 Ibid., pp. 9, 13–15; U. Im Hof, *Das Europa der Aufklärung* (Munich, 1993), pp. 34–8; U. Herrmann, 'Familie, Kindheit, Jugend', in N. Hammerstein and

122   *Mathis Leibetseder*

U. Herrmann, eds, *Handbuch der deutschen Bildungsgeschichte. Vol. 2: 18. Jahrhundert. Vom späten 17. Jahrhundert bis zur Neuordnung Deutschlands um 1800* (Munich, 2005), pp. 69–96, especially p. 84.

15 J.M. von Loen, *Der redliche Mann am Hofe, oder, die Begebenheit des Grafen von Rivera, in einer auf den Zustand der heutigen Welt gerichteten lehr- und Staats-Geschichte* (Frankfurt am Main, 1740).

16 Müller, *Die Aufklärung*, pp. 14–15, 53.

17 Ibid., p. 52.

18 Ibid., p. 48.

19 *Dansk Biografisk Leksikon* (hereafter DBL) (Copenhagen, 1979–84); see vol. 12, p. 157.

20 A.F. Büsching, *Beyträge zur Lebensgeschichte denkwürdiger Personen, insonderheit gelehrter Männer*, 4 (1786), pp. 73–218; DBL 9, pp. 233–5; G. Jansen, *Rochus Friedrich Graf zu Lynar, königlich-dänsicher Statthalter der Grafschaften Oldenburg und Delmenhorst* (Oldenburg, 1873).

21 On the completely different constitutional statuses of *Reichs-* and *Landadel*, see, for example, R. Endres, *Adel in der Frühen Neuzeit* (Munich, 1993), pp. 4–37.

22 On pietistic networks see H.-W. Erbe, *Zinzendorf und der fromme hohe Adel seiner Zeit* (Leipzig, 1928); C. Hinrichs, *Preußentum und Pietismus. Der Pietismus in Brandenburg-Preußen als religiös-soziale Reformbewegung* (Göttingen, 1971), pp. 174–215; M. Brecht and K. Deppermann, eds, *Der Pietismus im achtzehnten Jahrhundert* (Göttingen, 1995).

23 W. Neugebauer, 'Einleitung: Staatlicher Wandel. Kulturelle Staatsaufgaben als Forschungsproblem', in W. Neugebauer, ed., *Kulturstaat und Bürgergesellschaft im Spiegel der Tätigkeit des preußischen Kultusministeriums* (Berlin, 2012), pp.ix–xxix, especially p. xix.

24 Leibetseder, *Die Kavalierstour*, pp. 189–95; for further detail on the networks conveyed on this tour, see M. Leibetseder, 'Attici Vettern in Paris. Pietismus, Jansenismus und das Netz von Bekanntschaften auf der Kavalierstour', in Babel and Paravicini, *Grand Tour*, pp. 469–84.

25 The second tour was the 1740–1 excursion of Heinrich XI. ä. L. (1715–1800). Geusau's manuscript diary of this tour is to be found in the Staatliche Bücher- und Kupferstichsammlung Greiz, DB. 2316; see Leibetseder, *Attici Vettern*, p. 471.

26 P. Hoffmann, *Anton Friedrich Büsching (1724–1793). Ein Leben im Zeitalter der Aufklärung* (Berlin, 2000); Büsching, *Beyträge zur Lebensgeschichte*, 2 (1784), pp. 31–368.

27 H. Kürbis, 'Kavalierstouren des brandenburg-preußischen Adels (1550–1750). Quantitative Überlegungen', *Jahrbuch für brandenburgische Landesgeschichte*, 61 (2010), pp. 61–82.

28 M. Maurer, *Aufklärung und Anglophilie in Deutschland* (Göttingen and Zurich, 1992).

29 T. Grosser, *Reiseziel Frankreich. Deutsche Reiseliteratur vom Barock bis zur Französischen Revolution* (Opladen, 1989).

30 For travellers from Germany, L. Schudt, *Italienreisen im 17. und 18. Jahrhundert* (Vienna and Munich, 1959) is still useful.

31 BLHA, Rep. 37, SchlossA Lübbenau, Nr 4873.

32 Ibid., Nr 5065, 16 Sep. 1731.

33 A. Chales de Beaulieu, *Deutsche Reisende in den Niederlanden. Das Bild eines Nachbarn zwischen 1648 und 1795* (Frankfurt am Main 2000), pp. 82–5.

34 BLHA, Rep. 37, SchlossA Lübbenau, Nr 5065, 18 Sept. 1731.

35 Tilgner, 'Die Adelsreise', p. 66; W. Siebers, 'Von der repräsentativen zur aufgeklärten Kavalierstour? Reflexion und Kritik adlig-fürstlichen Reisens in der

Educational travelling and court culture 123

zweiten Hälfte des 18. Jahrhunderts', in Rees, Siebers and Tilgner, *Europareisen*, pp. 25–40; J. Rees, 'Wahrnehmen in fremden Orten, was zu Hause Vortheil bringen und nachgeahmet werden könne. Europareisen und Kulturtransfer adeliger Eliten im Alten Reich 1750–1800', in Babel and Paravicini, *Grand Tour*, pp. 513–40.

36 BLHA, Rep. 37, Schloss A Lübbenau, Nr 5065, 18 Nov. 1731 (Lynar).

37 Cf. C.B. O'Keefe, *Contemporary Reactions to the Enlightenment (1728–1762). A Study of Three Critical Journals: the Jesuit 'Journal de Trévoux', the Jansenist 'Nouvelles ecclésiastiques', and the Secular 'Journal des Savants'* (Genf and Paris, 1974), pp. 9–21; R. Taveneaux, *La vie quotidienne des Jansénistes aux XVIIe et XVIIIe siècles* (Paris, 1973), pp. 235–40.

38 E. Beyreuther, *Der junge Zinzendorf* (Marburg, 1957), pp. 161–201; D. Meyer, 'Zinzendorf und Herrnhut', in Brecht and Deppermann, *Der Pietismus*, pp. 5–106, especially pp. 13–16; Leibetseder, 'Attici Vettern', pp. 477–82.

39 Both Hamburg and Copenhagen at that time were centres of exchange for clandestine scriptures; M. Mulsow, *Präkeres Wissen. Eine andere Ideengeschichte der Frühen Neuzeit* (Berlin, 2012), pp. 111–15. Lynar's or Reuß's connection to those circles, however, still needs to be verified.

40 Leibetseder, *Die Kavalierstour*, pp. 114–21.

41 Bender, *Die Prinzenreise*, pp. 288–309.

42 J. Voss, *Universität, Geschichtswissenschaft und Diplomatie im Zeitalter der Aufklärung. Johann Daniel Schöpflin (1694–1771)* (Munich, 1979), pp. 146–50.

43 BLHA, Rep. 37, SchlossA Lübbenau, Nr 5065, 9 Sep. 1731.

44 Ibid., 30 Aug. 1731.

45 Ibid., 4 Sep. 1731.

46 'Staats Sachen'; BLHA, Rep. 37, SchlossA Lübbenau, Nr 5065, 12 Sep. 1731.

47 On the financial, legal and structural difficulties German petty-courts had to face in entertaining diplomatic envoys, see the case study of J. Matzke, 'Außenpolitische Handlungsspielräume und Gesandtschaftswesen der Sekundogenitur fürstentümer', in M. Schattkowsky and M. Wilde, eds, *Sachsen und seine Sekundogenituren. Die Nebenlinien Weißenfels, Merseburg und Zeitz (1657–1746)* (Leipzig, 2010), pp. 183–206.

48 M. Zollinger, *Geschichte des Glücksspiels. Vom 17. Jahrhundert bis zum Zweiten Weltkrieg* (Cologne, Vienna and Weimar, 1997), pp. 58–60.

49 BLHA, SchlossA Lübbenau, Nr 5065, 6 Dec. 1731.

50 Ibid., 22 Dec. 1731.

51 BStA München, FATörring-Seefeld, Litt. T. T. 1 Nr 4, Joseph Albert de Materne to Felix Ignaz Joseph Count of Törring-Jettenbach, Paris, 21 Mar.1737.

52 Leibetseder, *Die Kavalierstour*, pp. 78–9.

53 'in SchlafRöcken'. BLHA, Rep. 37 SchlossA Lübbenau, Nr 5065, 25 Aug. 1731.

54 'bekannt wegen einem graßlichen Anblick von Todt–Gerippen u. ausgestopften Menschen, die zum Theil in wunderl. posituren aufgestellet seyn'. Ibid., 28 Aug. 1731.

55 'machine seines Cörpers'. Ibid., 27 Aug. 1731.

56 On the concepts of *Wissenspräkariat* and *Wissensbourgeoisie* see Mulsow, *Präkeres Wissen*, pp. 33–6.

57 Siebers, 'Von der repräsentativen zur aufgeklärten Kavalierstour?', p. 39; see also Rees, 'Wahrnehmen in fremden Orten', p. 538.

58 Bender, *Die Prinzenreise*, p. 181. This applies not only to German travellers on a *Kavalierstour*, but to international travellers on a Grand Tour as well. See, for example, E. Chaney and T. Wilks, *The Jacobean Grand Tour: Early Stuart Travellers in Europe* (London, 2014), pp. 207–15.

124   *Mathis Leibetseder*

59 J. Towner, 'The Grand Tour: a key phase in the history of tourism', *Annals of Tourism Research*, 12 (1985), pp. 297–354, especially p. 302.

60 Bender, *Die Prinzenreise*, p. 182.

61 B. Bock, *Baedeker & Cook – Tourismus am Mittelrhein 1756 bis ca. 1914* (Frankfurt am Main, 2010), pp. 78–9.

62 'Weil die Wege zu lande von hier an sehr beschwerlich und bergicht werden, auch auf dem Rhein zu fahren profitabler ist und geschwinder gehet'. BLHA, Rep. 37 Lübbenau, Nr 5065, 7 Aug. 1731.

63 'Wir passirten die schönsten Gegenden und Oerter am Rhein'. Ibid.

64 'woselbst das über die Felsen, wovon gegen das Ufer einige hervorragen, herüber schießende Waßer ein starckes Geräusch und Wellen machet'. Ibid., 8 Aug. 1731.

65 'auf einer kleinen Insul mitt im Rhein ein altväterisches, aus Qvader Stücken erbautes und mit ein Hauffen Spitzen versehenes Schloß lieget'. Ibid.

66 Bender, *Die Prinzenreise*, pp. 181–4. Quotation, see L. Bély: 'La società dei principi', in C. Dipperand and M. Rosa, eds, *La società dei principi nell'Europa moderna (secoli XVI–XVII)* (Bologna, 2005), pp. 13–44.

67 'Reichs Grund Gesetz'. BLHA, Rep. 37 Lübbenau, Nr 5065, 6 Aug. 1731.

68 During the early modern period, the election of the *rex romanorum* and the coronation of the emperor were amalgamated.

69 B. Stollberg-Rilinger, *Des Kaisers alte Kleider. Verfassungsgeschichte und Symbolsprache des Alten Reiches* (Munich, 2013), pp. 174–5.

70 'Es fielen uns dabey die Worte ein: Mein Hauß ist ein Bethauß pp.'. BLHA, Rep. 37 Lübbenau, Nr. 5065, 7 Aug. 1731.

71 'ausgedört'. Ibid., 10 Aug. 1731.

72 'sehr schmächtiger Herr von Leibe und Gesicht'; 'nach Art der Bayerschen Printzen den Mund etwas offen stehen läßet'. Ibid., 6 Aug. 1731.

73 Leibetseder, *Die Kavalierstour*, pp. 117, 129–34.

Part II
Travel for leisure and business

7 The Petit Tour to Spa, 1763–87

Richard Bates

Introduction

During the 'golden age of Spa' (1763–87), an astonishing 23,271 of the European elite, of whom 5,257 (22.5 per cent) were British, travelled to Spa in the independent bishopric of Liège, located in today's southern Belgium.[1] Visitors were attracted to Spa's health-giving waters, the recently developed leisure facilities that could be enjoyed in convivial, cosmopolitan and aristocratic company, and by the prospect of a short, safe journey that was interspersed with opportunities for cultural tourism. Travel to Spa has been largely ignored by historians in favour of the Grand Tour to Paris and Italy. However, on average a noteworthy 210 Britons visited Spa during its short three-month summer season compared to the estimated 1,000 Britons who visited Paris each full year.[2] As such it exemplifies a pattern of travel that was clearly distinguishable from the Grand Tour, and yet has received little scholarly attention. Jeremy Black, for example, promises 'to devote due attention to tourism outside the parameters set by travel to Paris and Italy'; only four out of 365 pages of his study, however, are devoted to Spa.[3] Continental historians, such as Kees van Strien, have covered British travel in northern Europe but only up to 1720, which unfortunately excludes the dramatic expansion of Spa after 1763.[4] And although local Spa historian Albin Body (1836–1916) wrote extensively about the city and the activities of its visitors, he did not cover the journey to Spa and his works are now dated.[5]

This chapter will argue that the British travel culture relating to Spa was clearly distinguishable from the longer, more physically demanding, aristocratic and classically focused Grand Tour. Using a proposographical analysis of lists of visitors to Spa, a series of case studies drawn from travellers' diaries, the patient case notes of a resident physician, Dr Jean Phillipe Limbourg (1726–1811),[6] guide books and related literature, this chapter will explore the distinctive nature of British travel to Spa, through analysing the profile of British visitors, their reasons for visiting Spa, the accompanying 'Petit Tour' in terms of its route, attractions and supportive nascent travel industry, and, finally, the reasons behind the abrupt decline of British travellers to Spa in the 1780s.

128   *Richard Bates*

Spa was particularly attractive to the British because of its promise of a medical cure, its picturesque and healthy setting and its exclusive social cachet, which itself was the consequence of the resort's small size and the social profile of many of its visitors. However, travellers were also attracted by the comfort and convenience of travelling to a continental location within easy travelling distance of Britain: the journey was an attraction in its own right. Surviving evidence shows that a well-established route to Spa emerged in the eighteenth century, which offered a highly distinctive, pleasurable six-week travel experience that mirrors the tours enjoyed by the French or the Dutch identified by van Strien and Gerrit Verhoeven.[7] For the purposes of this chapter, this short pleasurable journey has been dubbed the Petit Tour. Unlike the classical Grand Tour, which was dominated by young men and their tutors in the pursuit of classical antiquity, travel to Spa was undertaken primarily by family groups and even by single women. This chapter suggests that the popularity of Spa with a broad array of ages and family groups was both supported by and encouraged the development of an incipient travel industry, via a well-developed infrastructure of travel, tourism services and entertainment industries.

Profile of British visitors

The profile of the British visitors to Spa has been facilitated by the online publication of the printed visitor lists for each of the 25 seasons from 1763–87, with arrival dates, names, nationalities and titles.[8] These 'Lists' were part of an exclusive concession to print visiting cards, granted by the Prince-bishop of Liège. The concessionaire would profit from the sale of the visiting cards and from the 'small ads' that appeared in the printed lists, which were distributed among the visitors.[9] At the end of each season the Lists were collated, totalled and published, with a commentary on the season's numbers and sometimes the identity of incognito visitors. They were primarily a marketing tool by the state authorities to publicise elite visitors, and were not designed to record each and every foreigner in Spa. An analysis of the Lists provides, among other insights, a profile of the British visitors in terms of their social composition, gender and nationality. For example, the majority (88 per cent) gave their nationality as English, a sizeable minority (11 per cent) gave their nationality as Irish (although there is evidence that the Irish numbers are understated),[10] only 1 per cent gave their nationality as Scots, and none declared themselves to be Welsh.

The lists contain the names and titles of 1,662 female visitors, and provide particularly valuable and rarely attained insight into female participation in travel. As could be expected in a male-dominated society, analysis shows that fewer females than males travelled from Britain to Spa, though women did make up over 30 per cent of the total. Taking the Lists at face value, a third of these females (10 per cent of all British visitors) travelled

The Petit Tour to Spa   129

without husbands. Female relatives such as wives and daughters formed 22 per cent of British visitors. This considerable female presence is perhaps indicative of Spa's reputation for respectability. These statistics of female travel are particularly interesting since historians rarely appear to have reliable large-scale data available to them. As a comparison, Daniel Roche comments that female travellers of any nationality in Paris were 'rare' (5.2 per cent), but this is based on police surveillance reports that seldom exceeded 10 per cent of all visitors which makes the validity of these statistics questionable.[11]

The British who appear in the Lists represented a wide cross-section of the elite. The majority of British visitors are recorded as simply 'Gentlemen' or 'Ladies' (73 per cent) and only a minority were titled (13 per cent), yet the Lists named members of the royal family, dukes, lords, members of parliament, prime ministers, lord justices and an Irish archbishop. There were numerous famous individuals among the visitors, including the dukes of Gloucester and Cumberland, the prime ministers William Cavendish, Charles James Fox, William Pitt the elder and Lord Shelburne, the 'Bluestockings' Sarah Lennox, Elizabeth Montagu and Elizabeth Carter, the diarists Mary Hamilton and Lady Coke, the abolitionist campaigner William Wilberforce, the proponent for Irish legislative independence Henry Grattan, the notorious courtesan Elizabeth Armistead, the bigamist duchess of Kingston, the naval officer who defeated the French fleet during the American War of Independence Admiral Rodney, the diplomat, antiquary, archaeologist and volcanologist Sir William Hamilton, the playwright Richard Sheridan, the actor-manager David Garrick, the leader of fashionable society Georgiana, duchess of Devonshire, the portrait painter Joshua Reynolds and many more.[12]

The Lists appear remarkably accurate, as cross-checking from British visitors' diaries and letters with the database has demonstrated. There are some omissions. For example, a simple cross-check against travellers' diaries proves that the Lists omit servants. Visitors who decided not to appear in the Lists are a more serious omission, but there exists independent data that permits this lacuna to be estimated. Comparisons with Mary Hamilton's diary from 1776 and the medical case notes of Dr Limbourg show that approximately 20 per cent of British visitors were omitted from the Lists.[13] For example, a clearly deliberate omission is Robert French of Cork, Ireland, who is shown in Dr Limbourg's notes as 'staying at the Glacière and does not wish to appear on the list'.[14] It would be logical for certain persons to avoid having their names shown on the lists, such as those fleeing their creditors or travelling with a mistress or lover. Some British visitors travelled incognito, and Dr Limbourg's case notes show three patients travelling as such.[15] However, despite these caveats, the Lists are a rich and robust source of primary material that allows a unique quantitative insight into the popularity of Spa and the composition of its clientele.

130   Richard Bates

To add a deeper insight into individual reactions, experiences and itineraries, seven travellers who compiled diaries of their travels have been selected for closer analysis. The surviving British documentation of visitors' diaries and letters is, as can be expected, skewed towards the titled minority. For example, the letters and diaries, including those referring to their Spa travels, of Georgiana duchess of Devonshire, the Spencer and Devonshire families and the Bluestocking group have been carefully preserved for historians. It is tempting to select examples of visitors from these high-profile 'titled' individuals, although as members of the aristocracy their experiences were not necessarily representative. However, some 'non-titled' visitors' accounts have also survived, and are analysed here in order to reflect the actual composition of visitors in the Lists. The number of diarists chosen is too few, and their method of selection such, as not to allow statistically valid conclusions. However, a more qualitative analysis of this material complements the statistical findings drawn from the Lists. For example, a comparison between the overall profile of the British on the Lists and that of the seven diarists and the 14 family and friends who accompanied them shows a remarkably good correlation.

A brief profile of each of the seven diarists follows: Richard Twining[16] visited Spa in August 1781. He was 32 years old, a London tea merchant and an enthusiastic traveller accompanied by his wife and 11-year-old daughter, all in good health. Horace Townsend visited Spa in August 1781;[17] aged 31, he was a Church of Ireland clergyman and author, travelling with two unnamed young gentlemen. All three were in good health accompanying an elderly sick relative and all four were from Ireland. Jane Hamilton visited Spa in July 1772 in her late 30s and in poor health.[18] She was of Irish descent, a mother of two separated from her disreputable husband, and accompanied by her daughter of approximately six years old and a young female companion. John Macdonald visited Spa in 1767 aged 26.[19] He was a Scottish servant travelling with John Craufurd,[20] aged 25, an English MP and inveterate gambler in poor health; Stephen Weston visited Spa in August 1771 aged 24, travelling as tutor to Sir Charles Bampfylde, aged 18.[21] Both were Oxford graduates and both in good health, visiting Spa as part of a longer Grand Tour.[22] Lady Coke visited Spa in 1762, 1764, 1765 and July 1767 aged 35, 37, 38 and 40 years respectively.[23] She was an aristocrat, well connected in the London and European courts, an idiosyncratic wealthy widow with a taste for travel; Mary Hamilton visited Spa in August 1776, a future 'Bluestocking', aged 20, full of enthusiasm on her first trip abroad and travelling with family friends, the wealthy Lord and Lady Dartrey, who were also accompanied by Lord Dartrey's son, and two young boys, the 'Master Penns' with their tutor, Mr Foster.[24] All were in apparent good health, with the exception of Lady Dartrey.[25]

Analysing the material relating to these seven travel parties reveals three striking features that cannot be deduced from the Lists, namely the diversity of the participants' backgrounds, the number of young people and family groups and the high number of travellers accompanying sick persons. Of the 21 people travelling, four were children: Sidney Hamilton, a girl aged between six and seven, Mary Twining aged 11 and the two boys travelling with Mary Hamilton aged 14 and 16.[26] Only four individuals were visiting Spa for their own health (the elderly invalid with Townsend, Jane Hamilton, Craufurd and Lady Dartrey) and all had been advised by their British doctors to take the Spa waters.[27] The majority of individuals were either relatives or friends who accompanied these four sick persons, and therefore, overall, 14 of the 21 travellers, two-thirds, were visiting Spa for the benefit of their own or someone else's health. Several of those accompanying the sick, such as the diarist Mary Hamilton who was in good health, and more conventional Grand Tourists such as Weston and Bampfylde, clearly took advantage of their stay in Spa to drink the waters and enjoy its social attractions.

Reasons for choosing to visit Spa

Spa had a number of attractions: the salubrious, health-giving properties of its location and waters, the exclusive social company, comfortable, entertaining amenities and the opportunity for gambling. The following section will consider each of these in turn.

The main reason for visiting Spa, as noted above, appears to have been related to health. The major health benefits of visiting Spa were its internationally famous mineral waters and its exceptionally healthy environment in the forests of the Ardennes. Its mineral waters were looked upon as uniquely beneficial for health and, despite the stiff competition from British spas, an industry that had shown dramatic growth in the eighteenth century, Spa had attracted British visitors from the time of the waters' discovery in the early sixteenth century.[28] They represented the 'gold standard' for chalybeate waters (mineral waters with a high iron content drunk for medical reasons).[29] The reputation of Spa water was such that it was imported into Britain in large quantities: the British Customs recorded imports of 123,000 bottles in 1730.[30] Spa's reputation was enhanced by newspapers announcing the departure of the elite to take its waters for their health: 'The Duke of Gloucester [the brother of George III], with his Duchess, will soon set out for the German Spa by the advice of his physicians'[31] or, as a further example; 'Lord Audley will set out ... for the German Spa by the advice of his physicians, for the recovery of his health.'[32] An added attraction was Spa's proximity of 25 miles from Aix-la-Chapelle (Aix), whose sulphurous hot waters were judged by Philip Thicknesse as the best in Europe.[33] A series of travel guide books published in both French and English illustrates this association of Spa with Aix.[34] Visitors not only drank the chalybeate waters at Spa but also bathed in the hot waters at Aix: of the seven diarists only Lady Mary Coke failed to visit Aix either before or after Spa.

132   Richard Bates

Spa not only offered its renowned Spa waters. It also offered opportunities to regain or improve health through its exceptionally healthy environment in the forests of the Ardennes, and through the opportunity for a regular, balanced routine of good air, exercise, sleep, food and drink and company. In other words, Spa was a location that encouraged the correct balance of the 'non-naturals' that were believed necessary to health maintenance and restoration, codified by the Roman physician Galen.[35]

The location of Spa in the forests of the Ardennes, for example, provided good air in a quiet idyllic setting, particularly as, by the 1770s, tastes had changed and areas of 'atrocious solitude' such as the Ardennes were newly discovered as having 'romantic charm'.[36] Mary Hamilton waxed lyrical: 'We had a delightful ride for 3 hours. The little horses here climb like cats ... We enjoyed the delicious breezes on the tops of mountains and was [sic] amused by seeking paths through the close growing woods.' The next day she rode again: 'we climbed up some of the highest mountains and had charming views of the countryside – subjects for a Poussin (my favourite landscape painter) ... Some spots romantically pretty.'[37]

Twining was equally enchanted at 'discovering' these forests of Shakespeare's *As You Like It*: 'To an Englishman the country about Spa is classic ground, for there he may say with the gentle Rosalind "Well! This is the forest of Arden."'[38] Alongside riding, there were also forest walks that British visitors had created by subscription.[39] Many walks started from directly behind the hotels. By contrast, the air of Bath was criticised by Thicknesse in 1778.[40] The acknowledged superiority of both the drinking waters of Spa and the hot baths of Aix, together with the outdoor exercise in the fresh air of the Ardennes, made Spa a healthier choice than its rival British resorts.

Spa also attracted visitors on account of its social exclusivity and the charm of its sociability and entertainments, distractions that were also understood to aid recovery of health. Spa's small size would have accentuated its exclusivity, and, despite being one sixth the size of Bath, it could still offer its visitors international levels of comfort, amenities and security within a much smaller, intimate infrastructure.[41] The short summer season of Spa also restricted numbers, whereas Bath was in theory open all year. It seems that Spa's exclusivity, due to its small size, its short season and the cost of travelling across Europe, meant that the British elite could relax among their own rank. There was an ambiance of small circles of friends on holiday, as shown by an extract from Lady Coke's diary:

> The Duke of Roxborough and Mr. Craufurd [of Errol, an MP] came up to me, and persuaded me to walk with them up the Mountain, a very pretty walk, but a little fatiguing [the walk up and back this steep hill adjacent to the centre of Spa takes about 45 minutes]. I think, however, I performed rather better than either of my companions, and

The Petit Tour to Spa 133

when they politely offered me to lean upon them by way of assisting me, I thanked them, but said they seemed rather to stand in need of assistance themselves than to give it to others. In the walk we met Lady Sarah Bunbury [the notorious Sarah Lennox, then aged 22], two other ladies, and three or four gentlemen. Monsieur Wangenheim [a Baron, captain of the Queen's Light Dragoons of the British army, later guardian to Prince Edward, fourth son of George III[42]] was towing up Lady Sarah and complained it was hard work.[43]

Because of this, the ambience at Spa was informal, and court etiquette was dropped. Thicknesse's travel guide explained that: 'One of the agreeable circumstances of Spa is that everybody lays aside their high rank, and are masters and mistresses *of their own ceremony* [his italics].'[44] Spa differed fundamentally from Bath in not having a Master of Ceremonies. Bath's Richard 'Beau' Nash occupied this role from 1705–61 and introduced rules of conduct and dress in 1716.[45] The frequent use of incognitos at Spa avoided the need for court etiquette and the informality of dress delighted the diarists. Jane Hamilton enthusiastically described: 'different dresses, hoops and no hoops, hats and no hats, gowns, sacks, polleneese, men with whiskers, others without, green hats, high sort of turban, with a waving feather like a tragedy King'.[46]

As 77 per cent of its visitors were not British, Spa also offered the perfect opportunity for socialising with the international elite. Again, this was an attraction that British resorts could not compete with. Townsend was delighted with the mix of nationalities:

Not the least of Spa's charms was the circumstance of it being an epitome of all the upper classes of Europe's inhabitants. In one group were collected Russians, Prussians, Danes, Swedes, Italians, Germans, French and British meeting together every day in the same rooms, and on terms of apparent equality. This produced an easiness of communication and freedom of manner that banished all the insipid restraints of formality and reserve.[47]

Finally, the company were provided with numerous distractions. By 1770, Spa boasted two casinos, including the 'very elegant and superb' Vauxhall, an assembly room that opened in 1763 and a theatre from 1769.[48] Twining noted that there were 'balls four nights in the week and plays the other three'.[49] In terms of space, the Vauxhall's ballroom was almost two-thirds the size of Bath's Upper Rooms, which were opened one year later.[50] Although gambling was essential to Spa's economy and shaped its reputation quite decisively, despite the well-known passion of the British for this activity, the travellers examined in this chapter do not appear to have been drawn to Spa for gambling. Rather, the attraction of Spa lay in its reputation for health-giving waters and social exclusivity.

134   *Richard Bates*

In summary, Spa's attractions were manifold: renowned chalybeate drinking waters, proximity to the Aix hot water baths, healthy air in a romantic forest setting, exclusivity, appealing informality among a circle of friends and peers, the cosmopolitan flavour of the European elite, the intimacy of a 'small village' and the benefit of modern, secure facilities and international standards of distractions.

The journey to Spa

Part of Spa's appeal was the relatively straightforward, quick and safe nature of the journey from Britain. Visiting the Continent unavoidably required sea travel, but the majority of diarists restricted this to a minimum by taking the shortest Channel crossing of Dover to Calais. Happily, the season for drinking Spa waters was during the calmer summer months. Exceptions to the Dover–Calais route were born of necessity, as in 1781, when Calais closed due to the American War of Independence. Horace Townsend and Richard Twining therefore chose Ostend in the neutral Austrian Netherlands, despite the safe conduct through France negotiated by the Prince-bishop of Liège for British travellers to Spa. All seven diarists chose roughly the same 200-mile geographically direct route from the channel ports to Spa, which was also the route recommended by travel guides.[51]

Travel from the English Channel to Liège or Maastricht was, by contemporary standards, fast, although uncomfortable. Mary Coke noted that letters from London to Spa took five to six days; independent travellers might make the journey even more swiftly.[52] It was over a good, paved road network, and Mary Hamilton judged the 180 miles from Calais to Maastricht 'equal to our best turnpike roads in England'.[53] The paved roads, the *pavés*, were the motorways of the period, linking major cities by a route that was safe, with post stops approximately every six miles for brief pauses, refreshments, fresh horses, drivers and postilions. The *pavé* might have been fast, but was not considered comfortable: Thicknesse was convinced that 'Frenchmen of fortune and fashion, do not suffer from the gout, stone, etc. as Englishmen do' due to the jolting carriage ride over the *pavé*.[54] It was the final half-day journey of the 20 miles from Liège to Spa, or the 25 miles from Aix to Spa, over normal, unpaved roads that were considered difficult, mainly due to the steepness of the hills surrounding Spa. Lady Coke described the road from Liège to Spa as 'very fatiguing; one always stops half way to rest the horses for one cannot change them', and the road from Spa to Aix as 'chiefly up and down rocks and mountains; you may judge one cannot go fast and it is fatiguing to the horses'.[55]

The diarists kept strictly to the main *pavés* that were organised by the government for the post and government officials. They could expect to travel in reasonable comfort when keeping to the main routes and cities. As the major cities were fortified, travellers had to arrive before the closure of the gates or risk poor accommodation and meagre food outside. Travellers

The Petit Tour to Spa   135

used route books with distances and estimated travel times to avoid being caught out by the curfew. Staying in small towns or taking minor routes and deviations were avoided, hence Lady Coke's frustration with being delayed at Calais: 'This was a great hindrance; it prevented my reaching Lille that night and obliged me to lie at Bethune, a dirty miserable place.'[56] Getting off the beaten track was neither easy nor desirable. As Twining noted: 'We travelled along a *pavé* .... passing on the left the city of Tongres [a town with Roman remains on the ancient route from Cologne to the English Channel] ... We should gladly have deviated from the high road ... but the unwieldiness of our equipages, and an approaching storm obliged us to give up the excursion.'[57] This was the only case in the seven diaries where a deviation from the main route was even contemplated.

The journey to Spa appears to have been very safe. Gerrit Verhoeven's analysis of travel books between 1675 and 1750 showed that travel in England and the Low Countries was viewed as more secure than some of the other countries through which the Grand Tour ran.[58] With the exception of Lady Coke, none of the seven diarists experienced either accidents or incidents during the combined 1,400 miles that they travelled to Spa. The travel-seasoned Lady Coke's problems arose when she deliberately took risks, losing a wheel when 'going very fast' or being forced to stay at a dubious hotel on arriving late at Liège after ignoring the city gate closing times.[59] Both problems were quickly resolved. The damaged wheel with a bent axletree occurred while on the main Brussels–Louvain–Liège route and repairs were carried out within three hours, which probably reflects the wisdom of keeping to the main routes. The dubious hotel where 'one of the men pursued me, and took hold of my arm to force me back' was quickly changed for another Liège hotel, highlighting the advantage of staying only in major cities with a choice of accommodation.[60] Jane Hamilton, a woman travelling without an accompanying gentleman, suffered no mishap of note, although her diary reveals indecision and inexperience at every step. Arriving too late for the gates at Calais, for example, she had to stay at an unsatisfactory inn outside, whereas, when Lady Coke arrived late at Liège, 'a little money easily opened them'.[61]

The ease and safety of the trip is underlined by the fact that, as mentioned above, the profiles of the diarists and their companions included high numbers of women and children, some very young, undertaking the journey. As a further example, when Lord and Lady Spencer travelled to Spa in 1763, they left their youngest children, aged two and five at home, as 'both considered too young to undertake such a long journey', but brought their six-year-old daughter Georgiana, who later became the well-known duchess of Devonshire.[62] Although Georgiana was judged old enough for the journey to Spa, she was left in her grandmother's care at Antwerp rather than accompanying her parents, who continued from Spa to Italy, a trip of approximately five to six weeks almost inevitably over the Alps.[63] Occasionally even younger children made the journey to Spa. In 1785 the

136   Richard Bates

newspapers reported that: 'Sir Cecil Bishop ... with his Lady, and son of three years old, sets off for the German Spa.'[64] The journey would therefore appear to have been safe, comfortable and unadventurous, allowing even single unaccompanied women and children to travel across northern Europe to visit Spa.

The nascent travel industry

This easy and safe journey was clearly facilitated by an incipient 'travel industry'. The first signs of this can be seen at Calais's large hotels that specialised in servicing the needs of the British travellers. The Hôtel d'Angleterre at Calais, run by Monsieur Dessein, was a well-known favourite among the fashionable British. Mary Hamilton stayed at 'Dessein's celebrated hotel' and noted 'it is a spacious mansion and contains 111 beds, the floors are dirty but the linen is white and clean, and the waiters are clever and attentive'.[65] Hamilton also stayed at the Hôtel d'Angleterre in Brussels and Hôtel d'Angleterre in Antwerp. Calais, and especially Dessein, provided another essential service of foreign exchange, although Thicknesse was highly critical of Dessein's foreign exchange practices, recording Dessein's offer to British travellers: 'I will give you, Sir, *L'dors* ... for your guineas, and on your return, I will give you guineas for your *L'dors*.'[66] As the *Louis d'or* was normally worth less than a guinea, and the British traveller returned with very few *Louis d'or* unspent, Dessein made a good profit.

Travellers could purchase guide books specifically catering for the journey to Spa. For example, *A Tour to Spa through the Austrian Netherlands and the French Flanders* was 120 pages in length, cost only two shillings, and gave the bare bones of the routes, accommodation and sightseeing.[67] A more extensive guide book of over 500 pages, written by the verbose and opinionated Thicknesse, was published in London and detailed guide books of specific cities, such as the *Description of the Principal Paintings and Sculptures of Antwerp*, were also available.[68] Local expertise was also sought, such as sightseeing guidance and private guides, who crowded around new arrivals' carriages at the major cities offering to show the visitors the main attractions.[69]

Travellers who had not brought their own carriage could rent one at Calais. Stephen Weston wrote in his journal: 'We hired a chaise with three horses for as many guineas to convey us to Antwerp, two masters and a man, provided we should return it to Dessein at Calais in the month of October, that is in three months.'[70] None of the diarists took the diligences or public coaches mentioned by Verhoeven, possibly to avoid contact with the lower orders, or possibly because the British guide book recommended public coaches only 'if a male party'.[71] The only public transport used was the barge from Bruges to Ghent, which was slow but renowned for its luxury. Three of the diarists, Lady Coke, Mary Hamilton, who travelled in

The Petit Tour to Spa   137

the carriage of Lord Dartrey, and John Craufurd, all had their carriages 'put on-board the packet [boat]': Lord Dartrey's party being large, more than one carriage was transported.[72] There were some disadvantages in travelling by private carriage, like unloading the carriage from the boat, which could be frustratingly slow: 'I could not get away till after nine o'clock. I waited for my equipage; it could not be disembarked and got ready before this time.'[73] Private carriages, however, were also status symbols that could be displayed while travelling or at Spa, and would ensure that hoteliers and others were 'attentive'. Thicknesse observed that the hotelier at Calais, Dessein, would 'mak[e] you a very low bow, if you come with your *own* [his italics] carriage'.[74]

As today, local luxury goods manufacturers existed from whom travellers could buy souvenirs: Flanders, for example, was renowned for its high-quality lace and textiles, and shopping for these was a favourite occupation, especially for Lady Coke, who purchased for both her friends and herself: 'I hope to send you your lace, Lord Stafford's ruffles, and four pair of the French leather shoes by [way of] Lady Sarah Bunbury, who will be in England before me.'[75]

Signs of a nascent travel industry that supported the Petit Tour can therefore be discerned: food and accommodation, money exchange, rental of carriages, horses, drivers, postilions, public transport services such as coaches, diligences and luxury barges, guide books, guides, local luxury goods and souvenirs.

The Petit Tour

Travel to Spa could provide a pleasurable six-week Petit Tour for the British traveller as an alternative to the more expensive, extensive and physically demanding Grand Tour. Of the seven diarists, five opted for combining their journey to Spa with a Petit Tour while en route.[76] This Petit Tour typically consisted of culturally touring the wealthy cities of Flanders by using the modern road network of northern Europe, before returning to Britain by way of Paris. According to Black, the Low Countries offered 'the third most important group of places visited by British travellers' after Paris and Italy.[77] The cities of Lille, Ghent, Antwerp, Brussels and Liège were among the jewels of northern Europe, with their art treasures, magnificent churches, colourful religious processions and surprisingly numerous English convents. The diarists took approximately ten to 14 days to travel from Calais to Spa. As this journey was possible in about three days, this left seven to 11 days for cultural sightseeing or socialising with friends en route. The profiles of the diarists indicate that the Petit Tour had attracted very different participants from the Grand Tour. Just under half of the participants in the Petit Tour, from among the diarists and their companions, were either female or children under 18. The high number of women and children participants, and the mixture of invalids and their companions,

138   *Richard Bates*

indicate that travel to Spa was a pleasurable short excursion for all of the family. Importantly, it was an integral part of the healing process. It distracted the invalid from their illness and was particularly useful for combating *l'ennui*. New places, new acquaintances and new experiences revitalised the invalid and entertained their numerous accompanying family and friends.

A guide book of 1777 proposed 'an agreeable Tour of about six weeks' to Spa, arriving via Brussels, staying two weeks at Spa and returning by way of Frankfurt and Reims.[78] This short absence from Britain, compared to the Grand Tour, would have better suited busy men of the period, like businessmen such as Twining, MPs with parliamentary duties, or landowners taking a more active interest in their estates.[79] Women would also have appreciated a shorter and safer tour, which would allow them to take their children with them, as did Mrs Twining, or leave children at home with a guardian while remaining in touch by letter over the relatively short distance, as did Lady Dartrey.[80] The lower cost of the Petit Tour encouraged repeat visits and made it accessible to family groups, rather than just the eldest son. Its main cultural asset was its art, particularly paintings, which would have been more accessible to women whose lack of classical education often meant that they were unfamiliar with the antiquities of Italy.[81] Finally, the majority of Petit Tourists returned via Paris, the fashion capital of Europe, a visit that would almost certainly have appealed to British women.

The Petit Tour of Flanders resembled the Grand Tour in Italy but in miniature, with travellers visiting large, famous cities for cultural education. The sociologist John Urry has defined the character of the Grand Tour as being 'based on the emotionally neutral observation and recording of galleries, museums and high culture artefacts', a definition that fits perfectly the Petit Tour recorded by the diarists.[82] Antwerp was a 'must-see' city for the diarists and Mary Hamilton, the most enthusiastic and knowledgeable of the Petit Tourists, noted that she 'saw no pictures to rival those at Antwerp'.[83] The Rubens masterpiece in Antwerp Cathedral, *The Descent from the Cross*, for example, appears in most diaries and guide books. The well-respected art critic, Roger de Piles (1635–1709), considered Rubens as one of the three greatest painters ever, on a par with Leonardo da Vinci and Michelangelo, whose works were an essential part of the Grand Tour of Italy.[84]

The colour and richness of the impressive churches and cathedrals in the wealthy cities of Flanders, containing ornate altars, jewel encased relics, stained glass windows and paintings by Dutch and Flemish masters, understandably attracted the travellers. As Black suggests, 'Religion, as much as language, food and currency, helped to make the Continent foreign.'[85] Mary Hamilton energetically visited churches to view their interior and, above all, their art. She recorded 27 visits to churches and five visits to convents during her trip.[86] In a single day at Liège, the city known as

The Petit Tour to Spa 139

'the paradise of priests' due to its enormous number of religious establishments, she visited five churches and a convent. In addition, she and her group of travelling companions attended Catholic services. After private Protestant prayers on a Sunday, the group went several times to Catholic services, including a mass at St Omer, vespers at Louvain and sermons at Spa.[87] Religious street processions were looked upon as enjoyable, exciting sightseeing events, a spectacle to be enjoyed rather than a religious event to be contemplated. Jane Hamilton recorded her impressions of a procession at Louvain but 'as it was the first, [I] was too much flurried to observe particularly' although this did not stop her from recording in great detail the participants, their clothing and the decorated figure of the Virgin Mary.[88] The majority of diarists, all Protestant, visited Catholic churches to view their interiors and contents without any thought of their religious significance.

There are a large number of comments on religious encounters in the diaries, but the majority are seemingly indifferent to theological differences between Protestantism and Catholicism. Travel to a Catholic state does not appear to have been criticised at court. For example, Lady Coke recorded a conversation with George III: 'His majesty was very gracious. ... He said "What is your plan, do you go again to the Spa?" My answer was that I was not sure ... He was afterwards very merry, and said if I made haste I might arrive time enough to see one day of the great fête at Ghent.'[89] The fête at Ghent was apparently well known to the English nobility. The manservant, Macdonald, noted that: 'the Duchess of Northumberland was there, and many other English ... The Duchess and my master [John Craufurd, a member of the George Selwyn circle] went to see all the preparations, and all the churches, when ornamented. The beauty of the procession was beyond description.'[90] In her diary Mary Hamilton did not criticise even the more unusual Catholic practices that she encountered. For example, at the English convent of Liège the nuns prayed for the sins of souls in Purgatory, selecting at random sins written on tickets: 'one of the nuns desired me to draw a ticket out of the box, which I complied with. It was for those who had never given alms for the love of God.'[91] Mary Hamilton's diary appears to have been used for drafting letters to her mother and may not reflect her own religious judgements. As Sweet notes, 'there was always the expectation that they would be circulated around family members at least' and it is possible that Mary Hamilton's circle of family and friends included Catholics.[92] The diarists could continue to practise in private their Protestant religion en route and at Spa without hindrance, despite being in Catholic states. Mary Hamilton recorded attending private prayers, each Sunday without fail, with Lord Dartrey's party while travelling and also at Spa. For example, at Aix: 'After breakfast Mr Foster (the young gentlemen's tutor) said prayers very well and gave us a good sermon.'[93] For whatever reasons, all of the diarists bar one were uncritical of their encounters with Catholicism.

140   *Richard Bates*

The visitors were extremely curious concerning the lives of nuns in convents. Visiting convents was very popular, especially the many English Catholic convents to be found in Flanders: six of the seven diarists described their visits to these institutions.[94] As Caroline Bowden and Liesbeth Corens have shown, the English Catholic religious orders that fled in the sixteenth century to the safety of Flanders (the then Spanish Netherlands) created English Catholic convents that still existed in the eighteenth century but were essentially regarded by the diarists as tantamount to 'tourist attractions'. These English convents continued throughout the seventeenth and eighteenth centuries to maintain their 'Englishness', due partly to the active support of rich English families as well as to other factors. The Council of Trent in 1563 required convents to be established in towns for reasons of security, and enclosed for reasons of propriety, which naturally isolated the nuns from outside influences. English convents were additionally isolated from their local communities, as their foundation was only permitted by the local town governments if they were self-financing and not reliant on local funding or begging. As Bowden argues, the convents maintained English language and English Catholic practices in the devout expectation that the nuns would return to England.[95]

Almost all the nuns had come directly from England, and this connection between English titled families and English convents is illustrated by Twining, who wrote: 'I had a letter to a lady in the Convent of the English Augustines [Bruges] … the lady portress … when she found out that I was acquainted with her kinsman, Sir William Jerningham in Norfolk, she seemed to forget the letter I had put in her hands.'[96] During Lady Coke's visits to the Continent she had formed a long-term friendship with a nun at Brussels. On 25 June 1764 she wrote, 'I passed all yesterday evening with my nuns; one of them is the most agreeable woman I ever knew.'[97] The convents accepted visitors as a matter of course, possibly because they sold small handmade goods such as purses in Calais or artificial flowers in Liège, and possibly because they welcomed visits from wealthy fellow countrymen.[98] Neither the nuns nor the visitors discussed religion or questioned whether Protestants could be allowed into a Catholic convent. As Corens argues, the 'English public opinion towards Catholics had quietened considerably' after the 1720s.[99] The diarists' accounts show that by the late eighteenth century the Catholic religion excited more curiosity than fear or repugnance among the British elite travelling to Spa.

The decline of Spa as destination

Even before the 1789 French and Liège revolutions made travel unsafe, Spa's attraction had begun to diminish. By the mid-1780s, Spa's 'business model' was now fundamentally flawed. Its dramatic growth destroyed the fashionable 'small village' image, and the gambling concessions, which

The Petit Tour to Spa 141

generated the funds needed for growth, led to violent disputes over profit shares at the Prince-bishop's court and between concessionaires.[100] The British were embroiled in these disputes through a British gambling club, known as the English Club. Although tolerated by the Prince-bishop, Spa's official casinos rightly saw the Club as a rival for the custom of the British rich, 'deep' gamblers. The Club had been formalised in 1766 under the patronage of George III's brother, the duke of Cumberland. Over the next 20 years it attracted over 500 members, mainly of the British elite.[101] In anonymous letters to the Prince-bishop the casinos attacked the Club and, especially, Count Rice, notorious as a gambler and duellist, who frequented both Spa and Bath.[102] Mary Hamilton described Rice in 1776 as 'a dashing Irishman in the Emperor of Germany's service, he plays well at games and fights duels. He is tall and genteel in his person and address.'[103] In 1778 Rice shot dead a friend and fellow gambler, Vicomte du Barré, in a duel at Bath and was tried but found not guilty of manslaughter.[104] In 1784 the Club, and in particular Rice, entered into a dispute over the authorisation of a third casino. A further dispute over end of the season gambling caused an open conflict with the two authorised casinos and the Prince-bishop. In 1785 Rice was expelled from Spa and went into temporary exile at Aix. A travel guide written in 1785 reported: 'When I arrived at Spa, (although it was the height of the season) it was very thin, owing to a quarrel which subsisted, at that period, between the English and the Liegeois.' The guide continues: 'Aix ... is not, in general, much frequented by the English; this year, however, owing to the aforementioned quarrel at Spa, it was remarkably full of English.'[105] The sharp fall of visitors can be seen therefore as British visitors expressing solidarity and taking advantage of a nearby alternative, Aix.

It is possible that Spa's reputation in Britain had already become tarnished, and this contributed to a decline in visitors.[106] The presence of the rich on holiday attracted an increasing number of imposters, charlatans, crooks, rascals, professional gamblers and cardsharps. A London newspaper wrote in 1783:

> Whoever visits the German Spa at this time, sees an abstract of Europe and the world in miniature. ... Peers and Pimps, hand in hand, Bishops and Beggars, Judges and Jugglers, and women of every denomination, as the chain that holds them together![107]

In 1787 the struggle between vested interests at the Liège court for shares of the gambling profits resulted in the assault by the Prince-bishop's troops of the unauthorised third casino. This was reported in the London press in July 1787, just as the Spa season started: 'A very serious procedure has taken place at the German Spa ... he [the Prince-bishop] sent a party of 50 soldiers into the town, to which number he has since added sixty more, with the accompaniment of two 12-pounders.'[108] Reports of armed conflict

142 *Richard Bates*

at Spa would have deterred British and non-British visitors alike: it was the harbinger of the Liège revolution and the end of the 'golden age of Spa'.

Conclusion

Travel to Spa in the late eighteenth century exemplifies a different type of travel in northern Europe which inextricably mingled health and leisure purposes. The case study shows how health and leisure travel were often part of the same journey and that they cannot therefore be viewed as two distinct types of travel. The British medical profession recommended leisure travel as a distraction for the wealthy sick: the physically undemanding and short, cultural Petit Tour to Spa was exactly 'what the doctor had ordered'. Once at Spa, the sick and their family and friends could all benefit from its internationally famous mineral waters, its healthy and attractive environment in the forests of the Ardennes and its social diversions among an exclusive company. Studying travel to Spa highlights the extent to which travel could involve entire families, men, women and even small children, and allows scholars to look beyond the exclusive demographic of young elite male Grand Tourists. The highly developed *pavé* road system that linked the channel ports to Spa allowed a safe cultural sightseeing tour of the rich and peaceful cities of northern Europe with their fabulous art, fascinating foreign Catholic customs and unfamiliar society. The culture of British travel to Spa and the extent of its popularity was an essential factor in the development of an early leisure and travel industry to support the Petit Tour.

This chapter has begun to outline some of the fruitful research avenues, but there remains potential for further research in numerous directions. For example, the extensive patient case notes held at Spa will be of interest to medical historians. In addition, social historians could usefully look at the reliable detailed lists of the men, women and children that travelled there with or without family and friends. Safe travel with an established support system allowed even single women with children to make the journey. The Petit Tour answered the rising demand of the aspiring British middle classes, including women, for a practical way of participating in foreign leisure travel. Spa was a viable alternative to the Grand Tour undertaken by the rich sons of British aristocrats. The popularity of a visit to Spa is clearly demonstrated by the astonishing numbers of the British elite that travelled there during its 'golden age' between 1763 and 1787, and provides historians with an excellent example of health and leisure tourism in this period.

Notes

1   The period 1763–87 has been selected for this study as it represents the period between the opening of the first public casino and the effective desertion of Spa by the British, following the attack on an unauthorised casino by the Prince bishop and the start of the Liège Revolution. Numbers have been extracted from

The Petit Tour to Spa   143

contemporary printed lists of visitors: Anon., *Liste des seigneurs et dames qui sont venus aux eaux minerales de Spa*, ed. F.J. Desoer (Liège, 1763–87).

2 Between 1763 and 1787 almost 90 per cent of British visitors to Spa arrived in the three high-summer months: June (26 per cent), July (36 per cent) and August (27 per cent). Daniel Roche estimates that between 1772 and 1787 approximately 3,800 foreigners visited Paris annually, of which 25 per cent (950) were British. Daniel Roche, *La ville promise* (Paris, 2000), pp. 236, 238. Spa arrivals for the seasons between 1763 and 1787 averaged 930 visitors, of which 22.5 per cent (210) were British.

3 J. Black, *The British Abroad: The Grand Tour in the Eighteenth Century* (Stroud, 2003), pp. v, 194–6. Brian Dolan's discussion of Spa in *Ladies of the Grand Tour* (London, 2001) is limited to three pages (pp. 129–31).

4 C.D. van Strien, *Touring the Low Countries: Accounts of British Travellers, 1660–1720* (Amsterdam, 1998).

5 Albin Body compiled an extensive bibliography of Spa in 1875: *Bibliographie spadoise et des eaux minérales du pays de Liège* (Verviers, 1981), which has since been updated by Jean Toussaint in *Bibliograhie spadoise, I. 1754–1784. Essai de mise à jour et de correction de la Bibliographie spadoise d'Albin Body* (Liège, 1970). The British Library has published a collection of Body's works. Albin Body, 'Spa, histoire et bibliographie', in *British Library Historical Collection* (London, 2011).

6 The descendants of Dr J.-P. Limbourg (1726–1811) generously gave permission to access the private archives of this outstanding eighteenth-century Spa physician, writer and entrepreneur.

7 Van Strien, *Touring the Low Countries*; G. Verhoeven, 'Transport innovations and the rise of short-term pleasure trips in the Low Countries, 1600–1750', *Journal of Transport History*, 30:1 (2009), pp. 78–97.

8 Société wallonne d'étude du dix-huitième siècle asbl (Swedhs). http://www.swedhs.org

9 P. Thicknesse, *A Year's Journey through the Pais Bas; or, Austrian Netherlands*, 2nd edn (London, 1786), p. 111.

10 L. Chambers, 'Les confessions au carrefour', in D. Droixhe, ed., *Spa, carrefour de l'Europe des lumières* (Paris, 2013), pp. 35–66.

11 Roche, *La ville promise*, pp. 241, 254.

12 Lists 1763–87. Because 73 per cent of the entries in the published lists simply record 'Gentleman' or 'Lady' it was not possible to complete further analysis of the less illustrious visitors who represented a majority.

13 Limbourg, *Case Notes*.

14 Ibid., 1784, p. 38.

15 Ibid., 1771, p. 6: 1772, p. 18: 1780, p. 3.

16 T. Twining, *Selections from Papers of the Twining Family* (London, 1887); T.A.B. Corley, 'Twining, Richard (1749–1824)', *Oxford Dictionary of National Biography* (*ODNB*) (Oxford, 2009), http://www.oxforddnb.com/view/article/27908 [accessed 21 March 2014].

17 H. Townsend, 'Recollections of a trip to Spa', *Blackwood's Edinburgh Magazine* (1827), pp. 281–300; E. Baigent, 'Townsend, Horace (1750–1837)', *ODNB*.

18 J. Hamilton, 'Jane Hamilton, Tour of France and Germany, 1772', National Library of Ireland, MS 1706, typescript; C.J. Woods, 'Archibald Hamilton Rowan (1751–1834)', in *Dictionary of Irish Biography* (Cambridge, 2014).

19 K. Turner, 'Macdonald, John (*b.*1741)', *ODNB*; J. Macdonald, *Travels in Various Parts of Europe, Asia, and Africa* (Dublin, 1791).

20 E. Haden-Guest, 'Craufard, John (?1742–1814), of Errol', http://www.historyofparliamentonline.org/volume/1754-1790/member/craufurd-john-1742-1814 [accessed 10 March 2014].

144   *Richard Bates*

21 S. Weston, *Two Sketches of France, Belgium, and Spa* (London, 1817); A. Sherbo, 'Weston, Stephen (1747–1830)', *ODNB*.
22 J. Ingamells, *A Dictionary of British and Irish Travellers in Italy 1701–1800* (New Haven and London, 1997), p. 47.
23 J. Rubinstein, 'Coke, Lady Mary (1727–1811)', *ODNB*; J. Home, ed., *The Letters and Journals of Lady Mary Coke* (Bath, 1970).
24 A. Baker, 'Hamilton, Mary (1756–1816)', *ODNB*; M. Hamilton, 'Diary of trip to Spa', John Rylands Library, University of Manchester, HAM/2/1, 2011.
25 M. Hamilton, 'Diary of trip to Spa', 30 Jul. 1776.
26 Limbourg, *Case Notes*, 4 Sept. 1772. Twining, *Selections from Papers of the Twining Family*, p. 8; M. Hamilton, 'Diary of trip to Spa', 30 Jul. 1776.
27 Townsend, 'Recollections of a trip to Spa', p. 281; J. Hamilton, 'Tour of France and Germany, 1772', 22 Jul. 1772; Macdonald, *Travels*, p. 90; M. Hamilton, 'Diary of trip to Spa', 10 Sep.1776: with reference to the waters of the Géronstrère source, Mary Hamilton noted that 'it is the water of this fountain that she [Lady Dartrey] is prescribed to drink'. As the diary does not note any visit to a local doctor in Aix or Spa it has been presumed that an English doctor prescribed the treatment.
28 P.M. Hembry, *The English Spa 1560–1815* (London, 1990), pp. 8–10.
29 L.M. Crismer, *La fabuleuse histoire des eaux de Spa* (Spa, 1983), p. 8.
30 Ibid., p. 31.
31 *St James Chronicle*, 11 Feb. 1775.
32 *Gazetteer and New Daily Advertiser*, 13 Feb. 1781.
33 P. Thicknesse, *The New Prose Bath Guide* (London, 1778), p. 97.
34 K.L. Pöllnitz, *Les amusemens de Spa: or the Gallantries of the Spaw in Germany*, 2nd edn (London, 1737); Pöllnitz, *The Amusements of Aix La Chapelle* (London, 1748).
35 William Coleman, 'Health and hygiene in the *Encylopédie*', *Journal of the History of Medicine and Allied Sciences*, 29:4 (1974), pp. 399–421; A. Emch-Dériaz, 'The non-naturals made easy', in Roy Porter, ed., *The Popularization of Medicine, 1650–1850* (London, 1992), pp. 134–59.
36 É. Hélin, 'Aux origines du tourisme contemporain: les amusements de Spa', in R. Boterberge, ed., *Histoire d'eaux: stations thermales et balnéaires en Belgique* (Brussels, 1987), p. 83.
37 M. Hamilton, 'Diary of trip to Spa', 25–26 Sep. 1776.
38 Twining, *Selections from Papers of the Twining Family*, p. 35.
39 The British were by far the most numerous in providing money for walks and other public facilities. Of 22 persons who had subscribed in 1766, 19 were British: Lists 1766, pp. 3–4.
40 Thicknesse, *The New Prose Bath Guide*, p.105.
41 Estimates of Bath visitor numbers are few and far between and are probably unreliable. According to one estimate there were 8,000 visitors at Bath in 1791 compared to Spa's 1,241 in the peak year of 1780. E. Clarke, *A Tour through the South of England* (London, 1793), p. 141.
42 Lists 1767, p. 10; R. Fulford, *Royal Dukes* (London, 1973), p. 163.
43 Coke, *Letters and Journals of Lady Mary Coke*, p. 68.
44 Thicknesse, *A Year's Journey through the Pais Bas*, p.104, footnote.
45 Hembry, *The English Spa*, p. 136.
46 J. Hamilton, 'Tour of France and Germany', 3 Aug. 1772.
47 Townsend, *Recollections of a Trip to Spa*, pp. 292–3.
48 J. Trusler, *The Habitable World Described* (London, 1788), p. 144.
49 Twining, *Selections from Papers of the Twining Family*, p. 28.

The Petit Tour to Spa 145

50 L. Marquet, *À l'âge d'or de Spa* (Verviers, 1985), p. 80; Hembry, *The English Spa*, p. 125.

51 See, for example, Anon., *A Tour to Spa through the Austrian Netherlands and the French Flanders* (London, 1777).

52 Calais to Liège was approximately 180 miles, or about 30 posts. Lady Coke managed 17 posts in a day, travelling between Paris and Calais in a breakneck journey to return to London on the death of a friend. Coke, *Letters and Journals of Lady Mary Coke*, pp. 56, 122.

53 M. Hamilton, 'Diary of trip to Spa', 15 Aug. 1776. The paved road network of Brabant had been started in 1704 and by 1780 extended to all the most important towns. B. Blondé, 'At the cradle of the transport revolution? Paved roads, traffic flows and economic development in eighteenth-century Brabant', *Journal of Transport History*, 31:1 (2010), p. 90.

54 Thicknesse, *A Year's Journey through the Pais Bas*, p. 29.

55 Coke, *Letters and Journals of Lady Mary Coke*, pp. 60, 72.

56 Ibid., p. 50.

57 Twining, *Selections from Papers of the Twining Family*, p. 22.

58 Verhoeven, 'Transport innovations and the rise of short-term pleasure trips', p. 81.

59 Coke, *Letters and Journals of Lady Mary Coke*, p. 58.

60 Ibid., p. 59.

61 Ibid., p. 58.

62 A. Foreman, *Georgiana, Duchess of Devonshire* (London, 1999), p. 11.

63 Their return trip from Rome started approximately 11 June 1764 and their arrival at Spa was approximately 12 July 1764. Ingamells, *Dictionary of British and Irish Travellers*, p. 883.

64 *General Advertiser*, 10 Nov. 1785.

65 M. Hamilton, 'Diary of trip to Spa', 2 Aug. 1776.

66 Thicknesse, *A Year's Journey through the Pais Bas*, p. 8.

67 Anon., *A Tour to Spa*.

68 Ibid., p. 17.

69 M. Hamilton, 'Diary of trip to Spa', 8 Aug. 1776.

70 Weston, *Two Sketches of France, Belgium, and Spa*, p. 11.

71 Anon., *A Tour to Spa*, p. 5; Verhoeven, 'Transport innovations and the rise of short-term pleasure trips', p.79.

72 M. Hamilton, 'Diary of trip to Spa', 1 Aug. 1776.

73 Coke, *Letters and Journals of Lady Mary Coke*, p. 50.

74 Thicknesse, *A Year's Journey through the Pais Bas*, p. 8.

75 Coke, *Letters and Journals of Lady Mary Coke*, p. 62.

76 These were Thomas Twining, Horace Townsend, Mary Hamilton, Jane Hamilton, Stephen Weston.

77 Black, *The British Abroad*, p. 51.

78 Anon., *A Tour to Spa*, p. 113.

79 Katherine Turner notes: 'Not so much the "Grand Tour" as a variety of shorter, humbler tours offered themselves to the leisured middle classes, for whom the consumption of culture abroad as well as at home was becoming increasingly fashionable.' K. Turner, *British Travel Writers in Europe, 1750–1800: Authorship, Gender and National Identity* (Aldershot, 2001), p. 3.

80 M. Hamilton, 'Diary of trip to Spa', 29 Aug. 1776. Mrs Twining was travelling with only her eldest daughter, Mary aged 11: Twining, *Selections from Papers of the Twining Family*, p.8, footnote.

81 R. Sweet, *Cities and the Grand Tour: The British in Italy, c.1690–1820* (Cambridge, 2012), p. 51.

146 *Richard Bates*

82 J. Urry, *The Tourist Gaze* (London, 2002), p. 4.
83 M. Hamilton, 'Diary of trip to Spa', 12 Aug. 1776.
84 R. de Piles, *The Art of Painting, and the Lives of the Painters* (London, 1706), dedication.
85 Black, *The British Abroad*, p. 273.
86 M. Hamilton, 'Diary of trip to Spa', 12 Oct. 1776.
87 Hamilton attended private Protestant prayer meetings each Sunday during her 12-week stay on the Continent.
88 J. Hamilton, 'Tour of France and Germany', 3 Oct. 1772.
89 Coke, *Letters and Journals of Lady Mary Coke*, p. 23.
90 Macdonald, *Travels*, p. 91.
91 M. Hamilton, 'Diary of trip to Spa', 12 Oct. 1776.
92 Sweet, *Cities and the Grand Tour*, p. 19.
93 M. Hamilton, 'Diary of trip to Spa', 18 Aug. 1776.
94 There were 21 English convents along the routes from the channel ports to Spa: Aire, Alost, Antwerp, Bruges (2), Brussels (2), Cambrai, Dunkirk (2), Ghent, Gravelines, Liège (2), Lierre, Louvain, Nieuport, Saint Omer, Termonde, Vilvorde, Ypres. P. Guilday, *The English Catholic Refugees on the Continent 1558–1795* (London, 1914), p. 40.
95 L. Corens, 'Catholic nuns and English identities. English Protestant travellers on the English convents in the Low Countries, 1660–1730', *Recusant History*, 30:3 (2011), pp. 441–59; C. Bowden, 'The English convents in exile and questions of national identity *c.*1600–1688', in D. Worthington, ed., *British and Irish Emigrants and Exiles in Europe, 1603–1688* (Leiden, 2010), pp. 297–314.
96 Twining, *Selections from Papers of the Twining Family*, pp. 14–15; Bowden, *English Convents in Exile*, p. 310.
97 Coke, *Letters and Journals of Lady Mary Coke*, p. 8.
98 M. Hamilton, 'Diary of trip to Spa', 12 Oct. 1776.; J. Hamilton, 'Tour of France and Germany', 1 Oct.1772.
99 Corens, 'Catholic nuns and English identities', p. 442.
100 P. Bertholet, *Les jeux de hasard à Spa au XVIII siècle* (Dison, 1988), pp. 182–98.
101 Body, 'Le club anglais de Spa', pp. 299, 321.
102 Ibid., pp. 321, 333.
103 M. Hamilton, 'Diary of trip to Spa', 30 Sep. 1776.
104 D. Murphy, 'Rice, James Louis (1730–*p.*1793)', in *Dictionary of Irish Biography* (2014).
105 An English gentleman, *An Entertaining Tour* (London, 1791), pp. 124, 134.
106 R. Bates, 'Spa and the "Petit Tour": British visitors to Spa, 1763 – 1787', University of Leicester MRes dissertation (2014), pp. 86–9.
107 *Morning Herald and Daily Advertiser*, 7 Aug. 1783.
108 *Whitehall Evening Post*, 5 Jul. 1787.

8 Amsterdam as global market and meeting place of nations

Perspectives of seventeenth- and eighteenth-century French travellers in Holland

Madeleine van Strien-Chardonneau

The purpose of this chapter is to analyse how Amsterdam, the 'Venice of the north', competed in the minds of the French with its sister city in the south during the *ancien régime*. The analysis will be based on a large corpus of travel narratives, alongside published travel guides and writings frequently consulted by travellers at the time. This chapter will, first, briefly review the increasing popularity of the 'trip to Holland' and its connection to Franco-Dutch relations from the late sixteenth century – the birthdate of the Dutch Republic – to the early nineteenth century. It will then focus on the eighteenth century, where the early signs of what would become the more 'leisurely' trips of the nineteenth century can be observed. Finally, the chapter will offer a close textual 'reading' of the French traveller's perception of Amsterdam, exploring the accounts, impressions and itineraries in surviving travel narratives to uncover the reasons behind Amsterdam's popularity.[1]

The French in Holland

Since the Renaissance, Italy held an undeniable appeal to northern European travellers, including the French. This was still the case at the end of the eighteenth century, as is evident in the comment of Cardinal de Bernis, French chargé d'affaires from 1769–91, that the French embassy in Rome was 'the French inn at Europe's crossroads'.[2] Nevertheless, the Republic of the Seven United Provinces, from its birth at the end of the sixteenth century to the end of the nineteenth century, was also a popular destination for the French, for a number of political, economic, religious and intellectual reasons.[3]

Unlike British travellers, who typically viewed the United Provinces as the first stopover of their Grand Tour to Italy, the French often travelled through the southern Low Countries and considered the Republic their final destination.[4] Throughout the seventeenth century, Holland increasingly outgrew its role as a stop on the Grand Tour itinerary and became a fully fledged destination in its own right.[5] This was not to the exclusion of other

148   *Madeleine van Strien-Chardonneau*

places, as the French also travelled to Italy, England, Germany and Switzerland. It is also noticeable that journeys completed in the seventeenth century took place over two to three consecutive years; in the eighteenth century one person might undertake a number of separate journeys, but these were less often a part of a single European Grand Tour.[6]

The 'Dutch miracle', admired by the Duke of Rohan in 1600, attracted French travellers well before the influx of Huguenot refugees during the revocation of the Edict of Nantes (1685).[7] The Franco-Dutch alliance in the first half of the seventeenth century facilitated and encouraged travel: French soldiers entered the service of the States General and Prince Maurice of Nassau, such as Descartes (1618–19), who would later return in search of a place that would permit him to engage in his scholarly work (1628–48). Economists eager to unravel the secrets of the Dutch miracle, diplomats, professors and students who were attracted to the innovative teaching methods at the University of Leiden (founded in 1575), were also attracted to Holland.[8]

Louis XIV's anti-Dutch and anti-Protestant politics cooled relations between the two countries and brought many French Huguenots to Holland in 1685. After the Treaty of Utrecht (1713), which brought back peace to Europe, and the death of Louis XIV (1715), travel resumed and continued throughout the eighteenth century. Once again, there were diplomats, priests, scholars, military personnel and refugees seeking sanctuary for religious as well as for rather more mundane reasons. Student numbers, however, declined significantly, as did the number of refugees.[9] As Paul Hazard noted, 'the tragic image of the refugee tends to fade; there are no outcasts; there are cosmopolitan people instead'.[10] At the beginning of the eighteenth-century the growing popularity of Dutch and Flemish painting also brought art lovers, eager to visit the rooms of private collectors.[11] Furthermore, 'mundane' journeys had become more widely accepted by the second half of the eighteenth century,[12] as some French travellers, like the British (as discussed by Bates in this volume), would combine a trip to Holland with a visit to Spa, which was enjoying increasing popularity due to its thermal waters and its gambling tables.[13]

At the end of the century, *émigrés* – forced to travel because of the revolutionary turmoil – hit the road, and large numbers of French people found sanctuary in the United Provinces, only to have to flee again when the French revolutionary armies invaded in 1795. The so-called Batavo-French period, from 1795–1813, while failing to promote what the two peoples had in common, did not hinder travel. In the nineteenth century, the Napoleonic wars contributed to the development of a national, and also a European, awareness, and this expansion of known horizons developed a passion for travel among the young French of the Restoration period.[14] The nineteenth century is also considered as the century in which modern tourism was born.[15] The development of new means of transportation – steamboat and train – facilitated longer journeys, and in that sense France

Amsterdam as global market   149

and Holland drew closer to each other. For the French, Holland continued to appeal. The rediscovery of the art of the 'golden age', popularised by the Louvre's exhibition of Stadtholder William V's collection (confiscated in 1795) attracted numerous visitors.[16]

Journeys for pleasure in the eighteenth century

As Gerrit Verhoeven has demonstrated in his analysis of Dutch travellers, there was a steady increase in relatively short pleasure trips during the eighteenth century.[17] These were quite different from the traditional, long Grand Tour that had been popular among the younger members of the elites since the sixteenth century. These leisurely trips were much shorter and closer to home, and were usually undertaken by older people of both sexes from more diverse backgrounds. The same characteristics can be seen in the travellers that are the focus of this study.[18] Although this phenomenon cannot be labelled 'tourism' in the sense that the term would acquire in the nineteenth century when a true 'industry' developed, the reasons for these trips – pleasure, rather than a specific purpose, with an emphasis on entertainment (gambling, theatre, opera), culture (art collections) and nature (seaside, gardens, picturesque landscapes) – anticipated the next century.

Of course, although the specific purpose was different, travel had been undertaken for pleasure long before the eighteenth century.[19] Yet, even if the weight of the 'educational' dimension – one must learn something while travelling – was still apparent in the eighteenth-century narratives, the trip made purely for leisure particularly benefited from Europe's peaceful atmosphere following the end of the Seven Years' War (1763), and from improved logistics. In France, for example, the renovation of the network of roads from 1738, and the invention of the diligence in the 1760s, facilitated travel significantly.[20]

In the United Provinces, the network of canals and other waterways, which had developed since the early seventeenth century, provided a regular, comfortable and economical system of transportation. From 1665, the most important towns in the province of Holland – Dordrecht, Rotterdam, The Hague, Leiden, Haarlem and Amsterdam – were part of this network and were served by horse-drawn barges on a regular, reliable and frequent basis.[21] Fares and timetables were listed in the travel guides, which eliminated unpleasant bargaining with contractors.[22] This means of transportation was by far the most popular because hiring a coach, which some people opted for in order to avoid the company of unfamiliar persons, was burdensome and uncomfortable on the bumpy roads. People who were in a hurry could, however, use the services of the stage coach; the one between Amsterdam and The Hague was known for its speed but was expensive.[23] In the southern Low Countries, which were part of the itinerary chosen by most travellers, a network of roads linking Antwerp, Brussels, Leuven and

150 *Madeleine van Strien-Chardonneau*

Mechelen had been developing since the late seventeenth century.[24] The stage coach from Antwerp to Rotterdam, introduced in the middle of the eighteenth century, provided, if not comfortable, reasonably swift transportation.[25]

These practical details stimulated travel. And whereas numerous travellers emphasised the difficulty of entering the Republic, they were more enthusiastic about the well-organised transportation within the country.[26] Nobody stated specifically that these facilities prompted him or her to select the trip to Holland, but the accessibility, by boat, of this province's towns definitely contributed to the strengthening image of 'the beautiful trip to Holland that everyone takes, that is, the trip to its beautiful towns'.[27] The United Provinces, geographically rather close to France but in many ways a 'peculiar' region – one of Europe's rare republics – did, indeed, arouse curiosity, especially for the enlightened minds who were in search of a better government.[28]

Amsterdam's fame

The United Provinces' towns took great care of their public image. In the early seventeenth century, descriptions of towns, often embellished with illustrations, maps, views from a distance and images of public buildings, were already in circulation.[29] These descriptions led to more practical publications, guides that borrowed a certain amount of information from them while adding practical details regarding itineraries, inns and timetables and fares of the horse-drawn barges. In the eighteenth century, especially after 1750, we find numerous publications of engravings that illustrated the special attractions of each town.[30] There were several for Amsterdam that had Dutch-French titles and captions such as: *103 afbeeldingen van de wijd-vermaarde koopstad Amsterdam: alle naar het leeven getekend – Recueil des édifices d'Amsterdam dessinés d'après nature* (1775), by Petrus Fouquet (1729–1800). Some works were devoted exclusively to Amsterdam's city hall, the most impressive building in the city.[31]

Of course, Amsterdam was also mentioned in the guides that covered the entire Republic, as well as in those describing the northern and southern provinces. Some writers, such as Pierre-Jean Grosley (1718–1785), who travelled in 1772, still referred to Latin works, but French texts prevailed.[32] And the towns boasted their own individual guides. For example, the *Guide d'Amsterdam* or *Guide ou nouvelle description d'Amsterdam* went through a large number of editions.[33]

Two publications played a particularly important role in developing Amsterdam's image because of their editorial success and their longevity. Pierre Leffen published the *Délices de la Hollande* by Jean Nicolas (de) Parival in 1651 and the work saw 14 editions between 1651 and 1728.[34] In his *Délices*, Parival followed the tradition of chorography – that is, the geographical and historical description of a country, a region, or a town,

Amsterdam as global market   151

during which he referred twice to a description by Marcus Zuerius Boxhorn, *Le Théâtre des villes d'Hollande* or *Theatrum sive Hollandiae comitatus et urbium nova descriptio* (1632).[35] Parival's work, much less scholarly and more accessible, helped shape the image of Holland and, more specifically, its towns for several generations of travellers.

Wishing to pay tribute to the city that had welcomed him, Parival started his description of Holland's towns with Leiden, 'which he loves and respects profoundly, as though it were a mother who had nurtured him',[36] and put Amsterdam in second place: 'Holland's most famous cities and best known in all of Europe are Leiden and Amsterdam.'[37] But even though he devoted only 14 pages to Amsterdam (compared to 26 on Leiden), he began his description by enthusiastically singing that city's praise:

> We are going to see this powerful city from which Neptune takes his orders and which is now in control of his empire: yes, it might even rob his brother of his very own estates if the air were as favourable to ships as salt water is. This city, which has no equal anywhere in the habitable world, if we consider its commercial activity, the convenience of its port, its power and its ability to equip very large fleets.[38]

Les Délices des Pays-Bas, first published in 1697 by Jean-Baptiste Cristyn, brought together descriptions of the United Provinces and of the Southern Netherlands.[39] As travellers often crossed the Spanish (and later on the Austrian) Netherlands before reaching Holland, this work was consulted relatively frequently. Information on Holland is more concise than in Parival's, yet the image sketched is quite flattering, especially with regard to Amsterdam.[40] As in Parival, the city's maritime and commercial power was emphasised, with a particular emphasis upon the port's activity and its international scale. In the overall presentation of Cristyn's guide, which focuses on a very large number of churches and monasteries, the special character of Amsterdam as *Le magasin de l'univers* (the global store) was all the more evident.

Amsterdam's attractions

Well prepared by what they may have read, travellers, once they were on the Republic's soil, easily reached Amsterdam by stage coach or barge. Some of them had acquaintances or brought letters of recommendation, but most stayed at inns. Amsterdam offered quite a few: between 1748 and 1795, our travellers mention 13 in total.[41] The Aux Armes d'Amsterdam, on the Kloveniersburgwal, was managed by a Frenchman – a certain Thibault, 'a very good fellow' – and received the highest honours.[42] Inns provided a 'valet service', interpreters or guides for those visiting the city; however, as Jean-Marie Roland de la Platière put it, they were not very popular.[43] Instead, people preferred to rely on friends or other connections.

152 *Madeleine van Strien-Chardonneau*

However, not everyone had such connections and, even if one did, these connections were not necessarily willing to devote their time to foreign guests.[44] Thus, it was difficult to avoid professional guides, especially if one did not speak Dutch. Only travellers with a sense of independence tried to obtain maps and precise descriptions, and to venture into town on their own.[45]

If visitors did not have personal contacts in Amsterdam, this did mean that they had fewer resources with which to entertain themselves. Public walks, such as the Plantage, were not spectacular and in the inns the air was polluted because of heavy pipe smoking. There was also the theatre, which was very popular in France; travellers were eager to go, but deplored the mediocrity of both the venues and the Dutch repertory. However, they did attend performances regularly, either in Amsterdam's theatre on the Keizersgracht or in the French theatre located outside the city walls. Programmes began at four or five o'clock in the afternoon and were over between nine and ten. To end the evening in a city where, thanks to night watchmen, it was safe to walk when it was dark, visitors might go to one of the many 'musicos'.[46] These venues were established in Amsterdam from the mid-seventeenth century. The local population would go to dance and drink, as would prostitutes looking for customers. A visit to these musicos became, with most honourable intentions, part of the traditional programme for tourists in Amsterdam. Even if the surviving descriptions do not necessarily assert that these places formed Amsterdam's principal attraction, they were nevertheless considered to be an undeniable (though disappointing) 'speciality', as is evident in a letter addressed to Pierre-Jean Grosley, which contained practical information for his trip: 'In Amsterdam, go visit [...] the city hall, its clock [...] the stock exchange at one o'clock, the Jewish neighbourhood on Friday at six in the evening, and the musico on Saturday evening around eleven.'[47]

During the day, there was the opportunity to go shopping, but only a handful of travellers mentioned this in their diaries. 'There is an abundance of new temptations, all the time,' wrote the Duc de Croy, who spent large sums of money on English prints, sampled some melons and coconuts, and bought a good supply of tobacco and of green tea.[48] People also brought back from Amsterdam various kinds of fabric, such as indiennes and mousselines, as well as porcelain trinkets from the Indies, which were very popular in France during the 1760s. Beautiful linens for the home, textiles and fine Dutch pottery were greatly valued as well. For book lovers, too, Amsterdam was of interest. Even towards the end of the century, when the United Provinces had become less important in this respect, in Amsterdam 'one still finds some of those beautiful works that, in the past, could be found all over Holland'.[49]

Amsterdam's entertainment remained rather limited, though, and was in no way comparable to that offered by London, Brussels, or even The Hague, where the diplomatic world added a certain style to the city's everyday life.[50] In fact, it was the city of Amsterdam itself, with its port, its cosmopolitan population, its public monuments, its canals and its extraordinarily lively atmosphere, that provided the most beautiful spectacle.

Amsterdam's modernity

As they discovered Amsterdam's architectural ensemble, ranging from the city hall, the stock exchange, patrician houses, places of worship and charitable institutions to the offices of the East and West India Companies, visitors 'read' the political organisation, social structure, tolerance and affluence of the city and, by extension, of the entire country.

The city's commercial, financial and maritime power, which already was seen as a feature of modernity in the seventeenth century, was still impressive, despite a certain decline, and continued to be embodied in the stock exchange and the port. In the words of the abbé de Saint-Pierre (1712),

> Amsterdam is the largest global marketplace, where one finds in abundance all the conveniences of life and one constantly gets news from all over the world, all the most desirable objects, for senators as well as princes whose business is quite diverse.[51]

French travellers frequently branded Amsterdam as *magasin, marché, l'entrepôt de l'Europe et même de l'univers* (the warehouse or the market of Europe or even the universe); it was considered to be the third European metropolis after London and Paris. They frequently overestimated the number of inhabitants, but however imprecise these numbers might have been, they very accurately reflect their impression that Amsterdam's affluence and activity exceeded what might be observed in other Dutch and European towns.[52]

During their wanderings in the city, they saw the stock exchange and the port as two key places. Amsterdam occupied a central place on the European capital market and its role as financial capital was embodied in the stock exchange, 'the circus where various games of fortune are combined'.[53] Built in 1608–11 by Hendrik de Keyser (1565–1621), the building attracted little attention in the eighteenth century for its architecture, but the enormous activity and variety of people were fascinating. Pierre Famin, a merchant who visited around one o'clock in the afternoon, when activity was reaching its peak, noted in his diary:

> I was there one day when the stock exchange was open. I went up to the window in a gallery and from there, at a glance, I saw 4,000 heads move. The sound and movement imitate the ebb and flow of the sea.[54]

154   *Madeleine van Strien-Chardonneau*

For Bernardin de Saint-Pierre, the power of the entire country was reflected in the pillars around the interior court of the stock exchange:

> It is a large square, surrounded by a row of pillars. Each of them is the commercial centre of some part of the world and bears the name of Suriname, London, Archangel, Bordeaux, etc. Those truly are the pillars of the Republic, which relies for its business on the most important cities in the world.[55]

A visit to the port, 'one of the largest, safest and busiest in the world', constituted another highlight.[56] From the top of city hall's tower one had a bird's-eye view and from the Nieuwe Brug, which spanned the Damrak, a beautiful glimpse of the port. Although mindful of Holland's decline as a maritime power, people remained impressed by the number of ships in the port and by the enormous amount of activity. The Admiralty, the Arsenal and, especially, the buildings of the Dutch East India Company, whose warehouses were filled with porcelain and spices which brought back the colours and aromas of the Far East, had great appeal for visitors. Visitors could take leisurely walks near the port and they liked to return there regularly. Pierre-Claude de Poterat, for example, could not get enough of watching 'the prodigious activity everywhere, the loading and unloading of large numbers of vessels of all sizes, that leave and arrive from all corners of the world'.[57]

The city's modernity was also visible in its layout, which visitors could see from the top of the city hall. They admired its originality, especially in the new neighbourhoods with the three concentric canals, the Prinsengracht, Keizersgracht and Herengracht. These enclosed the old centre and were connected to each other by a network of small streets and narrow canals: in the meshes of this network the long and narrow apartment blocks reminded visitors of an open fan. The city hall, designed by Jacob van Campen, was located right in the middle of town. The first stone had been laid in 1648 and construction was finished at a time when Amsterdam was reaching the peak of its prosperity. Called the eighth wonder of the world by Constantijn Huygens, it retained its prestige and popularity in the eyes of eighteenth-century visitors: they admired the large Burgerzaal (burghers' hall) with its imposing dimensions and its sumptuous decorations, which were unusual in the United Provinces.[58] Consulting the *Description de l'Hôtel de Ville d'Amsterdam*, visitors tried to decipher the political message found in the group of statues, the paintings and the inscriptions that decorated the building. Because of its multiple functions as headquarters of the city's civil, judiciary and financial divisions, it not only represented the municipal government's power, but also, for our travellers, the Republic's power. The seven entrances on the principal façade – some observers would have preferred one monumental entrance instead – were sometimes interpreted as the symbolic representation of the seven provinces and, because of the presence of a bank and a prison, the building was considered to serve both as the repository of wealth and as the protector of social order.

This social order rested, among other things, on two important pillars: the decision to look after weak or dangerous people who might threaten society's cohesion and the emphasis on tolerance, which allowed the co-existence of different religious groups. As they walked through the city, visitors became aware of this through the many attractive-looking charitable institutions (hospitals, hospices, orphanages) and penitentiaries, such as Amsterdam's new workhouse (Werkhuys), built in 1785 and so beautiful 'that one might think it was the home of a prince'.[59] Two visitors from Valenciennes expressed similar surprise when, in 1789, they noted in their diary:

> Maintained in a way that we never see in such places in our country, these facilities, just seen from outside, even look somewhat sumptuous and so well-kept that a stranger would take these charitable institutions for large hotels or think that they were public monuments of a very different kind.[60]

And indeed, especially in the eighteenth century, majestic buildings were erected, which the municipal authorities proudly showed to foreigners. The sight of them strengthened the image of a well-ordered society that made its vagrants and beggars do useful work in special facilities and that provided decent accommodation for the elderly and for orphans. As for the numerous places of worship – Calvinist, Lutheran, Anabaptist, Armenian and Moravian, as well as the four synagogues, that formed a unique ensemble in Europe because they stood out so prominently – they clearly illustrated in this urban landscape the notion of religious tolerance, which was the Republic's distinctive mark and the envy of many (the Catholic church, which was not allowed a public space, was excepted). While the abbé de Saint-Pierre stated that this religious tolerance was 'excessive', he also emphasised that it attracted all those persecuted people who were 'constrained elsewhere' and who then found 'the country with the greatest freedom'; they brought with them 'their merchandise, their money and their business'. Religious freedom was an economic boon.[61]

Because of its liveliness, its cosmopolitan character, its enormous commercial and financial activity and its infrastructure, Amsterdam was, from the seventeenth century, seen as a highly modern place. For the enlightened minds of the eighteenth century searching for a better society, the various places of worship and the social institutions also constituted marks of modernity. In the beautiful layout of the city some, like the Marquis de Goyon, discerned 'the beautiful painting of the equality, wealth and advantage that a republican state provides'.[62]

156 *Madeleine van Strien-Chardonneau*
Conclusion

In the nineteenth century, Amsterdam remained a popular destination but its image had changed. The port continued to fascinate people but 'its ships loaded with riches and filled with products from the Far East'[63] made people mostly dream of exotic faraway places.[64] The French travellers of the Romantic period did not know how to deal with their own fast-modernising society and set out to look for the past, hoping to find in Holland localities that had not yet been contaminated by the industrial revolution.[65] The city's modern character no longer appealed. Instead travellers were attracted to the quaintness of old neighbourhoods.[66] Seen through the prism of the Dutch 'golden age', the city was perceived as a series of paintings that restored its glorious past.[67] In that sense, the 'Venice of the north' competed still with the 'old queen of the Adriatic'.[68]

The strong artistic element in the representation of nineteenth-century Amsterdam is reminiscent of the image of Italy that emerges from earlier guides and travel narratives. Thus, in making a comparison with Venice, Parival referred to the affinities between the two maritime and merchant republics, but sought to emphasise the growing supremacy of the Dutch, who had made 'their reputation well-known and glorious across the entire world', as opposed to the empire of Venice, which was 'limited to the south and to Italy'.[69] During the seventeenth century, new relationships developed between northern and southern Europe, not only on the political and economic, but also on the cultural and intellectual level. 'It is from the north that the enlightenment is coming to us': paraphrasing Voltaire's words in a letter to the Empress Catherine II of Russia, Paul Hazard was also referring to the English and Dutch scholars who promoted the crisis in Europe's conscience between 1680 and 1715.[70] If eighteenth-century Italy delighted French travellers with its grandiose landscapes, its ancient and modern monuments and its artistic riches, this grandeur was often relegated to a cultural and artistic past that was cut off from the present. For the many travellers looking for a new kind of society, a bourgeois republic – exemplified by Amsterdam, where rationalism, pragmatism, virtue, business and enterprise prevailed – was favoured.[71]

Acknowledgments

Translation by Margriet Lacy-Bruijn.

Notes

1 The 'trip to Holland' was certainly popular not only among the French; numerous foreigners visited the United Provinces. Studies of travellers from Great Britain and Germany have pointed out Amsterdam's appeal: thus, according to William Lord Fitzwilliam (1663), 'Amsterdam is one of the most

Amsterdam as global market   157

famous cities of the world': K. van Strien, *Touring the Low Countries: Accounts of British Travellers, 1660–1720* (Amsterdam, 1998), p. 2), and according to Johann Herman Diehelm (1744), 'Die Perle aller Städte in der Welt' [the pearl of all cities in the world] cited in A. Chales de Beaulieu, *Deutsche Reisende in den Niederlanden. Das Bild eines Nachbarn zwischen 1648 und 1795* (Frankfurt am Main, 2000), p. 77. And, of course, there were visitors from other countries as well who came to Amsterdam (J.N. Jacobsen, *Reizigers te Amsterdam* (Amsterdam, 1919, Supplement, 1936)).

2 H. Harder, *Le Président De Brosses et le voyage en Italie au dix-huitième siècle* (Geneva, 1981), p. 158.

3 The Union of Utrecht, concluded in 1579 by the northern provinces of the Netherlands that had been in revolt against Spain, was, in a sense, the birth certificate of the new state.

4 R. Sweet, *Cities and the Grand Tour: The British in Italy, c.1690–1820* (Cambridge, 2012), p. 2.

5 G. Bertrand, *Bibliographie des études sur le voyage en Italie: voyage en Italie, voyage en Europe, XVIe–XXe siècles, Les Cahiers du CRHIPA*, 2 (2000).

6 See, for example, in the case of Dutch travellers, R. Linderman, Y. Scherf and R. Dekker, *Reisverslagen van Noord-Nederlanders, uit de zestiende tot begin negentiende eeuw* (Rotterdam, 1994), and R. Dekker, 'Nederlandse reisverslagen van de 16e tot begin 19e eeuw', *Opossum, Tijdschrift voor Historische en Kunstwetenschappen*, 4 (1994), pp. 8–25.

7 H. duc de Rohan, *Voyage du duc de Rohan faict en l'an 1600 en Italie, Allemagne, Pays-Bas, Angleterre et Escosse* (Amsterdam, 1646), pp. 151, 160.

8 R. Murris, *La Hollande et les Hollandais aux XVIIe et XVIIIe siècles vus par les Français* (Paris, 1925); A. Nijenhuis, 'Les "Voyages de Hollande." La perception française des Provinces-Unies dans la première moitié du XVIIe siècle', PhD thesis, Free University [VU], Amsterdam (2012).

9 M. Zoeteman, *De studenten populatie van de Leidse Universiteit, 1575–1812* (Leiden, 2011).

10 P. Hazard, *La Pensée européenne au XVIIIe siècle de Montesquieu à Lessing* (Paris, 1968), p. 247.

11 J.-B.-P. Lebrun, *Galerie des peintres flamands, hollandais et allemands* (Paris, 1792), pp. viii–ix. V. Lee Atwater, 'The Netherlandish vogue and print culture in Paris, 1730–50', *Simolius: Netherlands Quarterly for the History of Art*, 34: 3–4 (2009–10), pp. 239–50.

12 N. Broc, *La Géographie des philosophes: géographes et voyageurs français au dix-huitième siècle* (Lille, 1972).

13 British travellers showed the same interest in Dutch and Flemish painting and for Spa: see van Strien, *Touring the Low Countries*, pp. 238–56 and van Strien, *Britse en Franse reizigers in Holland en Vlaanderen, 1750–1795* (Utrecht, 2001), pp. 208–10, 249–56.

14 W. Guentner, *Esquisses littéraires: rhétorique du spontané et récit de voyage au XIXe siècle* (Saint Genouph, 1997), p. 30.

15 S. Venayre, 'Le siècle du voyage', *Société et représentations*, 21:1 (2006), 'Présentation'.

16 F. Boyer, 'Une conquête artistique de la Convention: les tableaux du Stathouder (1795)', *Bulletin de la Société de l'histoire de l'art français*, 1970, pp. 149–57; 'Le transfert à Paris des collections du stathouder (1795)', *Annales historiques de la Révolution française*, 43 (1971), pp. 389–404.

17 G. Verhoeven, 'Foreshadowing tourism? Looking for modern and obsolete features – or a missing link – in early modern travel behavior (1600–1750)', *Annals of Tourism Research*, 42 (2013), pp. 262–83. This development is

158   Madeleine van Strien-Chardonneau

European, rather than specifically Dutch: 'Eighteenth-century customs office registers from Paris show that French noblemen were less eager to embark on long voyages to Italy, though they appeared to have become spellbound by newly discovered attractions in England, the Low Countries and the German Empire' (ibid., pp. 268–9).

18 Of the 117 travellers (authors of narratives and those accompanying them) identified in 1748–95, 62 took a short leisurely trip, some 40 persons travelled by themselves and the others travelled as a family or with friends; there were few women (12) or young people: see M. van Strien-Chardonneau, '*Le Voyage de Hollande': récits de voyageurs français dans les Provinces-Unies 1748–1795* (Oxford, 1994), pp. 15–24.

19 Murris, *La Hollande et les Hollandais aux XVIIe et XVIIIe siècles*; A. Frank-van Westrienen, *De Groote Tour. Tekening van de educatiereis der Nederlanders in de zeventiende eeuw* (Amsterdam, 1983), 'Toerist in touw', pp. 243–312.

20 Broc, *La Géographie des philosophes*, p. 555.

21 J. de Vries, *Barges and Capitalism: Passenger Transportation in the Dutch Economy, 1632–1839* (Utrecht, 1981), pp. 26–34, 81–90; G. Verhoeven, '"Een divertissant zomertogje': transport innovations and the rise of short-term pleasure trips in the Low Countries, 1600–1750', *Journal of Transport History*, 30: 1 (2009), pp. 78–97, 84.

22 Strien-Chardonneau, '*Le Voyage de Hollande*', p. 30.

23 J. de Vries, 'Barges and capitalism', *A.A.G. Bijdragen*, 21 (1978), p. 106.

24 Verhoeven, 'Een divertissant zomertogje', p. 87.

25 Vries, 'Barges and capitalism', p. 106.

26 D.A.F., marquis de Sade, *Voyage de Hollande en forme de lettres fait en l'année 1769*, *Œuvres complètes du marquis de Sade* (Paris, 1973), vol. 14, pp. 87–107: 'Nothing is more convenient than using these barges that I just mentioned. In all towns in Holland they have been organized in such a way that every hour you can take one to go to another town. Apart from that, if you have a lot of luggage, two boats carrying them leave every day from all these towns and they are reliable. What a good way to do business and how convenient for the people living there' (97).

27 Letter dated 27 July 1776 from Malesherbes to Vergennes, quoted in P. Grosclaude, *Malesherbes, témoin et interprète de son temps* (Paris, 1961), p. 520.

28 On French views on republican models of government (Venice, Switzerland, United Provinces and America) in the eighteenth century, see A. Jourdan, 'La république d'avant la République (1760–1791). Voyages français en terre de liberté', in G. Bertrand and P. Serna, eds, *La République en voyage 1770–1750* (Rennes, 2013), pp. 47–70.

29 See E. Verbaan, *De woonplaats van de faam. Grondslagen van de stadbeschrijving in de zeventiende-eeuwse Republiek* (Hilversum, 2011).

30 B. Bakker, *Amsterdam getekend. Tekeningen en aquarellen uit vier eeuwen in de historisch-topografische atlas van het Gemeentearchief* (The Hague, 1978), p. 17.

31 Thus, Pierre Coste d'Arnobat (1731–1808), travelling around 1789, referred to the *Maison de ville d'Amsterdam représentée en 109 figures*, 1719; Feller (1775) mentioned a similar, older work in Dutch: *Afbeelding van 't stadhuys van Amsterdam*, 1661, but also a *Relation imprimée de la maison de ville d'Amsterdam*. See Nijenhuis, *Les Voyages de Hollande*, who noted numerous editions in Dutch, French, German and English (pp. 385–8).

32 For example, two titles among several: A. Boussingault, *La Guide Universelle de tous les Pays-Bas ou les dix-sept provinces* (Paris, 1665, 1673); *Guide de Flandre et de Hollande* (Paris, 1779).

Amsterdam as global market 159

33 Nijenhuis, *Les Voyages de Hollande*, p. 387, n. 1038. In 1778 Louis Desjobert used a recent *Guide d'Amsterdam* (1772), as well as a booklet with the names and addresses of the city's merchants (*Naamregister van alle de Heeren kooplieden der stad Amsterdam* (Amsterdam, 1767–1838).

34 Parival is the first to have used the title *Délices* in French (in the sixteenth and early seventeenth centuries there were many *Deliciae*), launching a series of *Délices* published by Pieter van der Aa in Leiden.

35 On Boxhorn, see Verbaan, *De woonplaats van de faam*, pp. 70–1.

36 Parival, *Délices* (1655), p. 37.

37 Ibid. (1651), p. 157.

38 Ibid. (1685), p. 95.

39 Editions were published in 1697, 1700, 1711, 1713, 1743, 1769, 1786; the same text was reprinted in *Histoire générale des Pays-Bas, contenant la description des XVII provinces* (Leiden, 1720).

40 Amsterdam is, without a doubt, the most mercantile city in the world, the global marketplace, a seat of opulence, the place where one finds exclusive and splendid products from countries all over the world. Foreigners see all this with surprise, are taken by its beauty and delighted by its magnificence. It is as though the four corners of the world had exhausted their resources to enrich the city and to bring to its port all their rarest and most singular products. If one compares the city today to what it was a century ago, one will be surprised to see that it has been able to acquire, in so little time and from such humble beginnings, the grandeur, beauty, and magnificence that it displays today (*Les Délices des Pays-Bas/Histoire générale des Pays-Bas* (Brussels, 1720), vol. 4, pp. 37–8).

41 In The Hague, where people also liked to stay, only seven inns were mentioned for the same period (Strien-Chardonneau, 'Le Voyage de Hollande', pp. 37–8).

42 Archives Départementales du Loiret, fonds Poterat 12, J 45, J 48, Pierre-Claude, marquis de Poterat, 'Voyage dans le Nord' (March–November 1781), 'Voyage en Suisse, Allemagne, Pays-Bas, Angleterre' (1789). Poterat stayed at this inn during his two trips, in 1781 and 1789. The *Guide de Flandre et de Hollande* (1779) stated: 'People stay at the inn managed by Thibault: it is the place to go to, where one finds the largest number of Frenchmen.'

43 BNF, Papiers Roland, Ms n.a.fr 6242, 1768, Jean-Marie Roland de la Platière, 'Voyage en Flandre et en Hollande', fols. 163–224: 'In each town servants are available to interpret and to provide transportation, but their knowledge is so poor and they show so little interest that one would easily be fed up with them.'

44 See, for example, Sade, *Voyage de Hollande en forme de lettres, fait en l'année 1769*, p. 102.

45 For example, Louis-Charles Desjobert, 'Voyage aux Pays-Bas en 1778 [...] publié par le vicomte de Grouchy', *De Navorscher* (1909), pp. 524–40. Poterat, 'Voyage dans le Nord' (1781) and 'Voyage en Suisse' (1789). In the *Délices de la Hollande* (1685), maps were provided for each city, with numbers indicating the most important buildings and sites.

46 Malesherbes noted in 1766 that Amsterdam's police was quite superior to the police in Paris see Grosclaude, *Malesherbes*.

47 Municipal Library, Troyes, Ms 2469, no. 56, 57, Pierre-Jean Grosley, *Itinéraire en Hollande* (1772).

48 Institut de France, Ms 1657, 1761, Emmanuel duc de Croy, *Mémoires de ma vie* (1718–84), vol. 17, 'Voyages de Zélande et de Hollande', f. 13 r.

49 Municipal Library, Douai, Ms. 1206, 'Voyage de Brabant, Hollande et Flandre par deux Valenciennois du 8 juin au 20 juillet 1789', 4 vols, ii, p. 257.

50 See, for instance, A.-M. Du Boccage, *Lettres sur l'Angleterre, la Hollande et l'Italie*, in *Recueil des Œuvres de Madame du Boccage* (Lyon, 1762).

160 *Madeleine van Strien-Chardonneau*

51 *Le Projet pour rendre la paix perpétuelle en Europe* (Utrecht, 1713), quoted in L. Bély, *Espions et ambassadeurs au temps de Louis XIV* (Paris, 1990), p. 725.

52 The numbers mentioned by travelers range from 200,000 to 400,000 inhabitants. According to A. van der Woude, 'La ville néerlandaise', in J. Meyer, ed., *Etudes sur les villes en Europe occidentale du milieu du 17e à la veille de la Révolution française* (Paris, 1983–4), vol. 2, pp. 320–80, Amsterdam had a population of 104,932 in 1622, 200,000 in 1675 and 217,024 (379) in 1795.

53 Bély, *Espions et ambassadeurs au temps de Louis XIV*, p. 525; G.-F, Abbé Coyer, *Voyages d'Italie et de Hollande* [1769] (Paris, 1775), p. 246.

54 BNF, Ms.fr.14626, 1760, Pierre Famin, 'Itinéraire du voïage d'Hollande fait en 1760 par Pierre Famin de Paris', p. 45.

55 H. Bernardin de Saint-Pierre, *Observations sur la Hollande* [1762], *Œuvres complètes* (Brussels, 1820), vol. 1, p. 275.

56 F.-C. de Tellier, marquis de Courtanvaux, *Journal du voyage de M. le Marquis de Courtanvaux* [1767] (Paris, 1768), p. 245.

57 Poterat, 'Voyage en Suisse, Allemagne, Pays-Bas, Angleterre', p. 140.

58 Bély, *Espions et ambassadeurs au temps de Louis XIV*, p. 388.

59 Municipal Library, Lille, Ms. 226 Rig.530, p. 80, 1786, Anon, 'Journal de mon voïage en Hollande avec monsieur de Mortemart'.

60 Municipal Library, Douai, Ms. 1206, 'Voyage de Brabant, Hollande et Flandre par deux Valenciennois', vol. 2, p. 239.

61 Bély, *Espions et ambassadeurs au temps de Louis XIV*, p. 723.

62 Municipal Library, Nantes, Ms 870, f· 29r., c.1789, marquis de Goyon, 'Voyage d'Hollande'.

63 Ch. Baudelaire, 'L'invitation au voyage' [1857], *Petits poèmes en prose* (Paris, 1969), pp. 48–52.

64 M. van Strien-Chardonneau, 'La vision exotique de la Hollande dans les récits de voyageurs français (XVIIIe–XIXe siècles)', in N. Demir, and G. Çetin, eds, *Journées internationales d'études sur l'exotisme, 10–11 mai 2007, Actes* (Ankara, 2009), pp. 79–89.

65 Guentner, *Esquisses littéraires*, pp. 36–8.

66 Th. Gautier, *Un Tour en Belgique et en Hollande* [1846, 1849] (Paris, 1997), p. 38.

67 Thus, Maxime Du Camp, upon arriving in Amsterdam in 1857, evokes *le Marché aux herbes* (1660–2) by Gabriel Metsu, admired at the Louvre: 'Today I took a walk in Amsterdam, and it has confirmed my first impression; it is indeed the city that we see in *le Marché aux herbes*, it has not changed; brick houses, windows painted black, a gable roof with a pulley sheltered under small painted wooden eaves, tree-lined canals where boats without sails are passing by, and stands displaying vegetables.' *En Hollande, lettres à un ami* [1857] (Paris, 1859), pp.109–10.

68 Du Camp, *En Hollande, lettres à un ami*, p. 159.

69 *Les Délices de la Hollande* (Leiden, 1660), p. 177. For a comparison of the United Provinces and Venice, see Nijenhuis, *Les Voyages de Hollande*, pp. 147–55, and for that of the United Provinces and Italy, pp. 344–8, pp. 379–82.

70 P. Hazard, *La crise de la conscience européenne, 1680–1715* (Paris, 1961).

71 Harder, *Le Président De Brosses et le voyage en Italie*, p. 435.

9 The European 'Grand Tour' of Italian entrepreneurs

Corine Maitte

We are gradually gaining a better understanding of men's *wanderlust* in the early modern period.[1] Their motives were as varied as the routes they took and the processes by which they put their narratives down on paper. In this vast galaxy of travels, which extends far beyond the nobility's Grand Tour, we have a fairly good idea of the movements of a number of representatives of the 'economic community', in particular those of merchants and ship owners who tended to write for their friends and family rather than for posterity. This fact sets them apart from 'scientists', whose travels could help establish their reputation and were for this reason often published.[2] The latter contributed, moreover, to the development of more specialised travel practices in the last quarter of the eighteenth century, like those of naturalists, archaeologists, alpinists and statisticians.[3]

There is, nevertheless, a type of journey that is rarely addressed in eighteenth-century European travel historiography: that of merchants or manufacturers tracking the products they manufactured or purchased, or the technical innovations that interested them. These journeys, though probably quite numerous, did not necessarily become the focus of developed narratives: hence the appeal of examining the few we do possess with a view to obtaining a detailed analysis of the routes, peoples and cities they encountered, as well as the often complex processes that led them to record these experiences.[4] Emphasis will be placed on the routes Italians took through Europe: a sort of reverse Grand Tour. In the dense network of relations between the peninsula and the rest of Europe, industrial and commercial exchanges were always crucial. But in the eighteenth century, just as Italy was losing its industrial primacy, its invention of new products and processes was also flagging. Among the numerous accounts of travellers who criss-crossed the peninsula at that time, few offer appraisals of Italian industry except perhaps to speculate on the reasons for its decline, in what had become a common theme.[5]

The Italians – a generic term that had little meaning at the time – were perfectly aware of the recent weakness of their industries: one need only read the reports of Venetian, Florentine or Piedmontese government agencies to realise as much. Consequently, a number of Italian governments and

162   Corine Maitte

more or less isolated individuals could sometimes combine their efforts and go looking for information at the source: the manufactories on the other side of the Alps in the small, middling or large cities where new manufacturing techniques had been invented. There was nothing 'cultural' about such journeys, and the narratives often omitted descriptions of 'tourist attractions', whether natural or manmade, in order to focus on the economic side of things.[6] Indeed, all of these texts implicitly contributed to the wider appreciation and representation of an *industrial geography* of Europe.[7]

Rather than an exhaustive inventory of these journeys, which would be impossible to compile,[8] this chapter aims to study a handful of them qualitatively in order to paint a few portraits of the 'entrepreneur-traveller', to analyse the purpose of their journeys and to evaluate the way these particular travellers described some of the cities they passed through.

Traveller profiles and forms of travel/travel narratives

From among the large spectrum of Italians who fanned out across Europe in the eighteenth and early nineteenth centuries for economic reasons, we have chosen four travellers who set out on tours of manufacturing Europe at fairly regular 20-year intervals: Gian Battista Xaverio Moccafy from Piedmont, who travelled between 1766 and 1767 and whose journals we have published elsewhere for the first time;[9] Marsilio Landriani, from Lombardy, who made his trip just before the start of the French Revolution (1787–8);[10] and, finally, two Tuscans, Giuseppe Morosi, whose trip was a pure product of the Napoleonic Empire (1806–7),[11] and Gaetano Mazzoni, who left Florence in June 1828 and did not return until January 1830.[12] Though we have used the very vague term 'entrepreneur', these travellers actually represent fairly distinct types, and their concerns varied accordingly, even if they were all motivated by a desire to see the latest production techniques on the other side of the Alps.

Categories of traveller

None of this group really fits the five categories of Italian merchant journeys devised by Gilles Bertrand.[13] Gian Battista Moccafy was a cloth merchant whose chronicle indicates he was aware of new technology, but who was mainly tuned into the quality of textiles and sales methods. Speaking of himself in the third person, he recalled the purpose of his journey in 1773:

> In 1766, he resolved to, and did, make the rounds of drapery manufactories in Normandy, Picardy, England, Flanders, Holland and Champagne at his own expense, so as to obtain the knowledge necessary for anyone who wishes to be abreast of the quality and substance of the merchandise.[14]

The 'Grand Tour' of Italian entrepreneurs   163

Here we are apparently dealing with the classic case of a merchant visiting the manufacturing sites of the products he acquires to hone his expertise and thus avoid being fooled by the many knock-offs. Moccafy hoped to learn more about the local conditions of sale and eventually cut out the middlemen with whom he undoubtedly had to deal until then. Finally, the trip could help him build or strengthen his network of contacts, which was crucial for commerce.[15]

Giuseppe Morosi was a self-described 'mechanic'. Indeed, he was a product of the importance attributed to the 'practically applied sciences' by Tuscan intellectual circles under Grand Duke Peter Leopold and it was a field which he sought all his life to develop. In 1794, he was officially made a paid member of the *Imperial Regio Museo di Fisica e Storia Naturale* (the Imperial-Royal Museum for Physics and Natural History of Florence).[16] Along with many other Italians, of whom the best known are Fabbroni, Dandolo and Volta, the French Revolution had afforded him the opportunity to go to Paris, where he came into contact with scientific circles and, in particular, Berthollet and Chaptal. He was even recruited for a job at Paris's new *Musée des machines des Arts et Métiers* as 'machine demonstrator', but ended up accepting the title of 'national mechanic' which the government of the Kingdom of Italy in Milan offered him. He was henceforth at the centre of technical and industrial projects and particularly advocated the creation of 'an Arts and Manufacturing Academy' based on the French model. Still, it was after requesting a temporary leave of absence from this role that he set out on two journeys, first in 1806–7 and then again in 1811, the purpose of which was to observe machines and reproduce models of them.[17] Indeed, on his first trip, Morosi drew diagrams of more than 130 machines: the manuscript preserved in Florence is illustrated with a whole series of sketches made in red pencil, most of which are roughly drawn and not to scale. These sketches not only represent machines, but also locals and their costumes, and even 'instruments of torture and torment', all of which merit further study. Upon his return, Morosi had more than 400 drawings of machines executed.[18] He, indeed, acted as a mediator for information on new machines between the Empire and the Kingdom of Italy, but also the Principality of Lucca, where his presence was requested by the Grand Duchess in 1808 and where he returned after the Bourbon Restoration, as well as to Florence, which remained a centre for mechanisation projects.[19]

Gaetano Mazzoni was an entrepreneur-traveller of the Restoration. Like many of his fellow industrialists, he sought to observe European achievements first-hand in order to put them to work in the firm he and his brother had inherited from their father.[20] He was, moreover, in contact with Morosi about mechanisation projects in his company.[21] In 1828, leaving his brother behind to run their manufactory located between Livorno and Prato in Tuscany, he set off towards northern Italy, and then decided to undertake a tour of Europe. Observing new production techniques was an

164   *Corine Maitte*

essential part of his journey, though he always relates them back to more general characteristics of the way factories were run.

The fourth traveller, who was second chronologically, differs from the others in several important ways. Marsilio Landriani was neither merchant nor commoner, but came from a patrician Lombard family. In 1776, when he was 25, he began teaching at the Universities of Brera and Pavia, Padua, Como and Varese. A 'scientific' figure, he was made president of the Patriotic Society in 1782, and embarked that same year on a journey to woo foreign entrepreneurs to settle in Lombardy, but to no avail. In 1783, he was hired by the Court of Vienna with the express mission of seeking out 'the most useful information' on the sciences (and notably chemistry); social welfare institutions; production, specifically agricultural (about which he says almost nothing); 'the state of factories, with a special emphasis on machines, especially the simplest ones'; 'economic and social conditions'; and 'cultural and scientific progress'.[22] The journey was finally completed in two stages: a first leg from the summer of 1787 until December 1788 and a second one between 1789 and February 1790, apparently in Hungary. Its goals were explicitly set forth in a number of gazettes at the time, a fact he complained about because the publicity surrounding the journey closed certain doors to him.[23] He was one of those scientific travellers who published multiple texts which met rather different editorial and critical standards than the others. But the text he drafted upon his return, which also included several sketches, was not intended for publication but for the edification of his backers. Indeed, it would not be published until the end of the twentieth century.[24]

Public vs private: the ambiguity of who organised trips and the nature of narratives

None of the other narratives was published: we only know of a rough draft of Moccafy's 'travel narrative', incomplete in places, which ended up in a collection of miscellanea at the Royal Library of Turin.[25] It is doubtful that Moccafy had publication in mind. However, the text was certainly intended to be read and, indeed, was at the highest levels, as he himself reminds the reader:

> Upon his return, after a ten- or eleven-month journey, he gives an account of his voyage, his observations on the merchandise manufactured, the methods observed, commercial practices and the exchange of currencies. This report had the good fortune of being seen by His Majesty Charles Emmanuel, by Your Majesty, and by the director of the Chamber of Commerce.[26]

The report was thus written to inform those who were not acquainted with the wool sector, with an obvious instructional focus, particularly

The 'Grand Tour' of Italian entrepreneurs 165

when Moccafy explained the major principles of drapery-making in broad strokes. It was, moreover, accompanied by a book of samples presented with the utmost care, its ornamentation more that of a precious object in its own right than that of a typical merchant's catalogue, and doubtless intended for important figures.[27] Using these samples, Moccafy in a sense taught his readers to recognise textiles by placing them before their very eyes and fingers. It is not hard to fathom all the work that went into collecting and labelling samples before the scrapbook could be compiled, and it is this that leads one to suspect that Moccafy was directly solicited to take the journey. The Count Bogin – Charles Emmanuel's principal minister to whom Moccafy offered his drapery register[28] – was the impetus behind several journeys in other domains, such as mining and metallurgy, which helped Piedmont emulate foreign models. Indeed, in 1749, he sent the Count Robilant and four young engineers to study the metallurgy schools of Saxony, Hanover, Brunswick, Hungary and Tyrol, in view of the founding of the Royal Armoury of Turin's own institute, museum and laboratory of chemistry and metallurgy two years later.[29] In 1751, the same count was sent on a mission to supply the Piedmont government with information on 'several manufactories located in Venice'.[30] The possibility thus remains that Moccafy was not alone in organising the trip, but that high-ranking government officials were at least partially responsible for it.

This ambiguity was quite common, for governments were often wary of officially backing missions that could potentially cause diplomatic problems or raise suspicions about the traveller – a fate which befell Landriani, for example. Morosi's situation was quite similar to Moccafy's: he was the Italian Kingdom's official 'national mechanic', and his trip was announced by Interior Minister Ludovico De Breme in August 1806. The latter gave him quasi-official letters of introduction and called on him to 'look, examine, record, draw and write'. Morosi thus sent him and the Viceroy letters during his journey, which he nevertheless embarked upon in a private capacity and without pay after requesting a leave of absence, as we have already mentioned. This ambiguity led to problems upon his return since he considered himself 'proprietor' of the observations he made and sought to have them published.[31] He doubtless believed, like Chaptal or François de Neufchâteau, that publicising and disseminating information, including statistics, was the best way to encourage private enterprise.[32] The government of the Kingdom of Italy, in this instance Viceroy Eugène de Beauharnais, and doubtless to an even greater extent his father-in-law the Emperor, were not willing to let him publicise mechanical observations which were still deemed confidential.[33] An *a posteriori* agreement was therefore reached declaring the state sole proprietor of Morosi's observations. In exchange, he received a bonus for relinquishing the right to publish and agreeing to turn all his observations over to the government, which was free to do with them as it saw fit.[34]

166   *Corine Maitte*

Three of these travellers thus set out on their trips in close contact or even cooperation with the states from which they hailed, whether this information was public or not. They doubtless oriented their narratives – which in each case was only completed after their return – around the goals that had been set, even if these were not clearly stated, except in the case of Landriani. As was common practice at the time, none cited possible sources for complementary information contained within their texts. Detecting evidence of what they may have read would necessarily require a side-by-side comparison with other sources, which currently there is no way of identifying.[35]

Some excerpts from Landriani's correspondence offer a glimpse into more personal concerns and interests; unfortunately the remainder have probably been lost.[36] This is not the case for Gaetano Mazzoni's letters, which give us a sense of his concerns, interests and the kinds of people he encountered. Two caveats, however: first, the correspondence is not evenly distributed over the duration of his travels – of the 78 letters he wrote to his brother, 57 were penned during the first six months while he was still in Italy; and second, he only wrote one letter each from Paris, London and Amsterdam, which are, moreover, largely illegible. The same man who set out with the stated goal of improving the family business and who one would assume to be the most pressed for time, only returned 20 months later, having made the longest journey out of the four. That said, he remained quite a long time in northern Italy (more than six months) where he decided to learn English in order to communicate with the British, whom he had arranged to meet. Indeed, it was (already) a foregone conclusion in Landriani's day that 'the English merchant is naturally cold and reserved, does not speak foreign languages or want to take the trouble to learn them, and does not like to converse with foreigners'.[37] Despite this fact, they all travelled to England – except for Morosi, who was laid up on the Continent due to a blockade – though we do not know if they all spoke the language. Indeed, there is no mention at all of linguistic difficulties in their accounts, though this does not necessarily mean they were accomplished polyglots.[38]

The travellers' routes

The breakdown of the journeys

The only information we have about travel itineraries is that recorded in letters or in the texts themselves. With the exception of Gaetano Mazzoni, we lack the specifics of the routes, roads and byways taken, the means of transport utilised and the precise timing of the journey. We cannot determine whether the travellers had company or, on the contrary, travelled alone, as was the case with Mazzoni.[39] Thus almost all details of the journeys and their vagaries elude us.[40] Our sole source, the three texts

The 'Grand Tour' of Italian entrepreneurs   167

themselves, are presented as a list of cities with descriptions. They adhere to a very old structure, modelled on the numerous travel narratives that preceded them: it is impossible, however, to know if our authors had read them.[41]

It is equally impossible to know if our travellers made use of guide books, which had become increasingly popular.[42] At the time of Moccafy's departure, the best-known guide book in Italy doubtless remained Gio Maria Vidari's *Viaggio in pratica*, first published in 1718 and then in a second edition in 1764, while F. Locatelli's *Il viaggiatore moderno* (Venice, 1775) was published only a handful of years after his return. The latter work is clear evidence that the interests of the modern 'traveller-researcher' were being placed to the fore, including 'the quality of places, the predominant spirit of peoples; ports and places where commerce is most important; fruits of the land, minerals, arts and manufacturing, money, weights and measures, frets and finally anything related to merchandise'.[43] However, nothing allows us to determine whether our authors had slipped these guide books into their bags, or even read them.

There are two additional uncertainties. First, we do not know whether the itinerary and the duration of the trips were decided beforehand. All of these journeys were fairly long due to the highly specific nature of their goals. Despite varying widely in duration – between six and 20 months – they were, nonetheless, far longer than the average merchant journey at the time.[44] This may be attributed to another unknown: that of the network of contacts these travellers called upon. Did they know in advance whom they would meet? Did Moccafy, Morosi and Mazzoni use their pre-existing network of commercial contacts to orient their travels, make introductions, gain entrance to factories? It is possible and even probable, but no information is explicitly given in this regard.

Moccafy, in particular, offered no clues about it in his writing. He often gives us the sense of heading first and foremost for cities renowned for their wool textiles, rather than visiting the manufacturers he might already know, but at no point did he mention prior knowledge of any of them. To evaluate his personal contacts prior to the journey, one must necessarily have knowledge of the circumstances in which he ran his business in Turin: was he in direct contact with the manufacturers whose products he purchased or did his stocks come from intermediary importers? No document provides evidence one way or the other. The individuals with whom he conferred during his journey remain for the most part unknown. Indeed, the names of manufacturers are only rarely cited.[45] Why this silence? Moccafy must have thought, perhaps in error, that his text's intended readers were not interested in the names of the manufacturers he met. This information must have seemed too far removed from the sphere of interest of the politicians he was addressing. Rather, he saw his mission as that of a clearing house for qualitative information on products, techniques and organisations, but not on people. At the same time, the implication was

168 *Corine Maitte*

that his role as practitioner and the reality of his observations were sufficient to make him a credible source, without his needing to prove his claims with precise information about those who allowed him to gain this knowledge.

In contrast, Gaetano Mazzoni's letters go into great detail about the people he met, the proprietors of the factories he visited and so on. In so far as his brother was his sole reader, there was a strong need to supply nominative information. One of the goals of the narrative, then, was to report back on the network of contacts consolidated during the completed expedition. The number of contacts made was also a measure of the journey's importance to the shared business, since the brother who stayed behind had to bear the burden of running the business alone, and the journey kept getting longer. As for Landriani, his contacts clearly belonged to other circles, tending to include more men of letters and learning. He also described certain entrepreneurs he met, reserving praise for some and vitriol for others. Indeed, the text sets out to forge the reputations of author and subject alike.

The appeal of northwestern Europe

As Gilles Bertrand points out, what set merchant journeys apart is that they conformed neither to the timing nor the roadmaps popularised in guide books, and no two were alike.[46] But there is no doubt that it was above all 'northwestern Europe' that our four travellers sought to behold with their own eyes – a region which had not yet been conceptualised in this way, but towards which all 'curious manufacturers' and, to an even greater extent, direct economic actors, gravitated. It included France north of the Loire (except for Lyon), England, the Low Countries, the United Provinces and a small part of western Germany. Table 9.1, which gives the number of cities visited in each country, offers a preliminary indication of the focus of each voyage, albeit a rough one (highlighted in bold).

Table 9.1 Numbers of cities visited by Italian entrepreneurs

Number of cities visited in each country (% in parentheses)	Moccafy	Landriani	Morosi	Mazzoni
France	**15 (42.85)**	13 (26)	18 (32.72)	3 (6.38)
Low Countries/Belgium	6 (17.14)	2 (4)	**10 (18.18)**	1 (2.12)
United Provinces (current Netherlands)	8 (22.85)	2 (4)	**13 (23.63)**	5 (10.63)
Germany	2 (5.71)	11 (22)	6 (10.90)	12 (25.53)
Switzerland	0	4 (8)	7 (12.72)	8 (17.02)
England/British Isles	4 (11.42)	**18 (36)**	0	3 (6.38)
Italy	0	0	1 (1.8)	**15 (31.91)**
Total cities visited	35	50	55	47

The 'Grand Tour' of Italian entrepreneurs 169

If we were able to count the number of words pertaining to each city, it would doubtless further accentuate each traveller's orientation, as it does for Moccafy, who devoted more than 51 per cent of his narrative to France. We are thus struck by Moccafy's penchant for France and Landriani's for Britain. It was doubtless the latter's desire to be comprehensive in this domain that led him to Scotland and Ireland, which none of our other travellers visited.[47] While he predicted that the Scots would soon rival the English – thanks not only to their abundant raw materials (coal, iron, lead, wool and flax), but also their industriousness and cunning – he was less optimistic about Irish manufacturing. Even though his narrative ends with Dublin, his description becomes sparser here; in fact, he does not follow the order of his actual itinerary. The text is, moreover, silent on the Low Countries and the United Provinces, even though he passed through them on his way back through Vienna. By contrast, Morosi's inability to visit England doubtless shifted his focus towards northern Europe (though Zaandam was the northernmost city he visited), and especially the regions which had just been annexed by France.[48] As for Mazzoni, he paradoxically remained the most Italian of the four.

The diversity of cities

On the subject of cities visited, it is worth beginning with a few statistics: Moccafy describes a total of 35 cities, Landriani nine more (44, though we know he passed through at least 50), Mazzoni comes in just short at 47, while Morosi is the most loquacious with 55 cities mentioned or described, that is 20 more than Moccafy. As we can see, the itineraries overlap in places, since 23 of the cities visited by Moccafy (nearly 64 per cent) were also visited by at least one of the others. Some of these are almost mandatory stopovers – Lyon if you leave Italy by way of France (Moccafy) and Geneva if you leave through Switzerland (Landriani, Morosi). But the cities were such important manufacturing centres that Landriani and Mazzoni passed through one *and* the other. Dijon was obviously merely a stop on the way to Paris; likewise, Calais and Dunkirk were only visited by Moccafy and Mazzoni because they booked passage to England through its ports.

By contrast, however, only two cities, Paris and Amsterdam, were visited by all four Italians, even though Landriani did not comment on the latter. But the number of cities each traveller was alone in visiting represents a relatively high portion of the total: a little more than a third for Moccafy, but about 60 per cent for Landriani and Mazzoni. Without a doubt, the geography of European manufactories was a multifaceted reality and each traveller could carve out a route based on his own interests.

Figure 9.1 shows the routes most likely taken by each traveller and tries, in Moccafy's case, to measure the importance of each city by the number of words used to describe it in the narrative. For Mazzoni, for whom we know

170   *Corine Maitte*

Table 9.2 Cities visited and described by Italian entrepreneurs

	Moccafy	Landriani	Morosi	Mazzoni
No. of cities visited/described	36	44/51	56	48
No. of cities visited by all four	2	2	2	2
No. of cities visited by Moccafy and one of the other three	–	9	18	8
No. of cities visited by at least two travellers	23	11	10	10
No. of cities described/visited by only one traveller (% in parentheses)	13 (36)	31 (60.78)	27 (46.55)	30 (62.5)

the travel dates, the graphic shows the number of letters sent from, and time spent in each respective city.[49]

Deciphering the routes: an industrial geography in flux?

Let us now turn to the detail of each traveller's route. Certainly, they probably all would have incurred the wrath of Mario Pieri, who denounced the traveller 'looking for new wealth, his mind marred by the promise of profit, who does not deign to give the major cities of Europe a second glance, but places Trieste before Rome and Ancona before Florence'.[50] In fact, Moccafy had only one clear interest – wool manufacturing – whether carded, combed, fine or ordinary, the quality of its products and techniques, the way its manufactories were organised, as well as its sales methods. This exclusive focus defines the specificity of his journey and narrative, in which there is rarely commentary of the sort so commonly found elsewhere – on routes, landscapes and 'attractions'. For example, he barely even mentions Lyon's silk industry. In Paris he was only interested in the Gobelins Manufactory and the postal system. He only deviates from his preferred subject at Rouen where the velvet and cotton manufactories hold his attention somewhat. The route he chose was thus dictated by this one interest alone. He set out to visit the main wool centres of northwestern Europe – those he already knew because he had bought their products or because they had served as models for Piedmontese manufactories (notably those in Reims), and those he probably stumbled upon along the way, and which he is often the only one of the four to name (Les Andelys, Darnétal, Aumale in Normandy, Tilburg, Borcette (Burtscheid), Bouillon between the Federated Provinces and the Empire). As he laments at the end of his account, his tour lacked the centres of southern France, undoubtedly due to lack of time. This Mediterranean oversight is symptomatic of the draw of northwestern Europe, which has already been pointed out.

The 'Grand Tour' of Italian entrepreneurs 171

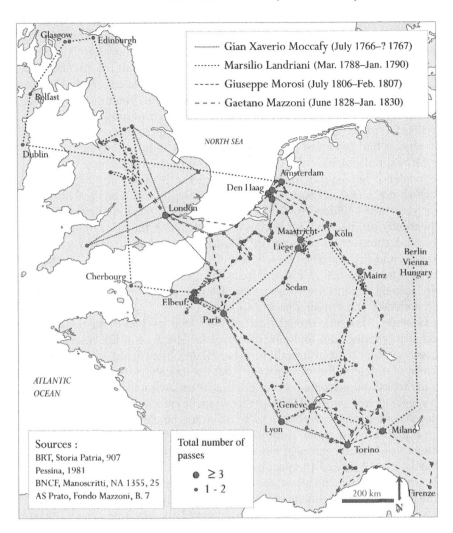

Figure 9.1 Map of Italian entrepreneurs' travels in Europe, 1766–1830.

By contrast, Landriani's route bears the mark of the multitude of goals he was pursuing. Of the many missions Landriani was given, the most significant, as we have seen, was the careful observation of machines. This explains why he passed through Moncenis/Le Creusot, which he describes at length, or Ratingen, whose cotton mills were worth the detour. The most striking difference when comparing the itineraries of Moccafy and Landriani is the contrast in the routes along which they travelled in England. While the former visited Leeds, Norwich, Exeter and the traditional centres of the wool industry, where he apparently had no trouble gaining entrance to manufactories, the latter went to Birmingham,

172   *Corine Maitte*

Coalbrookdale, Coventry, Derby, Belper, Bakewell and, above all, Manchester, Liverpool and Halifax, even though he makes much of the difficulties he had getting inside English factories.[51] Cotton mills and the most recent spinning jennies were, of course, the focus of his attention. He describes Arkwright's invention and character at length,[52] and places particular emphasis on the importance of the firm Boulton and Watt.[53] Assuredly, Landriani and Moccafy had very different mental maps of industrialised Europe. In the 20 years which had elapsed between their trips, awareness had grown of the importance of new industrial dynamics.

Morosi did not have the opportunity to report on what was happening in England, but he did roam the north of the Napoleonic Empire where English machines had been widely imported or copied. Though France did not yet count 130 departments when he left, the unification underway was apparently an incentive for taking this route, even though it only covered the westernmost part of Germany. Though France had already vanquished Austria and Prussia when he left, and the Confederation of the Rhine was formed ten days before his departure, he did not leave this western zone. He seemed mainly to follow the Rhine, before reaching the Swiss Confederacy and crossing back into Italy.

Gaetano Mazzoni, though just as interested as Landriani in studying recent mechanisation, undoubtedly spent far less time in England. It seems he was content to head straight for Manchester, by then already a renowned centre of industry. But he apparently cut his stay short, perhaps after being made to feel unwelcome by the 'English bears', whose language he admits to speaking very poorly. He nevertheless spent even less time in France (two months compared with three and a half in England), where he only visited Lyon and, for just short of two weeks, Paris. What is striking is the total absence of French centres of wool production from his list, despite the fact that he manufactured the product. There are two possible hypotheses for this, neither of which can be verified, since he never explained his choices. The first, which is highly improbable, was to study the case of a country left behind in economic terms; the second, more likely, was that he already had some familiarity with France thanks to ties forged during the Empire and which Morosi, among others, helped maintain.

What were the images of the cities?

It is obviously impossible to go into the specifics of what each traveller reports back about the cities they visited, so we will only look at Amsterdam as seen through the eyes of Moccafy and Morosi.[54] Along with Paris, it was one of the few cities that all of our travellers visited, even if they did not all describe it. Though historians today consider it to have been in decline, starting in the latter half of the eighteenth century, this was not necessarily the way contemporaries perceived it – for them it remained the warehouse of the world.

The 'Grand Tour' of Italian entrepreneurs   173

Amsterdam

Moccafy, oddly enough, had quite a lot to say about Amsterdam. The same man who deemed the Gobelins and the Paris post office worthy of mention attempted a relatively classic 'description' which strayed far from his abiding interest in wool manufactories, which Amsterdam, moreover, lacked. His general appraisals were quite brief when it came to air quality ('the air is unhealthy because of the stench of the canals'), the comfort of the city ('there's nothing enjoyable inside the city'), the exorbitant expense of country houses ('instead of being useful to the inhabitants, they are such a great expense that, without the impressive returns that commerce brings them, all the traders would be in trouble'). Moccafy thus soon came to the secret of the city's wealth: its commerce (its Jewish brokers and stock exchange, the role of Catholics and merchants, the nature and direction of trade, tariffs on merchandise, and exchange practices), its port and its channels of communication. While he mentioned the city's 'remarkable edifices' – the admiralty, warehouses and the Dutch East India Company are named first – the city's royal palace is only mentioned later and in passing. What is even more surprising, and unusual, to tell the truth, is the detail he goes into regarding property rentals and the city's dampness.[55] Moccafy here verges on the anecdotal, which is rarely the case elsewhere in his narrative. But after all, air quality was a predominant theme in hygienist literature of the period, and he seems to demonstrate his receptiveness to it.

Though Moccafy made mention of Amsterdam's prisons, his view of them apparently differed from Morosi's, in whose description of the city they figure prominently. Like Landriani, in many cities Morosi zeroed in on correctional institutions, hospices and orphanages which could potentially put youth to work. In Amsterdam, he was far less attentive than Moccafy to the city's commerce and general living conditions, but dwelt instead on orphanages, hospitals, hospices and houses of correction.[56] Perhaps the sketches he slipped into the manuscript depicting methods of torture and 'ordinary and continued suffering' were meant to illustrate the Rasphuis Prison, which he considered a place of 'unsurpassed horror'.[57]

All in all, comparing their two accounts only serves to highlight better their very different perception of things. There is little they agree on: one city, but two very different visions. Perhaps the lack of common references has something to do with this? Without going through all the cities in detail, it seems useful to end with a few broad observations about the image these travellers had of cities in general.

Cities interrelated and compared

The narratives, reports and letters all present an archipelago of cities interconnected by channels of communication. This was obviously an important point for any traveller, but even more so for our investigators, who were

174   *Corine Maitte*

concerned with the comparative advantages of one city over another. Proximity to raw materials and ease of commerce were the two recurring criteria by which urban economic potential was evaluated, and this, of course, comes as no surprise. Nor is it surprising that none of the travellers appears to have been concerned with the countryside, even though the physiocratic movement was in full swing when Moccafy set out, and part of Landriani's assignment was to study agriculture. All remained for the most part preoccupied with urban manufacturing and, in the case of the first two, sang the praises of Colbert. The large-scale production of consumer goods represented the real productive sector for them; crafts did not hold their attention at all. This was in keeping with the highly 'mercantilist' orientations of the major states of the Italian peninsula, for whom the main concern was to 'resist' encroachments into their market by outside manufacturing. Protecting, nurturing and stimulating manufactories seemed the only possible means to this end.

We rarely find a portrait of a city in its entirety. Among the diverse forms of writing studied here, descriptions of cities themselves are only rarely given any importance, and this is even more the case for the biggest and best-known ones. None really follows the customary travel narrative, which is why we only rarely find mention of a monument or the description of a cathedral. Major industries constitute the main focus of the narratives, followed, in Landriani and Morosi's case, by institutions of charity and public assistance. Most often, each city is summed up as a set of juxtaposing production processes, and sometimes producers.

Moccafy's book of samples is a good indicator of this tendency to identify a city with a set of products, in this case exclusively woollen ones. Here, for example, is the list of topics addressed by Morosi in Rouen:

> Cranked looms, bleaching of cotton, blue dye cauldron, bleaching of canvas, dye, topographic and commercial details, methods of flax growing, churches and public edifices, cotton velvet works, the double flying shuttle, a manufactory for steel combs for canvas weaving, orphanages, canvas-glazing calendar, windmill, a continuous spinning jenny, an extraordinarily large bell.[58]

On rare occasions, we find very general descriptions of a city's socioeconomic characteristics. This is what Moccafy attempted at the beginning of his visit to Normandy, when he gave a lengthy description of Louviers' streets, houses, manufactories and the diet of its workers.[59] After this first visit, he quickly became more concise.

Cities are, above all, described through their industry, whose merits are almost systematically compared, rather than through their material conditions or inhabitants. This culture of comparison was, moreover, an explicit part of the agenda assigned to Landriani since he was tellingly asked to 'draw comparisons between us and others and to *determine if we are equal*

The 'Grand Tour' of Italian entrepreneurs 175

or better than them in such-and-such an area',[60] which was part of the political calculations made with regard to the arts and sciences.[61] These comparisons were immediately used to make value judgements and to establish of a scale of merit.[62] Though less explicit in their plans, Moccafy, Morosi and Mazzoni did the same thing. Comparisons shaped the way each of the travellers saw and understood what they had seen, and at every level: countries, cities and producers were all evaluated and compared using the benchmark of the products they produced. We are therefore dealing with a *product culture*; what ultimately counted was not the machines, profit, or general wellbeing, but rather the quality and beauty of the product, which the machines could perhaps render more efficiently or better.

Moccafy thus compared the organisational specificities of manufacturing in the 'French method' with that of the 'English principle', or domestic system, attributing successful results to each in its own area of specialisation.[63] Then he compared cities – that is, the products made in their manufactories: Louviers, Sedan, Elbeuf, Abbeville and Leyde, for example, for carded drapery and Exeter, Lille, Amiens and Reims for combed drapery. Finally, he compared the merits of the most renowned manufacturers within each of these centres (Paignon, Rousseau and Labauche in Sedan, for example).

As for Landriani, he declared 'the superiority of English wool manufacturers'. Contrary to historians, he did not attribute this to machines, but, like Moccafy, to the quality of the cardboard used in the finishing presses.[64] He also explained how, according to him, the recent Eden Treaty (1786) 'revived the French nation's industry' even as it 'held back the English', in addition to making them even more suspicious of foreigners.[65] Landriani's opinion may seem strange given the prevailing view that the Eden Treaty dealt a major blow to French manufacturing.[66] But Landriani, who was convinced of the virtues of competition, saw it instead as a salutary lash of the whip.

In the race to the top, there were necessarily winners and losers in the eyes of our travellers. Competition and emulation did not guarantee a perfect market where resources and production were harmoniously distributed: not one of them truly believed in the liberal credo. By way of an example, Landriani visited the cities of Normandy after Moccafy, but concluded that Abbeville and Van Robais had lost their edge, despite having 'long competed successfully with the best English manufactories'.[67] Competition, falling behind, getting ahead: Europe as seen through its industrial cities was a place of constant battle.

Conclusion

Can we speak of a mercantile or 'entrepreneurial' travel culture? It is difficult to say when individual outlooks appear, on the face of it, so different. There is a major risk of reifying a nonexistent category whose virtual

176　*Corine Maitte*

members did not have the same culture, education, or interests. But the narratives studied here surely have a few things in common: the abiding attention paid to manufacturing and its evolution, the constant assessment of economic advantages and impediments, the sidelining in the narrative of any comments of a strictly 'cultural' nature. Certainly, our four travellers were not alone in focusing overwhelmingly on the economy of the countries visited. La Rochefoucauld or Arthur Young, for example, may have come from very different backgrounds and experiences, but basically shared very similar visions, if not judgements. Each speaks to the construction of the economic domain as a specific field with its own mechanisms.

We must dig deeper into what these views owe to the culture of administrative investigation which was developing, for example, in Piedmont, Lombardy and Tuscany, starting at the beginning of the century, in a very loose 'dialogue' with intendants, French inspectors and German cameralists. Though they fall squarely within the 'narrative genre', these texts seem to refer implicitly, not so much to the classical travel literature with its model of the nobleman's narrative, but rather to the questionnaires and enquiries on the 'state of the kingdom' that preceded those developed by the Napoleonic Statistical Office (1806).[68] The travellers did not tally, they described, but they did so to explain: they were looking for the causes of what they saw. They were more often observers of the economy than of social conditions, and in either case gave short shrift to what made a city unique. They contributed, in any case, to the creation of an 'industrial geography' of Europe, which the *Journal des Arts et manufactures* called for in 1794.[69]

Conforming to these models, which all (except Mazzoni) were familiar with thanks to their proximity to the administrative institutions, each interpreted them in his own way: their texts were tools for action. First-hand observation was the *sine qua non*: it was knowledge based on *seeing* and even *seeing things being done*, which alone made reproduction possible. To succeed, such observations had to be stripped of all subjectivity to favour a faithful recording of the data.[70] Moreover, samples and sketches served the same purpose. Such action could be taken by the travellers themselves who, having returned to their country, attempted to copy the techniques, to reproduce the products or the machines observed in the cities they visited. But it could also be the reforming action of governments who got hold of the writings and were responsible for implementing improvement (or even modernisation) programmes that were suggested, if not directly proposed by these travellers. They thus also attest to 'the emergence of a veritable audience of experts or professionals involved in the wider and more rapid circulation of economic information'.[71] Finally, these texts were the tools of a much more individually oriented goal: by writing them, their authors hoped to be recognised in this role of expert, and nurtured ambitions of professional and social ascension. On this last point, they mostly succeeded.

The 'Grand Tour' of Italian entrepreneurs 177

Notes

1 D. Roche, *Humeurs vagabondes* (Paris, 2005); G. Bertrand, ed., *La culture du voyage. Pratiques et discours de la Renaissance à l'aube du XXe siècle* (Paris, 2004); R. Sweet, *Cities and the Grand Tour: The British in Italy 1690–1820* (Cambridge, 2012).

2 See, for example, D. Roche and F. Angiolini, eds, *Cultures et formations négociantes dans l'Europe moderne* (Paris, 1995); G. Bertrand, *Le grand tour revisité. Pour une archéologie du tourisme: le voyage des Français en Italie (milieu XVIIIe s–début XIXe siècle)* (Paris, 2008), especially chapter 11 'les marchands en voyage' on the former; A. Simoes, A. Carneiro and M. Diogo, eds, *Travels of Learning: A Geography of Science in Europe* (Dordrecht, Boston and London, 2003); S. Collini and A. Vannoni, eds, *Les instructions scientifiques pour les voyageurs: XVIIe–XIXe siècle* (Paris, 2005) on the latter.

3 G. Bertrand, 'Voyage et altérité. L'émoi italien des Français en Italie du nord au XVIIIᵉ siècle', in *Identités et cultures dans les mondes alpins et italiens* (Paris, 2000), pp. 37–67. See also F. Wolfzettel, *Le discours du voyageur. Le récit de voyage en France du Moyen Age au XVIIIe siècle* (Paris, 1996), especially pp. 231–42, 266–76.

4 See, for example, P. Bertholet, 'Les industries d'Aix-la Chapelle, Eupen, Hodimont, Maestricht, Monjoie, Stavelot-Malmédy, Verviers et leurs environs vus par un négociant français vers 1755', *Bulletin de la Société verviétoise d'archéologie et d'histoire*, 61 (1980), pp. 117–35; S. Chassagne, 'Un voyage d'espionnage industriel en juin 1813', in A. Becchia, ed., *La draperie de Normandie du XIIIe au XXe siècle* (Rouen, 2003), pp. 253–62, and more generally C. Blanckaert, ed., *Le terrain des sciences humaines (XVIIIe–XIXe siècle)* (Paris, 1996).

5 See, for example, Y. Hersant, *Italies. Anthologie des voyageurs français aux XVIIIe et XIXe siècles* (Paris, 1988). In the section 'economy', one of the shortest, Hersant chose this passage from Lullin de Châteauvieux, dated 1813: 'What is hard to understand is the reason all these workers, born with so much intelligence and skill, have become incompetent, inept and uninventive. We can attribute this to a general decline in the industrial arts in Italy. When the decline has reached a certain point, emulation is lost alongside hope and courage.' Hersant, *Italies*, p. 795. Still, it is true that the merchants fanning out across the peninsula have quite a different view, Bertrand, *Le grand tour*, pp. 480 et seq.

6 We should note up front that is not where their uniqueness lies, for other travel narratives of the same period took stock of these same elements, which were increasingly the subject of research and international comparison. One need only think of Arthur Young, of course, *Travels during the Years 1787, 1788 and 1789, Undertaken more particularly with a View of Ascertaining the Cultivation, Wealth, Resources and National Prosperity of the Kingdom of France* (London, 1792) or F. de la Rochefoucauld, *Voyage en France (1781–1783)* (Paris, 1833). The latter would, moreover, go to England to meet with Young and complete a tour of England, and perhaps also Scotland and Ireland cf. de la Rochefoucauld, *La vie en Angleterre au XVIIIe siècle ou mélanges sur l'Angleterre* (Paris, 1784).

7 D. Margairaz, 'De Colbert à la statistique générale de la France', in Margairaz and P. Minard, eds, *L'information économique, XVIe–XIXe siècle* (Paris, 2008), pp. 143–53. She cites p. 149: *Journal des Arts et manufactures*, vol. 1, pt. 3 (unpaginated prospectus).

8 For purposes of comparison, A. Belmar and J. Sanchez, 'Constructing the center from the periphery: Spanish travelers to France at the time of the chemical revolution', *Boston Studies in The Philosophy of Science*, 233 (2003), pp. 143–88, discusses 80 Grand Tours of Europe by Spanish scientists between 1770 and 1830.

178   Corine Maitte

9   C. Maitte, 'Au coeur des manufactures lainières européennes du XVIIIe siècle. Le voyage de Gian Batta Moccafy, 1766–1767 – Relation de voyage de G.-B. Moccafy', *Documents pour l'histoire des techniques*, 18 (2009), pp. 151–200.

10 On Landriani, see S. Pugliese, 'I viaggi di Marsilio Landriani', *Archivio Storico Lombardo*, 51 (1924), pp. 145–95; M. Pessina, ed., *Relazioni di Marsilio Landriani sui progressi delle manifatture in Europa a fine Settecento* (Milan, 1981); S. Escobar, 'I viaggi di informazione tecnico-scientifica di Marsilio Landriani. Un caso di spionnaggio industriale', in A. De Maddalena, E. Rotelli and G. Barbarisi, eds, *Economia, istituzioni, cultura in Lombardia nell'età di Maria Teresa*, vol. II, *Cultura e società* (Bologna, 1982), pp. 533–44; Archivio di Stato di Milano, Commercio, busta 32.

11 On Morosi, see A. Moioli, 'Tra intervento pubblico ed iniziativa privata: il contributo di Giuseppe Morosi al progresso tecnico della manifattura lombarda in età francese', in A. Carera, M. Taccolini and R. Canetta, eds, *Temi e questioni di storia economica e sociale in età moderna e contemporanea. Studi in onore di Sergio Zaninelli* (Milan, 1999), pp. 153–204; A. Cova, 'Giuseppe Morosi e i problemi dell'innovazione tecnica nel napoleonico Regno d'Italia', *Rivista milanese di economia*, 26 (1988), pp. 108 et seq.; L. Funaro, 'Mezzi, metodi e macchine. Notizie su Giuseppe Morosi', *Nuncius. Annali di storia della scienza*, 13:1 (1998), pp. 77–137. Funaro wrote an intellectual biography of this Tuscan technician. His travel narrative is handwritten: 'Viaggio tecnologico del cav. Morosi in Francia, Olanda e Germania', Biblioteca Nazionale Centrale di Firenze (BNCF), Manoscritti, NA 1355, 25. This was not the only journey he took, for that matter. For example, he left again for Switzerland and France in 1811. There is also important correspondence preserved in Milan, notably at the Archivio di Stato di Milano (ASM), Studi, 272.

12 This journey was unique. Archivio di Stato di Prato (ASP), Fondo Mazzoni, busta 7: on this family and its importance in Prato, see C. Maitte, *La trame incertaine. Le monde textile de Prato, XVIIIe–XIXe siècle* (Villeneuve d'Ascq, 2001).

13 Bertrand, *Le grand tour*, p. 451, and the following: 1) those who were permanently itinerant, 2) those meeting a relative in a city, 3) those whose family sent them to be trained in a factory, 4) trips for leisure and cultural edification and 5) merchants passing through Italy by chance.

14 Biblioteca Reale di Torino (BRT), Storia Patria, 907, s.f.

15 On this point, see, in particular, J. Hirsch, *Les deux rêves du commerce* (Paris, 1991).

16 Notably after building an automaton chess player, see Funaro, 'Mezzi, metodi', p. 82.

17 The 1811 trip was the shortest and focused mainly on Switzerland and then on Strasbourg, Châlons sur Marne and Paris, between January and March. Funaro, 'Mezzi, metodi', pp. 110–11. Due to water damage sustained in 1966 by the National Library of Florence, the manuscript is almost unreadable. He made a final trip through Austria, Hungary and Bavaria, on Imperial orders, from June 1832–June 1833: ibid., pp. 118, 127–31; the manuscript is at the BNCF, N.A., 1355/7, 34 p. with many other drawings. After returning to Tuscany in 1833, he travelled again in 1834, this time to the Grand Duchy in the region of Maremma, Elba and the various mines of Tuscany: Funaro, 'Mezzi, metodi', pp. 131–3 and in the manuscript at the BNCF, N.A., 1355, 14.

18 In addition he noted the term 'executed' in the margins of the sketches once they had been completed.

19 He remained employed by the Lombardy administration after the Bourbon Restoration and finally returned to Tuscany in 1832.

The 'Grand Tour' of Italian entrepreneurs   179

20 On the Mazzonis, Maitte, *La trame incertaine*, pp. 195–225 and 419–25. At approximately the same time, Pietro Sella, from Biella in Piedmont, and Francesco Rossi, from Schio in the Venetian Republic, also left to observe technical and industrial Europe in order to adapt its principles to the reality of their firms: see, in particular, G.L. Fontana, 'L'Europe de la laine: transferts de techniques, savoir-faire et cultures d'entreprise entre Verviers, Biella et Schio', in Fontana and G. Gayot, eds, *La laine. Produits et marchés (XIIIe–XXe siècle)* (Padua, 2004), pp. 687–746; R. Gobbo, 'The transfer of knowledge between Verviers and Biella based on documents taken from the files of Sella wool mill in Croce Mosso', ibid., pp. 747–59.

21 Maitte, *La trame incertaine*, pp. 243–54

22 Landriani, *Relazioni*, pp. 34, 47.

23 Landriani regretted that his mission was made public by 'certain gazettes in Italy and Germany that announced my trip and the major goals I had set for it', ibid., p. 233.

24 See footnote 10: in 1981.

25 The report ends abruptly with Moccafy discussing industry in Abbeville and picks up again with his description of the samples from London.

26 BRT, *Storia Patria*, 907, without dates (1772) and unpaginated.

27 This notebook was found in the collection of the Forney Library in Paris, which it entered in 1924 after a strange and mysterious journey. It was donated by Mr David-Weill, then Honorary President of the 'Société des Amis de la Bibliothèque Forney'. He had purchased it for 3,000 francs. Information graciously supplied by Ms De Angeli Cayol. The first page of the book of samples includes the note 'mostre raccolte viaggiando dal signor Moccasi mercante di panni e nel suo ritorno verso il 1760 presentate al Conte Bogino'.

28 G. Ricuperati, *Lo stato sabaudo nel Settecento. Dal trionfo delle burocrazie alla crisi d'Antico regime* (Turin, 2001), pp. 202–12.

29 *Enciclopedia Biografica Italiana*, Bogino.

30 Archivio di Stato di Torino (AST), Materie economiche, IV, M. 13.

31 The BNCF manuscript is doubtless proof of this *Viaggio tecnologico*.

32 He had, moreover, already stated his desire to write in order to make technology 'more familiar, accessible and useful, and able to be studied with more confidence by young people, even if they are lack the gift of genius'. On the importance of the publication of statistics, notably for Chaptal, see M.-N. Bourguet, *Déchiffrer la France: la statistique départementale à l'époque napoléonienne* (Paris, 1989); D. Margairaz, *François de Neufchâteau* (Paris, 2005); Margairaz and Minard, *L'information économique*, and especially Margairaz's contribution, 'De Colbert à la statistique', pp. 143–53.

33 Funaro, 'Mezzi, metodi', p. 102, citing Archivio di Stato di Milano, Autografi, M., cart 146, fasc 8: 'M. Morosi travelled for the profit of Italian manufactures and not at all to the detriment of French manufactories.' Between 1807 and 1810, Morosi had to entrust the papers and drawings surrounding his trip to De Breme. He also kept a portion of them, which nonetheless remained unpublished and thus ended up in the manuscripts acquired by the National Library in Florence.

34 The government of the Kingdom of Italy disseminated Morosi's drawings widely through the Prefects and Sub-Prefects in an attempt to encourage industrialists to build machines, which led to a certain amount of suspicion. Be that as it may, a hierarchical model of economic administration still prevailed, far from the free circulation of men, ideas and machines and the new era of 'communicational action'. See Margairaz, 'De Colbert à la statistique', p. 148.

35 Unlike certain merchants studied by Gilles Bertrand, we know nothing about the possible libraries of these individuals. I compared the work of Duhamel du

180   *Corine Maitte*

Monceau, *Art de la draperie*, published in 1765, to Moccafy's narrative, but found no evidence of copying.

36 Pugliese used this correspondence with the Count Antonio Greppi, which was not publically available, but to which a descendant of the family granted him access. Pugliese cited, for example, Landriani's interest in climbing Mont Blanc. According to him, he would have willingly joined Balmat's third expedition, which brought Horace-Benedict de Saussure to the summit for the first time in August 1787, were it not for driving rain, which forced him to stay in town. He also related the observations of de Saussure from conversations he had with the man: 'The air is so thin that, after 20 or 24 steps, you fall into a sort of syncope or *deliquio*. The sky does not have that wonderful azure color we see down below: it is almost black, and the moon looks like a ball of fire above an immense piece of ebony.' Pugliese, 'I viaggi di Marsilio Landriani', p. 150.

37 Landriani, *Relazioni*, p. 233: 'difficulty gaining entrance into the English manufactories'.

38 We know that, at the time of his trip in 1832–3 for example, Morosi corresponded in Latin with the director of the mines of Halle, see Funaro, 'Mezzi, metodi', p. 130. The anonymous author of *L'art de voyager utilement*, published in Amsterdam in 1668, recommended not learning native languages to avoid becoming too familiar with the locals, cited by S. Collini, 'Practical advice and theoretical orientations in the instructions for travellers (XVIIIe siècle)', in Blanckaert, *Le terrain des sciences humaines*, p. 59.

39 Morosi began his travels in the company of Isimbardi and Prina on 22 July 1806, see Funaro, 'Mezzi, metodi', p. 96, but we do not know if they remained with him throughout his journey. Indeed, the opposite is highly probable.

40 In the case of Morosi, the manuscript of his trip includes succinct details about travel conditions themselves (whether slow, good, accident-ridden). In the case of Landriani, it was the correspondence with Greppi, of which we find only very indirect clues in Pugliese's article, which might have given such indications.

41 As Grimm sarcastically observed in 1769: 'our Frenchmen can no longer set foot in Italy without making us a present of a journey', cited by Y. Marcil, 'Lecture critique du voyage en Italie dans la presse littéraire de la seconde moitié du 18e siècle', in Bertrand, *La culture du voyage*, p. 181. In the science travel genre, recall that Linnaeus had published his *Instructio Peregrinatoris* in 1759.

42 The bibliography on travel guides is impressive, see, in particular, G. Chabaud, E. Cohen, N. Coquery and J. Penez, eds, *Les guides imprimés du XVIe au XXe siècle. Villes, paysages, voyages* (Paris, 2000).

43 F. Locatelli, *Il viaggiatore moderno* (Venice, 1775), cited by Bertrand, *Le grand tour*, p. 435.

44 Bertrand, *Le grand tour*, p. 464, points out that they tended to be shorter than those of noblemen or other travellers: five to seven weeks for most of those studied. Mazzoni's letters allow us to piece together his timetable with some precision: he stayed for the first six months in Italy and in the neighbouring Swiss cantons, then spent two months in France, three and a half in England, one and half months between the United Provinces and Germany, another two and a half months in Italy before returning to Florence/Prato. The lion's share of the voyage was therefore spent, surprisingly enough, in Italy.

45 No more than a dozen in all, essentially in France: Julienne, titular owner of the Gobelins in Paris; Lefebvre d'Elbeuf whose new products he described; Lambert, dyer in Rouen with whom he discussed the possibility of establishing one of his nephews in Piedmont; Van Robais in Abbeville whose manufactory he described at length, 'for he has the most magnificent of all he has seen'; Paignon and Rousseau, the two privileged Catholics from Sedan whom he accused of

The 'Grand Tour' of Italian entrepreneurs   181

'selling their name rather than their quality'; Louis Labauche, their Protestant competitor, whom he, on the contrary, praised. Outside France, one name alone was cited: that of Ellia Hanssen in Maastricht, in order to report on an offer made by the manufacturer.

46 Bertrand, *Le grand tour*, p. 464, and in particular the following pages.
47 For a comparison with French travellers who travelled at about the same time, see J. Gury, ed., *Le voyage outre-manche. Anthologie de voyageurs français de Voltaire à MacOrlan du XVIIIe au XXe siècle* (Paris, 1999), A. Coyer, *Nouvelles observations sur l'Angleterre par un voyageur* (Paris, 1779), and M. de Bombelles, 'Journal de voyage en Grande-Bretagne et en Irlande, 1784', compiled and presented by J. Gury in *Studies on Voltaire*, The Voltaire Fondation (Oxford, 1989), p. 269.
48 For purposes of comparison, the French perception of the United Provinces in the eighteenth century has been the focus of study by A. Nijenhuis, notably 'Les voyages de Hollande et la perception française des Provinces-Unies dans la première moitié du XVIIe siècle', Free University Amsterdam PhD thesis (2012).
49 For cities from which we have only one letter, there is no guarantee that he stayed longer than a day. We have, however, assumed two days as a low estimate for each city from which he sent a letter. It is impossible to know with any more accuracy.
50 M. Pieri, 'Dei viaggi', in G. Silvestri, ed., *Operette varie in prosa di Mario Pieri. Corcirese* (Milan, 1821), p. 208, cited by Bertrand, *Le grand tour*, p. 437.
51 Landriani, *Relazioni*, p. 233.
52 He criticised 'the hardness of his stubborn, ungracious and boorish character, and the greed with which he tyrannised all trade in Manchester, the cruel persecution with which he hassled those who tried to profit from his discovery and a thousand other similar circumstances which earned him the hatred and indignation of his fellow city-dwellers, who rather than feeling grateful – *grati* – to a man who did such a great service to the manufacturing nations, hate him intensely', see Pugliese, 'I viaggi', p. 179.
53 Ibid., pp. 180–2
54 Landriani, as we have said, passed through it, but did not write about it. The letters that Gaetano Mazzoni sent to his brother from the city are, unfortunately, illegible: the paper, too thin, has let the ink seep out. We would like to know what producer he got them from.
55 For example: 'In their bedrooms, they have to leave the beds unmade and the windows open from morning till mid-afternoon so the humidity [which he must have found extremely uncomfortable] doesn't rot the furniture.'
56 The index of his manuscript alludes to his wide-ranging interests: 'Arrived in the city. Took a walk, bridges, waterfalls, a large concert, theatre, etc. Long-burning candles for studying. Detail on the direction of water in the methods of building cataracts and embankments in Holland. Institute for Sciences and Arts called Filix Meritis. Ribbon factories, theatre, shipyards and arsenal, general orphanage, Orondelles (?), music halls, late-night café, Royal Palace, Marine Academy, mill for grinding cacao, Protestant orphanage, City Hospital, House of Correction, House of Correction for distinguished people, hospices for poor old Lutherans, orphanage for Catholics.'
57 BNCF, Mss, NA 1355, 25.
58 BNCF, Mss, NA 1355, 25, Rouen.
59 C. Maitte, 'Les yeux dans la laine: la Normandie sous le regard italien', in A. Becchia, ed., *La draperie en Normandie du XIIIe au XXe siècle* (Rouen, 2003), pp. 229–51.
60 Landriani, *Relazioni*, p. 47, emphasis added.

182 *Corine Maitte*

61 It was also clearly the case for a number of journeys made by Spanish scientists with the support of their government, see Belmar and Sanchez, 'Constructing the Centre', pp. 143–88.

62 This would, moreover, remain the case in historiography for a long time, particularly in terms of 'industrial' development cf. on the general comparison in historical practices, see M. Aymard, 'Histoire et comparaison', in H. Atsma and A. Bruguière, eds, *Marc Bloch aujourd'hui* (Paris, 1990), pp. 271–8; L. Pérez, 'Technique, économie et politique entre la France et l'Angleterre (XVIIe–XIXe siècles)', *Documents pour l'histoire des techniques*, 19:2 (2010), pp. 9–29.

63 The English system was summarised by Moccafy: 'wool shops are opened to give labourers work, which the latter complete at home. Twice a week a market is held for those who purchase the wool with their own funds to sell their items to whomever they want, and for those returning pieces to the agents from whom they had previously obtained the equal weight of wool for the price of their labor alone.' *Relation de voyage*, p. 186. This is what is now called the domestic or putting-out system. Both the French and English systems favoured the role of merchants over manufacturers.

64 Landriani, *Relazioni*, p. 282.

65 Ibid., p. 233.

66 For a contemporary opinion, see S. Cliquot de Blervache, *Considérations sur le traité de commerce entre la France et la Grande-Bretagne du 16 septembre 1786* (London, 1789). For historical analyses: M. Donaghay, 'Textiles and the Anglo-French commercial treaty of 1786', *Textile History*, 13:2 (1982), pp. 205–24, or J. Horn, *The Path Not Taken: French Industrialization in the Age of Revolution, 1750–1830* (Cambridge, 2006).

67 Landriani, *Relazioni*, p. 201.

68 See, for purposes of comparison, Bourguet, *Déchiffrer la France*; V. Denis, 'Surveiller et décrire: l'enquête des préfets sur les migrations périodiques, 1807–1812', *Revue d'Histoire Moderne et Contemporaine*, 47: 4 (2000), pp. 706–30, and, particularly, Margairaz and Minard, *L'information économique*. We can also compare them with another type of journey: that of explorers, see Collini, 'Conseils pratiques'.

69 Margairaz, 'De Colbert à la statistique', p. 149; *Journal des Arts et manufactures*, vol. 1 pt 3, unpaginated flyers.

70 S. Collini comments on the growing importance of this faithful recording of the data in instructional travel texts of the eighteenth century, Collini, 'Conseils pratiques', pp. 66–7.

71 Margairaz, 'De Colbert à la statistique', p. 145.

Part III
New patterns of travel

10 Young cosmopolitans

Flemish and Dutch youths and their travel behaviour (from the late sixteenth to the eighteenth century)

Gerrit Verhoeven

Journael van de reys na Flaederen – literally, the journal of a trip to Flanders – is an unremarkable travel journal, barely six folios in length and written in a clumsy, childish hand. It was found together with the last will and other papers of Johan Vultejus, bailiff of Liesveld and IJsselstein, and tells the story of an anonymous Dutch boy, who embarked on a summer trip to the Austrian Netherlands in 1731. At first sight, it is a highly conventional narrative, with bland descriptions of the cathedral in Ghent, the archducal court at Brussels and the lace-shops in Antwerp, yet, it is, in a sense, also unique, as the *journael* provides a rare insight into the travel experience of an early modern child.[1] Moreover, it hints at the emergence of a new travel culture that was as different to a traditional Grand Tour as chalk from cheese. Experts have only recently begun to trace the rough outlines of these emergent travel patterns, that were, slowly but surely, taking shape in the eighteenth century. New destinations emerged, as London, Paris and Amsterdam – and, on a lower level, Berlin, Dresden, Brussels or Nancy – became favourite *termini* for brief leisure trips,[2] while a *cours pittoresque* (a picturesque journey) along the Rhine also became fashionable.[3] Domestic travel was also on the rise. During the eighteenth century, British travellers discovered Wales, Scotland and the Lake District; a similar trend reshaped French, German, Dutch and Flemish travel behaviour.[4]

As the map of early modern travel behaviour was inch by inch – or better, mile by mile – redrawn, the social profile of travellers also changed radically in the eighteenth century. Leisure trips, let alone a classic Grand Tour, remained a privilege of the elites, as wealthy and often noble families still predominated; yet, at the margins of the group portrait, middle-class travellers began to emerge.[5] Travelling evolved from an (almost) exclusively male activity into a mixed experience, as women began to embark on short trips to Amsterdam, London and Paris, or even set off on a full-scale Grand Tour to Italy.[6] It has been suggested that children and adolescents also cropped up more frequently. Family trips became increasingly fashionable in the eighteenth century.[7] Yet, the evidence to substantiate such a claim remains scanty. Textbook-wisdom has it that the Grand Tour was teeming with

186   *Gerrit Verhoeven*

young men in their early 20s, but less is known about other modes of early modern youth travel. Were children and teenagers taken along on trips to London, Paris and Amsterdam? Did they enjoy a *cours pittoresque* along the Rhine? Or were they limited to domestic excursions?

It comes as no surprise that these questions are hard to answer, as children and young adolescents are barely visible in the sources.[8] Yet, this problem is less acute for the Low Countries, where all sorts of diaries, letters and ego-documents have been preserved, including literally hundreds of Flemish and Dutch travel journals.[9] Eleven travel accounts were selected from a larger sample, providing a rare and compelling insight into early modern youth travel. In some cases, children and young adolescents crafted their own travel journal – as was the case with the *Journael van een reys na Flaenderen* – yet, on most occasions, it was their father, mother or another relative, who recorded the journey.[10] As a result, a lot of information on youth travel is second-hand, which is a serious methodological drawback.[11] Moreover, the issue of representativeness looms large, given the tiny sample of travel journals of children and adolescents that has survived. Hence, the findings should be taken as indicative rather than as rock-solid evidence. Even though the sources disclose all sort of fresh detail on youth travel – allowing us, for instance, to outline the social profile of these 'small cosmopolitans' (their age, gender and class); to trace their travel destinations and motivations; and to explore their writing habits – this chapter aims to move beyond simple description by raising some analytical questions. Why, for instance, was youth travel on the rise in the eighteenth century? Did it mirror a surge in parental love and new family relations or was it rather the – unexpected – outcome of transport innovations?

The chapter then aims to identify the main differences or similarities between youth and mainstream travel behaviour. Was a distinct travel culture taking shape? Last, but not least, the research also considers the longer-term consequences. The experience of youth travel may been directive for later travel behaviour. According to the French geographer Jacques Lévy, children and young adolescents acquire a *compétence spatial*, as they are gradually familiarised with new destinations, activities and ways of travelling through their childhood excursions. It is often assumed that this *compétence spatial* is to a large degree directional for travel behaviour later in life.[12] Does Lévy's theory also hold for early modern Flemish and Dutch minors? Were their youth experiences decisive for their more mature travel behaviour?

New ways

Young men and adolescents were ubiquitous on the Netherlandish Grand Tour (Figure 10.1), as was also the case among English, German and other European travellers.[13] Famous humanists, such as the Louvain scholar, Justus Lipsius, had labelled the *peregrinatio academica* as the acme of an

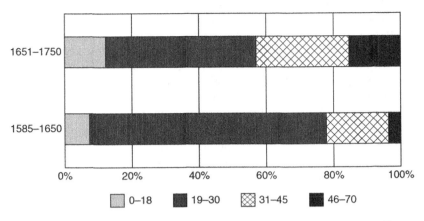

Figure 10.1 Netherlandish travellers and their age (1585–1750) (n = 183)[19]

aristocratic education in the late sixteenth century. Flemish and Dutch Grand Tour travellers were usually of an age somewhere between 20 and 25, although younger *peregrines* in their late teens or older travellers in their late 20s were not uncommon either. By contrast, children and younger teenagers were rarely if ever sent on a Grand Tour. Pieter Corneliszoon Hooft, scion of a wealthy Amsterdam merchant family, was barely 17 when he embarked on his *Groote Tour*, yet Hooft was an exception rather than the rule.[14] Clearly, the age limits and the planning of the Grand Tour fell in line with classic ideas on the stages of life. For early modern Netherlandish society, youth stretched to 28 or even – in some cases – beyond 30, even though young men officially reached manhood on their 25th birthday. Marriage or the start of one's career were deemed more informal markers for maturity,[15] whereas the Grand Tour functioned as a *rite de passage* or a coming of age ritual.[16] Young travellers usually set off after the completion of their formal university education, which means that most Grand Tour travellers were in their early 20s or even slightly older.[17] Moreover, humanist intellectuals strongly advised against travelling at a younger age.[18]

In the late seventeenth century, the tide was slowly but surely turning, as children and young adolescents cropped up among Netherlandish travellers. It would be unwise to label the trend as decisive – due to the lack of statistical data, the evolution is barely even measurable in percentages – yet, it is beyond doubt that Dutch and Flemish minors, between ten and 18 years old, were travelling alongside their elders with increasing frequency (see Figure 10.1). In the following section, this chapter will focus upon this younger unit. Unfortunately, there are no comparable figures for England, France, or the Holy Roman Empire, yet the scattered evidence seems to point in the same direction. Family excursions to the Lake District, Wales, or Scotland were not uncommon among British elites in the eighteenth

188   *Gerrit Verhoeven*

century, while children were also taken along on more physically demanding trips to the Continent and even – on the eve of the French Revolution – on a full-blown Grand Tour.[20] Clearly, the anonymous boy who wrote the *Journael van de reys na Flaenderen* was no exception, but rather a follower of fashion (or at least, his family was). It is unusual, however, that he recorded his travels himself. There are some other exceptions, but, as mentioned above, most travel journals were written by older family members who had taken their offspring on a family excursion. Obviously, this may obscure the role of children and young adolescents in early modern travel behaviour, as the adult writers were not always very informative about their younger travel companions. Children and adolescents often slipped through the net.[21]

Pieter de la Court, a well-heeled cloth merchant from Leiden, provides an illustrative example. During the summer of 1700, he left for Paris, together with his 12-year-old son Allard and his brother-in-law Jan Poelaert. In one of his first letters to his wife, Pieter wrote proudly that young Allard *zich seer kloeck hield* (had kept a stiff upper lip), while cousin Veen, who was much older, had been overcome by homesickness. More information about Allard is, however, hard to find, as Pieter was almost completely absorbed by the endless list of monuments, museums, churches and other entertainments in Paris. Notes on Allard and the other travel companions are thus extremely scarce.[22] Due to this 'dark number', it is likely that children and young adolescents may have been (much) more numerous than the paltry figures suggest.

Family excursions with mother and father, brothers and sisters and even – in some cases – with an assortment of other relatives were increasingly common or – *mama en papa, broers Meinard en Egbert, tante en oom Baeckman* – in the words of Pieter Johan Macaré, who embarked on a trip to Holland (*een reijsje*) in the spring of 1749. Even though Pieter Johan was 16 years of age, his journal was written in a rather childish way and imbued with warm feelings of familial bonding. Family travel was, in a sense, the exact opposite of the Grand Tour, where young travellers learned to fend for themselves.[23] Other types of youth travel were less common. Youngsters in their late teens sometimes pooled their resources together to hire a coach for a round trip through the Low Countries or a brief excursion to London or Paris. In 1742 Jason Bruijningh, a 14-year-old scion of a wealthy family of Amsterdam wine merchants, embarked on a *cours pittoresque* along the Rhine, together with some of his friends from Amsterdam, who were some years older. It is not unlikely that the boys travelled alone, as the journal fails to mention an accompanying adult, yet it is more plausible that they were chaperoned by a manservant, who kept an eye on his young masters.[24] After all, this was standard practice on the Grand Tour.[25] Jason travelled without his family, but they were not entirely out of the picture. Frequent letters were sent to *papa* (his father), while other relatives also repeatedly crossed his mind.[26]

Young cosmopolitans 189

Teenage trips were not unheard-of, but Netherlandish children and young adolescents predominantly travelled with their family.[27] In the late seventeenth century, these family excursions became even more fashionable among Dutch *burghers*. Some decades ago, historians would have referred to the classic theory of Philippe Ariès to explain the sudden upsurge in family excursions. According to the French historian, parental love was at its lowest ebb in the early modern period, due to extremely high child mortality rates. It was not until the eighteenth century, that the tide began to turn. However, Ariès' hypothesis is most unlikely, as personal letters, diaries and other ego-documents of seventeenth-century Netherlandish parents already brimmed with love, pride and other warm feelings towards children.[28] Fathers were increasingly incorporated into family life and leisure activities.[29] As domestic trips and frequent excursions to nearby metropolises became an essential part of the leisure and lifestyle of Netherlandish elites in the late seventeenth century, Flemish and Dutch families not only spent their vacation together at their country house, but also embarked on more daring trips and (beloved) children were simply taken along.

Group portrait

Family excursions provided an opportunity for children and young adolescents to travel, yet there were some restrictions limiting their participation. Their agency was curtailed according, to age, gender and class. Balthasar II Moretus's journey illustrates these limitations. The Antwerp printer left on a pilgrimage to the local sanctuary of Scherpenheuvel (in the southern Netherlands) in the summer of 1668, together with his wife Anna Goos, his sons Balthasar III junior, Johannes Jacobus, Franciscus and his daughter Maria Isabella. Having barely arrived at the shrine, Bathasar left his wife and the younger children Franciscus and Maria, who were 14 and 13, to return safely home, while he set off on an excursion to the Dutch Republic with the older boys.[30] Flemish and Dutch parents had rather clear-cut ideas about the most favourable age for travelling, although the unwritten law was tailored according to the risk and discomfort involved. Twelve was apparently deemed the absolute minimum age for travel, which seems to echo more widespread thoughts about the transition between childhood (under 12) and adolescence.[31] Youthful travellers were, however, in most cases, some years older, as boys of 16 and 17 predominated.[32] Family trips with children in their 20s were also fashionable.[33] These findings corroborate the hypothesis that early modern parents maintained warm relations with their offspring, even after they had left the home some years earlier.[34]

Gender was also an issue. Not that girls were entirely excluded – Maria Isabella Moretus serves as a counterexample – but there were obviously fewer girls than boys travelling along, while their agency was much more curtailed. This imbalance mirrors some entrenched gender inequalities in

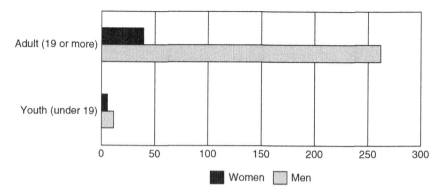

Figure 10.2 Netherlandish travellers and gender (1650–1750) (n = 320)

adult travel behaviour (Figure 10.2). Women were still scarce among Netherlandish travellers in the late seventeenth century, even though the tide was gradually turning. Classic conceptions of gender – as voiced, for example, by Johan van Beverwijcks' *Uytnementheyt des vrouwlicken geslachts* (Dordrecht, 1643), who confined women to the domestic sphere as *hun sachter vleesch* (their weaker vessels) hampered them from coping with bad roads, foul weather and other ordeals on their way – became gradually obsolete,[35] but other ideas proved much more persistent. Letters, diaries and ego-documents reveal that most parents still favoured boys above girls, even though the times were changing.[36]

New social and cultural morals thus provided an opportunity for more female travellers, yet, at the same time, girls were still treated differently. However, as time passed by, these young women set off a chain reaction. Adriana de la Court, daughter of the Leiden textile merchant Pieter mentioned above and beloved sister of Allard, provides a textbook-example. Barely 18 in age, Adriana travelled to London in 1714 chaperoned by her brother-in-law Johan Meerman. Apparently, she acquired a taste for travelling, as the trip to London was soon followed by a series of journeys to the Austrian Netherlands and the Holy Roman Empire.[37] Thanks to their childhood excursions, young ladies such as Adriana mastered a *compétence spatial*, which left an imprint on their later travel behaviour. Female travellers, as a result, became ever more numerous in the eighteenth century.[38]

Last, but not least, there were obvious social restrictions which constrained youth travel. Moretus, de la Court and the other families able to treat their children to excursions to London, Paris or Berlin, or, at least, to a domestic trip in the Low Countries, belonged to the Netherlandish high society. They were all settled *burghers*, who had made their fortune in trade or politics.[39] Wealth was a prerequisite for a classic Grand Tour, but even the shortest excursion through the Dutch Republic or the Austrian

Young cosmopolitans 191

Netherlands ran easily into hundreds of guilders for lodgings, transport and souvenirs. This represented a considerable sum, even for the most wealthy Netherlandish *burghers*. The presence of children would have been an additional financial burden, so they were only taken along by the wealthiest families. Likely, some parents were swayed by such financial considerations to leave their daughters at home.[40] Family trips may thus have served as a status symbol. In contrast, lower civil servants, barristers, clergymen, small entrepreneurs and other middle-class travellers had to plan their excursions before marriage or simply left their offspring at home during occasional outings.[41]

Space and time

Flemish and Dutch travel behaviour evolved radically in the late seventeenth century. Classic formulae such as the traditional Grand Tour to Italy and France, obviously lost ground, but other modes of travelling were on the rise. London, Paris and Berlin became favourite destinations for the Netherlandish elite, while a *cours pittoresque* along the river Rhine also proved fashionable. Moreover, *speelreijsjes* (leisure trips) and *divertissante somertogjes* (pleasurable summer trips) in the Low Countries likewise thrived.[42] Youth travel not only adhered to these evolving travel patterns, but also bolstered new developments. Nonetheless, the geographical range of children and young adolescents was rather limited. They were sometimes taken to London and Paris, but hardly if ever any further. For example, the Mechlen nobleman Corneille-Jean-Marie van den Branden travelled to Paris in 1736 together with his wife and daughters, while the 14-year-old Jason Bruijningh saw Mainz, Frankfurt and Cologne on his *cours pittoresque* in 1742.[43]

Most youth travel was, however, restricted to the Low Countries: Dutch *burghers* were dazzled by the baroque splendour of the Austrian Netherlands, while Flemish elites travelled northwards to the Dutch Republic. A case in point was Gerard Hinlopen, scion of a wealthy regent family from Hoorn [North-Holland], who embarked on a *speeljacht* (a pleasure yacht) sailing to the southern Netherlands in 1662. Barely one week later, he returned home with a trunk full of memories of Antwerp and Brussels.[44] It was an unremarkable journey in terms of length. Most children and young adolescents covered fewer than 100 miles, with 250 miles as the absolute maximum.[45] Longer trips are likely to have been deemed unsuitable not only because their length was at odds with conventional programmes of education, but also because of safety issues. With each mile travelled, the (anticipated) risk and discomfort rose.[46]

A closer look at the itineraries may confirm this hypothesis. Dutch travellers of the eighteenth century were not only fascinated by the baroque core of the Austrian Netherlands – especially the collections of paintings by Rubens in Antwerp, Brussels and Ghent – but were equally attracted by the

192   *Gerrit Verhoeven*

rugged landscapes of its southern fringe. A *cours pittoresque* along the river Meuse was the latest *vogue* in the early eighteenth century, including breathtaking panoramic views over rock-faces, wooded hills, lush meadows and ruined castles, while a detour to Spa, amid the Ardennes, proved fashionable too. Filthy inns, bad roads and barren landscapes seasoned these excursions with a pinch of adventure, but made these trips less suitable for children.[47] Children were, as a result, rarely if ever taken along. Family excursions were usually restricted to the lowlands of Holland, Flanders and Brabant, where transport was comfortable, safe and relatively cheap thanks to its modern infrastructure. From the seventeenth century onwards, trackboats were operating between the principal Dutch towns, while a dense grid of stone-slab paved roads opened up the Austrian Netherlands in the eighteenth century.[48] It is likely, that these slow-burn transport revolution(s) paved the way for more family trips, as it was much easier to take the children along than it had been a century before.[49]

Youth travel, once again, provided a *compétence spatial* that left an imprint on later travel behaviour. Memories of childhood excursions and teenage trips to London, Paris, Brussels or Amsterdam may have bolstered their growing repute. Pieter Johan Macaré's trip to Holland in 1749, when he was 16, became a stepping stone for later excursions to the Austrian Netherlands. Allard de la Court was barely 12, when his father took him to Paris in 1700, yet it was a brief foretaste of excursions to London (in 1710), to Köln (Cologne) and Düsseldorf (1724) and to the Austrian Netherlands (1728).[50] Flemish and Dutch travellers were, from childhood on, introduced to a new travel culture – they sampled up-and-coming destinations such as London, Paris, Amsterdam, Brussels – which became directive for later travel behaviour. Due to this effect, the lure of Dutch Republic and the Austrian Netherlands grew rapidly in the eighteenth century, when 78 per cent of the Netherlandish travellers opted for a domestic excursion, while barely 4 per cent embarked on a classic Grand Tour to Italy and France.[51]

Youth travel was not only distinctive in space, but also in timing. A classic Grand Tour to Rome easily extended for months, or even years, on end; a family trip with children or young adolescents lasted barely more than two or three weeks.[52] Young travellers were thus familiarised with less time-consuming ways of travelling, while the recurrence also increased. Balthasar III Moretus was, in his youth, taken on family trips to northern France and the Dutch Republic, which laid the foundation for a life full of travelling.[53] The same held true for the Leiden textile merchant Allard de la Court.[54] Moreover, jaunts and journeys were increasingly planned during the summer recess, or – less commonly – in the late spring or early autumn, thereby slowly but surely evolving into an adumbration of the modern-day vacation. As a concept, *vacance* was only coined in the late eighteenth century, but equivalents such as *speelreijsje* (leisure trip) and *divertissant somertogje* (pleasurable summer trip) began to circulate earlier. They were an unmistakable indicator for the leisurely nature of these excursions.[55]

Motives

In the late sixteenth century, the stern, humanist ideal of *utilitas* had fuelled the classic Grand Tour. Long and costly journeys to Rome were only deemed reasonable when they yielded knowledge, skills and *savoir faire* that could be useful in later life. Youthful travellers were expected to obtain an academic degree from a famous French or Italian university; to enrol in a foreign academy in order to master the noble arts of dancing, fencing and horsemanship; to refine their diplomatic skills and other talents. For Netherlandish parents, the concept of *utilitas* was elastic and could easily embrace trade and business.[56] Not surprisingly, education was also a vital motive in youth travel of boys in their later teens. Balthasar II Moretus, an Antwerp publisher, took his first-born son – the 14-year-old Balthasar III – to Paris in 1660. Moretus junior and senior wandered around Nôtre Dame, the Louvre and other classic sights; they visited Fontainebleau, the theatre and the royal zoo. Yet, more serious matters also cropped up, as Balthasar took the time to introduce his son – and future successor – to Cramoisy, Leonard and other Parisian printers, who were Moretus's most significant business partners in France. Through invitations to dine and convivial toasts new trading alliances and old friendships were celebrated. Together they visited the royal printing office, which was a sworn rival of Moretus's firm in the niche market of expensive and luxurious books. In a sense, the journey could thus be labelled as a sort of apprenticeship or even as industrial espionage.[57]

Multi-purpose trips, in which business and leisure were merged, also left an imprint on the travel journals of Johannes Samuel Cassa. Barely 18 years of age – on the cusp of adolescence – he travelled to Aachen in the retinue of the Dutch envoy, who sought to endorse the peace treaty of Aix-La-Chapelle in 1748. Being one of the younger clerks, Johannes's days were filled with writing letters, reports and other minor administrative duties. Meanwhile, he was able to observe the negotiations and diplomatic sparring, while he was inducted into ambassadorial protocol and *savoir faire*, thereby absorbing knowledge and skills, which would prove valuable in his later political career.[58] Yet, there was also enough spare time to visit the main sights in Aachen and other medieval towns, to go to the theatre or to take the waters, or even – in the sweltering summer months – to plan a leisure trip to Liège and Spa.[59] Moreover, Johannes's journal evidences a third motivation, as he approached the ride to Aachen as a *rite de passage*.[60]

Filthy inns and stale bread, long rides on horseback, grim publicans, cold nights on straw and other adventures punctuated Johannes's journal and were, in his own words, classic ingredients to turn a boy into a man. In his opinion, a relatively long separation from home was essential to steel oneself and to wash away the weakening influence of too much mothering.[61] Apparently, Cassa saw no contradiction between such bragging about manhood and some earlier lines in in his journal, where he confessed

194   *Gerrit Verhoeven*

that he had wept *heete traenen* (bitter tears), when he had bid *mama en papa*, brothers, sisters and other relatives farewell.[62] Manhood, perseverance and the ability to fend for oneself were also subthemes in Jason Bruijningh's *cours pittoresque* along the Rhine. Teetering on the edge of adolescence, Jason travelled with his Amsterdam friends, but without his parents.[63] Youth travel – as opposed to that of younger children – was, in this regard, not very different from a classic Grand Tour, that also functioned as a *rite de passage*.[64] It is not unlikely, that this overlap may have accelerated the eclipse of the Netherlandish *Grote Tour* in the late eighteenth century. Obviously, the theme was less pronounced in children's or young adolescents' travel behaviour, even though an excursion to London or Paris, such as Allard de la Court's trip to France at the age of 12, may well have served as a milestone between childhood and adolescence.[65]

Domestic trips had yet another purpose, which is illustrated by the *voorjaarsreijsje* (the spring excursion) of the 16-year-old Pieter Johan Macaré from Middleburg. While his father was caught up in endless business meetings and his mother was shopping her way through Holland, Pieter Johan and his brothers saw the sights. Leisure may have been their main motivation, but educational aims were not entirely ruled out, as the parents nudged their children with a gentle hand to see the iconic monuments and *lieux de mémoire* of the Dutch Republic, such as Amsterdam's city hall, the famous stained-glass windows in the church of Gouda, the Leiden *hortus botanicus*, the hall of the States-General in The Hague and the statue of Erasmus in Rotterdam. It is likely, that the educational value of viewing the memorials of a tumultuous past – such as the broadswords used by the Spanish troops to behead the rebellious citizens of Haarlem during the Dutch Revolt; the cuirass of Admiral Michiel de Ruyter, who had crushed the British fleet in the Anglo–Dutch wars; or the French banners from 1672, when the Republic had barely escaped total annihilation – was to awaken or bolster a feeling of Dutchness, while the visits to the Amsterdam Jewish synagogue and the *rasphuis* (bridewell) may have embodied national values of tolerance and discipline.[66] (Pre-)Nationalism[67] was also a strong motivation for British elites to focus on their own heritage and *lieux de mémoire* in the eighteenth century, when ruined medieval abbeys and neolithic stone circles turned into fashionable attractions.[68] Youth travel, thus, bolstered patriotism, working in conjunction with a surge of children's books on national history and geography. Education also increasingly focused on the national past.[69]

It is no coincidence that the educational theme became stronger in the eighteenth century, as pedagogical ideas were slowly but surely shifting. Formal schooling became less important, while education at home and more practical teaching methods were on the rise. Family trips were modified in accordance with these new educational ideas.[70] Youth travel was, however, also fuelled by leisure and pastime, as education and other serious motivations were barely more than a thin veneer or were, in most cases, completely absent. Corneille van den Branden, lord of Reet [in the Austrian Netherlands] travelled to Paris in 1736, together with his wife and daughters. They obviously saw Versailles, the Louvre and the other classic sights, but also spent hours on end shopping for fashionable evening gowns for the girls and a decent attire for him: 'Nous nous amusames a achetes [sic] des taftas pour trois habits de femmes en droguette et robe de chambre pour moi.'[71]

Moreover, they seized every opportunity to go the opera and the theatre.[72] Leisure also prevailed on the journey of Gerard Hinlopen to the Spanish Netherlands in the 1660s, as they embarked on their *speeljacht* (pleasure yacht) to Antwerp and Brussels. Pieter Johan Macaré even labelled his jaunt to Holland as a *plaisierreijsje* (a pleasure trip), replete with excursions and sightseeing, visits to family members and acquaintances, copious meals and breaks for coffee, board games, shopping and myriad other entertainments.[73] These easy-going leisure trips were poles apart from the stern ideals of *utilitas*, which had originally been the linchpin of the Grand Tour. By the late eighteenth century that ideal had been completely chipped away. Having been taken by their parents to London, Paris and other leisure hubs, these 'young cosmopolitans' became versed in a new travel culture that left its mark on their later travel behaviour. In the late eighteenth century, leisure became an even more powerful motive for travelling.[74]

Gazing

Children, it is assumed, travel differently. Memories of childhood excursions brim with reminiscences of sport and leisure activities, exotic food and unexpected encounters, while sightseeing is often recalled as tedious and mind-numbing.[75] Youth travel in the eighteenth century was not very different in this regard. Even though anecdotes and *petites histoires* were also to be found in the travel journals of grown-ups, they were ubiquitous in the travelogues of children and young adolescents. Pieter Johan Macaré dutifully described all classic sights in Amsterdam, Leiden and The Hague, but was much more verbose on the subject of his close encounter with a seal when they were sailing from Zeeland to Holland. The visit to the Leiden University collection of curiosities also left a deep impression, as he was mesmerised by the tiny shoes of Chinese women, the hipbone of a giant and a stuffed sea cow. The taste of a fresh salmon in Rotterdam was also worth a note.[76] According to humanist principles, early modern travellers were anything but free in their observations and descriptions, as the *artes apodemici* laid down a set of strict rules to lead the unpractised eye and the pen. In the late sixteenth century, travellers were advised to take notes on politics, law, economy, religion and other serious subjects. A checklist had to be used to portray towns, including notes on the walls and the gates, the harbour, the town hall and the main churches, the markets and numerous other items.[77]

196   *Gerrit Verhoeven*

Netherlandish travel behaviour was, on the whole, moving away from these humanist principles in the late seventeenth century, but the new tune was heard predominantly in the travel journals of younger travellers. Even though the anonymous writer of the *Journael van de reys na Flaenderen* dutifully described the classic sights in Antwerp, Brussels and Ghent, his attention was especially caught by a Catholic procession in Brussels, the brightly coloured banners and liveries of which he zealously recorded. A simple glass of Spa mineral water offered to him in Antwerp was also worth some paper and ink.[78] Younger travellers were more attentive to these *petites histoires* or felt less inhibited to scribble them down. Monuments, palaces and churches were rather superficially described in Jason Bruijningh's journal, but he was all ears for odd tales and side stories. Travelling through Amersfoort (still in the Dutch Republic) Jason bumped into a fellow traveller who spoke an unintelligible language, but was armed with a guide book and a satchel full of money.[79] Written down with relish, this trivial story was the first in a long sequence of similar *petites histoires* that punctuated his travel journal. More serious remarks on the monuments and sights of Frankfurt were preceded by a pleasantry on the piles of fried sausages and sucking pigs the hungry Dutchmen had wolfed down when they had just arrived after a long ride.[80] These stories were obviously no prerogative of children and young adolescents, yet it seems clear that these younger travellers (un)consciously subverted certain conventions. A similar observation could be made for personal letters. Correspondence between siblings was often extremely playful and blatantly ignored the rules for polite conversation.[81]

Conclusion

Young cosmopolitans – children and early teens – joined the ranks of Dutch and Flemish travellers in the late seventeenth century. Apparently, the Low Countries were in the vanguard, but scattered evidence suggest that British travellers were soon to follow, while French and German elites only joined in later. Despite this increasing popularity, youth travel was still the exception rather than the rule. Moreover, the agency of these 'young cosmopolitans' was constrained by restrictions on age, gender and social class, as young children, girls and middle-class children were rarely if ever taken along. During the eighteenth century, a distinctive travel pattern was slowly but surely taking shape. Youth travel not only differed fundamentally from a classic Grand Tour, but also diverged from mainstream – and thus adult – travel behaviour due to its specific timing, motivations and destinations. Family and teenage trips had a shorter range, as 200 miles was considered the absolute maximum, and they were completed in a brief timespan of some weeks or – *in extremis* – some days. Moreover, they adhered more to leisurely and educational motives, although their function as *rite de passage*, business trip, or other motivations should not be downplayed.

Looking back, it is no coincidence that youth travel became more popular in the eighteenth century. Transport (r)evolutions, such as stone-slab paved roads, track-boats and stage coaches, made travelling much safer, cheaper, more comfortable and facilitated the participation of younger travellers. Moreover, changes in family relations – and more especially the fact that domesticity and leisure became increasingly intertwined – bolstered the rise. Young cosmopolitans also seem to have benefited from the fresh pedagogical ideas that loomed large in the eighteenth century, which stressed the importance of practical training and family education. Finally, it seems important to consider the effects of youth travel in the long term. Much more research is obviously needed, yet the preliminary evidence drawn from Flemish and Dutch travel journals seems to suggest that these childhood or teenage trips really mattered. Young cosmopolitans were, from childhood on, versed in a new, trailblazing way of travelling. They acquired a *compétence spatial* or an intimacy with up-and-coming destinations, which left an imprint on their later travel behaviour. The same held true for timing, as Netherlandish youths were familiar with a more recurrent and less time-consuming way of travelling. Maybe, Netherlandish men became more tolerant towards female companions, thanks to childhood memories about family excursions. Finally, it seems plausible, that the shift from a humanist to a more personal way of writing and observing was cemented by the youthful scribblings, wherein little jokes, anecdotes and *petites histoires* closely intertwined.

Notes

1 Anonymous, *Journael van de reys na Flaenderen in't jaer 1731* (1731) [University of Amsterdam, coll. Hss. 31 Ed. no.7], pp. 1–6.
2 For instance, on the attraction of London as an up-and-coming travel destination for German, French and Netherlandish travellers: L. Bély, *Espions et ambassadeurs au temps de Louis XIV* (Paris, 1990), pp. 610–33; J. Rees, 'Wahrnehmen in fremden Orten, was zu Hause Vortheil bringen und nachgeahmet werden könne. Europareisen und Kulturtransfer adeliger Eliten im Alten Reich, 1750–1800', in R. Babel and W. Paravicini, eds, *Grand Tour. Adeliges Reisen und Europäische Kultur vom 14. bis zum 18. Jahrhundert* (Ostfildern, 2005), pp. 513–15; G. Verhoeven, *Europe Within Reach: Netherlandish Travellers on the Grand Tour and Beyond* (Leiden, 2015); G. Verhoeven, 'In quest for the new Rome: creative cities and early modern travel behaviour', in A. Miles and I. Van Damme, eds, *Unscrewing the Creative City* (London, 2015).
3 J. Towner, 'The Grand Tour: a key phase in the history of tourism', *Annals of Tourism Research*, 12 (1985), p. 314; M. Heafford, 'Between Grand Tour and tourism: British travellers to Switzerland in a period of transition, 1814–1860', *Journal of Transport History*, 27 (2006), pp. 25–47; Verhoeven, *Europe within Reach*, pp. 200–1.
4 K. Grenier, *Creating Caledonia: Tourism and Identity in Scotland, 1770–1914* (Aldershot, 2005); I. Ousby, *The Englishman's England: Taste, Travel and the Rise of Tourism* (Cambridge, 1990); for an overview, see J. Brewer, *The Pleasures of the Imagination: English Culture in the Eighteenth Century* (London, 1997), pp. 621–41.

198   Gerrit Verhoeven

5 Towner, 'The Grand Tour', p. 310. For Flemish and Dutch travellers: Verhoeven, *Europe Within Reach*, pp. 106–14.

6 B. Dolan, *Ladies of the Grand Tour: British Women in Pursuit of Enlightenment and Adventure in Eighteenth-Century Europe* (London, 2001) pp. 7–8; T. Proctor, 'Home and away: popular culture and leisure', in D.Simonton, ed., *The Routledge History of Women in Europe since 1700* (Abingdon, 2006), p. 311; R. Sweet, *Cities and the Grand Tour: The British in Italy, c.1690–1820* (Cambridge, 2012), pp. 23–64; A. Vickery, *The Gentleman's Daughter: Women's Lives in Georgian England* (New Haven, 1998), p. 252.

7 Brewer, *The Pleasures of the Imagination*, p. 632.

8 On this methodological issue, see W. Frijhoff, 'Historians' discovery of childhood', *Paedagogica Historica*, 48 (2012), pp. 11–30; P. Griffiths, *Youth and Authority: Formative Experiences in England, 1560–1640* (Oxford, 1996), pp. 1–2.

9 Classic historical studies on Dutch children include: A. Baggerman and R. Dekker, *Child of the Enlightenment: Revolution Europe Reflected in a Boyhood Diary* (Leiden, 2009); B. Roberts, *Through the Keyhole: Dutch Child-Rearing Practices in the Seventeenth and Eighteenth Century. Three Urban Families* (Hilversum, 1998).

10 These 11 manuscripts were taken from an initial sample of 139 Dutch and Flemish travel journals that were written between 1585 and 1750. For more information on this sample, see Verhoeven, *Europe Within Reach*, pp. 21–7.

11 Frijhoff, 'Historians' discovery of childhood', pp. 11, 17.

12 P. Duhamel, ed., *Tourismes: lieux communs* (Paris, 2002), pp. 153–4.

13 J. Black, *Italy and the Grand Tour* (New Haven, 2003), pp. 140–2; S. Warneke, *Images of the Educational Traveller in Early Modern England* (Leiden, 1995), p. 79; Towner, 'The Grand Tour', p. 311.

14 P. Hooft, 'Reis-heucheniss', in J. van Vloten, ed., *Hoofts brieven* (Leiden, 1856), pp. 407–33.

15 Even for contemporaries, there were no clear distinctions between infancy, childhood, adolescence, youth and adulthood. I. Ben-Amos, *Adolescence and Youth in Early Modern England* (New Haven, 1994), p. 11; L. Pollock, 'Parent–child relations', in D. Kertzer and M. Barbagli, eds, *Family Life in Early Modern Times, 1500–1789* (New Haven, 2001), p. 198; B. Roberts, *Seks, Drugs en Rock'n'Roll in de Gouden Eeuw* (Amsterdam, 2014), p. 25; Roberts, *Through the Keyhole*, p. 162; Frijhoff, 'Historians' discovery of childhood', p. 19; Griffiths, *Youth and Authority*, pp. 5–6, 22–8.

16 A. Stannek, *Telemachs Brüder. Die höfische Bildungsreise des 17. Jahrhunderts* (Frankfurt, 2001), pp. 19–23; M. Leibetseder, *Die Kavalierstour. Adlige Erziehungsreisen im 17. und 18. Jahrhundert* (Köln, 2004), p. 13.

17 Verhoeven, *Europe Within Reach*, pp. 114–23.

18 L. Coulon, *L'Ulysse Francois, ou le voyage de France* (Paris, 1643), introduction; Anonymous, *Wegh-Wyser, aenwijsende de besonderste vremde vermaeckelijckheden die in't reysen door Vrankryck te sien zijn* (Amsterdam, 1657), introduction.

19 Verhoeven, *Europe Within Reach*, p. 118.

20 Brewer, *The Pleasures of the Imagination*, p. 632. See also the chapter by Richard Bates in this volume. In Germany, the evidence seems to point to a much later evolution. P. Prein, *Bürgerliches Reisen im 19. Jahrhundert. Freizeit, Kommunikation und soziale Grenzen* (Münster, 2005), pp. 17–21

21 Other exceptions include: P. Macaré, *Journaal van een voorjaarsreisje gedaan naar Holland* (1749) [Central Bureau for Genealogy, The Hague, FA Macaré 937]; J. Bruijningh, *Rysbeschryving van Amsterdam naar Frankfort*

Young cosmopolitans 199

en terug (1742) [Amsterdam City Archives, FA Heshuysen 364]. See, for this methodological issue, Frijhoff, 'Historians' discovery of childhood', pp. 11, 17.

22 Pieter de la Court, *Brieven van Pieter de la Court van der Voort aan Sara Poelaert tijdens zijn reis naar Parijs* (1700) [Leiden City Archives, FA De la Court 64], 3 Jun. 1700

23 Macaré, *Journaal*, pp. 1–4, 54, 120–2.

24 Bruijningh, *Rysbeschryving*.

25 A similar methodological problem arises with regard to domestic servants who travelled alongside their employers as they are virtually invisible in the sources. For more information on 'itinerant' domestic staff, see Verhoeven, *Europe Within Reach*, pp. 82–104.

26 Bruijningh, *Rysbeschryving*, pp. 2, 10.

27 Nine journals from the 11 manuscripts in our sample record a family excursion. The exceptions are the journal of Jason Bruijningh and the report of Samuel Cassa of a diplomatic mission: Bruijningh, *Rysbeschryvinge* (1742); Johan Cassa, *Journaael van mijn reis na Aaken* (1748) [City Archives The Hague, Ov. Verz. Hs. 161[a]]

28 For the initial hypothesis and the proof to the contrary: P. Ariès, *Centuries of Childhood: A Social History of Family Life* (New York, 1960); Frijhoff, 'Historians' discovery of childhood', p. 23; Roberts, *Through the Keyhole*, pp. 140–2, 162; S. Schama, *Overvloed en onbehagen. De Nederlandse cultuur in de Gouden Eeuw* (Amsterdam, 1989), p. 485: J. Brouwer, *Levenstekens. Gekaapte brieven uit het rampjaar 1672* (Hilversum, 2014), pp. 251–9. Virtually the same seems to have been true for Great Britain: see Pollock, 'Parent–child relations', p. 201; Griffiths, *Youth and Authority*, pp. 2–3.

29 Roberts, *Through the Keyhole*, p. 142; Schama, *Overvloed en onbehagen*, pp. 541–2. On the rise of family excursions, see Verhoeven, *Europe Within Reach*, pp. 119–21.

30 B. Moretus, *Reijse ghedaen door Balthasar Moretus* (1668) [Museum Plantin-Moretus, Antwerp, M90²:III-IV] pp. 12r–13r.

31 Griffiths, *Youth and Authority*, pp. 22–3; Pollock, 'Parent–child relations', p. 198; Ben-Amos, *Adolescence and Youth*, p. 11; Roberts, *Seks, drugs en rock'n'roll*, p. 25.

32 From our sample, 12 young cosmopolitans could be linked to an exact age: 12 (2), 13 (2), 14 (2), 16 (1), 17 (4), 18 (1). These Netherlandish examples seem at odds with the British experience, as Richard Bates argues that even (very) young children were accompanying their parents in the eighteenth century. See his contribution in this volume.

33 See, for instance: Moretus, *Reijse* (1668); P. Hulft, *Verslag van een reis naar de Zuidelijke Nederlanden* (1682) [Amsterdam City Archives, HA Marquette 366]; C. van den Branden, *Voijage de Paris* (1736) [National Archives Brussels, I 196:15b].

34 Roberts, *Through the Keyhole*, p. 162; Pollock, 'Parent–child relations', p. 201; I. Ben-Amos, 'Reciprocal bonding: parents and their offspring in early modern England', *Journal of Family History*, 25 (2000), pp. 291–312.

35 Quoted in D. Haks, *Huwelijk en gezin in Holland in de 17de en 18de eeuw* (Utrecht, 1986), p. 151. On the growing number of female travellers in Britain, see Proctor, 'Home and away', pp. 299–340; Vickery, *The Gentleman's Daughter*, pp. 251–2; Z. Kinsley, *Women Writing the Home Tour, 1682–1812* (Farnham, 2008). It seems likely, that the growing female participation in travel culture was part of a wider trend, which gave Dutch and Flemish women more elbow room: M. van der Heijden, E. Nederveen Meerkerk and A. Schmidt,

200 Gerrit Verhoeven

'Terugkeer van het patriarchaat? Vrije vrouwen in de Republiek', *Tijdschrift voor Sociale en Economische Geschiedenis*, 6 (2009), pp. 26–52.

36 Brouwer, *Levenstekens*, pp. 251–9.

37 G. Meerman, *Gedetailleerde genealogie van het oude geslacht Meerman* (1757) [National Library The Hague, 75 B 26]. More information on later trips: A. de la Court, *Beschryving van een reis door Brabant en Vlaanderen* (1740) [High Council of the Nobility, The Hague, FA Van Spaen 183]; de la Court, *Beschrijving van een reis naar Hamburg* (1743) [High Council of the Nobility, The Hague, FA Van Spaen 184]; de la Court, *Beschrijving van een reis naar Maastricht, Spa en Kleef* (1733) [High Council of the Nobility, The Hague, FA Van Spaen 182].

38 Verhoeven, *Europe Within Reach*, pp. 123–9. For literature on British women, see Dolan, *Ladies of the Grand Tour*, pp. 7–8; Proctor, 'Home and away', pp. 299–340; Vickery, *The Gentleman's Daughter*, pp. 251–2.

39 For more information on the wealth of these elite families see K. Degryse, *De Antwerpse fortuinen. Kapitaalsaccumulatie, -investering en –rendement te Antwerpen in de 18de eeuw* (Antwerpen, 2005), p. 145; K. van Zandvliet, *De 250 rijksten van de Gouden Eeuw. Kapitaal, macht, familie en levensstijl* (Amsterdam, 2006), p. 123; G. Verhoeven, *Anders reizen?Evoluties in de vroegmoderne reiservaringen van Hollandse en Brabantse elites* (Hilversum, 2009), pp. 64–8.

40 An illustrative example is Adriaan van Assendelft, who paid 145 guilders for a nine-day trip through the Dutch Republic in 1696. In addition to his wife, brother and sister-in-law, his two daughters also travelled along. See A. van Assendelft, *Journaal van een reis door Holland* (1696) [High Council of the Nobility The Hague, FA van der Lely 421].

41 J. van der Streng, *Memorij van een plaisierreijsje* (1731) [University Library Leiden, Ltk. 862].

42 Verhoeven, 'Foreshadowing tourism?', pp. 262–83; Verhoeven, 'In quest for the new Rome'.

43 Bruijningh, *Rysbeschryving* (1742); de la Court, *Brieven van Pieter de la Court* (1700).

44 G. Hinlopen, *Reijse gedaan met ons speeljacht naar Brabant, Hulst in Vlaanderen, Zeelandt ende Uijtrecht* (1662) [University Library Amsterdam, coll. Hss. VIII E[1]].

45 Prein's research seems to bolster this hypothesis, as German youngsters also travelled only a relatively short distance. Prein, *Bürgerliches Reisen*, pp. 17–21.

46 Verhoeven, *Anders reizen?*, p. 315.

47 Examples of travellers taking pleasure in these adventurous features include: A. de la Court, *Beschrijving van een reis naar Maastricht, Spa en* Kleef (1733) [High Council of the Nobility The Hague, FA Van Spaen 182], pp. 2–3; Van der Streng, *Memorij van een plaisierreijsje*, pp. 25–43; P. Van Dorp, *Kort verhaal van het divertissant somertogje en pleijsier-reisje* (1732) [Central Bureau for Genealogy, The Hague, FA Mispelblom 47] pp. 92r–94r.

48 T. Barker and D. Gerhold, *The Rise and Rise of Road Transport, 1700–1900* (Cambridge, 1993); J. de Vries, *Barges and Capitalism: Passenger Transportation in the Dutch Economy, 1632–1839* (Utrecht, 1981); B. Blondé, 'At the cradle of the transport revolution? Paved roads, traffic flows and economic development in eighteenth-century Brabant', *Journal of Transport History*, 31:1 (2010), pp. 89–111.

49 G. Verhoeven, '"Een divertissant somertogje." Transport innovations and the rise of brief pleasure trips in the Low Countries (1600–1750)', *Journal of Transport History*, 30:1 (2009), pp. 78–97.

Young cosmopolitans 201

50 For example: A. de la Court, *Aanteekening ofte journaal van myn reys naar Londen* (1710) [Regional Archives Leiden, FA De la Court 104]; de la Court, *Reis naar Luik, Keulenen Dusseldorf* (1724) [University Library Amsterdam, coll. Hss. IV J 10 :2]; de la Court, *Kassaboek* (1728–38) [Regional Archives Leiden, FA De la Court 142] 11 Sep. 1728.
51 Verhoeven, *Anders reizen?*, p. 360.
52 Ibid., p. 147.
53 Moretus, *Reijse ghedaen*, 1668; B. Moretus, *Itinerarium Parisiense* (1660) [Museum Plantin-Moretus, Antwerp, M.90²:VIII]; B. Moretus, *Reyse nae Walschquartier* (1663) [Museum Plantin-Moretus, Antwerp M. 90²: XI].
54 For references, see note 39 above.
55 For instance, Anonymous, *Speelreis door sommige steden van Vlaanderen en Brabant* (1724) [University Library Amsterdam, coll. hss. E 32ᵃ]; Dorp, *Kort verhaal*.
56 The Netherlandish *Groote Tour* was, in this regard, very different from the British *Grand Tour*, where business and trade were deemed incompatible with a genteel lifestyle. Verhoeven, *Europe Within Reach*, pp. 52–81.
57 Moretus, *Itinerarium Parisiense*, pp. 3r–4v, 7r.
58 Cassa, *Journaael van mijn reis na Aaken*, pp. 6–7, 48, 53, 85.
59 Ibid., pp. 42–5, 50, 55, 67–79
60 A. Van Gennep, *The Rites of Passage* (Chicago, 1960).
61 A similar argument was used in classic texts on the *Grand Tour* by Maximilian Misson and Richard Lassels: see, for example, R. Lassels, *The Voyage of Italy* (Paris, 1670), preface.
62 Cassa, *Journaaal van mijn reis na Aaken*, pp. 1, 27–28, 32.
63 Bruijningh, *Rysbeschryving*, pp. 7–10, 119.
64 Stannek, *Telemachs Brüder*, pp. 19–23; Leibetseder, *Die Kavalierstour*, p. 13.
65 The lines quoted above, in which Pieter praises his son's courage in overcoming homesickness, seems to suggest that this trip was also a kind of test: P. de la Court, *Brieven van Pieter de la Court*, 3 Jun. 1700. At the age of 12, the sons of Netherlandish middle-class or lower-class burghers usually left home to start as an apprentice, while the elite enrolled in Latin or French boarding schools. Roberts, *Through the Keyhole*, p. 136.
66 Macaré, *Journaal*, pp. 15, 28–9, 35, 57, 75, 82, 91–3.
67 C. Kidd, *British Identities before Nationalism: Ethnicity and Nationhood in the Atlantic World, 1600–1800* (Cambridge, 1999), pp. 1–5; A. Smith, 'Nationalism in early modern Europe', *History and Theory*, 44 (2005), pp. 404–15. Patriotism was also important in the anti-Grand Tour discourse: Warneke, *Images*, pp. 11–14.
68 R. Sweet, *Antiquaries: The Discovery of the Past in Eighteenth-Century Britain* (London, 2004); Brewer, *The Pleasures of the Imagination*, pp. 632–7; Ousby, *The Englishman's England*, pp. 9–12; Vickery, *The Gentleman's Daughter*, pp. 251–2.
69 For children's books, see M. Grenby, *The Child Reader, 1700–1840* (Cambridge, 2014).
70 M. Hilton and J. Shefrin, 'Introduction', in M. Hilton and J. Shefrin, eds, *Educating the Child in Enlightenment Britain: Belief, Culture, Practice* (Farnham, 2009), pp. 8–9.
71 'We enjoyed ourselves by buying *taffeta* [sort of silk] for three women's robes and a dressing gown in *drugget* [a half-woollen fabric] for me.' Hinlopen, *Reijse gedaan*, pp. 1–6.
72 Branden, *Voijage de Paris*, pp. 3v, 7r.
73 Macaré, *Journaal*, pp. 1, 25, 28, 31, 35, 41, 66–7, et seq.

202   *Gerrit Verhoeven*

74 Verhoeven, 'In quest for the new Rome'.
75 J. Small, 'The absence of childhood in tourism studies', *Annals of Tourism Research*, 35 (2008), pp. 772–89.
76 Macaré, *Journaal*, pp. 8, 12, 36.
77 J. Stagl, 'Un système de literature normatrice des voyages au XVIe siècle', *Les guides imprimés*, pp. 34–44; Warneke, *Images*, pp. 3–4, 31–51; J. Stagl, 'The methodizing of travel in the sixteenth century: a tale of three cities', *History and Anthropology*, 4 (1990), pp. 303–38.
78 Anonymous, *Journael van de reys na Flaenderen*, pp. 3–4.
79 Bruijningh, *Rysbeschryving van Amsterdam*, pp. 1–2.
80 Ibid., pp. 12, 111–12, 125–6.
81 A. Harris, 'This I beg my Aunt may not know. Young letter-writers in eighteenth-century England, peer correspondence in a hierarchical world', *Journal of the History of Childhood and Youth*, 2 (2009), pp. 333–60. A similar observation can be made for female travel writing: see Sweet, *Cities and the Grand Tour*, pp. 46–7.

11 Revolutionary ruins
The reimagination of French touristic sites during the Peace of Amiens

Elodie Duché

The Revolution of 1789, and the destruction of the Bastille prison in Paris, left a debris field that generated a new touristic market of revolutionary relics in France, Great Britain and the United States in the decades following these events.[1] Myriad pieces of ruins, such as fragments of walls, stones, doors and keys of the fortress, were extracted from the rubble to circulate widely as material testaments to the liberating force of the Revolution. The dissemination of these remains was facilitated by one entrepreneur, Pierre-François Palloy, who arranged the demolition of the building and orchestrated touristic practices on the worksite. Not only did he employ tour guides to direct visitors through muddy dungeons, and help them detach stones from scathed towers, but he also launched a trade in Bastille-themed souvenirs. These ephemera included polished wall stones to adorn jewellery sets, medals and miniature models of the bastion carved in materials taken from the building itself.[2] These artefacts were meant to further the 'experiential dimension' of the Revolution through iconoclastic and reconstructive rituals, which, as the recent studies of Keith Bresnahan and Richard Taws have shown, were part of a patriotic agenda of myth-making.[3] This symbolic performance aimed to elongate a provisional reversal of power, by maintaining the visual memory of a tyrannical site that was bound to disappear, and therefore endanger the remembrance of a revolutionary momentum. Other historians, such as Lynn Hunt, have emphasised the affective power of this commerce of ruins in 'consolidat[ing] the new Nation that revolutionary rhetoric posited in the first place'.[4]

However, little attention has been given to the role of foreign travellers in the consumption of these revolutionary ruins, and their influence on the reimagination of French touristic sites during the period. Yet, it seems striking that various bits and pieces of the Bastille now populate British and American museums. Even items of a somewhat insignificant appearance, such as a small cube, cut from a wooden door, now feature in the Smithsonian's collections in Washington DC.[5] While the conditions of the transatlantic journey of this little piece remain unknown, it seems clear that material evidence of the Revolution circulated outside France, from the

204   *Elodie Duché*

1790s to the dawn of the nineteenth century.[6] Important figures accessed these goods through donations: the Marquis de la Lafayette, for instance, offered a Bastille key to George Washington, who proudly exhibited it at Mount Vernon.[7] Others, sometimes of a more modest nature, accessed these ruins directly by travelling *en masse* to the country during the Peace of Amiens, when hostilities temporarily ceased between France and Britain in 1802.[8]

This chapter intends to explore the impact of these migrations on touristic patterns, behaviours and imaginations in post-revolutionary France. As a gap between the Revolutionary and the Napoleonic conflicts, the Peace of Amiens led to a brief yet intense interlude of tourism, which was oriented both towards the resumption of financial connections with France and the first-hand contemplation of the remains of war and social unrest. British travellers were obsessed with ruins and collecting the remnants of the Revolution. They chronicled, in memoirs, sketchbooks and correspondence, their examination of scathed landscapes and mutilated churches in a direct, affective and sensory manner, which suggests that the peace further developed the 'experiential' memory of the Revolution mentioned above. Whereas the studies of Simon Bainbridge, John Richard Watson and Jeffrey Cox have illuminated the shaping force of the Revolutionary and Napoleonic Wars on English Romanticism, this chapter will reverse the perspective by examining how Romantic imaginations transferred antiquarian pursuits onto the construction of an 'immediate history' of the French Revolution at the eve of the First French Empire.[9]

Considered as a corpus, the narratives and watercolours produced by British travellers, along with French police records and guide books produced to shepherd them through revolutionary sites, offer the possibility to identify not only the reinvention of Grand Tour writing tropes in this episode of post-war tourism, but also the emergence of new spaces of touristic interest in France in 1802.[10] These sources highlight that the quest to contemplate revolutionary ruins had two consequences. First, it refashioned *ancien régime* touristic sites in a temporal dichotomy between before and after the revolutionary upheaval. New guide books systematised this tension, and fed imaginations of the recent past and reflections on the ravages of time. This led to another change: the emergence of new touristic sites within the traditional Grand Tour metropolis of Paris, but also beyond, in the provinces. Attempts to retrace Louis XVI's escape led, for instance, to the transformation of remote northern places in Lorraine, such as Varennes-en-Argonne, into touristic hubs where traces of past violence could be gleaned. To explore this two-fold dynamic, this chapter will first consider the itineraries and various social outlooks of British travellers to France during the Peace of Amiens, before investigating their collection of revolutionary ephemera and ruins. The last section will reflect on the shift these British migrations produced on the geography and meaning of tourism in post-revolutionary France.

Journeys and travellers

As Jenny Uglow and Cox have recently shown, the signing of the Peace of Amiens, on 25 March 1802, brought not only respite but also elation to a British population drained by war.[11] Festivities were organised throughout Britain to celebrate the truce: London was illuminated, shops and pubs advertised the imminent deflation of food prices, while mail coaches bore chalk inscriptions heralding 'Peace with France' across the country.[12] Britons also set sail to France with an unprecedented impetus. Within ten days following the treaty, 798 British passengers landed at Calais and, overall, 5,000 of these travellers were recorded as residing in the French capital during the truce.[13] In April, George Jackson, the sibling of the British envoy at the negotiations of Amiens, wrote that in Paris: 'all the hotels are overflowing with English; for we have an inundation of our shores since the signature of the Treaty, and the flood increases daily, and will no doubt go increasing'.[14] The environmental metaphor used by Jackson reveals that the peace was seen as a moment of heightened, if not overwhelming, mobility: what Cox terms a 'touristic expeditionary force'.[15]

This expedition was the product of war itself. The recent work of Renaud Morieux has shown how war did not suspend cross-channel migrations during the eighteenth century.[16] Rather, his study of the Channel has suggested the need to rethink patterns of transnational movements as being prompted and recorded by war. Inspired by Daniel Roche, his work has revealed the complexities of 'peaceful invasions' which 'make foreigners, who are usually invisible, suddenly visible'.[17] What made the 'overflow' of British visitors so visible in France in 1802 was the British and French systems of border control, which had been tested during the revolutionary wars and which came to be perfected, in various ways, during the peace.[18] The documents generated by this border surveillance reveal a two-fold phenomenon. First, migrations operated both ways, as evidenced by Madame Tussaud's ability to exhibit her waxworks in London in 1802. The 'Register of Passes' from the British Foreign Office suggests that 2,598 passports were given to English migrants wishing to visit France and 3,055 for French travellers traversing the Channel. These trans-channel migrations also involved other nationalities. Morieux has shown how the Channel constituted a global crossing between France and Britain, which was traversed by Italian, Swiss, German, Baltic and American visitors.[19] Second, the Peace of Amiens democratised temporary migrations, owing to less onerous modes of transport.[20] This democratisation of cross-channel tourism coincided with new attempts to ameliorate journeys across the Channel, exemplified by Albert Mathieu-Favier's project of an undersea tunnel.[21]

Much is known about the peripatetic elites who visited France for political and cultural affairs in 1802. These included myriad statesmen: not only Charles James Fox and the ambassador Lord Whitworth, but also twothirds of the British Parliament, with 82 past, current and future members

206 *Elodie Duché*

of the House of Commons and 31 peers.[22] Radicals, such as Thomas Paine and Helen Maria William, had already settled in France in the 1790s, and were visited by these new travellers. Reformers, lawyers and engineers were also prominently represented: Samuel Romilly, Thomas Malthus, Jeremy Bentham and James Watt were among them. Many Romantic authors and artists, such as Samuel Rogers, Maria Edgeworth, Thomas Daniell and William Turner, also hoped to explore Parisian museums and sketch the new acquisitions of the Louvre before the general public was admitted.[23] These select visitors produced vast quantity of writings, principally in the mode of private correspondence and memoirs, which explains the great attention their experience has drawn among historians.[24]

Conversely, little attention has been given to returning soldiers and more modest visitors, who crossed the Channel in the hope of finding employment or trade on the Continent. The lists of travellers compiled by the diplomat Anthony Merry reveal that members of the gentry constituted only 39.6 per cent of these travellers in 1802.[25] His records also suggest that 34.4 per cent were servants, 10.5 per cent soldiers and 6.8 per cent merchants. Yet, his compilation focused on travellers already in Paris in 1802, and requesting passports from him to return to Britain. Therefore, they do not account for the vast number of textile workers and dealers who contemplated a longer journey in France to develop their trade. Recent research has shown that the peace enabled the resumption of silk and muslin contraband between the two countries. These goods were extremely sought after, which explains why the French state was eager to encourage the arrival of British textile workers during the Peace of Amiens.[26] Procedures to obtain French citizenship were simplified for these migrants, who could freely circulate in the country and its new territorial extensions in Belgium, Rhineland and Piedmont. As a result, on 14 September 1802, an English textile technician named William Aitken was offered at Calais a passport 'to travel everywhere in the Republic'.[27] In May 1803, 132 British *'mécaniciens'* (an elusive term for skilled workers including master spinners, potters, candle makers, metal manufacturers) were counted in Paris, along with 59 textile dealers and merchant passengers.[28] Another group of travellers, more difficult to trace in the archives, is often left aside: the eloped and poor itinerants, sometimes in quest of employment, who journeyed without legal documents. Their journeys can be retrieved in other sources, such as judiciary reports and local newspapers, as is the case for Betty Amplett, an illegitimate girl from Worcestershire, who, aged 13, was placed under the care of 'some poor relations, and during the short interval of peace in 1802, went to France with an uncle, a shoemaker, who intended to settle there'.[29]

Overall, British travellers came to France to fulfil a variety of social interests. This led to a reinvention of pre-revolutionary patterns of movement, by remodelling older Grand Tour practices on interconnected business and cultural interests. In this respect, the example of William Humphrys, a

Birmingham merchant, is particularly apt. The Humphrys led a foreign trading house affiliated to the Levant Company, with close commercial ties with Europe, which the revolutionary wars had seriously damaged. The peace thus offered the family a perfect opportunity to canvass potential new trade partners and recover huge debts. Humphrys' project in November 1802 was colossal: assisted by his son, he aimed to find 120 French and Italian traders in Paris, and to write off an overall debt of £40,000. Claims required delicate arrangements, and necessitated copying a large amount of correspondence for the use of banking agents, which the father and son planned on accomplishing over six months.[30] Yet, during that time, the Humphrys also combined business with pleasure. Upon their landing at Calais, they chose to lodge at Monsieur Dessein's inn, which had inspired Laurence Sterne's famous novel *A Sentimental Journey through France and Italy* (1768).[31] Thence, they followed the coast to Montreuil-sur-Mer – also celebrated by Sterne – then Nouvion, Abbeville and Amiens, to see where the recent peace had been signed and which constituted another landmark in their attempt to follow Sterne's 'sentimental journey'. They stopped for several days at Amiens to observe the Gothic architecture of the cathedral which, in the words of Humphrys, was 'rendered interesting to the travellers by its being the *chef d'œuvre* of our countrymen during the Regency of the duke of Bedford'.[32] A common Franco-British history was sought in the contemplation of the landscape and famous châteaux, as they passed through Clermont and Chantilly. Their entrance into Paris epitomised this outlook, as the Humphrys chose to follow particular streets to obtain specific views of the capital. They made the decision to enter Paris in a two-stage itinerary, first by entering the metropolis from the north and passing by monarchical sites such as the Basilica of Saint-Denis and the former *Poste Royale*. Their progression to the centre of the city was equally codified: 'the course and point of entry into Paris being altered by desire of the travellers to the exterior Boulevards and *Barrière de l'Etoile* in order to view the capital from its finest approach through the *Champs Elysées*'.[33] Their Parisian entry formed a loop, as they then travelled back into Saint-Denis, to settle in the *Hotel de Bruxelles*. Their journey was clearly embedded in post-revolutionary tourism, or, at least, a highly symbolic itinerary to enliven business purposes.

(Re)collecting the ephemeral

Movement itself, in time and space, was the prime interest of British visitors. This movement was embodied in one specific kind of ephemera: the ruin, understood broadly as it was in the Romantic age, as an environmental and social phenomenon. Ruins acquired a different cultural value during the period. Previously conceived as artificial ornaments to fictionalise the gardens of aristocratic Europeans and elicit nostalgic sentiments about the power of nature over human endeavours, ruins came to be associated

208   *Elodie Duché*

with specific historical events to be commemorated. As Peter Fritzsche has convincingly argued:

> the ruins of the past were taken to be the foundations for an alternative present. The result, then, was that nineteenth-century contemporaries took ruins to be the debris of quite specific historical disasters ... and they anxiously attended to the preservation of these dated and provenienced ruins.[34]

Focused on French and Prussian responses to the Napoleonic Wars, Fritzsche's study has offered a compelling framework to consider changing perceptions of time and space during the period, which could be expanded to study British travelling behaviours in France during the Peace of Amiens. France was heavily scarred by the wilful demolition of churches, convents, castles and other sites of religious and feudal power that republicans aimed to obliterate. British visitors constantly commented on these ephemeral remains. Not only did they aim to collect evidence of these vestiges, but they also hoped to recollect the destructive force of the recent past. This was achieved by reading and discussing with the local population, but also by preserving, in their own writing, the transient historical message of these sites.

This process amalgamated previous travelling itineraries with a keen exploration of recent revolutionary debris. Indeed, the Peace of Amiens added a revolutionary detour to the Grand Tour. Travelling to France was not a novelty of the period; Paris and French academies had long been important educational points on the itineraries of Grand Tourists and their families towards Italy.[35] Yet, the cessation of war with revolutionary France enabled British travellers to resume this educational tradition with a twist. As Richard Ansell argues in his chapter on Foubert's Academy, looking beyond the Grand Tour 'is to examine the context of domestic preparations and alternatives within which foreign voyages took place'.[36] Looking at the preparation of English travellers, such as James Forbes, to revisit Grand Tour plans in 1802 is certainly fruitful. As his private correspondence suggests, the continental journey that Forbes elaborated for his family was not only meant to provide the 'last polish' to his daughter's education by exploring 'interesting scenes' in the Alps and Italy, but it also offered him and his wife the opportunity to visit formerly prohibited places in the north. Before setting sail in Harwich, he wrote to a friend:

> as I was prevented on my former tour from visiting Holland, Flanders, and France, by the war which then desolated so large a part of Europe, I shall avail myself of the present period of general tranquillity to pass through these countries ... It is our first object, therefore, to see the principal towns of Holland, and from thence shape our course through Flanders to Paris.[37]

They landed in Hellevoetsluis, as it was 'a place of considerable importance to the Batavian republic'; in Rotterdam, they visited the 'French and Dutch theatre' and Forbes observed the agricultural efforts of the locals, particularly the 'dykes, on which the very existence of the Republic may be said to depend'.[38] Although the family reproduced patterns of Grand Tour sociability, by exploring Gothic cathedrals, statues of Erasmus and meeting with exiled English and Scottish clubs, Forbes clearly stated in his letters to his sister that he was not in search of the 'picturesque' there.[39] The exploration of this 'flat' country responded to a different kind of aesthetics and touristic pursuit than his domestic touring of Wales or his appreciation of Italian sites. Rather, Forbes was interested in the infrastructures of 'revolutionised Holland', and he bought a 'statistical account published in Paris' to investigate 'the extent, population, agriculture, and commerce, of the Batavian republic', which he quoted in great length to his sister.[40]

Paris was equally visited for the revolutionary and military curiosities it hosted under the First Consul. The work of Holger Hoock has emphasised the importance of 'spoils of war' in shaping exoticism in the late eighteenth century.[41] This phenomenon was epitomised by the Peace of Amiens, which heightened the 'Egyptomania' and 'collecting furor' of British visitors eager to see Bonaparte's art loot, which filled the Louvre after his Egyptian and Italian campaigns.[42] Outside art galleries, British visitors had also an interest in contemplating the militarisation of French society through its landscape, particularly the war monuments populating the city. Many visitors commented on French war tablets, listing the fallen of the revolutionary conflicts. The painter Joseph Farington visited the Invalides for this purpose, and noted the democratic nature of these memorials where 'rank made no difference in the claim of distinction'.[43] This republican memory was associated with ancient Roman practices. Indeed, as Hoock argues, not only did Bonaparte's art booty embody a *translatio imperii* from Rome to Paris, but these war monuments were also perceived as 'a French variation on the Roman serial campaign relief carving'.[44]

This antiquarian perspective partly explains the obsession British visitors demonstrated for observing, drawing and touching ruins of the Revolution throughout the country. On his arrival to the north of France, the lawyer John Carr noted:

> We traced the desolating hand of the revolution as soon as we ascended the first hill. Our road lay through a charming country. Upon the sides of its acclivities, surrounded by the most romantic scenery of woods and corn fields, we saw ruined convents, and roofless village churches, through the shattered casements of which the wind had free admission.[45]

This romantic view of desolation encapsulates the tourism of absence that emerged among British visitors around three types of revolutionary

210   *Elodie Duché*

ruins: places of former monarchical glory, mutilated domestic settings and derelict confessional sites. Visiting the *Petit Trianon* in 1802 – a princely residence outside Versailles – Carr dedicated some time to the contemplation of the ruins of its farmhouse and mill, which he depicted in a watercolour. For Carr, the observation of the landscape functioned in a reimagining of what had been lost. 'A rivulet', he wrote, 'still runs on one side of it, which formerly used to turn a little wheel ... The apartments, which must have been once enchanting, now present nothing but gaping beams, broken ceilings, and shattered casements.'[46] The furniture bore the marks of other visitors' passages: 'the wainscots of its little cabinets, exhibits only a tablet, upon which are rudely penciled, the motley initials, love verses, and memorandums of its various visitors'.[47]

The contemplation of defaced convents and churches nourished melancholic musings among British visitors, whose perceptions were deeply influenced by reading and listening to music in their journeys. Visiting the chapel and gardens of a convent – which had been closed and turned into a musketry repository during the Revolution – Carr noted:

> the painful uncertainty of many years had occasioned the neglect and ruin in which I saw them. Some of the nuns were reading upon shattered seats, under the overgrown bowers, and others were walking in the melancholy shade of neglected avenues. The effect of the whole was gloomy and sorrowful, and fully confirmed the melancholy recital which I received from Mrs S.[48]

While music inclined his vision of ruinous landscapes, previous readings equally influenced the ways in which female travellers interpreted religious iconoclasm. In Calais, Anne Plumptre was struck by how the city contrasted with the travel accounts she had read before her journey, and which had depicted to her a populous place that 'abounded ... in monasteries and nunneries'.[49] Now, 'scenes of ruin' populated the city, revealing more broadly,

> the sad effects of that phrensy [sic] of destruction which at one fatal period of the revolution had taken possession of all France, and of which we never ceased to see continual and melancholy traces wherever we travelled in the French territory.[50]

These 'traces' were sought by British visitors, who recollected fragments of violence by systematically interviewing local inhabitants about their own direct experiences of the events. This was a two-fold process: it first involved enquiring about the meanings of surrounding ruins. On arriving at Montreuil, Mary Berry was struck by the desolation of the *Eglise Nôtre Dame*, and began, almost immediately, 'questioning the people at the inn at what time their church was *démolie*'.[51] She and her servants asked the

Revolutionary ruins 211

various customers, who 'denied it being demolished', before obtaining 'at last' the expected answer from 'the maid'. The latter 'owned that [the church] had been pulled down that a rich individual of the town had bought the church and meant to preserve it, but that the people of the place, *dans le temps de la terreur* (which they now all talk of as if it had taken place in the days of St Louis), had threatened him with the guillotine if he did not allow it to be destroyed'.[52] Reproducing the locals' speech flow, in a free indirect speech only interrupted by the historical insight of the visitor, further identified the French locals with the events.[53] Associating people with ruins was, in fact, the second aspect of this recollection. The Reverend Stephen Weston referred to the 'the long faces of the ruined' in Paris; Berry assessed a French theatre actress as *'une ruine que le temps n'a pas respectée'*; and Carr reflected on the fact that 'the barbarous jargon of the revolution is rapidly passing away. It is only here and there, that its slimy track remains.'[54] The ruin was double – both environmental and social – which the prolific writings and drawings of British visitors aimed to witness and translate onto paper.[55]

These accounts were infused by a variety of aesthetics and memories that coalesced into each other in the observation of revolutionary ruins. The main influence was that of French artists, who had already depicted the ruination of French landscapes during the Revolution. Inspired by Roman antiquities, Hubert Robert – nicknamed *'Robert des ruines'* after the Terror – had surveyed the obliteration of several Parisian landmarks in paintings such as *Les ruines de l'Abbaye de Longchamp en 1797*, and speculated on the destruction of the Louvre in *Vue imaginaire de la Grande Galerie du Louvre en ruine* in 1796.[56] Furthermore, the popularity of ruins, as a picturesque if not sublime sight, explains why travellers such as Berry, who had prior experience of Italy, praised the 'most picturesque ruined castles' of Avignon.[57]

However, there were clear tensions between the imaginings provoked by châteaux and churches. While the vision of castles mobilised positive visions of chivalric and rural felicity, mutilated Catholic churches revived Gothic myths about the Henrician Reformation. British travellers constantly associated the revolutionary closures and vandalising of convents with the dissolution of monasteries in England under Henry VIII. This is particularly evident in the trope of the 'idle monks' that permeated writings such as those of Plumptre, who saw them as 'idle, dissolute, and profligate race, and contributed not a little to the corruption of the country'.[58] This was embedded in a recurring comparison with domestic ruins such as Fountains Abbey, a Cistercian monastery in Yorkshire.[59] These parallels were owing to the fact that, because of the series of conflicts that kept the country at odds with the Continent, British Grand Tourists had refocused their activities on domestic sites, particularly English and Welsh ruins.[60] These comparisons were sometimes inflected by orientalism, to emphasise the forsaken nature of a post-revolutionary wasteland. Weston, for instance,

212 *Elodie Duché*

depicted a French Benedictine abbey as consisting of 'few remaining pillars and arches peeping through the trees like Palmyra in the desert'.[61] Overall, the exploration of revolutionary ruins crystallised a variety of imaginations, which were transferrable to new sites of tourism, beyond the traditional trajectories of the Grand Tour.

Changing geographies of tourism

British travellers loitered around sites of revolutionary significance which had not attracted much touristic interest prior to the events. The emergence of these new sites was owing to the heavily mediated nature of the Revolution, whose developments had been conveyed far and wide via letters, memoirs of combatants and continuous reports and illustrations in newspapers all over Europe.[62] This reshaped western concepts of historical continuity, and led to what Fritzsche has termed an 'inverted ventrilo-quism', whereby objects of a recent past contained mysterious historical meanings to be protected, interpreted and verbalised by their visitors.[63]

This disclosure of the past in obscure settings was facilitated by guide books, published in French and English between 1801 and 1803. These publications systematised a binary approach to various sites, comparing the Revolution with the *ancien régime*. Upon their return home, English travellers often published their letters or memoirs as guides to future visitors, which followed this dual perspective, as evidenced by a collection entitled *Paris As It Was and As It Is* (1803).[64] These guides often followed northern itineraries to Paris, from the Norman coasts to Picardy and Champagne-Ardennes, which highlighted previously neglected villages now bearing the marks of revolutionary ravages. Small towns, such as Clermont-en-Oise, inspired new entries in English guide books for their emptiness. Clermont was worth a detour because '[the] chateau is destroyed ... woods cut down, and that which was a terrestrial paradise is become a desert'.[65] Spatial emptiness lent itself to the 'pleasures of the imagination' of what was no longer there.[66] This was enabled by the description of the architectural structures that used to populate these locales: 'the chateau' in question 'was [the] domain of the duke de Fitzjames, who, during the revolution, [had] been an emigrant ... and [was] reduced to a miserable pittance'. Overall, these books emulated the French touristic guides that flourished with the cessation of hostilities, and which were specifically meant to guide foreign visitors through theatres of the Revolution.

These manuals highlighted 'modern Paris'. Pierre Villiers, a Parisian litterateur and former soldier, was prolific in publishing a whole series of these booklets, which included the multi-edited *Manuel du voyageur à Paris, ou Paris ancien et moderne*.[67] These displayed the new geography of Paris divided in 12 *arrondissements*, in the same fashion as the *Guide du voyageur à Paris*. Distributed in London and Paris, this guide book emphasised new 'public edifices' as improving the urban landscape and its

Revolutionary ruins 213

cultural value. The *Palais des Tuileries*, for instance, was said to have been embellished by the destructive impetus of the Revolution: 'the demolition of several buildings on the *place du Carouzel*, is finished; which means that, from whatever entry to the square, the visitor discovers the magnificent façade of the palace'.[68] A new Napoleonic Paris was under construction: the Louvre, renamed 'Napoleon Museum', was being expanded, while the nationalised *Palais Bourbon* was turned into a legislative assembly adorned by allegorical depictions of history in the making.[69] These guides encouraged visitors to explore places that had hardly been a source of touristic interest before the Revolution, such as the *Musée des Petits-Augustins*, a creation of the Revolution itself. There, mutilated remains of religious sculptures, books, clothes and funerary items had been collated since 1790, and reorganised chronologically to retrace the history of Paris from the Middle Ages to the present.[70] The museum was, in fact, very popular with British visitors, being open on Sundays and Mondays for the locals, and 'every day for foreigners equipped with passports'.[71] The Bastille was equally popular among these visitors, who, like James Forbes, 'frequently visited the Bastille, or rather the ruins of that celebrated fortress, and the buildings erected for various purposes from its dilapidation'.[72] The prison had hardly attracted any attention before 1789, yet its demolition site was now regarded as worth including in touristic guide books.

These new Parisian sights did not outshine previous places of tourism; rather they conflated past and new touristic interests. The Louvre attracted visitors mainly because Bonaparte's art loot came from Italy, and ancient Rome remained the key attraction. Second, within Paris, new sights linked to the Revolution altered, rather than replaced, more traditional sites such as the *Nôtre Dame* cathedral or the *Sainte Chapelle*. By putting the emphasis on new political sites, French guide books reframed – rather than erased – the classical hierarchy of destinations in Paris. *Le guide du voyageur à Paris* mentioned the traditional sites noted above, but it relegated religious buildings under the heading 'Edifices destined for the Catholic cult', and the former royal palace of the *Conciergerie* was meant to be visited as a 'prison'.[73] Most entries concerned spaces of recent political significance: new governmental buildings, places of social unrest such as the *Invalides*, revolutionary prisons such as the *Temple*, along with new state properties such as the *Hotel de Soubise*, the new *Banque de France*, national scientific institutes and places of symbolic display such as the *Champ de Mars* and the newly refurbished *Champs-Élysées*, which gained popularity during the Revolution for elegant promenades. A closer look at these entries shows how baroque architecture was considered as the main appeal of these locations. The *Hotel de Soubise*, for instance, was deemed 'worthy of the curiosity of travellers' because of its former '*éclat*', particularly the sculptures of Robert Le Lorrain and Guillaume Coustou the Younger which adorned its façade. Yet the *éclat* was even more valuable as the edifice had

214   *Elodie Duché*

become public property, and was displayed, in these guide books, as the wealth of a republican nation.[74]

Outside Paris, industrial sites became the source of new peregrinating interests, as entrepreneurs turned revolutionary ruins into textile factories. Exploring a derelict abbey near Rouen, Weston crossed the path of other British visitors, who came to France to develop their industry and were using the ruins of religious edifices for their trade. The abbey, he noted, 'is now occupied no more by lazy ecclesiastics, but by industrious mechanics who, under the direction of a company of English manufacturers there, weave velvets similar to those of Spitalfields. We learnt that there were several other establishments of the sort in the province.'[75] These reinvented spaces featured prominently in northern France, and calico factories embedded in ruins were advertised in various guide books. This under-pinned a growing industrial tourism among British visitors in France who perceived the social changes experienced by France through the trope of a manufacturing phoenix, which connected the country to Britain's industrial ebb and flow. 'In England', wrote Plumptre, 'the town of Manchester has risen to wealth and splendour on the ruin of Spitalfields; and, perhaps, in France, Chantilly, where cotton manufactories are established, may be destined to rise to opulence on the ruins of Lyons.'[76]

New itineraries were also traced by visitors who wished to relive the Revolution, not only in space but also in time. 'Having a wish to see Varennes,' wrote Forbes to his sister, 'the spot where the unfortunate Louis was arrested with his family in their flight from the capital, I was deter-mined to spend its anniversary in that town.'[77] The town attracted a grow-ing attention from foreigners, certainly owing to the various illustrations of the arrest that had largely circulated in print in France, Britain and Prussia in the 1790s.[78] There, they could inspect a house, a barn and a bridge, under the guidance of local tour guides.[79] A similar process was taking place across the Rhine, where Prussian farmers guided tourists around Revolutionary battle sites.[80] The British visitors remarked, in unison, upon the poor quality of the sights in Varennes: 'totally unworthy of notice on any other account', declared Major Blayney; 'it is a most insignificant place', wrote Forbes, 'but its connexion with the great events of the revolu-tion makes it interesting'.[81] To overcome this paradox, the latter scrutinised 'the spot', by examining 'the bridge over the Aire where the blockade was formed' and by 'reading the account of the arrest in different histories of the revolution'.[82] Their route to Varennes had already followed a specific historical trail in Lorraine, by passing through Valmy, where the Prussian Army had retreated, and following a military axis to Saint-Ménehould, to see the man who had identified the King on a coin. But it was only with the end of the peace, and the arrest of all British excursionists on French soil in May 1803, that Varennes emerged as a touristic hub for paroled British prisoners of war detained locally at Verdun. Police records and military archives reveal that captives were riveted by the town, and obtained, on a

Revolutionary ruins 215

regular basis, temporary permissions to visit 'the spot', which further suggests the close intimacy between war and tourism during the period.[83]

Conclusion

Historians have recently reappraised the need to 'look at the lesser "hot spots"' of the Revolutionary and Napoleonic period, in order to unravel the more complex contacts created by intermittent periods of truce, such as the Peace of Amiens.[84] This interlude has been reconsidered as a *'rattrapage'*, in the words of Morieux, namely a continuation of previous patterns of migrations suspended by war.[85] This chapter has further nuanced this picture, by revealing how the varied interests of British travellers in revolutionary ruins fed a reimagination of past travelling experiences. Itineraries of Grand Tourists took a northern turn, as the defaced confessional sites of France were perceived as another kind of historical ruins to be studied and collected. British travellers were active agents of the ongoing production and imagination of touristic spaces in France, by prompting the publication of new guide books and the emergence of touristic sites not only within Paris but also in northern provinces so far discarded for their lack of cultural refinement.[86]

This endeavour was facilitated by improving and less onerous modes of transport, which meant that thousands of British travellers of various ages, genders and social backgrounds (therefore not only genteel excursionists but also artisans, manufacturers and servants) crossed the Channel in the hope to witness the remnants of a historical milestone, and to develop financial connections abroad. Their migrations and interests triggered a long-lasting shift in the geography of tourism in France. Whereas Paris, Montpellier and watering places had previously gathered cosmopolitan travellers in search of intellectual refinements or a milder climate, more remote sites became the object of a novel interest. Travelling itineraries now included minor towns such as Varennes-en-Argonne, which had recently seen the arrest of Louis XVI. The northeast of France thrived with British peregrinators eager to discover landscapes mutilated by the Prussian invasion, and to render their experiences in diaries and sketchbooks.

These travelling behaviours were, in part, extensions of long-established practices. They drew mainly on the Catholic practice of reliquary and the cabinet of curiosity culture. Historians have shown that eighteenth-century tourists often took relics and fragments wherever they travelled: they chipped pieces of the stones at Stonehenge, picked up pieces of mosaic from tessellated pavements, or pocketed bits of pottery in Pompeii. Similarly, the writings of English travellers in post-revolutionary France echoed pre-existing tropes of travel writing. This is particularly evident in comments on women's clothing and comparisons made with ancient Rome.[87]

Yet, three elements distinguish the experience of revolutionary ruins from the classic Grand Tour. First, revolutionary ruins offered an immediacy of

216 *Elodie Duché*

contemplation that did not necessitate prior intellectual engagement with the Classics. In other words, the rawness and recent nature of the damage allowed for a more vivid reimagining than older, milder classical ruins. These revolutionary sites were readily accessible, both geographically and intellectually, to a variety of travellers, since there was little need for interpretation. Reading the post-revolutionary landscape could easily be done through the reading of newspapers and by conversing with the locals, which explains the popularity of these sites.

Second, this engendered a variety of emotional languages to narrate personal experiences in locations associated with the French Revolution. Victoria Thompson has recently shown how the Revolution forged new 'emotional landmarks' that were eagerly sought by British travellers visiting Paris in 1802, 1814 and after Waterloo.[88] The Revolution, she argued, led to a 'consistent use of strong and distressing expressions of emotions' among British travellers, who no longer perceived the ravages of time through the pleasurable contemplation of the picturesque, but from a negative emotional lens, a strong fear of revolutionary violence. This caused an unprecedented 'emotional community' in response to a 'cultural trauma'.[89] This chapter does not entirely concur with Thompson's conclusions, especially on the reinforcement of Franco-British alterity in these travels. Rather, this chapter has highlighted how the existence of endearing melancholy or sentiments of elation in witnessing the end of monarchical absolutism and 'idle monks' also permeated the writings of authors such as Berry and Carr. The assertion, penned by the latter, that 'every lover of pure liberty must leap with delight upon the disencumbered earth, where once stood that gloomy abode' to describe the demolition site of the Bastille, is a powerful reminder that British and French visions of freedom not only collided but also coincided in affective readings of the landscape.[90] Overall, this chapter has argued that the 'emotional community' of British travellers was, far from being homogeneously negative, providing a diverse, if not contradictory, vision of post-revolutionary France.

Third, these revolutionary ruins differed from classical remains in prompting new perceptions of time. Chloe Chard has shown that eighteenth-century Grand Tourists conflated femininity and antiquity in contemplations of classical ruins in Italy, in order to 'convert historical time', the 'remote, vanished nature of the past ... into personal time'.[91] Conversely, revolutionary ruins were seen as crystallising an accelerated time. They embodied the events of 'yesterday', a compressed 'space of time, hav[ing] crouded [sic] ages into years', in the words of an English traveller, which did not necessitate this 'conversion'.[92] Overall, the upheavals of the French Revolution caused a distinctive change, in the sense that pre-existing travel tropes and antiquarian pursuits were geared towards new reflections on social unrest, war and time, on a scale that was unusual and unprecedented in its focus.

In this respect, it seems clear that war and social unrest during the period subtly remodelled touristic practices. French revolutionaries were not the first to wreck castles and churches – the Seven Years' War had already left many scars in the country – but the fact that foreign visitors travelled *en masse* to France in 1802 to amble around specific sites of revolutionary ruins indicated a long-lasting change of perception, the fact that, in the words of Fritzsche, 'recent history had come to be dramatised as a sequence of abrupt endings and new beginnings'.[93] These 'abrupt endings' also meant that the touristic attraction of these revolutionary sites faded away within a few years. This is particularly perceptible in the rapid narrowing of anecdotes related to the *Tuileries* palace and garden in British travel accounts. While in 1802 the *Tuileries* featured as the most visited and commented site in narratives penned by British excursionists, the location only led to brief remarks in accounts published in 1814. Previously associated with five remarkable events – the deposition of the French royal family in residence in the palace, the meetings of the Convention and National Assembly, the 12 July 1789 riot of the *Tuileries* gardens and the defining invasion of the palace on 10 August 1792 – only the 10 August insurrection was mentioned in accounts in 1814.[94] But, perhaps most strikingly today, the spot where the Bastille once stood is no longer a prime site of touristic attraction.

Other sites fell into similar oblivion as the Napoleonic Wars led to new imaginings. The touristic surge of 1802 had, indeed, many successors, particularly following the first abdication of Napoleon. In 1814, British and American visitors flocked again *en masse* to France to witness what came to be known as the Hundred Days. Their exodus back into Britain in 1815 was only temporary, as visitors of all sorts, included women and children, again crossed the Channel in a post-Waterloo frenzy in 1816.[95] Literary figures, such as the Shelleys, but also merchants, artisans and scientists were eager to visit Belgian battlefields to relive the combats of Waterloo.[96] Such developments are a potent reminder of the versatility of interests that underpinned the reimagination, relocation and democratisation of peripatetic practices, beyond the Grand Tour, in northern France and Europe at the end of the eighteenth century.

Notes

1 On the religiosity of these artefacts, see K. Bresnahan, 'Remaking the Bastille: architectural destruction and revolutionary consciousness in France, 1789–1794', in J. Mancini and K. Bresnahan, eds, *Architecture and Armed Conflict: The Politics of Destruction* (New York and Abingdon, 2014), pp. 58–71.

2 Musée Carnavalet, Paris, S 503, 1790, Modèle réduit de la Bastille exécuté dans un bloc de pierre provenant de la Bastille.

3 R. Taws, *The Politics of the Provisional: Art and Ephemera in Revolutionary France* (Philadelphia, 2013).

4 L. Hunt, *Politics, Culture, and Class in the French Revolution* (Berkeley, Los Angeles and London, 1984), p. 124.

5 Smithsonian Institution, National Museum of American History, Kenneth E. Behring Center, Washington DC, PL*034262, Piece of the Bastille, Paris, France, 1380.

218 *Elodie Duché*

6 W. Bird, *Souvenir Nation: Relics, Keepsakes, and Curios from the Smithsonian's National Museum of American History* (New York, 2013), pp. 88–9.

7 Mount Vernon collections, Fairfax County, Virginia, 'Key to the Bastille'. http://www.mountvernon.org/research-collections/digital-encyclopedia/article/bastille-key/ [accessed 26 March 2015].

8 After the signature of a preliminary truce in Lunéville, the Treaty of Amiens (27 March 1802) was an agreement between France, Britain, Spain and the Batavian Republic (the Netherlands), achieving a European peace for 14 months.

9 S. Bainbridge, *Napoleon and English Romanticism* (Cambridge, 1995); Bainbridge, *British Poetry and the Revolutionary and Napoleonic Wars* (Oxford, 2003); J.R. Watson, *Romanticism and War: A Study of British Romantic Period Writers and the Napoleonic Wars* (Basingstoke, 2003); J.N. Cox, *Romanticism in the Shadow of War: Literary Culture in the Napoleonic Years* (Cambridge, 2014). On the 'immediate history' of the Revolution, see P. Bourdin, ed., *La Révolution 1789–1871. Écriture d'une Histoire Immédiate* (Clermont-Ferrand, 2008).

10 Owing to the extensive literature on the subject, newspapers and caricatures have not been explored for this chapter. See J.-P. Bertaud, A. Forrest and A. Jourdan, eds, *Napoléon, les Mots, et les Anglais: Guerre des Mots et des Images* (Paris, 2004).

11 J. Uglow, *In These Times: Living in Britain through Napoleon's Wars, 1793–1815* (London, 2014), pp. 169, 289–96.

12 Cox, *Shadow of War*, p. 25.

13 Ibid., p. 26.

14 *The Dairies and Letters of Sir George Jackson, K.C.H., from the Peace of Amiens to the Battle of Talavera*, 2 vols (London, 1872), p. 81, quoted in R. Morieux, '"An inundation from our shores": travelling across the Channel around the Peace of Amiens', in M. Philp, ed., *Resisting Napoleon: The British Response to the Threat of Invasion, 1797–1815* (London, 2006), p. 217.

15 Cox, *Shadow of War*, p. 26.

16 See Morieux, *Une mer pour deux royaumes: la Manche, frontière Franco-Anglaise (XVIIe–XVIIIe siècles)* (Rennes, 2008).

17 Morieux, '"An inundation from our shores"', p. 218.

18 Morieux, *Une mer pour deux royaumes*, pp. 298–9, 304.

19 Ibid., pp. 303–8.

20 On 'trough tickets' options, see J. Goldworth Alger, *Napoleon's British Visitors and Captives (1801–1815)* (London, 1904), p. 25, and R. Phillips, *A Practical Guide During a Journey from London to Paris: With a Correct Description of All the Objects Deserving of Notice in the French Metropolis* (London, 1802). Privileged travellers often shipped their own carriages, as was the case of Lord and Lady Tweeddale who declared to the Boulogne customs the possession of a lavishly adorned *berline*, with which he and his wife planned to travel comfortably during a 'fourteen-months sojourn in France'. National Library of Scotland, Edinburgh, Tweeddale papers, MS. 14527, f. 228, copy of a customs declaration, Boulogne, 26 Sept. 1802.

21 T. Whiteside, *The Tunnel under the Channel* (London, 1962), p. 17.

22 Cox, *Shadow of War*, pp. 26–7.

23 Ibid., p. 29.

24 See P. Gerbod, *Voyages au pays des mangeurs de grenouilles: la France vue par les Britanniques du XVIIIe siècle à nos jours* (Paris, 1991); H. Fauville, *La France de Bonaparte vue par les visiteurs Anglais* (Aix-en-Provence, 1989).

25 For an in-depth study of these lists, see Morieux, *Une mer pour deux royaumes*, pp. 307–8.

Revolutionary ruins 219

26 Ibid., p. 309. Yet, England deployed a stricter surveillance of French textile workers coming to London, owing to a fear of industrial espionage.

27 Ibid.

28 M. Audin, 'British hostages in Napoleonic France: the evidence with particular reference to manufacturers and artisans', unpublished MA dissertation, University of Birmingham (1988).

29 *Edinburgh Annual*, 21 Aug. 1810.

30 J.B. Macaulay, ed., *The Life of the Last Earl of Stirling: Gentleman, Prisoner of War, Scottish Peer, and Exile, with Extracts from his Original Manuscripts and Sketches* (London, 1906), pp. 8–9.

31 Ibid., p. 10.

32 Ibid.

33 Ibid., p. 11.

34 P. Fritzsche, *Stranded in the Present: Modern Time and the Melancholy of History* (Cambridge, MA, and London, 2004), p. 98.

35 See M. Cohen, 'The Grand Tour: constructing the English gentleman in eighteenth-century France', *History of Education*, 21:3 (1992), pp. 241–57.

36 See Richard Ansell's chapter in this volume.

37 J. Forbes, *Letters from France, Written in the Years 1803 and 1804*, 2 vols (London, 1806), I, pp. 1–2.

38 Forbes, *Letters*, I, pp. 9, 13, 24.

39 Ibid., pp. 13–14.

40 Ibid., pp. 27–8, 36–7.

41 H. Hoock, *Empires of the Imagination: Politics, War and the Arts in the British World, 1750–1850* (London, 2010), pp. 219–41.

42 Ibid., p. 223.

43 Ibid., p. 159.

44 Ibid.

45 J. Carr, *The Stranger in France, or, A tour from Devonshire to Paris* (London, 1803), p. 34. See also the manuscript diaries of Charles Throckmorton: Warwickshire County Record Office, Charles Throckmorton Papers, CR1998/ CD/Drawer 8/2, 1802–1805, memoranda.

46 Carr, *The Stranger*, p. 185.

47 Ibid., pp. 185–6.

48 Ibid., p. 142.

49 A. Plumptre, *A Narrative of Three Years' Residence in France, Principally in the Southern Departments, from the Year 1802 to 1805*, 3 vols (London, 1810), I, p. 15.

50 Plumptre, *A Narrative of Three Years' Residence*, I, p. 15; M. Berry, *Extracts of the Journals and Correspondence from the Year 1783 to 1852*, 3 vols (London, 1862), II, p. 126.

51 Berry, *Extracts*, II, p. 127.

52 Ibid., II, pp. 126–7.

53 See also Plumptre, *A Narrative of Three Years' Residence*, I, pp. 14–5.

54 Carr, *The Stranger*, p. 37; S. Weston, *The Praise of Paris, or A Sketch of the French Capital in Extracts of Letters from France, in the Summer of 1802* (London, 1803), p. vi.

55 On the publishing boom of memoirs, see C. Kennedy, *Narratives of the Revolutionary and Napoleonic Wars: Military and Civilian Experience in Britain and Ireland* (Basingstoke, 2013).

56 Musée du Louvre, Paris, R.F. 1975–11, Hubert Robert, *Vue imaginaire de la Grande Galerie du Louvre en ruines* (1796).

57 Berry, *Extracts*, II, p. 213.

220   *Elodie Duché*

58 Plumptre, *A Narrative of Three Years' Residence*, I, p. 16.
59 Weston, *The Praise of Paris*, p. 139.
60 On the domestic Grand Tour, see S. Lichtenwalner, *Claiming Cambria: Invoking the Welsh in the Romantic Era* (Cranbery, NJ, 2008).
61 Weston, *The Praise of Paris*, p. 30.
62 Fritzsche, *Stranded in the Present*, pp. 30, 37–9, 43.
63 Ibid., p. 7.
64 W. Blagdon, *Paris As It Was and As It Is, or a Sketch of the French Capital Illustrative of the Effects of the Revolution*, 2 vols (London, 1803); R. Phillips, *A Practical Guide during a Journey from London to Paris*, 2nd edn (London, 1802); G. Kearsley, *Kearsley's Travellers's Entertaining Guide through Great Britain* (London, 1803).
65 Kearsley, *Kearsley's Travellers's Entertaining Guide*, p. 789.
66 See J. Brewer, *The Pleasures of the Imagination: English Culture in the Eighteenth Century* (Chicago, 1997).
67 See P. Villiers, *Manuel du voyageur à Paris, ou Paris ancien et moderne*, 2 vols (Paris, 1802); Villiers, *De Paris et ses curiosités, ou le nouveau guide du voyageur à Paris* (Paris, 1802).
68 P.J. Alletz, *Le guide du voyageur à Paris: contenant la description des monuments publics les plus remarquables & les plus dignes de la curiosité des voyageurs* (Paris, 1802), pp. 4–5, 11.
69 Ibid., pp. 50–1, 58–9.
70 Villiers, *Manuel du voyageur à Paris*, pp. 301–12.
71 Ibid., p. 312.
72 Forbes, *Letters*, I, p. 31.
73 Alletz, *Le guide du voyageur à Paris*, pp. 59–61, 68.
74 Ibid., pp. 237–8.
75 Weston, *The Praise of Paris*, p. 31.
76 Plumptre, *A Narrative of Three Years' Residence*, p. 256.
77 Forbes, *Letters*, II, p. 294.
78 Bibliothèque Nationale de France, Paris, Département Estampes et Photographie: RESERVE FOL-QB-201 (125), 1796, Mariano Bovi, 'Louis XVI stopt in his flight at Varennes'; RESERVE QB-370 (23)-FT 4, 1794, Paul Jacob Laminit, 'Gefangennehmung des Koënigs Ludewig zu Varennes: den 22 Jun. 1791'.
79 Forbes, *Letters*, II, p. 294.
80 Fritzsche, *Stranded in the Present*, p. 122.
81 A. Blayney, *Narrative of a Forced Journey through Spain and France*, 2 vols (London, 1814), II, p. 198.
82 Forbes, *Letters*, II, p. 296.
83 E. d'Hauterive, *La Police Secrète du Premier Empire*, 7 vols (Paris, 1922), III, p. 296; IV, pp. 3, 177.
84 Cox, *Shadow of War*, pp. 1–24.
85 Morieux, *Une mer pour deux royaumes*, p. 306.
86 On the literary and imaginative production of space, see D. Massey, *For Space* (London, 2005).
87 See R. Sweet, *Cities and the Grand Tour: The British in Italy 1690–1820* (Cambridge, 2012).
88 V.E. Thompson, 'An alarming lack of feeling: urban travel, emotions, and British national character in post-Revolutionary Paris', *Urban History Review/ Revue d'Histoire Urbaine*, 42:2 (2014), pp. 8–17.
89 Ibid., pp. 9–11.
90 Carr, *The Stranger*, p. 192.

Revolutionary ruins 221

91 C. Chard, *Pleasure and Guilt on the Grand Tour: Travel Writing and Imaginative Geography, 1600–1830* (Manchester, 1999), pp. 133–4.
92 Thompson, 'An alarming lack of feeling', p. 14.
93 Fritzsche, *Stranded in the Present*, p. 98.
94 Thompson, 'An alarming lack of feeling', pp. 11, 14.
95 National Maritime Museum, Greenwich, 1816, 'Landing of English travellers at Calais. Low water'.
96 See C. Eaton, *The Days of Battle; or Quatre Bras and Waterloo* (London, 1853); M. Shelley, *History of a Six Weeks' Tour through a Part of France, Switzerland, Germany, and Holland* (London, 1817).

Index

Aachen 193 *see also* Aix la Chapelle
Abbeville 175, 179n25, 180n45, 207
academies 13, 34, 40, 46–64; curriculum 47, 50–1, 53; in England *see* Foubert's Academy; in French provinces 48, 68, 90, 96 in Geneva 57, 68–9; in Italy *see* Turin, *Accademia Reale*; in Paris 34, 40, 47–9, 55, 86–7, 90; student numbers 52–3
accommodation 135–6, 15; *see also* Hotel d'Angleterre
Aitken, William 206
Aix la Chapelle 3, 131, 132, 134, 139; treaty of 193
Albermarle, earl of 74
Aldworth, Richard 73
ambassadors, social role of 6, 68–71; *see also* diplomats
American Independence, War of 134
Amiens 39, 175; cathedral 207; travel during Peace of 203–21
Amplett, Betty 206
Amsterdam 6, 11, 15–16, 68, 111, 112, 148–60, 169, 172–3; accommodation at 151; Bohemian visitors to 88 92–3; charitable foundations 112, 153–5, 173, 194; entertainments 152–3; guidebooks 150–1; modernity of 153–5; places of worship 155
Angers (academy) 48, 55, 90
Ansbach 68
antiquarianism 32, 209
Antwerp 88, 135, 136, 137, 138, 149, 185, 189, 191, 195, 196
Ardennes, the 131–2, 192, 212
Ariès, Philippe 189
Arkwright, Sir Richard 172
Arran, James Hamilton, earl of 54, 56
ars apodemica (art of travel) 33

art (Dutch) appreciation of 138, 148, 154
August Clemens, elector of Cologne 118, 120
Ausson, François de Jaucourt, marquis d' 48, 53
Austrian Netherlands 3, 4, 9, 11, 114, 134, 137, 151, 185, 190–2; *see also* Flanders
Austrian Succession, War of 76, 97
Austria Hungary 4, 12, 178n; *see also* Holy Roman Empire
Avignon 211

Bampfylde, Charles 130, 131
Banks, Caleb 48
Bath, John Granville, first earl of 48
Bath 132–3, 133–4, 141
Beauharnais, Eugène de 165
Bély, Lucian 4
Berlin 3, 68, 69, 72, 92, 96, 110, 185, 190, 191
Bernis, Cardinal de 147
Berry, Mary 210, 211, 216
Bertrand, Gilles 30, 31, 33, 162, 168
Binger Loch 117
Birmingham 171
Black, Jeremy 128
Blayney, Major 214
Body, Albin 127
Boerhaave, Herman 115–16
Bogin, Count 165
Bonn 92, 96, 118, 119
Boulton, Matthew 172
Bourdieu, Pierre 40, 85
Boxhorn, Marcus Zuerius 151
Brabant 145n54, 192
Branden, Corneille-Jean-Marie van den 191, 195

Index 223

Brandenburg 68, 96, 110
Brisbane, John 49, 50
Britain *see* England
Brittany 34, 39
Bruges 136, 140, 146n95
Bruijningh, Jason 188, 191, 194, 196
Brunswick 68, 75, 165
Brussels 68, 86, 88, 89, 90, 93, 94, 96,
   111, 137, 140, 149, 191, 192, 195,
   196
Bunbury, Lady Sarah *see* Lennox, Lady
   Sarah
Burman, Pieter 115

Calais 39, 95, 134–5, 136–7, 140, 169,
   205, 206, 210; Dessein's Inn 136–7,
   207
Camden, William 37
Campen, Jacob van 154
Carr, John 209–10, 211, 216
Cartier, Jacques 27–8
casinos 133, 141; *see also* gambling
Cassa, Johannes Samuel 193
Castiligione, Baldassare 85
Champagne-Ardennes 212
Chantilly (manufactures at) 207, 214
Chappuzeau, Samuel 41
charity, travellers' observations on 155,
   173
Charles II, king of England 50, 51, 54,
   56
Charles Emmanuel III (duke of Savoy
   and king of Sardinia) 164, 165
Chavigny, duc de 34, 35
Chevreuse, duc de 34
children as travellers 9, 10, 15, 16–17,
   131, 135–6, 137, 142, 185–202, 217
Chotek, Johann Karl 94, 95, 100
Clarendon, Henry Hyde, 2nd earl of 48
Clermont-en-Oise 207, 212
Cohen, Michèle 3, 58
Coke, Lady Mary 129, 130, 131, 132,
   134–5, 136–7, 139, 140
Colloredo, Rudolf (Count) 70, 75
Cologne 88, 91, 92, 116, 118, 119,
   191, 192
Common Room Club 72–4, 81n84
convents 137; English 139–40, 146n95;
   ruins of 209–11
conversation, skills of 1, 71, 86–7,
   114, 119
Conway, Stephen 4, 75
Copenhagen 110

Corens, Liesbet 4, 140
Cosimo III (Grand Duke of Florence)
   67, 91
counter reformation, influence on
   travel 50–1, 87
Court, Allard de la 188, 190, 192,
   194
Court, Pieter de la 188, 190, 192
courts, as sites of elite formation
   13–14, 32, 66–72, 75–6, 84–5, 86–7,
   91, 96, 109, 110, 113–14, 118–20
Craufurd, John 130, 131, 132, 137, 139
Cristyn, Jean-Baptiste 151
cultural exchange 13, 47, 58, 84
Cumberland, Prince William Augustus,
   duke of 52
Cumberland, Prince Henry, duke of
   129, 141
Czernin, Franz Joseph 95, 99, 100,
   106n47 and n60, 107n61 and n62
Czernin, Herman Jacob 91, 92, 99,
   100, 105n38

dancing 1, 47, 50, 53, 56, 86
Dartrey, Lord and Lady 130, 131, 137,
   138, 139
Davenant, Charles 58
de Boufflers, Amélie, duchess de Lauzun
   75
de Breme, Ludovico 165
de Seta, Cesare 1
Degenfeld von, Count and Madame 70
Denmark 110
Descartes 148
Devonshire, Georgiana, duchess of 129,
   130, 135
Dijon 169
diplomatic revolution 70
diplomats, social role of 86–7, 113–14
domestic travel: in Britain 9–10,
   46–64; in Germany and Holy Roman
   Empire 14, 23n44, 96–7, 116–19; in
   the Netherlands and Low Countries
   10, 185–202
Dordrecht 149
Dresden 3, 68, 92, 96, 185
Du Soucy, François 29
Dublin 169
Dunkirk 169
Duplessis-Mornay, Philippe 34
Düsseldorf 91, 192
Dutch East India Company (buildings
   of) 95, 154, 173

224   *Index*

Dutch Republic 10, 11, 15–16, 93–5, 147–60, 189, 191, 192, 194; *see also* Holland and United Provinces

Eden Treaty 175
Edict of Nantes 27; revocation of 57, 148
Edinburgh 12, 38, 56
England, as destination of European travellers 4, 11; French visitors to 27–9, 32–45, 148; Bohemian visitors to 83, 87, 88, 91, 95, 106n51 and n53; German visitors to 111; Italian visitors to 166, 168, 169, 171, 172, 177n6; travel within 10, 187
English Channel: crossing 36, 47, 134, 205–6, 216–17
enlightenment, influence on travel, 12, 14, 70, 87–8, 109, 115, 118, 119–20
Erasmus 84; statue of 194, 209
espionage (industrial) 16, 193
Esterházy, Nikolaus I, Prince 70
Eton College 55
Evelyn, John 51

family strategy and travel 13, 46–7, 54–7
family travel 9, 10, 11, 15, 17, 128–31, 138, 142, 185–202, 208–9
Famin, Pierre 153
Farington, Joseph 209
fencing 47, 50, 53, 56, 86, 193
Fenwick, Samuel 54
Ferdinand, Prince of Brunswick 73
Ferrus, Abbé 112, 116
Fiennes, Celia 10
Flanders 137–8, 183–202; English convents in 140
Florence 67, 86, 89–91, 163, 170
Forbes, James 208–9, 213–14
Foubert family 46–64; Henri Foubert 47, 52–3, 57, 58, 59; Solomon Foubert 46–64
Foubert's academy 46–64; costs 54; curriculum 52–3; foreign students 57; in London 49–64; in Paris 47–9; student misbehaviour 53–4; student numbers 52–3
Fouquet, Charles Louis Auguste, duc de Belle Isle 75–6
Fouquet, Louis-Marie, comte de Gisors 75–6

Fouquet, Petrus 150
Fox, Charles James 129, 205
France, travel to 3–4, 17, 47–8, 50–1, 65, 83, 90–1, 111, 168–9, 170, 172, 194, 203–21; *see also* Paris
Frankfurt 88, 91–2, 96, 116, 117, 138, 191, 196
Franz Stephan, Grand Duke of Tuscany and Holy Roman Emperor 93, 96
Frederick the Great, King of Prussia 70, 72
French language, acquisition of 48, 49–50, 56, 93, 96
French Revolution 17, 163; impact of revolutionary wars 148, 207; travellers' interest in 203–21

Gallocentrism 32–6, 40
Gallomania 50
gambling 53, 114–15, 131, 133, 140–1, 148, 148
gardens 115, 149, 207
Geneva 8, 55, 57, 68, 72–3, 85, 88, 169
Gerbier, Sir Balthazar, 49, 51
Germany 34–5, 67–8, 72, 91, 111–24, 168, 172
Geusau, Anton von 110–20
Ghent 136, 137, 139, 185, 191, 196
Gibbon, Edward 76
Giro d'Italia 108
Glasgow 56
Goos, Anna 189
Gouda 194
Goyon, Marquis de 155
Graham family, dukes of Montrose 57
Grand Tour: as cultural capital 85; and elite education 8, 13–14, 83–107, 108–24; historiography of 1–6; as preparation for state service 84–5, 97, 110, 120; social purpose of 65–82; use of term outside Britain 6–8, 13–14, 30–3, 83–4, 108–9
Groote Tour 6, 8, 187
Grosley, Pierre-Jean 150, 152
grosse tour 108
Grotius, Hugo 114
guidebooks, use of 136–7, 138, 167, 204, 212–14

Haarlem 149, 194
Hague, The 68, 88–9, 92–3, 111, 113–14, 149, 194–5

Index 225

Halifax, George Savile, 1st marquis of 48, 55
Halifax 172
Halle 109–10, 112, 115
Hamilton, Jane 130–1, 135, 139
Hamilton, Mary 129–32, 134, 136, 138–9, 141
Hamilton, William, duke of 48
Hanover 68–9, 71, 75, 92, 96, 165
Harcourt, George Simon, viscount Nuneham (later 2nd earl Harcourt) 65, 66, 68
Harrach von, Ernst and Maria Josepha, Count and Madame 70
Hastings, George, 53–4
Hatzfeldt-Gleichen, Carl and Charlotte, Count and Madame 70
Hazard, Paul 148, 156
Hellevoetsluis 209
Herbert, George (later 11th earl of Pembroke) 75
Herbert, Henry, 10th earl of Pembroke 72, 75
Hesse-Cassel 68, 71
Hinlopen, Gerard 191, 195
hofmeisters 83–4, 89
Holland 95, 147–60, 208–9; see also Dutch Republic and United Provinces
Holles, Thomas Pelham, 1st duke of Newcastle 74–5
Holroyd, John (later 1st earl of Sheffield) 76
Holy Roman Empire 8, 13–14, 84, 88, 91, 92, 96–8, 116–20
Hooft, Pieter Corneliszoon 187
horse-riding (training in) 1, 46–7, 48–9, 50, 52, 53, 86, 90
Hotel d'Angleterre: in Antwerp 136; in Brussels 136; in Calais 136
Huguenots: as cultural mediators 58–9; in Holland 148; in Paris 48–9; see also Foubert
humanism (theories of education) 8, 27–8, 32, 39–40, 84–5, 186–7, 193, 195–6
Humphrys, William 206–7
Huygens, Constantijn 154

Inns of Court 49, 53, 55, 56, 58
inns see accommodation
Ireland 169
Italy (as part of Grand Tour) 1–3, 12, 28, 30, 40, 55, 67, 85–7, 90–1, 111, 192

Jackson, George 205
James I, king of England 40
James II, king of England 52
Jansenism 112–13
Jena 110
Jerningham, Sir William 140
Johnson, Maurice 53, 55
Joseph II, Emperor of Austria 71

Kaunitz von, Wenzel, Prince 70, 98
Kavalierstour 7, 14, 101n1, 108–22
Kaveliersreise 3, 8, 101n1
Keith, Sir Robert 68–9, 75
Keith, Sir Robert Murray 69
Keyser, Hendrik de 153
Kingsale, Almeric de Courcy, 23rd baron 53, 55
Königsmarck family 57

la Lafayette, the Marquis de 204
Länderreise 7, 108
Landriani, Marsilio 161–82
landscape, appreciation of 9, 117, 132, 149, 192, 207, 209–11
Lassels, Richard 30–1
Lausanne 68
Le Brun, Antoine 31
Leffen, Pierre 150
legal education 47, 56, 87–8, 90, 93–4, 96–7
Legge, George viscount Lewisham (later 3rd earl of Dartmouth) 69–71, 74–5
Legge, William, 2nd earl of Dartmouth 67–9, 71–2, 74–5
Leiden 68, 87, 93–4, 97, 111, 115, 148, 148, 151, 194, 195
leisure travel see pleasure
Lennox, Charles, 3rd duke of Richmond 68
Lennox, Lady Sarah 129, 133
Leuven 87, 89–90, 149
Liège 127, 134–5, 137, 138–9, 141, 193
Liège, Prince-bishop of 128, 134
Lille 135, 137, 175
Limbourg, Jean Phillipe 127, 129
Lipsius, Justus 186
Loen, Johann Michael von 109
London 3, 4, 6, 10, 12–13, 46, 88, 91, 92, 93, 95, 111, 152, 166, 185, 190, 191, 192; celebration of peace in 205; described by duc de Rohan

226 *Index*

36–8; English court at 119; Foubert's academy 49–64; Madam Tussaud's 205

Lorraine, duchy of 14, 55, 83, 87, 92–3, 96, 204, 214

lotteries 52

Louis XIV, king of France 50, 57, 114, 148

Louis XVI, king of France 204, 215

Louvain 135, 139

Low Countries 4, 5, 12, 15, 16, 67, 135, 137, 147, 149, 168–9, 186, 188, 190–1, 196; *see also* Austrian Netherlands and Flanders

Lunéville (academy) 55, 57, 93–4, 96, 111

Lynar, Rochus Friedrich zu 14, 110–24

Lyon 168, 169, 170, 172, 214

Macaré, Pieter Johan 188, 192, 194–5

Macdonald, John 130, 139

Mainz 88, 91–2, 116, 118, 191

Manchester 172, 181n52, 214

Mann, Sir Horace 67

Mannheim 68, 71, 92, 96

manufactures, observations on 161–2, 163, 164–5, 169, 170–2, 174–6, 214

Maria Theresa, Empress of Austria 70, 84, 93, 96, 97, 107n66

Markham, Gervase 49

Mathieu-Favier, Albert 205

Mayerne, Theodore de 34, 43n38

Mazzoni, Gaetano 161–82

Mechelen 150

Meerman, Johan 190

mercantilism 174

merchants/entrepreneurs as travellers 16, 17, 130, 153, 161–82, 188, 206–7, 217

Merry, Anthony 206

Meuse, river 192

Milan 39, 67, 94, 98, 163

Moccafy, Gian Battista Xaverio 162–82

modernity, ideas of 4, 5–6, 25–6; in Amsterdam 153–5

Molesworth, Robert 46

Montaigne, Michel de 28

Montreuil-sur-Mer 207; *Eglise Notre Dame* 210

Moretus, Balthasar II 189–90, 193

Moretus, Balthasar III 189, 192, 193

Moretus, Maria Isabella 189

Morosi, Giuseppe 161–82

Mont Blanc 180n36

Nancy 87, 88, 93–4, 96, 111, 185

Napoleonic Empire 162, 172

Napoleonic Wars 17, 148, 204, 208, 216–17; The Hundred Days 217; post-Waterloo travel 216–17

Netherlands (Austrian or southern) 2, 3–4, 9–10, 11, 14, 83, 90–4, 111, 114, 134, 151, 186, 189–92

Netherlands (Spanish) 140, 195

New World (in travel writing) 28, 31, 36

Nicholas, Edward 54, 55

Nicolay, Nicolas de 27–8

Noblesse de robe 27

Noblesse d'épée 12, 27, 34

nobility, bodily theories of 47–8, 50–1, 53, 57, 58, 86, 87, 90

Norborne, John 48

Normandy 47, 170, 174–5

North, Lord Frederick (later 2nd earl of Guildford) 67–9, 72, 74

North, William, 6th Baron North and 2nd Baron Grey 54

Nouvion 207

O'Brien, William O'Brien, 3rd earl of Inchiquin 56

O'Brien, Lucius 54, 56

O'Brien, Sir Donat 54

Orléans 48, 55, 90

Orrery, Lionel Boyle, 3rd earl of 48

Ossory, Thomas Butler, 6th earl of 52

Otway, Thomas 54

Oxford 55, 57, 111; riding school 52

Oxford, Robert Harley, first earl of 54, 55, 59

Padua 85, 90, 164

Palloy, Pierre-François 203

Paris, 3, 11, 68, 89, 92, 94–6, 111–13, 127, 138, 163, 169, 172, 185, 188, 191, 193, 195; academies in 40, 47–9, 54, 57, 86, 90; Bastille 203–4, 213, 216, 217; court at, 86, 90; Gobelins manufactory 170, 180n45; guidebooks to 212–3; Hotel de Soubise 213; Invalides 209, 213; Jansenism in 112–13; Louvre, the 5, 149, 160n67, 193, 195, 206, 209, 211, 213; Musée des Petits Augustins

Index 227

213; Nôtre Dame 193, 213; relics from 203–4; ruins of 211; social life at 69, 71, 75, 114; Tuileries, the 213, 217
Parival, Jean Nicolas de 150–1, 156
Parthenay, Catherine de 34
patriotism, as motive for travel 10, 17, 30, 32–3, 194, 201n67
Pavia 39, 164
Pelletier, Thomas 39–40
Pergen, Joseph and Philippina, Count and Countess 70
Peter Leopold, Grand Duke of Tuscany 163
Petit tour 11, 15, 127–46; attractive to women and children 137–8; contrasted with Grand Tour 127–8, 138; itineraries of 134–6; sightseeing on 137–40; transport infrastructure 136–7
Petty family 46
philanthropy *see* charity
physiocratic theory 174
Picardy 212
Pieri, Mario 170
Pietism, as influence on travel 14, 108, 109–10, 112, 114, 119, 120
Piles, Roger de 138
Platière, Jean-Marie Roland de la 151
pleasure trips 9, 14, 15, 149–50, 195
Plaisierreisjsjes see pleasure trips
Plumptre, Anne 210, 211, 214
Pluvinel, Antoine 40
Poelaert, Jan 188
Polish War of Succession 95, 96
Popish Plot 50, 54, 57
Poterat, Pierre-Claude de 154, 159n42
Potsdam 68, 70, 72
Prague 68
prisoners of war 214
Price, Robert 72

Radziwiłł, Prince 71
Ramus, Petrus 27
Rawdon, John 48, 54
Redford, Bruce 1
Republicanism (Dutch), 95
Residenzstädte 14, 86, 89, 91, 94, 96, 117
Reuß, Heinrich VI 14, 110–24
revolutionary battle sites 214, 217
Rhine, the (route along) 116–17, 118, 172, 185, 188, 191, 194

Rice, James Louis, Count 141
Robert, Hubert 211
Roche, Daniel 3, 129, 205
Rohan, Henri, duc de 12, 27–45; career of 33–4; influence of 39–4; travels in England and Scotland 35–9, 169
Roman Catholic churches, travellers' comments on 118, 139–40, 196, 211, 213, 215
Rome, as destination on Grand Tour, 1–2, 4, 28, 67, 89, 90, 94, 170; antiquities moved from 213; criticised by duc de Rohan 40; sociability in 67, 86
Rotterdam 68, 149, 209
Rouen 170, 174, 180n45, 214
Royal Society 51, 52, 53
ruins 17, 192; as souvenirs 203–4; of French revolution 207–17

Saint Ménéhould 214
Saint-Pierre, Bernardin de 153–4, 155
Salzburg 88, 91, 92, 94, 96
Schaffhausen, 116
Schaumburg-Lippe, Albert Wolfgang von, Count 19
Schaumburg-Lippe, William von, Count 74
Schlieffen von, Martin Ernst, General 73
Scotland 12, 35–6, 38–9, 169
servants (accompanying travellers) 3, 49, 50, 129–30, 139, 188, 199n25, 206, 215; *see also* Macdonald, John
Seven Years' War 75, 149, 217
shopping 137, 152, 194–5
Siena, 85, 90
Somertogjes 9, 16, 191–2; *see also* pleasure trips
Southwell, Sir Robert 51, 56
Southwell, Sir Thomas 56
souvenirs 137, 203–4
spa 3, 15, 127–46; attractive to women, 128–9; British visitors to 128–31; casinos, 133, 141; cosmopolitanism of 133; decline in popularity 140–2; English Club 141; exclusivity of 132; and health 131–2; visitor numbers 127; waters 131
Spanish Succession, War of 87, 90, 92, 95
Spencer family, dukes of Marlborough 66
Spencer, Lord and Lady 130, 135

228 *Index*

Sternberg, Adam Franz 95–6
Sterne, Laurence, *A Sentimental Journey* 207
Strasbourg 36, 88, 93, 111, 113
Switzerland 67, 88, 148, 168, 169

Thevet, André 27–8
Thicknesse, Philip, *A Year's Journey through the Pays Bas* 131, 132, 133, 134, 136, 137
Thirty Years War 111
Thun von, Maria Wilhelmine 70
Townsend, Horace 130, 133, 134
transport: barges, 136–7, 149, 150, 158n26; carriages 134–7, 218n20; coaches 136, 137, 149–50, 188, 197; diligence 136, 149; roads, quality of 134, 149, 192
travel and health 10, 11, 15, 127–46
Trier 92, 118
Turin: *Accademia Reale* 53, 57, 69, 76, 90, 105n38, 141; as a fashionable social destination 69, 70, 76; court at 86, 89; Royal Armoury 165; Royal Library 164
Turner, Katherine 7
tutors 48, 49, 53, 57, 65, 71, 72, 87, 91, 110, 114, 130; *see also* hofmeister
Twining, Richard 130, 132, 133, 134, 135, 140

United Provinces 91, 92–3, 112, 114, 168–9; *see also* Dutch Republic and Holland
universities 13–14, 68, 87; Geneva 68–72; Halle 110; Jena 110; Jesuit universities 89, 97; Leiden 93–4, 97, 115, 148, 195; Leuven 87, 89, 90; Oxford 55; Padua 90; quality of education at, 49, 56, 84–5; Salzburg 96; Siena 90, 91; Strasbourg 113

Utrecht 68, 88, 93, 111, 116; Treaty of 148

Valmy 214
Van Strien, Kees 4, 127
Varennes-en-Argonne 204, 214, 215
Venice 16, 67, 156, 165
Verdun 214
Versailles 5, 68, 86, 119, 195, 210
Vienna 13, 67–70, 72, 75, 88, 97
Villiers, George Bussy (later 4th earl of Jersey) 65, 66, 68, 75
Vitriarius, Johann Jacob 93–4, 96, 97, 115

Washington, George 204
Weston, Stephen 130, 131, 136, 211–12, 214
Whitehead, William 65, 66, 68
Wilhelmina Karolina, Landgravine of Hesse-Cassel 71
William III, king of England 52
William VIII, Landgrave of Hesse-Cassel 68
Williamson, John 72–3
Windham, William 73
Wolfenbüttel 68
Women as travellers 10, 128–9, 137–40, 190
Wrey, Sir Bourchier 74

Yarburgh family 55
Yorke, Philip, 2nd earl of Hardwicke 66–7, 72
Yorke, Philip (later 3rd earl of Hardwicke) 66–8, 69, 70, 71, 73
youth travel *see* children

Zaandam 169